The Soundtracks
of Woody Allen

# The Soundtracks of Woody Allen

*A Complete Guide to the Songs and Music in Every Film, 1969–2005*

ADAM HARVEY

*Foreword by* DICK HYMAN

McFarland & Company, Inc., Publishers
*Jefferson, North Carolina, and London*

"Serenade in Blue," lyric by Mack Gordon, music by Harry Warren, © 1942 (renewed) WB Music Corp. All rights reserved. Used by permission.

LIBRARY OF CONGRESS CATALOGUING-IN-PUBLICATION DATA

Harvey, Adam, 1964–
  The soundtracks of Woody Allen : a complete guide to the songs and music in every film, 1969–2005 / Adam Harvey ; foreword by Dick Hyman.
    p.    cm.
  Includes filmography, discography, bibliographical references and index.

  ISBN-13: 978-0-7864-2968-4
  softcover : 50# alkaline paper ∞

  1. Motion picture music — History and criticism.  2. Allen, Woody — Criticism and interpretation.  I. Title.
  ML2075.H35   2007
  781.5'42092 — dc22                                    2007001160

British Library cataloguing data are available

©2007 Adam Harvey. All rights reserved

*No part of this book may be reproduced or transmitted in any form or by any means, electronic or mechanical, including photocopying or recording, or by any information storage and retrieval system, without permission in writing from the publisher.*

Cover photograph ©2007 Comstock Photos

Manufactured in the United States of America

*McFarland & Company, Inc., Publishers*
  *Box 611, Jefferson, North Carolina 28640*
    *www.mcfarlandpub.com*

For my son,
Max

# Acknowledgments

Firstly, I would like to thank my wife, Ann, for her forbearance, understanding and literary advice. Others who have, in their own different ways, assisted with the production of this book include Christopher Ballam, Claudia Dumschat, Howard Friend, Simon Fuller, Robert Lindner, Tim Lole, Mundell Lowe, Tom Pierson, Tom Sancton, Cynthia Sayer, Mikhail Smirnov and especially Dick Hyman, who has kindly provided me with invaluable material and has given me much help and support. Finally, I would like to thank Woody Allen himself for inadvertently introducing me to so much wonderful music.

# Table of Contents

*Acknowledgments* ........ vi
*The Films Listed Chronologically* ........ ix
*Foreword by Dick Hyman* ........ 1
*Preface* ........ 3
*Introduction* ........ 5

## The Films

| | | | |
|---|---|---|---|
| *Alice* (1990) | 13 | *Hollywood Ending* (2002) | 70 |
| *Annie Hall* (1977) | 18 | *Husbands and Wives* (1992) | 73 |
| *Another Woman* (1988) | 21 | *Interiors* (1978) | 74 |
| *Anything Else* (2003) | 26 | *Love and Death* (1975) | 75 |
| *Bananas* (1971) | 30 | *Manhattan* (1979) | 78 |
| *Broadway Danny Rose* (1984) | 31 | *Manhattan Murder Mystery* (1993) | 84 |
| *Bullets Over Broadway* (1994) | 34 | *Match Point* (2005) | 87 |
| *Celebrity* (1998) | 37 | *Melinda and Melinda* (2004) | 91 |
| *Crimes and Misdemeanors* (1989) | 42 | *A Midsummer Night's Sex Comedy* (1982) | 95 |
| *The Curse of the Jade Scorpion* (2001) | 47 | *Mighty Aphrodite* (1995) | 98 |
| *Deconstructing Harry* (1997) | 50 | "Oedipus Wrecks" (from *New York Stories*) (1989) | 101 |
| *Everyone Says I Love You* (1996) | 54 | *Play It Again, Sam* (1972) | 105 |
| *Everything You Always Wanted to Know About Sex\* (\*but were afraid to ask)* (1972) | 62 | *The Purple Rose of Cairo* (1985) | 108 |
| *Hannah and Her Sisters* (1986) | 64 | *Radio Days* (1987) | 113 |

| | | | |
|---|---|---|---|
| *September* (1987) | 119 | *Stardust Memories* (1980) | 133 |
| *Shadows and Fog* (1992) | 123 | *Sweet and Lowdown* (1999) | 138 |
| *Sleeper* (1973) | 125 | *Take the Money and Run* (1969) | 146 |
| *Small Time Crooks* (2000) | 129 | *Zelig* (1983) | 148 |

| | |
|---|---|
| *Appendix 1: Soundtracks on Record or CD* | 157 |
| *Appendix 2: Most Popular Songwriters* | 174 |
| *Appendix 3: Most Popular Performers* | 176 |
| *Appendix 4: Most Popular Songs and Jazz* | 178 |
| *Appendix 5: List of Songs and Jazz* | 180 |
| *Appendix 6: Classical Music by Composer* | 185 |
| *Notes* | 189 |
| *Select Bibliography* | 197 |
| *Index* | 199 |

# THE FILMS LISTED CHRONOLOGICALLY

*Take the Money and Run* (1969)
*Bananas* (1971)
*Play It Again, Sam* (1972)
*Everything You Always Wanted to Know About Sex\* (\*but were afraid to ask)* (1972)
*Sleeper* (1973)
*Love and Death* (1975)
*Annie Hall* (1977)
*Interiors* (1978)
*Manhattan* (1979)
*Stardust Memories* (1980)
*A Midsummer Night's Sex Comedy* (1982)
*Zelig* (1983)
*Broadway Danny Rose* (1984)
*The Purple Rose of Cairo* (1985)
*Hannah and Her Sisters* (1986)
*Radio Days* (1987)
*September* (1987)
*Another Woman* (1988)

"Oedipus Wrecks" (from *New York Stories*) (1989)
*Crimes and Misdemeanors* (1989)
*Alice* (1990)
*Shadows and Fog* (1992)
*Husbands and Wives* (1992)
*Manhattan Murder Mystery* (1993)
*Bullets Over Broadway* (1994)
*Mighty Aphrodite* (1995)
*Everyone Says I Love You* (1996)
*Deconstructing Harry* (1997)
*Celebrity* (1998)
*Sweet and Lowdown* (1999)
*Small Time Crooks* (2000)
*The Curse of the Jade Scorpion* (2001)
*Hollywood Ending* (2002)
*Anything Else* (2003)
*Melinda and Melinda* (2004)
*Match Point* (2005)

# Foreword
# by Dick Hyman

When Adam Harvey phoned me several years ago and described his forthcoming book on music in Woody Allen films, I was pleased at the prospect of contributing what information I could. Mr. Harvey is a probing musicologist as well as a scholar of film, and in order to respond to his detailed questions, I had to re-immerse myself in material which I had not dealt with in many years. I consulted scores and work sheets and viewed film sequences which had both familiarity and, with the passage of time, an unexpected freshness. I am most grateful to Mr. Harvey for reminding me of a euphoric time in my career, when many things became possible. I am equally grateful to Woody Allen, whose confidence in my musical judgment enabled me to do my best.

*Dick Hyman is an accomplished jazz musician who, in his versatile role as composer, pianist or arranger, has worked on no fewer than fourteen of Woody Allen's films.*

# PREFACE

> I've noticed that whenever you use a pretty record in a movie, you're inundated for a year afterwards with people writing or calling or asking you, "What was that piece of Bach that you played?" Or "What was that Django Reinhardt record?"[1]

The above remark by Woody Allen provides the source of inspiration for this book: a comprehensive survey of all of the music used in his films from *Take the Money and Run* (1969) to *Match Point* (2005). Allen's films are covered alphabetically and examined, scene by scene, with each piece of music listed as it appears; the composers, authors and performers are given, together with a description of where the music can be heard. In this way, even if one is unfamiliar with the music, any piece can still be identified if the film from which it comes is known. Every film section includes its own specific commentary and an analysis of the score, together with any other salient features. (The author assumes that the reader has seen the respective film in question and is familiar with its content.)

Although some films do give a list of the music in the end credits, these lists can be incomplete and several contain errors. Also, if a piece of music or recording is not protected by copyright, there is no obligation for the film company to credit it and consequently such pieces are often omitted. Moreover, in several of Allen's earlier films, the credits only give a brief "Music by..." tag. A number of these films have specifically composed scores, but there are also films such as *Sleeper* and *Love and Death*, for instance, where the songs and music have been hitherto unidentified; they are listed here — in detail — for the first time. For those films with original scores, I have, with the help of some of the composers involved, given an analysis of each score, as well as listing all other pieces of music used in each film, some of which do not appear in the end credits.

There is a detailed introduction, which looks at some of the ways Woody Allen utilizes music in his films, including numerous quotes by Allen himself about this key aspect of his filmmaking. The book also contains a number of appendices including a complete alphabetical list of all the songs and jazz tracks used; a film-by-film list of all the available soundtracks on record and/or CD, together with suggestions about where omissions and tracks from films with no soundtrack can be found; and all of the classical music used, listed by composer.

Music is a significant part of any Woody Allen film, but previous commentators have merely touched upon this important area of his work. Such neglect is surprising, especially when one also considers Allen's active interest in music and his well-documented love of jazz. This book, then, is the first in-depth study of Allen's soundtracks to be published, and should provide fans and students alike with an interesting and informative guide.

# INTRODUCTION

Woody Allen has a special relationship with music; it is something that has been a part of his life, all of his life, and this has had a significant influence on his films. He was born on 1st December, 1935, at a time when America's popular musical culture was burgeoning. From an early age, music made a deep impression on Allen. "When I grew up, the popular music on the radio was Benny Goodman and Count Basie and there were songs from Gershwin, Cole Porter and Rodgers and Hart and Jerome Kern and Irving Berlin. And I found that beautiful and wonderful music. By the time I was ten years old, I could give you the tune on anything by Gershwin, Cole Porter, Kern, you know. And I loved all the music of the '20s and '30s. I like American songs very, very much. I think they're great."[1] Later, Allen's taste turned more specifically to jazz. "I started to listen to jazz in my teens.... When I was fourteen, fifteen — fourteen, maybe — I heard Sidney Bechet. On record. And I was very, very taken with it. And this gradually introduced me to more jazz recordings. I listened to Bunk Johnson and Jelly Roll Morton. And I got very, very interested in jazz. I loved it."[2]

This love of music also extends to performing. Allen took up playing the clarinet when he was fifteen, taking lessons from Gene Sedric (who had played with Fats Waller), and has practiced daily ever since. In 1970 he formed his own band — the New Orleans Funeral and Ragtime Orchestra — that began playing a number of New York clubs, including Barney Google's on East 86th Street. A review in the *New York Times* stated, "Mr. Allen's style on clarinet shows traces of his two favorites, George Lewis and Albert Burbank, and there are moments when one can detect echoes of Ted Lewis. He is a confident, surprisingly adept performer who holds his own with his band that rolls through tightly knit, lusty ensemble passages."[3] Eventually the band settled down to playing Monday night gigs at Michael's Pub on East 55th Street, where they played regularly until it closed in 1997; after that they moved to the Café Carlyle (a venue where Bobby Short also performed, as seen in *Hannah and Her Sisters*). The group has embarked on several tours including a number of successful trips to Europe (the one in 1996 was documented in the film *Wild Man Blues*).

6 / Introduction

With music meaning so much to Allen, it is not surprising that it plays such an important role in his movies. Several of his films have been either formulated specifically around musical themes (*Radio Days* and *Sweet and Lowdown*) or have showcased a certain composer (Prokofiev in *Love and Death*, Gershwin in *Manhattan*, Mendelssohn in *A Midsummer Night's Sex Comedy* and Weill in *Shadows and Fog*), and in 1996 Allen even fulfilled his desire to make a musical comedy with *Everyone Says I Love You*. Music is not simply background to Allen; he says, "I feel the use of music in films is a very, very important part of the tools that you're working with. Just like light and sound."[4] When asked by Tom Sancton how important music is to his life as an artist, Allen replied, "Oh, it's really important. It's important, first of all from a personal point of view, and important because I make movies, and my movies, unlike Bergman, who doesn't use music, it's a very big part of what I present to an audience. It really has an enormous effect on the material that I show them."[5] And the process of adding music to his films is clearly something he enjoys. "That's one of my favorite parts of filmmaking — going through my record collection and picking out which music I'm going to use for which scenes. Sometimes I know what I'm going to use, but more often than not, not. We shoot the scene, we come in here — there are a lot of records here — and I go through them and, you know, I've got a smorgasbord. You can pick out a Django Reinhardt or a Louis Armstrong or a Mozart, whatever you want."[6] "Selecting the music myself gives me control over a key creative facet of the film. I love it. To me, the most fun of the entire process of filmmaking is dropping the recordings in. I probably should have been a disc jockey."[7]

In his early films, Allen followed the normal practice of using a composer to write the musical score, initially employing a young Marvin Hamlisch. "In the first couple of movies I felt it was just a cliché. Everybody used somebody to score their movies. So I thought, here is this kid, he's very talented. And I used him and he scored my first couple of films."[8] Although Allen's next two films also had specially composed scores, he was never happy with using a composer. "I don't like the process. You know, the guy has to wait till the whole film's finished. He's got to see the film. And he's got to then go out and compose music, and he comes in and plays it and, hopefully, I've got to like it. And if I don't like it, I've got to tell him, 'I really don't like this,' and he's gonna be disappointed and get angry with me and go home and write another thing and come back."[9] It would appear that the score to *Everything You Always Wanted to Know About Sex* was the last straw for Allen: "I did one film ... with a score by Mundell Lowe. I didn't think much of it. I figured, this is ridiculous. I'm just gonna play my records, and score the way I want to score, when I want to score."[10]

Ralph Rosenblum had a significant influence on Allen at this time. Even as early as *Take the Money and Run*, he suggested using records to aid the editing process. "Ralph showed me many, many things. Not least of which was that I was never editing with music at all. I just edited the film. But he said, 'When you edit, take a couple of records, put them on tape and — it doesn't have to be the final music for the film — throw them in behind the scenes.' ... A little bit further down the line, I started to realize that every time I edit, I stick these records behind the scenes. And I like it better that way. I like the sound of the records. I can control it, I can do the music myself, right here in this room. There are all my records over there. I just pick up the world's greatest music and melodies, and I can choose whatever I want. And I need no finesse. I can turn it up when I want to. I can turn it off when I want to. So I started doing that and I never stopped."[11]

While Allen draws on various areas of popular music, it is his use of jazz that is most celebrated. The influence of jazz can be seen even in his earliest films — ragtime in *Take the Money and Run*; Oscar Peterson's especially composed "Blues for Allen Felix" in *Play It Again, Sam* and the Dixieland score to *Sleeper*. Throughout his films, we find many of the most notable jazz artists, ranging from Bix Beiderbecke and Louis Armstrong to Art Tatum and Thelonious Monk. This said, Allen tries not to use music that is most dear to him, as he feels that this would be inappropriate. "There are people I don't want to use because I'm too worshipful; I don't feel their music should accompany anything. Like Sidney Bechet, for example. Now I've used him twice, but in the most fleeting ways and not his great stuff. The only way I could conceivably see using one of those people would be untrammelled under the titles. I could never walk down the street with a Sidney Bechet tune bouncing behind me. I just feel, for me, that would be barbaric."[12]

Furthermore, Allen feels that using anything too pre-eminent would be overly diverting: "the great music I try not to use on a soundtrack, because it's too good and I think will subvert the picture rather than enhance it."[13] Of course, what Allen regards as "great music" is subjective. His taste leans towards authentic New Orleans jazz. "For all my love of these people, I've never used George Lewis in the background. I've never used Sidney Bechet or Johnny Dodds or Jimmie Noone.... I feel there is something about those New Orleans players that would distract you from the picture and get you too involved in the music."[14] While Allen, for the most part, steers away from this particular area of jazz, his films are nevertheless permeated with a plethora of historic recordings featuring a list of artists that runs like a who's who of jazz, including Louis Armstrong, Count Basie, Sidney Bechet, Bix Beiderbecke, Bunny Berigan, Dave Brubeck, Benny Carter, Buck Clayton, Bob Crosby, Tommy Dorsey, Roy Eldridge, Duke Ellington, Erroll Garner, Stan Getz, Benny Goodman, Bobby Hackett, Edmond Hall, Coleman Hawkins, Earl Hines, Billie Holiday, Harry James, Eddie Lang, Ted Lewis, Glenn Miller, Thelonious Monk, Gerry Mulligan, Red Nichols, the Original Dixieland Jazz Band, Wilbur de Paris, Oscar Peterson, Django Reinhardt, Artie Shaw, Art Tatum, Joe Venuti, Chick Webb, Ben Webster, Teddy Wilson and Lester Young, among others.

Allen's feeling of being "too worshipful" does not extend to other areas of jazz or popular music. "I usually use stuff that swings.... I've had no problems using great swing music and great, you know, cocktail music."[15] Indeed Allen happily uses classic tracks by many of the greatest exponents of big band music, and this also applies to the great American songwriters he has grown up with. Throughout his films there is a rich supply of some of the best songs by Gershwin, Kern, Rodgers and Hart, Berlin and Cole Porter (see appendix 2). *Manhattan* is a tribute to the songs of Gershwin. And Cole Porter, Allen's favorite songwriter, appears in no less than fifteen films, almost half his output. "Yes, you can say I'm addicted to Cole Porter."[16]

Essentially, Allen chooses music that he likes, and this is primarily from the first half of the twentieth century. "I grew up in a good era of popular music. I never like popular music, like in the '50s. I never really could get with it beyond 1950."[17] As a result, Allen's choice of music is invariably conventional, drawing primarily from popular dance music, Broadway, Tin Pan Alley and traditional jazz. Sometimes modern pop music does find its way into Allen's films by way of source music, but rarely, and his views on this type of music are in keeping with his old-fashioned tastes: "I got lost in the shuffle of contemporary music.... I'm sure it's me, but I like to think it's not. I love to see someone like Billie Holiday or Frank Sinatra singing a Cole Porter tune or a Jerome Kern tune or Gershwin, quietly, and you can hear the lyric and hear the melody. Today you see four guys with guitars and 10,000 people lifting their friends up over their shoulders, and the music is amplified beyond belief, and they dress silly and smash the guitars. It just doesn't mean anything to me. It's clear that I've been left behind."[18] Allen argues that the music on a soundtrack has to be easy to listen to, otherwise it can depreciate a particular scene. "If I'm walking down the street with a girl or chasing someone down the street or following somebody, and you put on John Coltrane or even less radical, even if it's earlier Miles Davis, it doesn't feel right. Whereas if you put on Ben Webster, then it's fine. It needs to be older."[19]

Of course, Allen's 1950 cut-off point is a generalization, and it should be pointed out that throughout his canon there is still a fair representation of music from artists beyond this date. In addition to Allen's use of "cocktail music" from performers such as Jackie Gleason, Carmen Cavallaro and Liberace, he has also included jazz from more modern exponents like Dave Brubeck, Erroll Garner, Stan Getz, Jim Hall, Thelonious Monk, Wes Montgomery and Gerry Mulligan. But although the recordings may be later, the songs performed predominantly come from Allen's preferred pre–1950 era. Picking up on his reference to Ben Webster, seemingly one of Allen's favorite jazz albums is that recorded by Webster with Art Tatum for Norman Granz as part of *The Tatum Group Masterpieces*. Tracks from this session feature in *September, Manhattan Murder Mystery* and *Deconstructing Harry*, but although the recording was made in 1956, the songs chosen all emanate from the 1930s — "My Ideal," "Night and Day," "Have You Met Miss Jones?" and "All the Things You Are." Allen's preference for accessible music can also be seen in his use of Dave Brubeck, a jazz artist who clearly postdates 1950. Brubeck's quartet appears in *Hannah and Her Sisters, Another Woman, Manhattan Murder Mystery, Mighty Aphrodite* and *Celebrity*, but again we find Allen using earlier standards such as "I Remember You," "Perdido" and "Tangerine" rather than any of their more progressive works. The one exception is "Take Five," which is the group's most popular hit and can be classed as a latter-day standard in any case.

The point is, of course, that Allen chooses music that he feels is most appropriate for a given scene or sequence, regardless of when it was written or recorded, and clearly much thought is given as to what type of music this is. While there are a few occasions when the music is simply background or source music, other times we find Allen using a certain song to reflect or comment upon what the audience sees on screen. This is achieved with great subtlety, as Allen, for the most part, employs songs in instrumental versions, so that the singing does not distract the audience from the dialogue. Consequently, a new dimension is added to the film, which will only be grasped by the members of the audience who are familiar with the song title and/or lyrics. The utilization of song as a subtext is an especially significant aspect of Allen's filmmaking process, and the reader will find numerous examples cited throughout this book.[20]

Allen's predominant use of instrumental versions of songs is in itself an interesting feature. If a particular rendition of a song is used which does contain singing, then this is almost always only ever heard over the opening or end credits, or during scenes where there is little or no dialogue. Otherwise, Allen uses either non-vocal versions or carefully edits out the singing of a particular recording. Examples of this latter process include "A Sailboat in the Moonlight" (*Zelig*), "Out of Nowhere" (*September*) and "I've Heard That Song Before" (*Hannah and Her Sisters*). There are situations, however, where the appropriate recording of a particular song is unobtainable or simply doesn't exist. In these instances, Allen will, on occasion, have the song(s) specially arranged as he did in *Manhattan*, *Radio Days*, *Bullets Over Broadway*, *Everyone Says I Love You* and *The Curse of the Jade Scorpion*, for example; otherwise he will employ a pianist such as Dick Hyman or Bernie Leighton to play the required song on the piano, as seen in *Hannah and Her Sisters*, *September*, *Another Woman*, *Husbands and Wives* and *Melinda and Melinda*, among others.

There are also a number of extended sequences in Allen's films where music is employed, but where there is no singing and no dialogue, and here Allen harks back to the silent film era. As these scenes are often slapstick or otherwise comic in nature, there needs to be a certain tempo to the music in order to make the scene funny (see Allen's remarks in the sections on *Take the Money and Run* and *Sleeper*). Therefore, the music used is often rhythmically driven and/or very upbeat, and Allen is a master at finding just the right piece of music to accompany such scenes. Good examples include "The Big Noise from Winnetka" in *Manhattan Murder Mystery*, when Carol (Diane Keaton) sneaks into her neighbor's apartment; Wilbur de Paris's lively rendition of "I've Found a New Baby" in *Mighty Aphrodite*, when Lenny Weinrib (Woody Allen) is looking frantically for the name of his adopted child's mother (note the use of subtext in the song title); and the recurrent use of Benny Goodman's "Sing, Sing, Sing," with Gene Krupa's pulsating drums ("Oedipus Wrecks," *Manhattan Murder Mystery* and *Deconstructing Harry*). This last piece is a particular favorite of Allen's and its frequency in his films has to do with the track's relentless energy, which makes it suitable for a wide range of comic scenes. (See the section on *Manhattan Murder Mystery* for Allen's own description of this piece.)

The consideration that Allen gives to how music should be applied is also demonstrated in how he uses it within the structure of his films. It is common to find the same piece of music at the beginning and end of a film, thus providing a frame, giving a sense of unity and completeness. Many of these tracks have been carefully chosen to complement the subject matter and are particularly pertinent to the storyline. With "I Want a Girl (Just Like the Girl That Married Dear Old Dad)" ("Oedipus Wrecks"), "What Is This Thing Called Love?" (*Husbands and Wives*) and "With Plenty of Money and You" (*Small Time Crooks*), for instance, Allen has selected songs that encapsulate the principal theme of each film. Sometimes this framing process will occur not over the titles, but over the opening and closing scenes. In *Radio Days*, for example, Harry James's version of "The Flight of the Bumble Bee," heard as the credits come up, is of less importance than the use of "September Song," which we hear during Allen's opening narration. Kurt Weill's appropriately nostalgic song then reappears as Allen gives his final monologue, thus providing a correlation between the beginning and the end of the film.

While popular music, and especially jazz, are clearly important elements in Allen's films, his use of classical music is also worthy of attention. Benayoun states, "Woody Allen pays the same rigorous attention to popular music that Kubrick does to classical and experimental music."[21] But classical music also plays a key part in Allen's films and is an area that is often overshadowed by his use of jazz, even though Allen has scored three complete films using music by specific classical composers (Prokofiev in *Love and Death*, Mendelssohn in *A Midsummer Night's Sex Comedy* and Kurt Weill in *Shadows and Fog*), and more recently has used opera to provide the musical backdrop to his 2005 film, *Match Point*.

Allen's treatment of classical music is similar to that of popular music. Again, we find the aforementioned framing process. In *Love and Death*, for example, Prokofiev's famous "Troika" is heard over the opening and closing credits, and within the film itself Allen uses "Song about Alexander Nevsky" to accompany Boris's opening and closing monologues. It should be pointed out that this latter example is a rare instance of singing and dialogue being heard simultaneously. For the most part, Allen uses instrumental classical music when scoring scenes with dialogue, corresponding to his use of popular music (as mentioned above). There are occasions where vocal works are present in his films, but these are generally all forms of source music, either sung by characters in the film or heard at the opera. The score to *Match Point* is a notable exception: Allen uses pre-existent recordings of opera extracts as an integral part of the soundtrack, but even here, the scored elements are rarely heard in conjunction with dialogue.

A good demonstration of how Allen carefully evades the sound of the human voice can be found in the score to *Shadows and Fog*. All of the music used in the film is actually vocal in origin, but Allen either uses authentic instrumental arrangements (Weill's own suite from *The Threepenny Opera* and Marek Weber's rendition of "Alabama Song") or carefully selects specific extracts. The opening from *The Seven Deadly Sins*, for example, is only heard for a few seconds and fades after only fourteen bars just before the singing begins. This highlights another common trait in Allen's scoring process, which can also be found in his use of popular music: if a section of a piece of music is right for the scene at hand, then this will be used regardless of how short or incomplete it is. Another example of this can be seen in *A Midsummer Night's Sex Comedy*, where the beautiful opening to the slow movement of Mendelssohn's Second Piano Concerto is used as a type of love theme for Woody Allen's character, Andrew. Here, Allen only requires the theme played by the full orchestra; he omits the opening piano introduction and fades the music out before the piano comes in afterwards. This process also correlates to Allen's use of popular song, where he will often exclude the introduction and start at the point where the main tune begins.[22]

In addition to the films with complete classical scores, individual pieces of classical music can also be found throughout Allen's work. Not surprisingly, it occasionally appears as source music, being performed at a concert or playing on a record. However, there are also numerous instances where classical music is used to good effect to underscore either slapstick or dramatic scenes. In Allen's early films, we find classical music accompanying visual gags. Examples include the slow motion 1812 Overture in *Bananas* when Fielding Mellish makes love to a female rebel; the use of Beethoven's "Tempest" Sonata for Miles's slow/fast eating scene in *Sleeper* and the exchange of lusty looks between Boris and Countess Alexandrovna at the opera during "The Magic Flute Overture" in *Love and Death*. These early examples are rare though, as normally more rhythmic music with a faster tempo is required to accompany slapstick scenes of this nature (as mentioned above). And even though he has succeeded here, Allen still believes it is difficult to combine these two contrasting elements: "If you put classical music behind comedy scenes, it's hard to find a piece that works right for the scene — that doesn't sap the energy of a scene. Usually, you want ... you know, years ago in the silent films, they had a piano player playing and he'd pick up the tempo under certain things. And you want that."[23]

As Allen's filmmaking developed, so did his use of classical music, which became increasingly more sophisticated. During the late 1980s, Allen produced a number of films of a more serious nature, and in several of these classical music features prominently, as it is well suited to films of this type. Subsequently, Allen has continued to utilize classical music regularly, whether employing it to enhance the dramatic impact, such as the use of Beethoven's Fifth Symphony to accompany the cry for help in *Celebrity*, or to represent upper-class culture, as seen in *Small Time Crooks*. Most recently, classical music has been used to good effect to emphasize the serious elements in *Melinda and Melinda* and *Match Point*.

Focusing on the late 1980s, we find that films such as *Crimes and Misdemeanors*, *Hannah and Her Sisters* and *Another Woman* provide excellent illustrations of how cultivated Allen's use of classical music can be. In *Crimes and Misdemeanors*, Allen deliberately chooses music by Bach and Schubert for the thought-provoking elements of the film, while popular songs and jazz accompany the comedic scenes. (A similar division of music can be seen later in *Melinda and Melinda*.) In particular, the use of the opening movement of Schubert's last string quartet is especially striking, adding depth and poignancy to the scenes surrounding the murder. In *Hannah and Her Sisters*, the slow movement of Bach's F Minor Harpsichord Concerto starts life as source music when Lee (Barbara Hershey) plays a recording of it to Elliot (Michael Caine). But the piece then becomes a love theme for the two characters, reappearing twice later in the film. A similar technique to this is used in *Another Woman* during the scene where Marion Post (Gena Rowlands) puts on a record of Bach's Cello Sonata No. 2. Again, this piece is used initially as source music, but then develops into scoring as it continues during a series of flashbacks. *Another Woman* actually contains almost as much classical music as it does jazz and includes such diverse composers as Bach, Satie, Mahler, Weill and Varèse. While discussing the use of Satie in this film with Stig Björkman, Allen allows us a brief insight into his classical music tastes: "I have many great favorites other than Satie in the classical world. Naturally I like those composers who most people like: Mozart, Beethoven. But I like Mahler very much and Sibelius still more. I love Sibelius. Outside of the old masters I would say that Mahler and Sibelius are my favorites."[24] It is interesting to note that Allen has never used Sibelius in any of his films and Mahler only appears twice, both times as source music. Perhaps he feels "too worshipful" toward these composers, as he does with exponents of authentic New Orleans jazz.

Throughout Allen's films then, music — be it classical, popular or jazz — clearly plays a significant role; much like the famous black and white titles, it has become a Woody Allen trademark. His enduring love affair with jazz and popular music from the "Golden Era" has meant that Allen's films are imbued with music he loves. However, this music is not merely decorative or diegetic, but is frequently functional. Allen utilizes music subtly and with great deftness to augment what we see on screen. "Woody Allen listens carefully to the ways music can enhance the thematic and emotive content of his films. His deliberate selection of pieces suggests that music is essential to understanding his works more fully."[25] While Allen's skills as writer, director and actor are widely acclaimed, his adeptness at editing his films with music generally goes unnoticed. As Eric Lax points out, "his talent as a scorer of movies is widely overlooked, or is so taken for granted that it passes unremarked. Music is such an integral part of Woody's presentation of a film, and his use of tunes from 1900 to 1950 so pronounced, that it is possible to recognize a Woody Allen film from the score alone."[26]

# THE FILMS

## *Alice* (1990)

*Music and songs from the repertoire.*

In many ways, *Alice* is a fanciful version of *Another Woman*. Allen conveys the same principal theme — a woman's journey of self-discovery — but presents it in a much lighter vein. Although the content in *Alice* is still thought-provoking, the tone is altogether more whimsical, and this is reflected in the soundtrack. *Another Woman* is one of a number of more serious films Allen had produced toward the end of the 1980s, and in them, he had adopted a starker musical approach. But in *Alice*, he revisits the type of score found in such films as *Hannah and Her Sisters* and *Radio Days*, where the music is more ebullient. Drawing primarily on his usual array of jazz, cocktail music and American popular song, Allen provides a wonderfully buoyant and romantic score that complements perfectly the film's magical nature and charm.

Originally, Allen had considered hiring a composer to write the music for the film. In the first draft of the script, he wrote, "We should allow for the possibility of an original score."[1] Although Allen eventually decided to supply the music himself in his accustomed manner, this would account for the fact that the film has more scoring in it than usual. In contrast to his previous film, *Crimes and Misdemeanors*, where the soundtrack was primarily made up of source music, virtually every piece of music in *Alice* is used for scoring. There is a wide selection of music here, ranging from dance bands (Ambrose, Wayne King) and swing (Artie Shaw, Count Basie) to 1950s mood music (Jackie Gleason, Paul Weston) and the unusually modern Thelonious Monk. Throw in a tango (the Castilians), some Dixieland (Firehouse Five Plus Two), Erroll Garner and the (by now) almost ubiquitous Bach and you have a wonderfully diverse soundtrack. The score is archetypal Woody Allen, and it is disappointing that a soundtrack album was not released for this film. (See appendix 1.)

The aptness of Allen's choice of music is immediately apparent from the opening credits when we hear Jackie Gleason's lively rendition of "Limehouse Blues." Although this jazz standard is more traditionally performed as an instrumental (as is the case with the two versions heard in *Alice*), it was originally written with the following lyrics:

> Oh, Limehouse blues,
> I've the real Limehouse blues.
> Can't seem to shake off,
> Those real China blues.
> Rings on your fingers,
> And tears for your crown,
> That is the story,
> Of old Chinatown.

Not only do these unheard lyrics reflect Alice Tate's (Mia Farrow) disposition at the beginning of the film — she has the blues (in the form of a back pain) which she "can't seem to shake off" — but the song's Chinese flavor also foreshadows her life-changing encounter with Dr. Yang (Keye Luke) later on ("This is the story of old Chinatown"), when a different version of the song is heard. These later Chinatown scenes are skillfully edited by Allen, who utilizes the more overt oriental affectations of Ambrose's delightful recording. "Each time Alice is driven in her limousine to Chinatown, the music slides from jazz, associated with the Upper East Side, to Asian motifs, connoting a downtown world bubbling with Eastern mysticism."[2] Gleason's version then returns at the end for the concluding voice-over. This song, then, holds an important place in the film's structure. As well as appearing centrally, it acts as both prelude and postlude, and thus emphasizes the significance of Alice's fateful visit to Dr. Yang. It should also be pointed out that Jackie Gleason's "Limehouse Blues" is not the schmaltzy stuff normally associated with "The Great One." This track and "Breezin' Along with the Breeze" are both taken from his album *Jackie Gleason Presents Lazy, Lively Love*, which is more upbeat and features, as the LP cover states, "an impressive list of top-notch jazz instrumentalists whose wonderful solo and ensemble work is tastefully employed against a rich background of strings."

Gleason's more characteristic recordings — with lush strings and Bobby Hackett's trumpet — are also used by Allen and appropriately accompany the scenes when Alice is visited by the ghost of her first love. On one level, the songs "I Remember You" and "Moonlight Becomes You" are used to provide the required dreamlike quality; when discussing the use of "I Remember You," Allen remarked, "It's so pretty, it's a very, very beautiful piece of music. The most romantic music is when Eddie appears, definitely."[3] On another level, Allen again uses songs where the lyrics, although not heard, are relevant to the scene. "I Remember You" refers clearly to Alice's fond memories of her old flame, Eddie (Alec Baldwin), while their moonlit flight over New York is aptly accompanied by "Moonlight Becomes You," which also relates to the two taking a nostalgic trip back in time to the Moonlight Casino.

Both these songs refer to dreams, and this is a pervasive theme throughout the film and consequently the score. Although there is no connection with *Alice in Wonderland*, Allen's film does include a number of dream and fantasy sequences. To accompany these, Allen adopts the same musical technique seen in a number of other films, notably *Stardust Memories* and *Deconstructing Harry*, where he uses songs with the word "dream" in the title and/or lyrics to reflect the images we see on screen. When Alice has thoughts about Joe Ruffalo (Joe Mantegna), we hear "I Dream Too Much." This sumptuous string version of the song performed by Paul Weston is comparable to the latter two Jackie Gleason tracks cited above, and likewise provides the appropriate dream-like quality required.[4] Furthermore, the title of the song nicely sums up Alice's feelings: she cannot help fantasizing about Joe, but is guilty about doing so. These reservations are reflected further in the song "Darn That Dream," which is heard when Alice and Joe finally make love. During this scene, Allen even includes a visual dream reference by showing the LP cover of the Thelonious Monk Quartet's Columbia album *Monk's Dream*.[5] Both these songs illustrate that, although Alice is unquestionably attracted to Joe, she has doubts as to whether this is what she is really looking for; Allen's subtle musical references hint that the affair will not work out, even before it has properly begun.

The romantic aspects of the film, attended for the most part by mood music, are contrasted by a number of more comical sequences. The accompaniment here is more upbeat, with good examples including the Firehouse Five Plus Two's "Southern Comfort" during the scenes when Alice and Joe are invisible, and the aforementioned "Limehouse Blues" when Alice visits Chinatown. But perhaps the most amusing instances in the film occur during the scenes when Allen uses the famous tango "La Cumparsita." This dance has been described as an "acting out" of the relationship between a woman and a man, and Allen aptly associates it with the on/off affair between Alice and Joe. The piece appears briefly in *Radio Days* when the lustful Mr. Manulis is on a date with Bea and his car conveniently breaks down. Here Allen takes the seduction theme and extends it, constructing two whole sequences timed to the total duration of the selected recording. The first of these occurs when Alice takes the first batch of herbs while in Valentino's on Madison Avenue.[6] We then cut to the school and the delightful scene when Alice, under the influence of the herbs, turns from meek society wife into a brazen seductress. As the tango softly continues in the background, Alice, with a magically acquired knowledge of jazz, tantalizingly imparts a number of provocative phrases such as, "You look like you blow tenor to me" and "I just love the sax." As she leaves, she says to Joe, "I remember the first time I heard Coltrane on soprano. Until then it had just been tenor.... It was such a moment, Joe.... [It] opened up a whole new world of harmonics for me." The sleeve notes to the Decca soundtrack to *Valentino* describe the tango as "delicate but virile, graceful but vigorous — and always captivating," and this could equally describe Alice in this scene. After a couple of brief appearances, Allen then plays the whole track again later in the film when Alice frantically gets ready for her illicit rendezvous with Joe. Both these sequences are delightfully funny and highlight an interesting feature of Allen's scoring technique: he will often edit his scenes to the music — marrying the two together — rather than simply tagging the music on afterwards. For him, the music is an integral part of the editing process and the two are seen as a cohesive whole.

Finally, a number of commentators have observed that *Alice* can be seen as Allen's equivalent to Fellini's *Giulietta degli spiriti* (1965).[7] As with *Stardust Memories* and *Otto e mezzo*, there are certain musical links between the two films. *Alice* includes circus music, the original compositions by Linda Hudes for the Big Apple Circus replacing Rota's "La ballerina del circo Snap"; the female protagonist's lover is a musician in both films — Giorgio's guitar-playing Spanish friend being substituted for Joe, a tenor sax–playing Italian; and the oriental inflections in Rota's "Vascello di Susi" have a counterpart in "Limehouse Blues," both of which accompany the characters in each film who are instrumental in bringing about a change in the eponymous heroine's life.

## "Limehouse Blues"

*Written by Philip Braham and Douglas Furber (1922). Arranged by George Williams. Performed by Jackie Gleason and His Orchestra, featuring Ruby Braff (trumpet), Buck Clayton (trumpet), Yank Lawson (trumpet), Buster Bailey (clarinet), Andy Fitzgerald (clarinet), Lawrence Brown (trombone), Claude Hopkins (piano), Al Caiola (guitar) and Milt Hinton (bass) (1960).*

Opening credits and opening scene where we see Alice fantasizing about kissing Joe Ruffalo in the penguin house. This version is reprised for the end sequence where Alice's "friends" are talking about her leaving her husband, going to Calcutta and then living downtown with her children. During this sequence we see a shot of a plane, shots of India and then finally Alice happily spending time with her kids. The final gong spells the end of the film before cutting to the end credits.

## "Breezin' Along with the Breeze"

*Written by Richard Whiting, Haven Gillespie and Seymour B. Simons (1926). Arranged by George Williams. Performed by Jackie Gleason and His Orchestra, featuring Ruby Braff (trumpet), Buck Clayton (trumpet), Yank Lawson (trumpet), Buster Bailey (clarinet), Andy Fitzgerald (clarinet), Lawrence Brown (trombone), Claude Hopkins (piano), Al Caiola (guitar) and Milt Hinton (bass) (1960).*

Heard as Dr. Yang is recommended to Alice by her trainer, cutting to Alice shopping at Krizia and then talking with friends at a beauty salon. A longer cue is heard later when Alice and Joe are sharing a bottle of wine in Barbetta's and they both become invisible after taking herbs.

## "I Dream Too Much"

*Written by Jerome Kern and Dorothy Fields (1935). Performed by Paul Weston and His Orchestra (1958).*

Heard as Alice is fantasizing about meeting Joe on the stairs at the school. The track is repeated a little later when Alice is waiting to pick up her kids, knowing that Joe will arrive as well.

## "Limehouse Blues"

*Written by Philip Braham and Douglas Furber (1922). Performed by Bert Ambrose and His Orchestra (1936).*

The second version of this jazz standard is heard on two occasions when Alice goes to Chinatown to see Dr. Yang.

## "Moonglow"

*Written by Will Hudson, Eddie DeLange and Irving Mills (1934). Performed by Artie Shaw and His Orchestra (1941).*

Heard during Alice's hypnotized flashback to when she first met her husband, Doug Tate (William Hurt).

## "La Cumparsita"

*Written by Gerardo Matos Rodriguez (1917). Performed by the Castilians (1951).*

This tango is heard first when we see Alice shopping and as she takes the initial batch of herbs. It continues as we see Joe at the school and then Alice arriving. She sits next to him and begins to flirt with him, becoming increasingly more forward, until they eventually agree to meet in the penguin house at the zoo (as per Alice's earlier fantasy). It then reappears when Alice cannot bring herself to meet Joe at the penguin house, and as Joe is walking down the street on his way to see his ex-wife, Vicki (Judy Davis). The final use of this track occurs when Alice is frantically getting ready to meet Joe without her husband knowing, continuing throughout the subsequent scene where Alice lies to Doug about why she is going out (after he has told her that his backgammon game has been cancelled) and as Joe waits for her in his car in the rain. It ends as Alice's taxi arrives.

### "Caravan"
*Written by Duke Ellington, Juan Tizol and Irving Mills (1937). Performed by Erroll Garner (piano), Wyatt Ruther (bass) and Eugene "Fats" Heard (drums) (1953).*

Heard briefly as an invisible Alice watches Joe seduce Vicki on the sofa in her office, and Alice unexpectedly reappears.

### "I Remember You"
*Written by Victor Schertzinger and Johnny Mercer (1942). Performed by Jackie Gleason and His Orchestra (1953).*

Heard after Alice has taken the second batch of herbs at midnight and wakes up to find the ghost of her first love, Eddie, in her apartment. It continues as they talk, ending at the point where Doug comes in. The song begins again as Doug goes back to bed, cutting to the school, where Alice points out Joe to Eddie.

### "Moonlight Becomes You"
*Written by James van Heusen and Johnny Burke (1942). Performed by Jackie Gleason and His Orchestra (1956).*

Heard as Alice and Eddie fly over New York, past the Chrysler Building, to the Moonlight Casino (which had burned down years ago). It is heard again a little later when they are dancing, during voice-over snippets of their former relationship, until Eddie fades away.

### "The Courier" and "World Music"
*Written by Linda Hudes. Performed by the Big Apple Circus Band.*

Being played at the circus, where Alice and Joe take their children on a "date."

### "The Way You Look Tonight"
*Written by Jerome Kern and Dorothy Fields (1936). Performed by Erroll Garner (piano), John Simmons (bass) and Shadow Wilson (drums) (1951).*

Heard during the sequence where Alice and Joe are walking in Central Park and visit the dinosaur house, cutting to the two having lunch on a rooftop overlooking Times Square.

### "Alice Blue Gown"
*Written by Joseph McCarthy and Harry Tierney (1919). Performed by Wayne King and His Orchestra (1940).*

This charming waltz is used to good effect during Alice's opium dream sequence, where she visits her sister, Dorothy (Blythe Danner). Note the similarity here to the family flashback in *Another Woman*. In the earlier film, Allen used Bach, but here opts for a warmer and more nostalgic piece. The whole track is reprised for the end credits, directly following on from the final gong of "Limehouse Blues."

### Violin Concerto No. 1 in A Minor, BWV 1041, 1st movement: Allegro moderato
*Written by Johann Sebastian Bach (1717). Performed by Pinchas Zukerman (violin and conductor) and the English Chamber Orchestra (1971).*

This is the fourth film in four years in which Allen has used Bach. Here the composer is employed in much the same way as he had been in Allen's previous film, *Crimes and Misdemeanors*, with the music accompanying documentary footage of a more serious nature; in this case,

Mother Theresa helping sick people in Calcutta.

### "Darn That Dream"

*Written by James van Heusen and Eddie DeLange (1939). Performed by Thelonious Monk (piano), Oscar Pettiford (bass) and Art Blakey (drums) (1956).*

Heard as Alice and Joe make love and then reassure each other about the other's "performance" afterwards. The track is heard again later when Alice is at her typewriter and her muse (Bernadette Peters) appears. It continues as they talk and as Alice speaks to a vision of her dead mother.

### "Southern Comfort"

*Written by the Firehouse Five Plus Two (1954).[8] Performed by the Firehouse Five Plus Two (1954).*

Heard as an invisible Alice and Joe get out of a cab and go into Ralph Lauren on Madison Avenue. It continues as she eavesdrops on her friends (and he peeps at Elle MacPherson) as they talk about Alice's affair and Doug's affairs, cutting to Alice reading *The New Yorker* in bed. (Note that Allen keeps the track going for a few seconds longer than one might expect after we have cut to Alice and Doug's apartment, presumably so that we get to hear the band's trademark siren.)

### "Mack the Knife"

*Written by Kurt Weill and Bertolt Brecht (1928).*

Played (briefly) by Joe's band during a rehearsal as he talks with Alice.

### "Flight of the Foo Birds"

*Written by Neal Hefti (1957). Performed by Count Basie and His Orchestra (1957).*

Being played at Dorothy's Christmas party as Alice arrives, continuing as they talk in the kitchen. (Note the similarity here to the opening birthday party in *Another Woman*.)

### "Will You Still Be Mine?"

*Written by Matt Dennis and Thomas M. Adair (1940). Performed by Erroll Garner (piano), Wyatt Ruther (bass) and Eugene "Fats" Heard (drums) (1953).*

Still at the party, this is now being played as we see a shot of the eggnog (again this is reminiscent of the opening birthday party in *Another Woman*, where we saw a shot of the birthday cake as the music changed), continuing through the subsequent scene where numerous men profess their love for Alice under the influence of magic herbs.

### "O Tannenbaum/We Wish You a Merry Christmas"

*Traditional. Performed by Liberace (piano) (1973).*

Heard briefly as Alice leaves Dorothy's Christmas party and walks home.

# *Annie Hall* (1977)

*Music and songs from the repertoire.*

Having explored the possibilities of using jazz and classical music in *Sleeper* and *Love and Death* respectively, Allen's attitude towards scoring radically changed in his next film:

In those days I was sort of still groping for a musical approach.... I wasn't sure yet what I really wanted to do musically, so I was trying this film without music. The only music in *Annie Hall* is source music. There's no scoring at all. It's either coming from a car radio or a party of something. But there is no music in the movie. I don't know, I was just experimenting, seeing what it would be like. To be very, very sparing with the music. I was so uncompromising in my feeling. I didn't care if the audience liked it or not. I just wanted to do what I wanted to do there, make some turning point. If I did the same film today, it would probably be full of music. There's also another possibility — I remember Bergman never used music, and I was so taken with his film-making in those days, I may have thought to myself, "Perhaps he's right about the use of music." But over the years I came to have a different feeling about music.[1]

Allen said much the same thing in his interview with Melvyn Bragg a few years later:

> Bergman said he stopped using music in movies years ago, saying that it was barbaric. And so I was so under the influence of Bergman when I made *Annie Hall*, I didn't use any music in *Annie Hall* at all. 'Cause I said, "Yeah, if he says it's barbaric, it must be." And I didn't use any music. The only time there's ever music in *Annie Hall* [is when] someone turns on their radio or if they're playing at a party — source music, where there's a justifiable source. There's no scoring in the picture. There's no music over the credits. There's no music in the picture. Then as I began to make more films, I began to realize that, while this is true for Bergman, I just didn't feel that way. I felt that music was, not only *not* barbaric for my films, but vitally connected with the material and vitally connected with the emotional feelings that I wanted at the time. And so, I just now overflow, and use music, you know, frequently and it became a major, major part of my films.[2]

Allen has clearly been affected by Bergman's attitude toward scoring in this film, but unlike *Interiors* (which is more heavily influenced by Bergman) one does not come away with the feeling that the film is as musically barren as Allen suggests. The absence of music is most noticeable over the opening and closing credits — obvious places for music — but throughout the film itself it is less perceptible. This is because Allen includes a number of examples of source music: Mozart and Christmas carols on the car radio; Tim Weisberg on the record player at Tony Lacey's (Paul Simon) party; Tommy Dorsey on the radio at cousin Herbie's welcome home party; and — most memorably — the songs sung live by Annie (Diane Keaton). While all of this music is diegetic, it nevertheless still gives the film a certain warmth — something that is lacking in *Interiors*. And in point of fact, there is one unequivocal use of scoring in the film where the music does not come from a "justifiable source," despite Allen's statements above. On the first hearing of "By the Sleepy Lagoon," when we flashback to Alvy Singer's (Woody Allen) youthful reminiscences, there is no explanation for where the music is coming from as the film cuts from various exterior shots to interior shots. This sequence, with Allen's voice-over relaying childhood memories accompanied by big band music, foreshadows similar scenes found in *Radio Days*. In addition, the most important piece of music in the film, "Seems Like Old Times," is, in a way, also used as scoring. Initially sung live by Annie in a nightclub, Allen then maximizes the song's wistful tone by reprising it during the film's closing montage of flashbacks to produce a poignant ending. The significance of this song in the context of the film as a whole is ably expressed by Maurice Yacowar:

At the two-thirds point in the film Keaton sings "Seems Like Old Times." This scene is a turning point in several respects. First, it proves Annie's talent and growth. Second, the nostalgia implicit in the choice of song concentrates the emotional tenor of the entire film in this scene. (The song is heard again, faintly, behind Alvy's concluding monologue, and it swells up to provide the very last word that we hear in the film, Annie's warm "you.") Third, the scene marks a crucial point in Annie's life. It follows her reconciliation with Alvy, when they celebrate her birthday by revisiting Alvy's childhood home in Coney Island. Thus the scene is associated with her birthday, the resurrection of her affair with Alvy, and Alvy's own fixation on the past. But the song also leads to Annie's meeting with Tony Lacy, the California musician-producer who will lure Annie away from Alvy romantically, philosophically, and professionally. The song bridges her reconciliation with Alvy and her meeting his successor. At the very moment that it expresses the comfort of their reunion, it contains the beginning of their final separation.[3]

The final sequence was not in the original script, but was actually tagged on later, as Allen explains: "The editor, Ralph Rosenblum, and I tried to think how to best end the film. And we thought that what felt best was a tie-up, bringing it up to where it began. And that's what we did. But that's something that we added later."[4] When co-writer Marshall Brickman first saw the movie with this new conclusion, he enthused, "I'll never forget, suddenly there was an ending there — not only that, but an ending that was cinematic, that was moving, with that simple recapitulation of some of the previous scenes, with that music.... The whole film could have gone into the toilet if there hadn't been that last beat on it."[5]

## "By the Sleepy Lagoon"

*Written by Eric Coates (1930). Performed by Tommy Dorsey and His Orchestra (1942).*

Eric Coates's light music classic, famous in England as the theme tune to *Desert Island Discs*, was popularized in the 1940s when it was transformed from a "Valse Serenade" (its alternative title) into a slow foxtrot by big band leaders such as Harry James, Ray Anthony, Al Hirt and later Tommy Dorsey.

It is heard first as we see Alvy's old house under a roller coaster, and continues throughout the following shots of men from the armed forces outside "Steve's Famous Clam Bar" and Alvy's father directing the bumper cars. It ends during the following school sequence at the point where a young Alvy kisses a girl in his class. The track is heard again later when Alvy, Annie and Rob (Tony Roberts) visit Alvy's house years later and witness the welcome home party in 1945 for Alvy's cousin Herbie, continuing through the scenes with Joey Nichols and Aunt Tessy.

## "It Had to Be You"

*Written by Isham Jones and Gus Kahn (1924). Sung by Diane Keaton, accompanied by Artie Butler.*

Sung at a club by Annie in front of "a tad restless" audience.

## Symphony No. 41 in C Major, "Jupiter," K. 551, 4th movement: Molto allegro

*Written by Wolfgang Amadeus Mozart (1788).*[6]

Heard briefly (on the car radio) as Annie and Alvy drive to Long Island.

## "Seems Like Old Times"

*Written by Carmen Lombardo and John Jacob Loeb (1946). Sung by Diane Keaton, accompanied by Artie Butler.*

Sung at a club by Annie, this time to great applause. The song is reprised at the end of the film, starting at the point where the actors kiss at the climax of Alvy's play and continuing through Alvy's final voice-over during the montage of flashbacks from the film, ending as the film ends just before the credits.

**"Christmas Medley: We Wish You a Merry Christmas/O Christmas Tree/God Rest You Merry, Gentlemen"**

*Traditional. Performed by the Do-Re-Mi Children's Chorus.*

Heard (on the car radio) as Rob drives Alvy and Annie through Beverley Hills at Christmas.

Allen uses the carols medley to emphasize that, in California, Christmas is celebrated in the blazing sun, rather than the more traditional winter weather found in New York (which is referred to in the dialogue — "It was snowing and really gray in New York yesterday"). Indeed, the whole sequence is one of several examples where Allen shows his disdain for the West Coast. Note that Allen accentuates this at the end of the sequence when the shot of a cinema showing *House of Exorcism* and *Messiah of Evil* is accompanied by the words, "To save us all from Satan's power, when we were gone astray" from the carol "God Rest You Merry, Gentlemen."

**"A Hard Way to Go"**

*Written by Chris Youlden (1970). Performed by Tim Weisberg (1971).*

Being played at Tony Lacey's party, as Alvy, Annie and Rob pull up to his house in Beverley Hills. It returns briefly later when Annie is dancing with Tony.

## *Another Woman* (1988)

*Music and songs from the repertoire.*

Undeterred by *September*'s lack of success (and the criticism afforded to *Interiors* ten years earlier), Allen's next film was another attempt at a serious drama. In much the same vein as Bergman's *Wild Strawberries* (1957), *Another Woman* explores themes concerning family and love, as it follows an academic's uncomfortable journey of self-discovery through a series of mysterious circumstances, finally forcing the characters to confront both their past and present. Musically, however, Allen eschews Bergman's view that music in film is "barbaric" and, moving away from the Swedish director's influence, includes a much larger amount of music in this film than he did in his previous Bergmanesque dramas, *Interiors* and *September*.

As with several other films during this period, the score for *Another Woman* combines both popular and classical music, but here Allen chooses more classical music than normal in order to reflect the film's serious make-up. In other works where classical music also features prominently, such as *Hannah and Her Sisters* and *Crimes and Misdemeanors*, Allen was able to provide a counterbalance by having jazz and other popular songs accompany the more comedic scenes. But as *Another Woman* allows no lighter moments, this is not possible, and so Allen incorporates popular music into the film by way of background music. An interesting feature of the score is the way in which Allen divides these two distinct styles of music to correspond to the intellectual and emotive elements of the film. Classical music is associated with Marion Post (Gena Rowlands) and her husband, Ken (Ian Holm), who are portrayed as being aloof and undemonstrative. Paralleling the various references to poetry (Rilke) and art (Klimt), Allen uses classical music to reflect their sophisticated and academic lives: Bach chamber music is heard when they are having dinner with Eleanor and Doctor Tom Banks; we see the two attending a Mahler symphony concert; and there are references in the dialogue to Ken's preference for opera. Conversely, the more expressive characters are accompanied by jazz: Jim Hall is heard as Mark (Bruce Jay Friedman) recounts how he and Lydia (Blythe Danner) made love on the living room floor; Erroll Garner accompanies Larry Lewis's (Gene Hackman) display of passion at Marion and Ken's engagement party; and Teddy Wilson is playing in the bar when Claire (Sandy Dennis) fervently tells Marion how she really feels about her.

Although the jazz and popular songs used are primarily heard as source music, their function is not always merely decorative. As with several other films, notably *September*, Allen again succeeds in utilizing music so that it plays an important role, despite the fact that, on the surface, it might appear inconsequential. Once again, his familiar technique of using certain songs or song titles to provide a subtext to the narrative is present. A good illustration of this occurs when Marion and her former lover, Larry, are together at the engagement party. In the background, we hear "A Fine Romance," where the ironic lyrics reflect their unsettled relationship: Marion has agreed to marry Ken, but is still involved with Larry. Later on at the same party, another Jerome Kern song, "Make Believe," echoes Marion's repressed feelings for Larry and her refusal to face reality.

Offsetting the diegetic popular music, the classical pieces that Allen chooses are invariably used for scoring, and one area in which this is particularly effective is during Marion's dream sequences and flashbacks. In *Stardust Memories* (and later in *Alice* and *Deconstructing Harry*), Allen used his favorite technique of reflecting dream sequences with songs that have the word "dream" in the title or lyrics. In *Another Woman*, however, Allen uses classical music instead, partly because it is more fitting for a serious drama, but also because it reinforces the aforementioned intellectual aspect of Marion's character. Once again, Bach is used to emphasize this relationship. When visiting her father (another academic), Marion plays an LP of Bach's D Major Cello Sonata.[1] The piece begins life simply as something Marion enjoys listening to, but then develops from source music into scoring as she reminisces about her childhood. Likewise, Bach is used again near the end of the film when Marion is in bed and recollects a happier time with her first husband, Sam (Philip Bosco), which is reflected in the elegiac "Allemande" that Allen chooses for this scene. All three Bach works used in the film involve a solo cello, and it could be that Allen was intending the instrument to symbolize Marion's isolated character. Furthermore, chamber music seems better suited to complement Marion's highbrow world; one gets more of an impression of dry academia with this type of music, and it provides a starker accompaniment than orchestral music. Even more unusually, Allen chooses Varèse's *Ecuatorial* for Marion's more disturbing fantasy sequences. The unsettling visions she has are effectively accompanied by this austere experimental work, which uses electrically generated sound. The inclusion of such an avant-garde piece marks a departure from Allen's normal choice of classical music, which is primarily mainstream, and this is a rare example of him utilizing a piece of music purely for its effect, rather than also being something he enjoys listening to.

As a contrast, Allen selects a more lyrical piece to accompany Marion's bittersweet reminiscences about Larry, a man whose passion she rejects for the "cold and stuffy" Ken. Satie's *Gymnopédie No. 1*[2] is, to all intents and purposes, used as a love theme for Marion and Larry; the fact that this piece frames the film and also appears in the middle of Marion's main dream sequence emphasizes its importance. When discussing the use of Satie in *Another Woman* with Stig Björkman, Allen remarked, "He's not my favorite composer, but I do like him. And I use a pretty piece of music, one of his 'Gymnopédies.' Because it fits."[3] However, this choice of music by Allen has been criticized. Brode finds that it has a "prissy, pristine quality,"[4] and then goes on to quote from Pauline Kael's review from *The New Yorker*:

> The opening music, Satie's *Gymnopédie No. 3* [sic], is like the soothing Vangelis arrangements used in commercials for Gallo wines — music that's selected because it couldn't upset the most delicate sensibilities. (It has the qualities of a digestif.) The audience laughs, taking the wine-country connection to be a joke. It's a jump ahead of Woody Allen, who must be so secluded from the world of commercials that he didn't anticipate the reaction. He has become so conventional in his tastes that this genteel slumber-party music is his idea of an artistic prelude.[5]

Misguidedly taking his cue from this statement, John Baxter comments:

> For the main titles he [Allen] used Erik Satie's *Gymnopédie No. 3* [sic], evidently not realizing that dozens of film-makers had already done so, including the director of a television advertisement for Gallo wines, which employed a particularly soupy arrangement by Vangelis. Audiences for *Another Woman* giggled, assuming a musical comment by Allen on the resemblance between Marion's unexamined life and the anodyne world of commercials; but insiders realized that Allen, who never watched network TV, simply didn't know the Gallo ad existed.[6]

Admittedly, *Gymnopédie No. 1* is Satie's most popular work, and it has been used in a number of TV commercials and films. However, Kael's "wine-country connection" is one of her own making, as this was not the actual piece used for the Gallo wines TV commercials. This was, in fact, "Hymne," an original composition by Vangelis, which, with its somewhat cloying theme and synthetically produced sound, is in no way comparable to Satie's wistful melody or Debussy's delicate orchestration. Moreover, it is irrelevant whether Allen is conscious or blissfully unaware of the music used in TV commercials. Kael misses (or chooses to ignore) the point. Allen selected this piece because it gave him the dreamlike quality he required. This is why he uses Debussy's impressionistic orchestration rather than the original solo piano version, which is how the work is most often heard. In this respect, this version of the *Gymnopédie* is particularly apt; Allen selects music that is meditative and ethereal, music that not only provides the required feeling of nostalgia, but also captures the regret Marion has for not making the right choice.

Of equal importance to Satie's *Gymnopédie* in the score is "The Bilbao Song," the most famous excerpt from Kurt Weill and Bertolt Brecht's last collaboration, *Happy End* (1929). This song is being played on the piano at the opening 50th birthday party. Seemingly, this is just background music, but significantly, it accompanies a scene between Ken and Marion where we are allowed to see — ever so briefly — the passion the two used to share before their marriage became sterile. In the kitchen, when the two are alone, Ken recognizes the song and says, "Take you back?" and Marion replies, "Oh yeah!" Later, the song takes on greater meaning when, near the end of the film, Allen reuses it to score the scenes when Marion finally meets Hope (Mia Farrow). This meeting acts as a catalyst for the final phase of Marion's transformation from her "cold, cerebral life" into one where she allows herself to feel, including the climactic discovery that Ken is having an affair with Lydia. It could be argued then that Allen uses this song to echo the repressed emotion in Marion's character; emotion that we glimpsed at the beginning of the film and that she eventually recaptures at the end, after her life-changing encounter with Hope. "The Bilbao Song" can also be seen as bridging the gap between the intellectual/classical and emotional/popular aspects; appearing in both contexts of the score, it forms a link between these two worlds as it accompanies Marion's journey from one to the other. Allen's use of Kurt Weill is fitting in this respect, as Weill was something of a crossover composer with a foot in both the classical and popular music camps. In addition, Bernie Leighton's pensive piano arrangement aptly provides the desired feelings of longing and nostalgia, enhancing further the moving scenes toward the end of the film.

### Gymnopédie No. 1

*Written by Erik Satie (1888). Orchestrated by Claude Debussy (1897). Performed by the Orchestre de la Société des Concerts du Conservatoire, conducted by Louis Auriacombe (1967).*

Opening credits. This piece is used later in two significant scenes where Marion is thinking about Larry and their past relationship. During Marion's main dream sequence, the music is heard at the mention of Larry's name, continuing as he appears with his wife (in the form of Claire) and he and Marion talk. It returns at the end of the film when Marion decides to read Larry's novel. The book has a character in it based on Marion, and it recounts some of the happier times Larry and Marion spent together. As she reads it, we see flashbacks of them together, culminating in a passionate kiss when sheltering from the rain in Central Park. The music continues as we hear Marion's final voice-over, before cutting to the end credits: "And I wondered if a memory is something you have or something you've lost. For the first time in a long time, I felt at peace."

### "Perdido"

*Written by Harry Lenk, Erwin Drake and Juan Tizol (1942). Performed by the Dave Brubeck Quartet: Dave Brubeck (piano), Paul Desmond (alto sax), Ron Crotty (bass)* and Lloyd Davis (drums) (live at Oberlin College, 1953).

Heard at the 50th birthday party.

## "You'd Be So Nice to Come Home To"

Written by Cole Porter (1942). Performed by Jim Hall (guitar), Chet Baker (trumpet), Paul Desmond (alto sax), Sir Roland Hanna (piano), Ron Carter (bass) and Steve Gadd (drums) (1975).

Continuing from the previous scene, this is heard as we see a shot of the half-eaten birthday cake, and continues as Marion and Ken listen to Mark telling them how he and Lydia made love on the living room floor.

## "Lovely to Look At"

Written Jerome Kern, Dorothy Fields and Jimmy McHugh (1935). Performed by Bernie Leighton (piano).

Being played on the piano at the birthday party by Bernie Leighton himself.

## "The Bilbao Song"

Written by Kurt Weill and Bertolt Brecht (1929). Performed by Bernie Leighton (piano).

Continuing from the previous scene, we hear this as Marion and Ken are talking in the kitchen. This song then takes on a more important role and recurs three times near the end of the film in the scenes with Marion and Hope. We hear it as Marion enters the antique store and finds Hope crying, and briefly, when Marion and Hope are walking down the street going to a gallery. Finally, it reappears as we see Marion's close-up after Hope has said, "I just don't wanna look up when I'm her age and find my life empty." It continues as we flashback to when Marion sees Ken and Lydia together at the restaurant, cutting to her at home crying, before Ken comes home. The song is reprised in full during the end credits.

## "A Fine Romance"

Written by Jerome Kern and Dorothy Fields (1936). Performed by Erroll Garner (piano), Eddie Calhoun (bass) and Kelly Martin (drums) (1976).

Heard at the engagement party where Marion and Larry are secretly kissing.

## "Make Believe"

Written by Jerome Kern and Oscar Hammerstein II (1927). Performed by Erroll Garner (piano), Eddie Calhoun (bass) and Kelly Martin (drums) (1976).

Heard at the same party later on, as an upset Marion lights a cigarette and then talks to Larry about Ken.

## Sonata for Cello and Piano No. 2 in D Major, BWV 1028, 4th movement: Allegro

Written by Johann Sebastian Bach (1721). Performed by Mischa Maisky (cello) and Martha Argerich (piano) (1985).

An LP of this is put on the record player by Marion before she goes through her mother's possessions with Laura (Martha Plimpton). The book of Rilke poems and photographs induce childhood memories, and the music continues during the subsequent flashbacks. The piece is heard again briefly later, when Marion is driving Laura back into town.

## "Smiles"

Written by Lee S. Roberts and J. Will Callahan (1917). Performed by Teddy Wilson (piano), Gene Ramey (bass) and Jo Jones (drums) (1956).

Being played in the bar where Marion goes for a drink with Claire and her husband, Jack (Jacques Lévy).

## "On the Sunny Side of the Street"

Written Jimmy McHugh and Dorothy Fields (1930). Performed by Teddy Wilson (piano), Gene Ramey (bass) and Jo Jones (drums) (1956).

Continuing from the previous scene, this is heard at the point where Marion and Claire start arguing about a former lover named David ("Then you do know!").

### *Ecuatorial*
*Written by Edgard Varèse (1934). Performed by Ensemble InterContemporain, conducted by Pierre Boulez (1983).*

This avant-garde piece is used twice during Marion's dream sequences. The first time, we see a black panther (a reference to Rilke's poem), a theatrical mask (a present she gave her first husband) and Klimt's painting *Hope* (foreshadowing Marion's meeting with the pregnant Hope later in the film). The piece returns briefly at the beginning of Marion's main dream sequence, as we shift to the front of the theater and she enters.

### "Roses of Picardy"
*Written by Haydn Wood and Fred E. Weatherly (1916). Performed by Frankie Carle (1948).*

Heard as Marion walks down the corridor into her brother Paul's office and they talk.

### Symphony No. 4, 1st movement: Bedächtig. Nicht eilen
*Written by Gustav Mahler (1901). Performed by the New York Philharmonic Orchestra, conducted by Leonard Bernstein (1960).*

A brief passage from the opening movement is heard at a concert attended by Marion, Ken, Mark and Lydia.[7] The camera is pointed at the audience, who are seemingly watching a performance of this symphony, although what we hear is a pre-existent recording.

### Sonata for Cello and Piano No. 3 in G Minor, BWV 1029, 1st movement: Vivace
*Written by Johann Sebastian Bach (1721). Performed by Mischa Maisky (cello) and Martha Argerich (piano) (1985).*

Heard during Marion's voice-over when she and Ken are having dinner with Tom and Eleanor Banks.

### Cello Suite No. 6 in D Major, BWV 1012, 2nd movement: Allemande
*Written by Johann Sebastian Bach (1725). Performed by Yo-Yo Ma (1983).*

Heard as Marion is in bed and we then see a flashback of her with Sam, her first husband. The music continues as a young Marion gives him an original mask from a French production of *La Gioconda* for his birthday; she puts it on and they kiss, the scene cutting back to Marion in bed.

# *Anything Else* (2003)

*Music and songs from the repertoire.*

As seen in his previous film, *Hollywood Ending*, the score to *Anything Else* primarily centers on a particular group of performers. In a similar manner to the way Jackie Gleason and Bobby Hackett were used together and separately in *Hollywood Ending*, here Allen uses Billie Holiday as the focal point for the soundtrack, to which he adds material by two of her closest jazz associates — Teddy Wilson and Lester Young. The scored elements of the film comprise six songs in recordings that involve each of these three musicians, either performing together or independently from one another. Holiday performs all three of her songs with Wilson's orchestra (Young features on "I Can't Believe That You're in Love with Me"), and these songs, which are all heard several times throughout the film, dominate the score. As with Holiday's recording of "Did I Remember" in *Celebrity*, Allen chooses material from the historic sessions recorded during the early phase of her career when she was in the company of a number of great soloists: "Billie's first three years of recordings constitute her finest period.... Most of these 1935–39 recordings, some with Teddy Wilson–led small groups, others under her own 'leadership,' are classics of jazz."[1] Supplementing these, Allen also includes "Honeysuckle Rose" from Teddy Wilson's 1937 session with Harry James and Red Norvo, and two tracks from Lester Young's 1952 session with the Oscar Peterson Trio, recorded at the twilight of his career. Clearly, then, Allen uses the link between this triptych of jazz luminaries to give the score a cohesive unity, and at the same time pay tribute to three of jazz's most eminent and iconic figures.

Each of the three songs sung by Billie Holiday have been used before by Allen and, as in earlier films, he uses them to reflect the feelings of the characters involved. In this case, the songs provide a subtext to the ups and downs of Jerry (Jason Biggs) and Amanda's (Christina Ricci) relationship. As used in a similar fashion by Allen in *Alice* and *Deconstructing Harry*, Jerome Kern's "The Way You Look Tonight" is heard as romance is about to blossom, while Jerry's surprise that Amanda shares his feelings is accompanied by "I Can't Believe That You're in Love with Me." The most important song, however, is Cole Porter's "Easy to Love," which ironically comments on the difficulty Jerry has in his relationship with Amanda. Twenty-three years earlier Allen used this same song in a similar fashion, when Sandy Bates was having comparable problems in his relationship with Dorrie in *Stardust Memories*. Just as Cole Porter's "What Is This Thing Called Love?" bookends *Husbands and Wives*, "Easy to Love" is heard significantly over the opening and closing titles (as well as throughout) and acts as the film's main theme. This familiar framing technique is a favorite of Allen's, and, as we have seen, has been employed in a number of other films. Cole Porter is also mentioned a number of times in the dialogue, and as with Schubert in *Crimes and Misdemeanors*, this creates a relationship between the narrative and the score.

The songs performed by Holiday's soulmate Lester Young are also relevant to Jerry and Amanda's troubled affair. "There Will Never Be Another You" reflects Jerry's gradual realization that his relationship with Amanda is coming to an end, while "I Can't Get Started" predicts Jerry's failed attempts at making love with Amanda in a hotel suite. Vernon Duke and Ira Gershwin's standard was a favorite of Young's. He recorded the song a number of times throughout his career, including a celebrated date in 1938 with Billie Holiday's orchestra. Significantly, Allen uses two of the slower, more serene tracks from Young's late sessions with Oscar Peterson in order to provide a romantic and less intrusive accompaniment. (Most of the songs on the *Lester Young with the Oscar Peterson Trio* album are faster bebop-like numbers.)

In addition to the aforementioned songs, which make up the main body of the score (along with "Honeysuckle Rose"), the remainder of the soundtrack comprises a few items of source or background music, either heard in a restaurant or party, with two songs sung live by Diana Krall and Stockard Channing respectively. These latter two songs are also pertinent to the storyline. At the Village Vanguard (a jazz haven since 1935, where Lester Young used to jam) Diana Krall sings a poignant rendition of "It Could Happen to You." This song, with its cautionary lyrics about falling in love, is heard at the point where Jerry is becoming increasingly infatuated with Amanda and is unable to resist her allure. As a counterpoint to this, Amanda's mother, Paula Chase (Stockard Channing), sings "There'll Be Another Spring" later in the film after Jerry and Amanda have had an argument. This song offers some hope that they will resolve their problems, but it also conveys an undertone of acceptance that perhaps the relationship is over and that the two need to move on.

The soundtrack to *Anything Else* ranks as one of Allen's most jazz-oriented scores. While the music concentrates on highlighting pre-eminent jazz musicians, with Billie Holiday as the central figure, it also contains a host of renowned songwriters. As we have seen, the inclusion of songs by the likes of Cole Porter, Jerome Kern and Harry Warren is normal practice for Allen. However, it is worth pointing out that this film provides some prime examples of how popular song and jazz were intertwined. It was common for jazz musicians to draw their material from the popular hits of the day; both "Easy to Love" from *Born to Dance* and "The Way You Look Tonight" from *Swingtime*, for example, were recorded by Billie Holiday in 1936, the same year that these films were released. And even though Allen includes some later examples of jazz — Wes Montgomery, Oscar Peterson, Lester Young — these too are heard performing standards that pre-date 1950. Of course, this is Allen's preferred period of music and so it is not too surprising to find most of the songs in *Anything Else* emanating from this era. This is further born out by Diana Krall's live performance. In the film's trailer, Krall is heard singing "The Look of Love," written in 1967 for Dusty Springfield. But in the actual film she sings "It Could Happen to You," an old standard used by Allen before in *Hannah and Her Sisters*. It is significant that he chooses a song which is more in keeping with his tastes as well as the tone of the film; a Burt Bacharach song would be out of place in a score which so ably brings together Allen's beloved jazz and favorite songwriters.

### "Easy to Love"

*Written by Cole Porter (1936). Performed by Billie Holiday, with Teddy Wilson and His Orchestra (1936).*

Opening credits, fading during the opening shot of Central Park. The song returns various times throughout the film: when Jerry first mentions Amanda and talks about meeting her, cutting to him waiting for her taxi in the rain; when Jerry and Amanda are in bed together at the Warwick Hotel; and finally at the end of the film when Jerry gets a final glimpse of Amanda as he is leaving the city in a cab, cutting to the end credits.

### "Gat I"

*Written by Ravi Shankar. Performed by Ravi Shankar.*

Background music in the Indian restaurant.

### "It Could Happen to You"
*Written by James van Heusen and Johnny Burke (1944). Performed by Diana Krall.*

Sung live by Diana Krall at the Village Vanguard.

### "Gone with the Wind"
*Written by Herb Magidson and Allie Wrubel (1937). Performed by Wes Montgomery (guitar), Tommy Flanagan (piano), Percy Heath (bass) and Albert Heath (drums) (1960).*

Background music at the Village Vanguard after Diana Krall's performance.

### "The Way You Look Tonight"
*Written by Jerome Kern and Dorothy Fields (1936). Performed by Billie Holiday, with Teddy Wilson and His Orchestra (1936).*

Heard first when Jerry is hanging around outside Amanda's apartment and then phones her to ask her if she wants to go to a record store to pick up some Billie Holiday records. Paralleling this, the song returns near the end of the film when Jerry is again following Amanda, but this time to see if she is having an affair.

### "I Can't Believe That You're in Love with Me"
*Written by Clarence Gaskill and Jimmy McHugh (1926). Performed by Billie Holiday, with Teddy Wilson and His Orchestra (1938).*

Heard as Jerry kisses Amanda in the record store. At this point Jerry even says, "I can't believe I'm in love with a smoker." The song returns when we see Jerry dating another girl after he and Amanda have temporarily split up, continuing as Amanda then returns and moves back in.

### "Honeysuckle Rose"
*Written by Thomas "Fats" Waller and Andy Razaf (1929). Performed by Teddy Wilson (piano), Harry James (trumpet), Red Norvo (xylophone) and John Simmons (bass) (1937).*

Heard when Jerry and Dobel (Woody Allen) are spending time together in Central Park and are "getting closer and closer." The track returns at the end of the film when Jerry is about to leave the city and we flashback to him and Dobel walking in Central Park, before cutting back to him in the taxi cab. The song segues into "Easy to Love" as Jerry gets one last glimpse of Amanda.

### "I Can't Get Started"
*Written by Vernon Duke and Ira Gershwin (1936). Performed by Lester Young and the Oscar Peterson Trio (1952): Lester Young (tenor sax), Barney Kessel (guitar), Ray Brown (bass) and J.C. Heard (drums).*[2]

Heard as Jerry and Amanda come out of a cinema and walk down the street.

### "Sunday (the Day Before My Birthday)"
*Written by Moby and Sylvia Robinson (2003). Performed by Moby (2003).*

Background music at the party when Jerry is introduced to Connie (Erica Leerhsen).

### "There'll Be Another Spring"
*Written by Peggy Lee and Hubie Wheeler (1959). Sung by Stockard Channing, featuring Cynthia Sayer (piano).*

Sung at the piano by Paula in Jerry and Amanda's apartment.

### "There Will Never Be Another You"
*Written by Harry Warren and Mack Gordon (1942). Performed by Lester Young and the Oscar Peterson Trio (1952): Lester Young (tenor sax), Oscar Peterson (piano), Barney Kessel (guitar), Ray Brown (bass) and J.C. Heard (drums).*

Heard when Jerry is walking by the river at night, cutting to the apartment where Amanda is cooking spaghetti with Connie.

## *Bananas* (1971)

*Original music composed by Marvin Hamlisch,
with additional music from the repertoire.*

For his second film Allen retained the services of Marvin Hamlisch, who was once again asked to compose an original score. Conscious of the mistakes he had made on *Take the Money and Run*, Allen's main concern with *Bananas* was being funny. As Allen's editor Ralph Rosenblum points out, "Woody packed *Bananas* so full of jokes that another movie could have been made from its outtakes."[1] Allen himself remarks, "I wanted to make sure that everything was funny and fast-paced. That was really what I was concentrating on. So if I shot or edited scenes almost cartoonlike, it was for that reason."[2] To complement the film's frenetic character, Hamlisch provides appropriately effervescent music, which not only keeps pace with the film's energy, but also enhances several of Allen's comic sequences. For Rosenblum, who again worked closely with the composer, Hamlisch "created one of the great unacknowledged film scores."[3]

With the Latin American associations in *Bananas*, it is not surprising that there is often a Spanish flavor to some of Hamlisch's music. The composer wrote both music and lyrics (in Spanish) for the song "Quiero la Noche," which is sung by the Yomo Toro Trio, and also had an input for its use over the opening titles: "Comedies are probably the most difficult type of films to score. The music cannot get in the way of the laughs, and yet it must support all of the different kinds of scenes in the film. When I came up with the whole idea of perforating the title sequence of *Bananas* with bullet holes, I brought the idea to Woody. He was very receptive and it really worked out."[4] As with *Take the Money and Run*, Hamlisch gives *Bananas* a main theme, which he then developed and used throughout the film in various guises. In addition to the vocal version, the song's melody also appears as a love theme played on solo piano during Fielding Mellish's (Woody Allen) scenes with Nancy (Louise Lasser), and as an upbeat Dixieland number. All of these variants permeate the score, and Hamlisch even reprises "Quiero la Noche" for the film's end credits, this time sung by Jake Holmes under the name "'Cause I Believe in Loving," with English lyrics by Howard Liebling. After such a fast-paced comedy, it is surprising that the film concludes with a calm and pensive ballad. On this subject, Yacowar remarks, "One sentimental refuge from the film's satirical tone can be found in the Liebling-Hamlisch song that closes the film. The singer declares that he is taken for a fool because he believes in loving, giving and sunshine. The nebbish hero of *Bananas* would like to live by this idealism, but the bananas world does not nourish those values. *Bananas* satirizes the variety of ways that man conspires to exploit others — politically, religiously, culturally, and romantically. The sense that this exploitation is a lunatic waste of life gives this chaos of comedy its remarkable and sober cohesion."[5]

For the remainder of the score, Hamlisch again shows his skill at writing music in a number of different styles, as he had done with *Take the Money and Run*. Paralleling Allen's sketch-like structure, much of this music appears as brief vignettes, which accompany the various free-standing scenes that make up much of the film's thin plot. These include typical 1970s incidental music when Fielding is looking at pornographic magazines; piano music in the style of a silent movie accompaniment heard when the two thugs get on the subway; and a bizarre choral piece followed by frantic sitar music during the weird dream sequence when monks are carrying Fielding on a cross. Besides "Quiero la Noche" and its variations, the only other substantial musical material in the score is the zany, kazoo-inflected music used exclusively during the scenes where Fielding is at the rebel camp. This theme is heard on a number of occasions, primarily in an up-beat form, and is linked to the various slapstick sequences when Fielding trains with Esposito's (Jacobo Morales) men, but it also appears as a slow blues number to accompany Fielding's seductive eating scene with the rebel girl, Yolanda (Natividad Abascal).

In addition to Hamlisch's soundtrack, the film also includes the following pieces of music, none of which appear in the end credits:

### "Tramp! Tramp! Tramp!" from *Naughty Marietta*

*Written by Victor Herbert and Rida Johnson Young (1910).*

Captain Dick's march-like song is heard as a recording of this operetta is played to a captured rebel as a means of torture. We also hear briefly the beginning of the next song, "Taisez-Vous."

### 1812 Overture, Op. 49

*Written by Peter Ilyich Tchaikovsky (1880).*

The climax to this orchestral piece is heard as Fielding and Yolanda remove their clothes in slow motion before making love.

### "O mio babbino caro" from *Gianni Schicchi*

*Written by Giacomo Puccini (1918).*

This is sung (a cappella) by Miss America (Dagne Crane) in the court room.

## *Broadway Danny Rose* (1984)

*Music and songs from the repertoire, including original songs by Nick Apollo Forte. Music supervisor: Dick Hyman.*

At New York's Carnegie Deli on Seventh Avenue, a group of borscht-belt comics gather and begin to tell stories about Danny Rose (Woody Allen), a two-bit talent agent who handles a number of dubious acts, including a one-armed juggler and a one-legged tap dancer. Eventually we hear "*the* greatest Danny Rose story," as told by Sandy Baron, which centers around Danny Rose's best act, Lou Canova (Nick Apollo Forte), an over-the-hill crooner who "made some noise" in the forties, and his mistress, Tina Vitale (Mia Farrow), a brash, blonde virago and ex–Mafia moll.

Given the predominant Italian theme, it is not surprising that the score is infused with Italianate music. The real-life singer-entertainer Nick Apollo Forte provides two original songs, "My Bambina" (also known as "Keep Italian in Your Heart") and "Agita," a song about indigestion. Both of these are in the style of Italian-American crooner songs of the 1950s and 1960s. "My Bambina" is a love ballad redolent of "Innamorata" and "Non dimenticar," while "Agita" is an upbeat novelty song in the manner of "Eh Cumpari" and "That's Amore." Indeed, the verse of "Agita" bears a striking resemblance to Lou Monte's 1962 hit, "Pepino, the Italian Mouse," which is perhaps the ultimate Italian novelty song.

Although there are two brief compositions by Dick Hyman in the score, here he acts primarily as music arranger and supervisor rather than composer. Both of Apollo Forte's songs are arranged in a variety of ways, with "Agita" dominating the score. To add to the Italian flavor, Hyman also incorporates a number of Italian standards, including "Funiculi Funicula" and "Torna a Surriento!" and features distinctive instruments such as the accordion and the guitar (played with tremolo in the manner of a mandolin).

The accordion solos are performed by the highly regarded Dominic Cortese, who also makes a cameo appearance during the Mafia party sequence where he plays several traditional dances and Neapolitan songs. Hyman and Cortese would work together again three years later on Norman Jewison's, *Moonstruck* (1987), and then again in 1996 on Allen's musical comedy, *Everyone Says I Love You*.[1] In actual fact, *Broadway Danny Rose* can, in some ways, be seen as forerunner to Hyman's score for *Moonstruck*. In the later film, Hyman not only arranges a number of Italian pieces (mostly from Puccini's *La Bohème*), but also composes a number of original compositions in the Italian style. No doubt, the experience gained working on this film stood him in good stead in this respect.

### "Agita"
*Written by Nick Apollo Forte. Performed by Nick Apollo Forte; also performed by Dick Hyman's Studio Orchestra: Dick Hyman (piano), Dominic Cortese (accordion), Don Arnone and Vinny Bell (guitars), John Beal (bass) and Ted Sommer (drums).*

This infectious song is heard first sung live by Lou Canova over the opening credits, continuing during the opening scene at the Carnegie Deli, and then reappears in various guises throughout the film. An up-tempo orchestral version is used as chase music (when Danny Rose and Tina Vitale are being pursued by Mafia hoods), and during traveling shots (when Danny and Tina drive out to New Jersey). There is also a slow accordion version heard when Danny and Tina are in the cab going home, having eluded the Mafia, and when Danny visits Barney Dunn (Herb Reynolds) in hospital. In addition, we hear part of the song again sung by Lou, this time at the Waldorf-Astoria. The orchestral version returns during the end credits.

### "The Band Played On"
*Written by Charles B. Ward and John F. Palmer (1895). Performed by Gloria Parker.*

Being played by the "water glass virtuoso" in Phil Chomsky's (David Kissell) office.

### "Catskill Cha Cha"
*Written by Dick Hyman. Performed by Dick Hyman (piano), John Beal (bass) and Ted Sommer (drums).*

Heard briefly when Danny is backstage trying to reassure the husband of an old Jewish lady who has been put in a trance by his hypnotist act, but will not wake up.

## "All of You"
*Written by Cole Porter (1954). Performed by Nick Apollo Forte.*

Being sung by Lou at a club, watched by adoring women.

## "Queens Club Trio"
*Written by Dick Hyman. Performed by Dick Hyman (piano), John Beal (bass) and Ted Sommer (drums).*

Performed by an unseen group following on from the previous song while Danny and Lou talk in his dressing room. It fades as the film cuts to Danny picking out a jacket for Lou.

## "You're Nobody Till Somebody Loves You"
*Written by Russ Morgan, Larry Stock and James Cavanaugh (1944). Performed by Nick Apollo Forte.*

Being sung by Lou on the stage of a cruise liner and then again later after Lou has left Danny and is being watched by Sid Bacharach (Gerald Schoenfeld) and a guilt-ridden Tina.

## "Tra Veglia e Sonno"
*Written by Luigi Canoro and P. Forte. Performed by Dick Hyman's Studio Orchestra.*

This Italian mazurka (which translated means "Between Dreaming and Waking") is heard in a plaintive mandolin-like version on two occasions: when Tina and Danny visit a fortune teller, and during the shot of the boat slowly floating off down the Hudson River. A fragment of the opening is heard briefly on solo accordion preceding "Agita" when Danny and Tina are creeping down the stairs after untying themselves. It is also the first tune played by Dominic Cortese on the accordion at the Mafia party (see below).

## "Funiculi Funicula"
*Written by Luigi Denza and Giuseppe "Peppino" Turco (1880). Performed by Dick Hyman's Studio Orchestra (as above).*

Heard first when Tina — and then a little later Danny — arrive at the Mafia party. We hear it again when the Rispoli brothers smash up Danny's car, cutting to Danny and Tina getting on a boat to cross the Hudson River. It is reprised in full during the end credits.

## "Tra Veglia e Sonno"
*Written by Luigi Canoro and P. Forte.*

Heard at the Mafia party when Danny talks to Rocco (Tony Turca), shortly after arriving. This is first of seven tunes played by Dominic Cortese on the accordion.

## "A Frangesa"
*Written by P. Mario Costa (1894).*

Heard as Danny talks to Vincent (Ronald Maccone) after speaking to Rocco.

## "Ciribiribin"
*Written by Alberto Pestalozza and Carlo Tiochet (1898).*

This is heard faintly from the garden outside, as Johnny Rispoli (Edwin Bordo) tells Tina that he loves her and recites a poem. It continues as the film cuts to a shot of the accordion player (Dominic Cortese) walking past outside.

## "Tarantella"
*Traditional tune played at Italian weddings.*

Heard as we see two men tearing up money, continuing as Danny and Tina are walking in the garden talking about Lou's performances of "Sorrento" and "That's Amore."

## "Luna mezzo mare" (aka "C'e la luna" or "Cella luna")
*Written by Paolo Citarella.*

This Sicilian tarantella is heard as Danny continues to talk to Tina in the garden.

### "O Sole Mio"
*Written by Eduardo di Capua and Giovanni Capurro (1899).*

The opening of this famous Neapolitan song is heard as Danny takes a sip of Tina's drink. We hear the opening bars of the more familiar chorus just before cutting to the next scene when Tina is talking on the phone to Lou.

### "Chella llà"
*Written by Sandro Taccani and Umberto Bertini (1957).*

Overlapping with the previous scene. This is heard as Tina is on the phone to Lou, cutting to a woman's face as she sees Johnny on the balcony (the accordion comes to an abrupt halt at this point).

### "Torna a Surriento!" (aka "Come Back to Sorrento")
*Written by Ernesto de Curtis and Giovanni Battista de Curtis (1902). Performed by Dick Hyman's Studio Orchestra (as above).*

Heard as we see a car shot of Danny and Tina leaving the party, cutting to the Rispoli brothers plotting revenge with Johnny's mother (Gina DeAngeles).

### "My Bambina" (aka "Keep Italian in Your Heart")
*Written by Nick Apollo Forte. Performed by Nick Apollo Forte; also performed by Dick Hyman's Studio Orchestra (as above).*

Sung by Lou at the Waldorf-Astoria. A slow and sad instrumental version is then heard at the end of the film when Tina turns up at Danny's Thanksgiving party, but is rejected by Danny and leaves. The music swells as Danny eventually decides to follow her and runs down the street (this is reminiscent of the end of *Manhattan*), catching her up outside the Carnegie Deli. The music softens as they walk off, continuing during the final voice-over to the end of the film.

### National Emblem March
*Written by Edwin Eugene Bagley (1906).*

Being played by the marching band during Macy's Thanksgiving Day Parade on Central Park West watched by Tina and Ray (Craig Vandenburgh).

### "Begin the Beguine"
*Written by Cole Porter (1940). Performed by Gloria Parker.*

Being played by the "water glass virtuoso" at Danny's Thanksgiving party.

# *Bullets Over Broadway* (1994)

*Music and songs from the repertoire.*

With *Bullets Over Broadway* Allen returns once again to his much-loved pre–War era, this time to 1920s New York where big-city mobsters and the Broadway stage collide. Drawing on jazz, dance music, Broadway show tunes and Tin Pan Alley, Allen provides a representative selection of the various types of popular music that were all the rage during the Roaring Twenties. The score dutifully complements Santo Loquasto's sets, Jeffrey Kurland's costumes and Carlo di Palma's cinematography, and it provides the perfect musical backdrop to the Runyonesque world that these components help create. Such a setting allows Allen to indulge his preferred musical tastes, and the film has been furnished with a number of songs by Allen's favorite songwriters, notably Cole Porter, Jerome Kern, Rodgers and Hart and George Gershwin.[1] Some of these composers are also referenced in the script, with Cole Porter, Jerome Kern, George Gershwin and Billy Rose all mentioned by one or other of the characters. The score also includes popular artists of the time, such as Al Jolson and Eddie Cantor, as well as some fine examples of jazz from this period by Duke Ellington, Red Nichols and Bix Beiderbecke.[2]

In addition to the pre-existent recordings, Allen also required a number of special period arrangements. For these, he again turned to Dick Hyman, whom he had not worked with since *Radio Days*. As with *Zelig*, Hyman produces authentic-sounding arrangements that blend in seamlessly with the 1920s setting. Under the name of the Three Deuces Musicians and Chorus, Hyman conducts all of the show tune numbers we hear performed at the Three Deuces Club. During the performance of "You Took Advantage of Me," Hyman can actually be seen conducting the stage band.[3] The name "The Three Deuces" may have been inspired by the real-life speak-easy at 222 North State Street in Chicago which flourished in the 1920s, as well as another club with this name which opened in New York City in 1937. The Chicago club often hosted jam sessions by a number of jazz musicians, including Bix Beiderbecke, Eddie Condon, the Dorsey brothers and a young Gene Krupa, among others. The Three Deuces Musicians and Chorus include a number of performers that Hyman would work with on Allen's next two films. In addition to arranging and conducting, Hyman also performs a solo piano version of "Thou Swell" and a duet version of "That Certain Feeling" with Derek Smith. Hyman and Smith have made a number of recordings together (including *At the Movies* and *They Got Rhythm*) and also worked together on *Hannah and Her Sisters*, *Radio Days* and *Everyone Says I Love You*.

Most of the music for the score is diegetic. While Allen still uses some songs that reflect what we see on screen, for example, "Let's Misbehave" when Nick (Joe Viterelli) feels like fooling around, most of the music is being performed in clubs or is heard in the background. The one notable use of scoring is "Lazy River," which accompanies the scenes where Cheech (Chazz Palminteri) takes his victims to the waterfront. This song was actually written in 1931, and so, strictly speaking, its inclusion is not historically accurate. However, as the song is expressly used for scoring purposes and not as source music, it is not technically an anachronism. The version Allen uses of "Lazy River" was taken from the 1988 album *Here Comes the Hot Tamale Man* by the New Leviathan Oriental Fox Trot Orchestra, a contemporary New Orleans–based group, who gave Allen the authentic performance he required.

## "Toot, Toot, Tootsie! (Goodbye)"
*Written by Gus Kahn, Ernie Erdman, Dan Russo and Ted Fio Rito (1922). Performed by Al Jolson with the Vitaphone Orchestra (1923).*

Opening credits.

## "Ma! (He's Making Eyes at Me)"
*Written by Con Conrad and Sidney Clare (1921). Performed by Eddie Cantor with Henri Rene and His Orchestra (1921).*

## Bullets Over Broadway (1994)

Heard briefly before Cheech and his fellow hoods shoot some rival gangsters.

### "You've Got to See Mamma Ev'ry Night (or You Can't See Mamma at All)"

Written by Con Conrad and Billy Rose (1923). Arranged and conducted by Dick Hyman. Performed by Dick Hyman and the Three Deuces Musicians with the Three Deuces Chorus.

Being sung and danced to at the club by the chorus line, as Nick is talking to his fellow gangsters about "business."

### "Make Believe"

Written by Jerome Kern and Oscar Hammerstein II (1927). Arranged by Walter Paul. Performed by Dick Hyman and the Three Deuces Musicians.

Being played at the club while Nick and Olive Neal (Jennifer Tilly) are arguing backstage.

### "That Jungle Jamboree"

Written by Thomas "Fats" Waller, Andy Razaf and Harry Brooks (1929). Performed by the Harlem Footwarmers (1929).[4]

Heard briefly at the Cotton Club where Julian Marx (Jack Warden) is talking on the phone to David Shayne (John Cusack) about the play. This 1929 recording of Duke Ellington is used to give the impression that the piece is being performed live at the Cotton Club, which would be historically accurate, as Ellington was resident at the club between 1927 and 1930.

### "Singin' the Blues (Till My Daddy Comes Home)"

Written by Con Conrad, Samuel M. Lewis, J. Russell Robinson and Joe Young (1920). Performed by Frankie Trumbauer and His Orchestra, featuring Bix Beiderbecke (cornet) (1927).

Heard while David and Helen Sinclair (Dianne Wiest) are talking about the play in a speakeasy.

### "Lazy River"

Written by Hoagy Carmichael and Sidney Arodin (1931). Performed by the New Leviathan Oriental Fox Trot Orchestra (1988).

Heard as Cheech takes a member of a rival gang to the waterfront and "bumps him off." The song returns later when he does the same thing to Olive.

### "Poor Butterfly"

Written by Raymond Hubbell and John L. Golden (1916). Performed by Red Nichols and His Five Pennies (1928).

Heard while David and Helen are on the roof drinking martinis and discussing the play.

### "Let's Misbehave"

Written by Cole Porter (1927). Performed by Irving Aaronson and His Commanders (vocal refrain by Phil Saxe and Chorus) (1928).

Heard as Nick fancies "a little action" with Olive, who is not in the mood. The track is reprised in full during the end credits.

### "You Took Advantage of Me"

Written by Richard Rodgers and Lorenz Hart (1928). Arranged and conducted by Dick Hyman. Performed by Dick Hyman and the Three Deuces Musicians, featuring Randy Sandke (trumpet).

Played at the club when David is celebrating his birthday.

### "When the Red, Red Robin Comes Bob, Bob Bobbin' Along"

Written by Harry Woods (1926). Arranged and conducted by Dick Hyman. Performed by Dick Hyman and the Three Deuces Musicians.

Continuing from the previous scene,

this is the next number played at the club as Cheech makes suggestions about the play to David.

### "Crazy Rhythm"
*Written by Joseph Meyer, Roger Wolfe Kahn and Irving Caesar (1928). Performed by Roger Wolfe Kahn and His Orchestra (1928).*

Heard as David narrates events during rehearsals, where the play is now working much better. We see Helen and Eden Brent (Tracey Ullman) seemingly getting on and Warner Purcell (Jim Broadbent) cheating on his diet; the sequence ends with Warner hiding a roll in his script.

### "Thou Swell"
*Written by Richard Rodgers and Lorenz Hart (1927). Arranged by Dick Hyman. Performed by Dick Hyman (piano).*

Background music (presumably being played on the piano) at Helen Sinclair's party.

### "At the Jazz Band Ball"
*Written by D.J. LaRocca and Larry Shields (1918). Performed by Bix Beiderbecke and His Gang: Bix Beiderbecke (cornet), Bill Rank (trombone), Don Murray (clarinet), Adrian Rollini (bass saxophone), Frank Signorelli (piano) and Chauncey Morehouse (drums) (1927).*

Heard as we see a shot of the train from Boston to New York, on which David and Helen are talking and drinking paint remover.

### "Nagasaki"
*Written by Harry Warren and Mort Dixon (1928). Arranged and conducted by Dick Hyman. Performed by Dick Hyman and the Three Deuces Musicians with the Three Deuces Chorus.*

Sung at the club by the chorus line while Nick and Julian discuss Olive's part in the play.

### "That Certain Feeling"
*Written by George and Ira Gershwin (1925). Arranged by Dick Hyman. Performed by Dick Hyman and Derek Smith (pianos).*

Being played at the club when Julian is reading out reviews of the play, leading into the scene where David is walking home and shouts up at Sheldon Flender's (Rob Reiner) apartment where he suspects Ellen (Mary-Louise Parker) is staying.

### "Who?"
*Written by Jerome Kern, Otto Harbach and Oscar Hammerstein II (1925). Performed by George Olsen and His Music (1926).*

Heard as David and Ellen get back together and as he admits that he is not an artist and proposes marriage. The track leads into the end credits.

## *Celebrity* (1998)

*Music and songs from the repertoire.*

The score to *Celebrity*, a social satire examining the pleasures and pitfalls of fame, draws from Allen's usual musical assortment of jazz and popular song. There is a slight emphasis on piano and mood music from the likes of Liberace, Carmen Cavallaro and Jackie Gleason, and several of the artists used have appeared before: Stan Getz and Gerry Mulligan (*Another Woman*), Jackie Gleason (*Alice*), Dave Brubeck (*Hannah and Her Sisters*, *Another Woman* and *Mighty Aphrodite*), Teddy Wilson (from the same sessions heard in *Another Woman*) Liberace ("Oedipus Wrecks" and *Crimes and Misdemeanors*) and Erroll Garner, who made his "debut" in *Another Woman* and has appeared regularly in Allen's films ever since. What is more, it could be argued that the reappearance of so many of the same performers is linked to the fact that "*Celebrity* ... replays many of the themes found in Allen's earlier films."[1] Reflecting this, the soundtrack has similarities or direct links to some of the scores to previous films. Like *Crimes and Misdemeanors*, most of the music appears as source music — either being sung or performed live at one function or another or being heard on the soundtrack of a film. In addition, the plot is largely episodical, and thus resembles the multilayered structure of *Deconstructing Harry*, which, as we have seen, also includes several songs heard in earlier films. In order to accompany some of the various encounters experienced by the film's main protagonist, Lee Simon (Kenneth Branagh) and his ex-wife, Robin (Judy Davis), Allen ascribes to these episodes their own musical theme, as he did in his previous film. Indeed, it may be significant that *Celebrity* and *Deconstructing Harry* have more repetition of songs and artists in them than in any of Allen's other films to date.

Perhaps the best example of an interrelationship with an earlier film can be seen in the way certain themes in *Celebrity* "evoke associations to *Manhattan*."[2] In particular, Schwartz refers to the black and white photography, bridge shots and self-destructive affairs. From a musical perspective, there are corresponding references in the score that also recall Allen's earlier film. Having used Gershwin exclusively in *Manhattan*, Allen has understandably avoided having his songs in subsequent films (*Bullets Over Broadway* is a notable exception). But here he includes two Gershwin songs on the soundtrack.

Moreover, *Celebrity* contains a scene in Elaine's, complete with a shot of the restaurant's name on the window. This is a direct quote from the opening scene in *Manhattan*, and the accompanying music is similar in each case. In addition to using the same style and genre — up-tempo jazz played by a piano-based trio — Allen also alludes to this scene in the title of the song he chooses: "Mine" in *Manhattan*; "Will You Still Be Mine?" in *Celebrity*.

As is common, Allen begins with an appropriate song over the opening titles. Dana Suesse (a rare female songwriter during the Tin Pan Alley era) and Edward Heyman penned "You Oughta Be in Pictures" for the *Ziegfeld Follies of 1934*. The song's movie related theme and references to wealth, fame and stardom are particularly apt for Allen's film. As well as being significantly used over the opening titles, the song also appears later in the film during the hectic sequence where Robin starts her new job working for Tony (Joe Mantegna). Here, the song is heard in full, including Little Jack Little's vocal, which is a rare example of Allen combining singing and dialogue; on the whole Allen will go out of his way to avoid such a clash, such as in the case of "Did I Remember" (see below).

Hirsch describes the film has having a "symphonic texture,"[3] and this is in evidence, from a musical aspect at least, right from the outset. After the opening titles, Little Jack Little is interrupted abruptly by the well-known strains of Beethoven's Fifth Symphony as we are plunged into what appears to be a dramatic cry for help. "Thus fate knocks at the door" is how Beethoven himself described the rhythmic opening to his most celebrated symphony, and this analogy can be extended to include Allen's use in *Celebrity*: the film's opening scene fatefully foreshadows Lee's "existential crisis"[4] seen at the end. As Schwartz points out, "The final images of the movie underscore how lost and out of control he has become, as Allen cuts from an on-screen, sky-written plea for HELP to a close-up of Lee alone at the screening of the movie whose filming begins *Celebrity*. Even the coaching for the skywriting scene given to the star, Nicole, now pertains to Lee."[5] Indeed, as Bailey observes, "The image of these letters recalls the instructions Nicole's director gave her while shooting the scene ... instructions which provide a perfect gloss for Lee's circumstances as he watches *The Liquidator*'s premiere. 'You see the skywriting.... You realize that everything has gone wrong, and you can't believe it because you thought you had it all figured out, but everything's chaos now.'"[6] Structurally, then, Beethoven frames the film in much the same way as Prokofiev's "Song about Alexander Nevsky" did in *Love and Death*, and this correlation between the opening and closing scenes adds to the film's sense of unity as a whole.

As already stated, most of the music in *Celebrity* is diegetic; however, there are a few scenes that are scored and these are done so in typical fashion. Taking Billie Holiday's classic rendition of "Did I Remember," Allen continues the "adoration theme" posited over the film's opening titles for the episode involving the supermodel (Charlize Theron). This song is heard four times in the film and it has been carefully edited so that the singing does not run into any dialogue. Note that during the scene where Lee and the supermodel are in the diner/bar — where there is constant talking — we hear the middle section of the song with instrumental solos, while the beginning and end of the song — when Holiday is singing — are used during scenes where there is no dialogue: on the catwalk; Lee cleaning his car; and walking away from the crash. Another instance of scoring shows Allen making good use of "On a Slow Boat to China." Here the song works on two levels. The romantic style of Jackie Gleason and the theme of desire (which Allen used to effect in *September*) combine to provide fitting music for Lee's affair with Nola (Winona Ryder). In addition, Allen takes the song's nautical imagery and humorously uses it to accompany the scene when Bonnie (Famke Janssen) — having been dumped for Nola — throws the only copy of Lee's novel into the Hudson River, as she floats slowly away on a riverboat. Later in the film Allen alludes to this earlier episode by reprising the song when Lee speaks to Philip Datloff (Larry Pine) about his novel and Bonnie.

As we have seen in a number of Allen's films, notably *September*, *Another Woman* and *Crimes and Misdemeanors*, some of the source music we hear is also used functionally. In *Celebrity*, Allen again employs the technique where unheard lyrics reflect the feelings of the characters on screen, thus providing a subtext to the narrative. At the book party in Elaine's, for instance, "Will You Still Be Mine?" is being played in the background, which is a question both Lee and Nola (who had flirted with each other earlier on the film set) are secretly asking themselves as they look at each other across the table. Another good example of this occurs during the scenes surrounding the wedding between Robin and Tony. Before the ceremony, we hear "Soon," a song with lyrics that are especially appropriate for such an occasion, echoing Allen's use of "Great Day" and "Because" at the wedding in *Crimes and Misdemeanors*. After Robin's non-arrival, the pianist then plays "For All We Know," and the unheard lyrics to this song aptly reflect Tony's feelings — he is uncertain if he will ever meet Robin again. These examples exemplify the precision with which Allen chooses music for his films. It would have been very easy to have inconsequential background music playing either side of the wedding scene, but Allen has carefully selected songs that are relevant to the storyline, even though ostensibly they appear to be insignificant.

### "You Oughta Be in Pictures"

*Written by Dana Suesse and Edward Heyman (1934). Performed by Little Jack Little (1934).*

Opening credits and then again during the hectic scenes when Robin starts a new job working for Tony Gardella at the studio, cutting to a birthday party at Tony's parents. The track returns near the end of the film when Lee Simon bumps into Robin in the foyer during the movie premiere.

### Symphony No. 5 in C Minor, Op. 67, 1st movement: Allegro con brio

*Written by Ludwig van Beethoven (1808). Performed by the Royal Philharmonic Orchestra, conducted by Rene Leibowitz (1961).*

Heard as the word "HELP" is seen written in the sky by a plane over New York City. As the music fades, we discover that this turns out to be a scene from a movie called *The Liquidator*, and the music is on the soundtrack to this film. The music returns at the end of the film as we see the same scene during the movie's premiere. The camera pans left over the audience, pausing at Lee's face before cutting to the movie screen where once again we see the word "HELP" written in the sky, before the end credits.

### "Tangerine"

*Written by Victor Schertzinger and Johnny Mercer (1942). Performed by the Dave Brubeck Quartet: Dave Brubeck (piano), Paul Desmond (alto sax), Eugene Wright (bass) and Joe Morello (drums) (1958).*

Heard during the traveling shots either side of Lee's episode with Nicole Oliver (Melanie Griffith) as they drive to the house where she grew up.

### "Kumbayah"

*Traditional. Performed by Janet Marlow.*

Sung by a nun at the Catholic retreat.

### "Did I Remember (To Tell You I Adore You)?"

*Written by Walter Donaldson and Harold Adamson (1936). Performed by Billie Holiday and Her Orchestra, featuring Artie Shaw (clarinet) and Bunny Berigan (trumpet) (1936).*

This song is used during the scenes involving Lee and the supermodel. It is heard first at the fashion show, as models walk up and down the catwalk. The track then returns three times: as Lee walks past the supermodel going to his car and she comes out and says, "Hey, nice car!"; when Lee and the supermodel are in a diner with some of her friends and he tells her how beautiful she is; and as the supermodel walks away from the car crash. The song is reprised in full during the end credits.

### "Chanel No. 5"

*Written by Michael Franano (1998). Performed by the Michael Moon Band (as the El Flamingo Band).*

Being performed (and badly mimed)

at a club where Lee and the supermodel are dancing.

### "Fascination"
Written by Filippo D. Marchetti and Dick Manning (1904). Performed by Liberace (piano).

Heard at the screening where Lee and Robin argue with each other. The music is used as the soundtrack to the film they are watching, during a scene where we see a couple on a beach.

### "Truckin'"
Written by Bob Weir, Jerry Garcia, Phil Lesh, and Robert Hunter (1970). Performed by the High School Reunion Band.

The first song we hear being played by the band at the High School Reunion.

### "The Impossible Dream"
Written by Mitch Leigh and Joe Darion (1965). Performed by Robert Cuccioli and the High School Reunion Band.

Sung by Monroe Gordon at the High School Reunion.

### "American Pie"
Written by Don McLean (1972). Performed by the High School Reunion Band.

Being played by the band at the High School Reunion, after Monroe Gordon's solo.

### "All Hail to You, Glenwood High"
Written by Eddy R. Davis. Performed by the High School Reunion Class.

Sung by the class at the High School Reunion.

### "I Got Rhythm"
Written by George and Ira Gershwin (1930). Performed by Teddy Wilson (piano), Gene Ramey (bass) and Jo Jones (drums) (1956).

Heard when Lee and Bonnie are at Philip Datloff's cocktail party.

### "That Old Feeling"
Written by Lew Brown and Sammy Fain (1937). Performed by Gerry Mulligan (baritone and tenor sax), Stan Getz (tenor and baritone sax), Lou Levy (piano), Ray Brown (bass) and Stan Levey (drums) (1957).

Also heard at Philip Datloff's party, when Lee is speaking to a woman about Irwin Shaw.

### "Will You Still Be Mine?"
Written by Matt Dennis and Thomas M. Adair (1940). Performed by Erroll Garner (piano), Wyatt Ruther (bass) and Eugene "Fats" Heard (drums).

Heard during the scene at the book party in Elaine's. Lee is already there with friends before Nola and David (Hank Azaria) arrive.

### "Lullaby of Birdland"
Written by George Shearing and George David Weiss (1952). Performed by Erroll Garner (piano), Wyatt Ruther (bass) and Eugene "Fats" Heard (drums) (1953).

Directly following on from the previous song, this is heard briefly at the end of the Elaine's book party scene, when David comes to find Nola, who has just arranged a liaison with Lee.

### "On a Slow Boat to China"
Written by Frank Loesser (1948). Performed by Jackie Gleason and His Orchestra (1965).

Heard as Nola comes out of the subway to meet Lee, continuing as they talk and eventually kiss, cutting to Bonnie at the apartment. The track then returns a little later when Lee realizes that Bonnie has taken the only copy of his novel and he chases after her only to see her throw it page by page into the Hudson River. We here the song again later when Lee bumps into Philip Datloff.

### "Cocktails for Two"
Written by Sam Coslow and Arthur John-

ston (1934). Performed by Carmen Cavallaro (piano).

Heard as Robin interviews celebrity diners in the Jean-Georges Restaurant for an episode of "Manhattan Moods."

**"Soon"**
*Written by George and Ira Gershwin (1930). Performed by Ray Cohen (piano).*

Played by the pianist at Robin and Tony's wedding before the service.[7]

**"Bridal Chorus" from *Lohengrin***
*Written by Richard Wagner (1848). Performed by Ray Cohen (piano).*

Played for the bride's procession at Robin and Tony's wedding, although Robin doesn't turn up. (Note that any pianist or organist at a wedding would not start playing until the bride had arrived and was about to walk down the aisle.)

**"For All We Know"**
*Written by J. Fred Coots and Samuel M. Lewis (1934). Performed by Ray Cohen (piano).*

Played by the pianist (we see a badly synchronized shot of Ray Cohen at the piano) at Robin and Tony's wedding after Tony has been jilted.

## *Crimes and Misdemeanors* (1989)

*Music and songs from the repertoire.*

As with *Manhattan* ten years earlier, the decade culminated with a film that was acclaimed by fans and critics alike. During the latter part of the 1980s, Allen's films had become increasingly serious in nature, dealing with more thought-provoking themes. With *Crimes and Misdemeanors*, this darker tone is still present, but unlike *September* and *Another Woman* (which were both heavily criticized), it is offset by a parallel storyline which provides the audience with some comic relief. As Brode observes, "Allen's technique in *Crimes and Misdemeanors* is to brilliantly balance the dramatic and comedic elements—moving self-assuredly from scenes of silly, sweet-spirited, characteristic Allenesque humor to confrontations that, as in the best of Bergman, transform the melodramatic into the allegorical."[1] A similar dual structure had been seen in *Hannah and Her Sisters*, but whereas the dramatic and comedic elements had been blended together in the earlier film, in *Crimes and Misdemeanors* the contrast is more distinct. Fundamentally, the latter film is made up of two disparate stories only tenuously linked, but with just enough of a connection to be joined at the end of the film. Corresponding to this, Allen selects a mixture of both classical and popular music, which he uses to distinguish the serious subject matter and the funnier aspects: Bach and Schubert accompany Professor Louise Levy's (Martin Bergman) documentary and the murder; jazz and popular songs are heard during the film's lighter moments involving Woody Allen's character, Cliff Stern.

While there is an abundance of music in *Crimes and Misdemeanors*, it is interesting to note that the majority of it appears as source music. Much of the music is performed live at one function or another, or is played on the record player, or on the soundtrack of something that a character is watching.

While much of this is purely background music, once again there are examples of certain songs being chosen which are used functionally and, in a similar fashion to *September*, often reflect or comment upon the feelings of the characters. (Examples of this are given below under the individual song titles.)

Although the actual scoring in *Crimes and Misdemeanors* is sparse, the little that is present is used to good effect. Without question, the most striking example of this involves Allen's utilization of Schubert's last string quartet. Allen does not actually show the murder itself in the film, but concentrates on the scenes before and after. The dramatic opening movement of the quartet serves to heighten the apprehension as we see the killer follow Dolores Paley (Angelica Huston) to her apartment, and then Judah's (Martin Landau) shock as he sets eyes on her dead body. "I've loved that piece of music for many years. And long before I wrote the story for *Crimes and Misdemeanors* I thought, 'What a wonderful piece of music, gripped with tension and gripped with portent.' So when I thought of music for that spot, this Schubert quartet came back to me and it was an instantly correct feeling for me. Then I went back into the script and changed one of the pieces of dialogue to include Schubert in it, so there was a relationship ... the strings are riddled with anxiety. That's a beautiful piece of music!"[2]

A key theme in the film is about seeing and sight. As Allen remarks, "eyes were a metaphor in the story. Judah was an eye doctor who heals people on one hand, but is willing to kill on the other. And he doesn't see well himself. I mean, his vision is fine, but his emotional vision, his moral vision is not good. The rabbi is blind in other things, to the realities of life. On the other hand, he can triumph over it because he has spiritual substance. *Crimes and Misdemeanors* is about people who don't see. They don't see themselves as others see them. They don't see the right and wrong of situations. And that was a strong metaphor in the movie."[3] To reflect this, Allen includes a number of songs in the score that refer to eyes or sight. One such song, "I'll Be Seeing You," was chosen for the film's final sequence, but although seemingly appropriate, it was not Allen's first choice, as he had used it in his previous film, "Oedipus Wrecks." Eric Lax states:

> Woody had planned to use "Always," but when he heard that Steven Spielberg was making a film with that title he checked with him to see if he intended to use the song. He did (although it turned out that Irving Berlin would not give permission to use it) and Woody said he'd find something else, a gracious act he now regretted because he couldn't find anything appropriate. An added problem was that with Ben's blindness, a title with "eyes" in it, such as "I Only Have Eyes for You" or "Jeepers Creepers," made an unintentional and inappropriate joke. (He ended up, however, using "I'll Be Seeing You" because he could find nothing better.)[4]

Lax then proceeds to quote a conversation between Woody Allen and Susan (Sandy) Morse (Allen's editor), which took place when the two were trying to find a suitable replacement. The following gives an interesting insight into how Allen chooses songs for his films:

> He and Sandy suggested songs to each other, occasionally getting up to check the backs of albums on the shelves

in a large case against the wall or to look through the ASCAP title book. He knows virtually every decent song written between 1900 and 1950 and has used hundreds of them in his movies. He has also seen and re-seen thousands of films and has retained their specifics with almost the same clarity as a chess grandmaster remembers thousands of moves.

"We've used 'Make Believe' before, in *September*," Woody said [sic — Allen means *Another Woman*]. "'We'll Meet Again,' but Kubrick used it in *Dr. Strangelove*. It has the right sort of schmaltzy sound. 'Speak to Me of Love.' 'If I Loved You.' 'I Only Have Eyes for You.'" He laughed. "I keep doing that by accident. It's too bad. It's such a pretty, schmaltzy song. 'As Time Goes By' can't be used. 'I Dream Too Much,' we've used. I wouldn't want to use Gershwin because of *Manhattan*. Cole Porter is the wrong person for this end music. 'Falling in Love Is Wonderful,' but an Irving Berlin song can't go beyond the picture [and into the credits]. How about 'I'm Confessin'?"

"That's in *September* also," Sandy told him.

"Okay." He paused. "I want something with the feel of 'Lara's Theme,' that's a waltz." He paused again. "'I'll Be Seeing You' is in *Oedipus Wrecks*. 'You Are Too Beautiful,' we've used. 'Bewitched,' we used. 'Isn't It Romantic?'..."

"You don't think *that* would have gotten away." (It's used in *Hannah and Her Sisters*.)

"Nothing by Vernon Duke? Certainly nothing by Duke Ellington. Too jazzy. Porter's too sexy, more of a Latin beat. That's not right. Anything of Leonard Bernstein's? 'On the Town.' 'My Sister Eileen.' There are so many to choose from."[5]

It should be noted that, despite his reluctance to repeat himself in this instance, Allen has used many songs or recordings more than once on several other occasions (see appendix 4).

## "Rosalie"

*Written by Cole Porter (1937). Performed by the Jazz Band: Warren Vaché (trumpet), Walt Levinsky (clarinet), George Masso (trombone), Derek Smith (piano), Major Holley Jr. (bass) and Charles Miles (drums).*[6]

Allen uses this live recording over the opening and closing credits. Later in the film we see the actual performance of the song, which was recorded live to camera by an ad hoc group at the bar where Cliff Stern (Woody Allen), his wife, Wendy (Joanna Gleason), Halley Reed (Mia Farrow) and Lester (Alan Alda) are having a drink together. This recording is also heard briefly when we see Cliff walking down the street with his niece, Jenny (Jenny Nichols), eating pizza.

## "Taking a Chance on Love"

*Written by Vernon Duke, John LaTouche and Ted Fetter (1940).*

Being played by the band at Judah's honorary dinner. The title of the track alludes to Judah's affair.

## "I Know That You Know"

*Written by Vincent Youmans, Anne Caldwell O'Dea and Otto Harbach (1926). Performed by Bernie Leighton (piano).*

Heard at the party at the Tavern on the Green, where Cliff and Wendy are with Lester and his date Lisa (an uncredited Daryl Hannah). Segues into...

## "Dancing on the Ceiling"

*Written by Richard Rodgers and Lorenz Hart (1930). Performed by Bernie Leighton (piano).*

Following on from the previous track, as Cliff and Lester walk off to discuss a documentary on Lester.

## English Suite No. 2 in A Minor, BWV 807, 1st Movement: Prelude

*Written by Johann Sebastian Bach (1715). Performed by Alicia de Larrocha (1972).*

Heard briefly on two occasions when we see video footage of Louis Levy.

## "Home Cookin'"

*Written by Hilton Ruiz (1987). Performed by the Hilton Ruiz Quartet.*

Hilton Ruiz's quartet make a brief cameo appearance at the club where Barbara (Caroline Aaron) is dancing with a man she had met through an ad in the personal columns. The track continues as they go back to her apartment.

## "I've Got You" (from the soundtrack of *This Gun for Hire*)[7]

*Written by Frank Loesser and Jacques Press (1942).*

## "Happy Birthday to You"

*Written by Mildred J. Hill and Patty Smith Hill (1893).*

Sung to Judah by his family as he comes downstairs.

## "Sweet Georgia Brown"

*Written by Maceo Pinkard, Ben Bernie and Kenneth Casey (1925). Performed by Coleman Hawkins and His All-Star Jam Band (including Benny Carter and Django Reinhardt) (1937).*

Heard as we see shots of Cliff filming Lester in the street and in his car. The track is reprised in full during the end credits.

## "This Year's Kisses"

*Written by Irving Berlin (1937). Performed by Ozzie Nelson and His Orchestra (1937).*

Heard after Cliff and Halley have watched the Louis Levy video and Cliff goes to get champagne (presumably he puts a record on at this point), continuing as they talk until Lester phones. Note that this song is used to reflect Cliff's situation: he realizes his marriage is over and is looking for love elsewhere, preferably with Halley.

## "All I Do Is Dream of You" (from the soundtrack of *Singin' in the Rain*)

*Written by Nacio Herb Brown and Arthur Freed (1934).*

Heard briefly as Cliff and Halley watch Cliff's 16mm print of *Singin' in the Rain* while eating Indian takeaway. The lyrics to this song also apply to Cliff's feelings for Halley.

## String Quartet No. 15 in G Major, D 887 (Op. Posth. 161), 1st movement: Allegro molto moderato

*Written by Franz Schubert (1826). Performed by the Juilliard String Quartet (1974).*

This is the most memorable piece of music in the film. The dramatic opening of Schubert's last quartet perfectly enhances the two scenes either side of the murder. First, as the assassin arrives in his car and follows Dolores to her apartment, and then as Judah, who is compelled to find out what has happened, drives to her apartment to find her dead body on the floor.

## "Beautiful Love"

*Written by Victor Young, Wayne King, Egbert van Alstyne and Haven Gillespie (1931).*

Played by a pianist at a restaurant where Judah is with his wife, Miriam (Claire Bloom), and daughter, and continues as Judah loses his temper and goes out to get some air.

## "Murder He Says" (from the soundtrack of *Happy Go Lucky*)

*Written by Frank Loesser and Jimmy McHugh (1943). Sung by Betty Hutton.*

Brief clip of this song sung by Betty

Hutton in the above film, watched by Cliff and Jenny.

### Incidental music from *The Last Gangster*

*Written by Edward Ward (1937).*[8]

Film watched by Cliff and Jenny at the cinema. The shots of Edward G. Robinson working in the prison laundry as the months pass by are used to reflect Cliff's feelings, after Halley has told him that she is going to London for three or four months. We then jump forward four months to the wedding of Ben's (Sam Waterston) daughter.

### "Great Day"

*Written by Vincent Youmans, William Rose and Edward Eliscu (1929). Performed by Bernie Leighton (piano).*

Being played at the wedding as Cliff and Miriam arrive, continuing as we see Judah and Ben, and as Cliff tells Barbara that he is calling it quits with his marriage to Miriam. The track ends at the point where Cliff has just seen Lester arrive with Halley, his new fiancée. On one level, the song befits a wedding and on another, it can be seen as an ironic comment on Cliff's situation with Halley. Segues into...

### "Star Eyes"

*Written by Don Raye and Gene DePaul (1942). Performed by Lee Musiker.*

Heard briefly, following on from the previous scene, as Lester tells other guests how he persuaded Halley to marry him, while Cliff looks on in shock.

### "Because"

*Written by Guy d'Hardelot and Edward Teschemacher (English lyric) (1902). Performed by Lee Musiker.*

Edward Teschemacher's lyrics — which express a vow of everlasting devotion — have made this song a favorite at weddings. The final four bars are heard on the piano as the bride and groom approach the altar.

### "Crazy Rhythm"

*Written by Joseph Meyer, Roger Wolfe Kahn and Irving Caesar (1928). Performed by the Wedding Band: Anthony Gorruso (trumpet), Tony Sotos (saxophone), Lee Musiker (piano), Peter Antell (guitar), Gary Allen Meyers (bass) and Tony Tedesco (drums).*[9]

The first of five tunes heard in succession played by the wedding band at the reception held in the Waldorf-Astoria. This song is heard as Barbara's friend tries to set her up on a date with a convict, and continues as Lester dances with Miriam and then as Cliff and Halley talk about why she got engaged to Lester.

### "I'll See You Again"

*Written by Noël Coward (1929). Performed by the Wedding Band (as above).*

Following on from the previous scene, this is heard as Cliff and Halley continue to talk and she returns his letter. In addition to the eye reference, the song is also used to reflect Cliff's acknowledgment at losing Halley.

### Hopak

*Traditional Ukrainian dance.*[10] *Performed by the Wedding Band (as above).*

Heard briefly as we see wedding guests attempting to dance the *kazatsky*.

### "Cuban Mambo"

*Written by Xavier Cugat, Rafael Angulo and Jack Wiseman. Performed by the Wedding Band (as above).*

Heard as Cliff and Judah meet each other by the piano and discuss the perfect murder, cutting to Lester and Miriam talking about Cliff.

### "Polkadots and Moonbeams"

*Written by James van Heusen and Johnny Burke (1939). Performed by The Wedding Band (as above).*

Following on from the previous scene, this is heard as Miriam tells Lester that she has met somebody else, cutting back to Cliff and Judah as they talk about Judah's "hypothetical" murder.

### "I'll Be Seeing You"
*Written by Sammy Fain and Irving Kahal (1938). Performed by Liberace (piano).*

The instrumental version of Liberace's theme song is heard at the end of the film as Judah's wife comes to find him and they kiss, leaving a forlorn Cliff on his own. The track continues as Ben dances with his daughter at the wedding and we hear a voice-over by Louis Levy talking about "choices" during a montage of clips from previous scenes. The song ends as the film ends.

## *The Curse of the Jade Scorpion* (2001)
*Music and songs from the repertoire.*

The year is 1940, the setting a Chandleresque New York. In homage to films of that period, Allen's *The Curse of the Jade Scorpion* is a blend of *film noir* and screwball comedy that draws primarily from such classics as *Double Indemnity* (1944), *The Big Sleep* (1946) and *His Girl Friday* (1940). The notion of using a scorpion may well have come from Bob Hope's spy spoof, *My Favorite Blonde* (1942), while the hypnotizing pendant idea has been lifted straight out of *The Road to Rio* (1947). As with a number of his earlier films (*Zelig*, *The Purple Rose of Cairo*, *Radio Days*, *Bullets Over Broadway* and *Sweet and Lowdown*), *The Curse of the Jade Scorpion* is set during the pre–War era, clearly a time that Allen looks back on with fondness. "I tend to like certain periods. The '20s, '30s and '40s were a very exciting time in New York. They were the decades of gangsters and gamblers — the music was great, the clothes were great... It's just a period that appeals to me."[1] Characteristically, Allen is fastidious about the film's look and sound. "The clothes, like the music, are there to help support the story. Everything has to contribute to making the tale work — it's true of any film I do, and I'm sure most directors feel the same."[2] As with earlier period films such as *Radio Days* and *Bullets Over Broadway*, Allen again worked with production designer Santo Loquasto, who comments, "He just loves the music. It is his inspiration. When we're discussing the look of any of his productions, our meetings are on top of his album collection. The breadth of his knowledge of music from that era is truly amazing."[3]

The score actually comprises only seven songs in total, with most of these originating from or around 1940, the year in which the film is set. The dearth of songs does not compromise the score, however, as several of these are replayed frequently. To frame the film, Allen uses Duke Ellington's 1940 Columbia recording of "Sophisticated Lady." This instrumental version has outstanding solos by Harry Carney (baritone sax) and Johnny Hodges (alto sax), and the sultry sound of saxophones adds to the film's ambience and, in particular, complements the scenes where *femme fatale* Laura Kensington (Charlize Theron) — a composite of Lauren Bacall and

## 48 / The Curse of the Jade Scorpion (2001)

Veronica Lake — appears. "I wanted a kind of private eye-ish '40s sound, and I got that from Duke Ellington's "Sophisticated Lady." That kind of metropolitan, sophisticated feeling."[4] In order to reflect the two main characters being hypnotized, Allen uses "Two Sleepy People," which was written for the 1938 Bob Hope film, *Thanks for the Memory*, and was a No. 1 hit in 1940 for Fats Waller. It should be noted that the film's setting antedates the Earl Hines version used here, however, as this was recorded in 1956, and so obviously could not have been playing on the radio. Perhaps Fats Waller's rendition would have been more exact, but as we have seen, Allen tends to favor instrumental versions so that the audience is not distracted from the dialogue by the words from the song. If the cue in which we first hear this song (during the scene in Rocky's Bar) had been shorter, then perhaps Allen would have used Fats Waller and edited out the singing (something he has done before on occasion). It would seem, though, that Allen has timed this scene to the Hines recording, and as a certain length was required, he would not have wanted Waller's unmistakable voice disrupting the banter between Briggs (Woody Allen) and Fitzgerald (Helen Hunt).

Two other significant songs in the film are Harry James's "Flatbush Flanagan" and Wilbur de Paris's Dixieland take on "In a Persian Market." "I had used 'In a Persian Market' before in *New York Stories*. But this version is special because it's by a great jazz musician, Wilbur de Paris."[5] As with the magician scenes in "Oedipus Wrecks," the banjo and drums introduction along with de Paris's irrepressible trombone provide just the right comedic quality.[6]

Once again, Dick Hyman makes a contribution, arranging and performing "Tuxedo Junction" and "How High the Moon" under the name of the Rainbow Room All-Stars. This group also includes a number of musicians who have worked with Hyman before on earlier Woody Allen films, including Howard Alden (guitar), who was featured in *Sweet and Lowdown*. Hyman himself makes a brief appearance in the film. We see him at the piano giving a downbeat at the beginning of "How High the Moon."

### "Sophisticated Lady"
*Written by Duke Ellington, Mitchell Parish and Irving Mills (1935). Performed by Duke Ellington and His Orchestra (1940).*

Opening credits. The song is then heard when Laura Kensington appears in the doorway as Briggs is going through her closet and then later when she is waiting for Briggs at his apartment. It returns at the end of the film when Briggs and Fitzgerald walk out of the office together, cutting to the end credits.

### "Two Sleepy People"
*Written by Hoagy Carmichael and Frank Loesser (1938). Performed by Earl Hines (piano), Eddie Durham (guitar), Dean Riley (bass) and Earl Watkins (drums) (1956).*

Background music in Rocky's Bar, where Briggs and Fitzgerald go for a drink (the song title subtly hints at what will happen later to the two characters). The track returns as the song on the radio when a hypnotized Fitzgerald comes on to Briggs, before falling asleep on his shoulder.

### "Tuxedo Junction"
*Written by Julian Dash, Erskine Hawkins and William Luther Johnson (1939). Arranged by Dick Hyman. Performed by*

*Dick Hyman and the Rainbow Room All-Stars.*

Being played at the Rainbow Room where the North Coast employees go to celebrate George's (Wallace Shawn) 50th birthday.

### "How High the Moon"

*Written by Morgan Lewis and Nancy Hamilton (1940). Arranged by Dick Hyman. Performed by Dick Hyman and the Rainbow Room All-Stars.*

Played at the Rainbow Room, as a hypnotized Briggs and Fitzgerald are made to think they are married. The song then returns, love theme–like, when Briggs lays his coat over Fitzgerald after she has passed out, and significantly at the end of the film, when Fitzgerald is seemingly hypnotized by Briggs as he inadvertently says "Madagascar."

### "In a Persian Market"

*Written by Albert Ketèlbey (1920). Performed by Wilbur de Paris (trombone), Sidney de Paris (trumpet), Omer Simeon (clarinet), Don Kirkpatrick (piano), Eddie Gibbs (banjo), Nat Woodley (bass) and Zutty Singleton (drums) (1953).*

This track is used during all of the scenes where Briggs, and later Fitzgerald, are re-hypnotized by Voltan Polgar (David Ogden Stiers) over the phone and are turned into burglars. It appears when Briggs breaks into the Kensington estate and then later the Dillworth mansion to steal jewels; when he takes the jewels to Grand Central Station and is arrested, continuing during the police interviews; when Fitzgerald robs the Adrian Greenwood mansion; and then when she takes the jewels to Chinatown, inter-cut with Briggs looking for Fitzgerald in her apartment.

### "Flatbush Flanagan"

*Written by Harry James (1941). Performed by Harry James and His Orchestra (1941).*

This track can be seen as "Briggs's theme." It is used exclusively for scenes involving him, often when he is investigating. The track occurs numerous times:

1) When he is talking to Charlie (Irwin Corey), one of his informers.

2) When he sneaks into Fitzgerald's apartment.

3) When he is in the corridor of the office just after Fitzgerald and Magruder (Dan Aykroyd) leave, cutting to him cooking in his apartment.

4) When he is kissed by Laura Kensington, who secretly slips him the key to the handcuffs, cutting to him escaping over the roof.

5) When he finds a jewel on the floor of Fitzgerald's apartment, continuing as he leaves and meets with his informers, including Charlie.

6) The final occurrence is during the climax to the film when Briggs has followed Fitzgerald to Chinatown and confronts Polgar, continuing as Polgar runs off as the police arrive and Briggs gets the opportunity to kiss Fitzgerald.

### "Sunrise Serenade"

*Written by Frankie Carle and Jack Lawrence (1938). Performed by Glenn Miller and His Orchestra (1939).*

This is heard briefly on the radio in the morning, and appropriately accompanies the scene when Fitzgerald wakes up, having slept on Briggs's shoulder all night.

# *Deconstructing Harry* (1997)

*Music and songs from the repertoire.*

*Deconstructing Harry* is without question Allen's most controversial film since *Stardust Memories*. In a stunning mélange of "real time" and fictionalized episodes, he presents a complex, multi-faceted narrative, employing jump-cuts, flashbacks and various different actors to play overlapping roles. Allen himself plays the film's writer-protagonist, Harry Block, a morally deficient character whom Allen describes as "a nasty, shallow, superficial, sexually obsessed guy."[1] In an attempt to capture Harry's neurotic personality, Allen was mindful of what music should play over the opening (and closing) titles, but had some difficulty finding exactly what he wanted. "At the beginning of *Deconstructing Harry*, I ended up using Annie Ross singing 'Twisted,' but I originally wanted to use one of those discordant modern jazz records, something fast by Charlie Parker and Dizzy Gillespie. I figured that would get the nervous craziness of the character. But it doesn't. It gets a darker side too. There's a dark streak. It kills your laughs."[2] Nonetheless, Allen's final choice is fitting, as Sander Lee points out: "The lyrics of the opening song, 'Twisted,' perfectly match the film's themes in their depiction of an egomaniac who others label crazy but who considers himself a misunderstood genius."[3] Referring to this song, Janet Maslin remarks in her *New York Times* review that Allen uses "a dearth of feel-good music to underscore his film's bitterness."[4] However, while this is certainly Allen's most acerbic film to date, the score actually remains faithful to his customary musical approach, with the soundtrack comprising a typical mixture of jazz and American standards.

In fact, much of the music in *Deconstructing Harry* is familiar. A number of commentators have pointed out that the film makes numerous references to several of Allen's earlier films. Girgus states, for instance, that "elements of the story resemble events, characters, and themes in Allen's other films starring Allen,"[5] while Schwartz remarks that "the film is replete with intertextual references to other works by Allen" and that Allen "elicits appropriate themes and emotions evoked by his earlier works and transposes them onto characters and situations."[6] This reworking of material appears to be echoed in the musical score, which includes a large number of songs and music used by Allen before. Schwartz himself gives the following example: "When Fay announces her forthcoming marriage to Larry, Allen inserts the same unsettling image of clouds covering the moon and the same ominous musical passage from Mussorgsky's *A Night on Bald Mountain* that he used to introduce the episode in *Stardust Memories* where Sydney Finklestein's hostility breaks loose and terrorizes Central Park. In this case, Allen's self-conscious, postmodern reference to his earlier film communicates Harry's emotional state after hearing Fay's news because, for viewers familiar with Allen's works, it signifies that Harry's anger is as intense and out of control as Sydney Finklestein's."[7]

Other examples are combined with some of Allen's typical musical techniques. "The Way You Look Tonight" is employed generally by Allen for its romantic qualities and is often heard at the beginning of a couple's relationship (*Alice* and later *Anything Else*). Here it is used in a similar fashion for the scene when Harry meets Fay (Elizabeth Shue) in the elevator. The Jerome Kern association is then continued as "All the Things You Are" subsequently becomes a love theme for these two characters (as it did for Sheldon and Treva in "Oedipus Wrecks"), appearing whenever they are together. Employing the *leitmotif* process he used to good effect in *Hannah and Her Sisters*, Allen thus provides a thematic link between Kern's songs and Harry's relationship with Fay. Further to those mentioned above, other songs that refer back to earlier Allen works include "Out of Nowhere" (*September* and *Manhattan Murder Mystery*), "Rosalie" (*Crimes and Misdemeanors*) and "When the Red, Red Robin Comes Bob, Bob Bobbin Along" (*Bullets Over Broadway*). This latter example also offers us another opportunity to hear Allen sing when he and his travel companions joyfully intone this 1920s standard during the car journey up-state. One suspects that this was a deliberate inclusion in light of the criticism he received for the "unprofessional" singing heard in *Everyone Says I Love You*, released the previous year.

As well as recycling songs, Allen also draws from specific recording sessions that have regularly appeared in earlier films as well. The 1937 Paris session by Coleman Hawkins and His All-Star Jam Band was used in *Crimes and Misdemeanors* ("Sweet Georgia Brown"), while the exact same recording of "Out of Nowhere" appears in *Manhattan Murder Mystery*. Likewise, Erroll Garner's 1951 Columbia recording of "The Way You Look Tonight" was previously heard in *Alice*, and Allen also used "I'm in the Mood for Love," taken from the same session, in *Manhattan Murder Mystery*. Art Tatum and Ben Webster's sublime rendition of "All the Things You Are" comes from *The Tatum Group Masterpieces* series, recorded for Original Jazz Classics/Pablo in 1956. This particular session featured prominently in *September* ("My Ideal" and "Night and Day") and also turned up in *Manhattan Murder Mystery* ("Have You Met Miss Jones?"). Allen even employs Benny Goodman's 1937 recording of "Sing, Sing, Sing" for an unprecedented third time. As in "Oedipus Wrecks" and *Manhattan Murder Mystery*, this "killer diller" is used to good effect, this time accompanying the dissolute "Hell scene," where Harry encounters the Devil (in the guise of Larry); the "slightly sinister" and "hot" qualities that Allen has described this piece as having (see the section on *Manhattan Murder Mystery*) are particularly fitting here. It is also interesting to note that *Deconstructing Harry* is the first Allen film in which "Christopher Columbus" has been credited. When "Sing, Sing, Sing" was first recorded by Goodman, the phrase "incorporating 'Christopher Columbus'" was appended to the title, as arranger Jimmy Mundy had worked in a fragment of this tune. The absence of any credit in "Oedipus Wrecks" is accurate, as the track fades before this fragment is heard. However, in *Manhattan Murder Mystery*, a longer cue is used and we do hear the "Christopher Columbus" section, but the song is not given in this film's end credits.[8]

In addition, Allen again utilizes certain song titles to provide a subtext to what is happening on screen. A good illustration of this occurs during the story about a female analyst named Helen (Demi Moore) who is a composite of Harry's second ex-wife and his overtly Jewish sister. The strange behavior she adopts — marrying her patients — is reflected in the subtle use of "She's Funny That Way," while her excessive Judaist Orthodoxy is accompanied by genuine Jewish klezmer music. (Note that Allen also uses the traditional Hebrew tune "Tzena, Tzena, Tzena" during his other Jewish story about Max Pinchus.) Another example involves Allen using "I Could Write a Book" and "Dream a Little Dream of Me" near the end of the film at Harry's make-believe award ceremony. Here, Harry imagines that all of his characters are present and, while he is being commended, he gets the idea of writing a new book based on a character that's "too neurotic to function in life, but can only function in art" (i.e. himself). "Dream a Little Dream of Me" then begins shortly after Harry says, "I feel like I'm in a dream. This, for me, is like the best dream I've had in months, ya know. The happiest dream." The latter is another example of Allen using songs with "dream" in the title to reflect fantasy sequences on screen (as seen previously in *Stardust Memories* and *Alice*).

### "Twisted"
*Written by Wardell Gray (1949) and Annie Ross (lyrics, 1952). Performed by Annie Ross (1952).*

Opening credits and again (this time complete) for the end credits. Segues into...

### "Out of Nowhere"
*Written by John Green and Edward Heyman (1931). Performed by Coleman Hawkins and His All-Star Jam Band (including Benny Carter and Django Reinhardt) (1937).*[9]

Heard during the opening barbeque scene, at which Ken (Richard Benjamin) and Leslie (Julia Louis-Dreyfus) secretly make love in the house.

### "The Girl from Ipanema"
*Written by Antonio Carlos Jobim, Marcus Vinicius da Cruz de Melo Moraes and Norman Gimbel (1962). Performed by Stan Getz (tenor sax), João Gilberto (guitar and vocals), Astrud Gilberto (English vocals), Antonio Carlos Jobim (piano), Tommy Williams (bass) and Milton Banana (drums) (1963).*

Used twice during the sketch where Harvey Stern (Tobey Maguire) has a tryst with a prostitute and is eventually visited by Death (Ralph Pope).

### "She's Funny That Way"
*Written by Richard Whiting and Neil Moret (né Charles N. Daniels) (1928). Performed by Erroll Garner (piano), John Simmons (bass) and Alvin Stoller (drums) (1949).*

Heard when Helen and Paul Epstein (Stanley Tucci) are together sitting on a bench in Central Park, cutting to their apartment.

### "Waiting"
*Written by Glenn Dickson (1993). Performed by the Shirim Klezmer Orchestra (1993).*

Heard as the now Orthodox Helen gives praise and thanks for everything. We hear it again later when Harry is talking to an imaginary Helen and they look in on Harry's sister, Doris (Caroline Aaron).

### "All the Things You Are"
*Written by Jerome Kern and Oscar Hammerstein II (1939). Performed by Art*

Tatum (piano), Ben Webster (tenor sax), Red Callender (bass) and Bill Douglass (drums) (1956).

Heard first when Harry and Fay are having a drink together and she tells him she is going to marry Larry (Billy Crystal). However, within the chronology of the story, the song is heard first being played on a jukebox as we flashback to Harry and Fay dancing and sharing their first kiss. It then becomes "their song" and reappears (with the exception of when they first meet in the elevator) whenever Harry is with, or thinking about, Fay: in his apartment discussing one of his stories before she gives him a baseball signed by the 1951 Giants; in jail talking with a dead Richard (Bob Balaban) before she turns up with Larry and they walk out of jail; and when the film cuts back to his apartment and he looks longingly at the baseball she gave him.

### *Night on Bald Mountain*
*Written by Modest Mussorgsky (1867). Performed by L'Ochestre de Suisse Romande, conducted by Ernest Ansermet (1964).*

The demonic opening to Mussorgsky's famous orchestral piece nicely befits the story where the Devil comes in the night to abduct Goldberg's "beautiful, blonde love."

### "The Way You Look Tonight"
*Written by Jerome Kern and Dorothy Fields (1936). Performed by Erroll Garner (piano), John Simmons (bass) and Shadow Wilson (drums) (1951).*

Heard when Harry meets Fay in the elevator.

### "When the Red, Red Robin Comes Bob, Bob Bobbin' Along"
*Written by Harry Woods (1926). Sung by Woody Allen, Bob Balaban, Hazelle Goodman and Eric Lloyd.*

Sung in the car by Harry, Richard, Cookie Williams (Hazelle Goodman) and Hilly (Eric Lloyd), as they drive up to Adair University for Harry's honoring ceremony.

### "Rosalie"
*Written by Cole Porter (1937).[10] Performed by the Savoy Hotel Orpheans, under the direction of Carroll Gibbons (1938).*

Heard twice at the fairground, first when we see shots of Hilly on rides and then when Harry is talking to Ken, his alter-ego.

### "Miami Beach Rumba"
*Written by Irving Fields, Albert Gamse and John A. Camacho (1946). Performed by the Stebbins Hall Band.*

### "Tzena, Tzena, Tzena"
*Written by Julius Grossman, Issachar Miron and Mitchell Parish (1950). Performed by the Stebbins Hall Band.*

These two songs are being played by the band at the *Star Wars* Bar Mitzvah during the "Max Pinchus's Dark Secret" story. "Miami Beach Rumba" is heard as the story begins and we see Max (Hy Anzell) at the Bar Mitzvah. "Tzena, Tzena, Tzena" is then heard in the background as the film cuts to Elsie (Viola Harris) sitting at a table, continuing as she beckons over Dolly Pinchus (Shifra Lerer) to tell her about Max.

### "Sing, Sing, Sing (with a Swing)"
*Written by Louis Prima (1936). Performed by Benny Goodman and His Orchestra (1937).*

Heard as Harry gets out of the elevator after he has descended down to Hell, continuing as he speaks with his father (Gene Saks) and then Larry (as the Devil).

### "I Could Write a Book"
*Written by Richard Rodgers and Lorenz Hart (1940). Performed by the Stebbins Hall Band.*

## 54 / *Everyone Says I Love You* (1996)

Being played at Harry's imaginary honoring ceremony as he arrives and is applauded by his characters. Segues into...

**"Dream a Little Dream of Me"**
Written by Wilbur Schwandt, Fabian Andre and Gus Kahn (1931). Performed by the Stebbins Hall Band.

This is heard briefly as the film cuts back to Harry in his apartment and he starts to think of ideas for a new novel.

## *Everyone Says I Love You* (1996)

*Music and songs from the repertoire, with original music by Dick Hyman.*

The film musical is a form for which Allen has a great admiration. "Some of my favorite films are musicals — *Gigi, My Fair Lady, Singin' in the Rain.*"[1] Throughout his work he has regularly incorporated songs from musical shows by great songwriters such as Berlin, Kern, Gershwin, Porter and Rodgers and Hart; and some of his films make reference to specific musicals or musical comedies — *Top Hat* (*The Purple Rose of Cairo*), *Duck Soup* (*Hannah and Her Sisters*), *Singin' in the Rain* and *Happy Go Lucky* (*Crimes and Misdemeanors*) and *Guys and Dolls* (*Manhattan Murder Mystery*) — which underlines further his fondness for this type of film. Given this, it is not entirely surprising that Allen embarked on a project to make a musical comedy of his own, even though the film musical had been dormant for a number of years.[2] Of course, it was not Allen's intention to revive the musical with *Everyone Says I Love You*, rather to pay homage to it. Allen is not adverse to making films with a deferential nod to certain film types, as seen in *Shadows and Fog* (1920s German expressionism) and *The Curse of the Jade Scorpion* (film noir); *Everyone Says I Love You* is purely a nostalgic look back at musicals and musical comedies of the Golden Age. Typically, the film is mostly set in modern-day New York, but Allen also travels to Paris and Venice, his two other favorite cities. Such glamorous locales are characteristic of some of the most famous film musicals — *An American in Paris* (1951), *Funny Face* (1957), *Gigi* (1958) and *Can Can* (1960) were all set in Paris, while *Top Hat* (1935) was mostly set in Venice. The old-time musical feel is enhanced further by Carlo di Palma's rich and luscious color, reminiscent of the great MGM musicals of the 1940s and 1950s.

Having said this, *Everyone Says I Love You* is not a musical in the same sense as, say, *Oklahoma!* or *West Side Story*. Basically, it is a Woody Allen comedy where the characters occasionally burst into song. As Paul Power points out, "it's as appropriate to describe *Everyone Says I Love You* as a musical as it is to term a Marx Brothers film — even their early ones like *The Cocoanuts* — a musical. Fundamentally, *Everyone Says I Love You* is a comedy, with (a lot of) musical numbers thrown in."[3] There are a few production numbers, but most of the singing is conversational rather than showy and the film is more akin to the musical comedies of the 1930s and 40s, like the films of Fred

Astaire and Ginger Rogers or Eddie Cantor. As Allen himself remarks, "This film is very experimental for me. I've never tried anything this musical before. The truth is I don't even think of it as a musical but as a comedy where the characters sing and dance."[4]

To emphasize the spontaneity of the film, Allen felt that the singing should be realistic rather than polished. "I just wanted it to come from the heart. I didn't want it to be slick and professional. I wanted it to be very natural."[5] So much so, in fact, that he cast the film regardless of whether or not the actors could sing. "I wanted to do a musical where the people sang when they wanted to sing. I couldn't care less whether they could sing or couldn't sing. Like when you sing in the shower or you sing to your kid or — I wanted actors, not singers, for the parts."[6] Some commentators have criticized the film for this approach. Hirsch remarks, "The loopy charm of Allen's musical concepts, however, is seriously compromised by the cast of delightful performers who happen to be tone-deaf singers. Tim Roth, Drew Barrymore, Edward Norton, Julia Roberts, along with Woody himself, are painful to listen to, even for a few bars.... What distinguishes the characters from those in regulation musical comedy is the fact that they are so patently unmusical. And the result is the desecration of the kind of popular American music of the past that Allen venerates. Would the film maker cast a comedy with performers who either don't get the jokes or don't know how to deliver them?"[7] And while even some of those working on the film were concerned, Allen's intentions are made clear: "The people in the music department were saying, 'They can't sing!' and the distributors were saying, 'They can't sing!' and I kept saying, 'Yes, I know, that's the point. If they can sing as well as they could in the shower, as well as you and I could sing, that's the idea. I don't want Edward Norton to start singing and sound like Pavarotti.'"[8]

This approach was reflected during the auditioning process. "When I cast this picture I never told people that they'd have to sing or dance, or even asked them if they could. I was only interested if they could act their role well; as far as dancing and vocals I just wanted an honest and simple emotion. Often the most interesting renditions of songs are done by people who don't really have particularly good voices but are good actors, full of feeling and a certain kind of charisma or emotion. That was much more important to me."[9] Whether or not the actors could sing was so inconsequential to Allen that he didn't even tell them that the film was going to be a musical until weeks after they had signed contracts. As Edward Norton recalls, "Woody entrapped us. He informed the cast that it was a musical a month before we started shooting. It was a phone call in the middle of the night so we could all wake up in the morning going, 'Was that a dream or am I really doing a musical?' I've always thought Woody should do a musical because music is such an integral part of his films anyway. He uses music in such a pointed way for emotional effect. He wanted it to be as if these characters were just singing to themselves."[10]

Despite the late notice, all of the actors were happy to sing with the exception of Drew Barrymore, who told Allen she was tone deaf; her singing was dubbed by New York schoolgirl Olivia Hayman. Allen himself sings in the film, albeit very briefly, and he had no qualms about doing it, even though singing is not his strong point. "I personified what I wanted to do in this, that I would croak out a song as best I could do. But I didn't give myself a whole song. I had mercy on the audience. I gave myself a half song to do."[11] On its release, *Everyone Says I Love You* received a positive critical response, and Allen was justifiably pleased. "I was very happy with it. Happy with the success of it. That people liked it and didn't say, 'Oh, nobody here can sing!' They got the idea. I was pleased, and I was encouraged that I wasn't crazy."[12] Richard Schickel in *Time* was particularly understanding of Allen's intent: "Most of the people can't sing any better than you or I, but that's part of the movie's charm and a lot of its point. They all want their life to be set to a soaring score by Kern or Gershwin.... They all hope for the kind of transformative musical epiphanies that would suddenly be vouchsafed Kelly or Astaire as they soft-shoed through their happier — or anyway more stylized — realities. But all they can manage is a wistful croak or an awkward shuffle."[13]

The concept of making a musical is something that Allen had been considering for sometime, as Lax points out, "For many years, Woody has talked about his desire to write an original musical. The problem is, the kind of music he likes went out of fashion forty or fifty years ago, and he has no desire to make a picture with a contemporary score. In *Manhattan* he was able to use many songs by George and Ira Gershwin to enhance the story, but that only whet his appetite for a more ambitious work."[14] With Allen's taste in music entrenched firmly in the first half of the century, he chose to use pre-existing songs, rather than employ modern songwriters. Musicals that have an especially composed score will usually include songs that augment the narrative, and Allen follows this practice. The songs used in *Everyone Says I Love You* were selected expressly because they either advance the plot or they articulate the sentiments of the characters. "The people in this film are singing the emotion of the story at the time. I tried to always keep the story moving."[15] Choosing appropriate music for a specific scene is something that is not new to Allen. As we have seen in many other films, he has used instrumental versions of songs regularly to reflect what we see on screen, where the song title and/or lyrics provide a subtext to the action. Now the music is brought to the foreground and the characters are simply able to sing about what they are thinking or feeling at the time. In this respect, *Everyone Says I Love You* has certain similarities with Dennis Potter's *Pennies from Heaven*. Potter's 1978 TV serialization starring Bob Hoskins also used musical numbers to convey the character's feelings, thoughts and dreams. However, the one major difference between the two is that Allen has his characters actually sing, whereas in *Pennies from Heaven* the characters lip-sync to pre-existent recordings, regardless of gender.[16]

Allen has chosen a selection of songs primarily from the 1920s and 1930s — arguably his favorite musical period — as witnessed by a number of earlier films such as *Zelig, The Purple Rose of Cairo, Hannah and Her Sisters, Radio Days, Bullets Over Broadway* and later, *Sweet and Lowdown. Everyone Says I Love You* rediscovers a few gems, notably, "All My Life" (a number one hit for Fats Waller in 1936), "I'm Thru with

Love" (a number three hit for Bing Crosby in 1931) and "Looking at You" (from Cole Porter's 1929 musical *Wake Up and Dream*). However, with the exception of the aforementioned Cole Porter and a brief quote from Rodgers and Hart, the songs selected by Allen do not come from what is generally regarded as the "A" list of American songwriters. There are no songs by Arlen, Berlin, Gershwin, Kern or Warren, and even the Cole Porter song is one of his lesser-known works, beautiful though it is. Nevertheless, these songs are still standard Broadway repertoire and most of the songs chosen have been penned by model Tin Pan Alley composers and lyricists. Several of the songs have been used by Allen before — "Just You, Just Me" (*Hannah and Her Sisters*), "Makin' Whoopee" (*Husbands and Wives*), "If I Had You" (*Hannah and Her Sisters*) and "Chinatown My Chinatown" (*Radio Days*). For the title song and the film's finale, Allen turned to his much-loved Marx Brothers. Burt Kalmar and Harry Ruby's "Everyone Says I Love You"[17] was written for the 1932 film *Horse Feathers*, while "Hooray for Captain Spaulding" (which became Groucho's theme song) comes from the 1928 show *Animal Crackers*, which the brothers later filmed in 1930. Allen also pays tribute to Maurice Chevalier, quoting three of his most popular songs, including his theme song "Louise," during the Paris sequence. (Chevalier starred in *Gigi*, one of Allen's favorite musicals, as noted above.)

Unsurprisingly, Allen turned to long-time collaborator Dick Hyman to arrange the score for the film. Hyman not only orchestrates, performs and conducts, but also composes two brief linking interludes. Working once again with Helen Miles (*Bullets Over Broadway* and *Mighty Aphrodite*) he produces a delightful score which combines amateur singers (the actors) with professional singers and dancers. In addition to the singing, Hyman also incorporates some of the thematic material from the songs into the fabric of the score. Many musical films of the 1930s and 1940s would use the melody of a song as incidental music to give the score continuity. In *Top Hat*, for example, the melody of "No Strings" is played softly under the scene leading up to Astaire's performance of the song, and then again afterwards. Similarly, "Isn't This a Lovely Day?" is repeated a number of times following Fred and Ginger's routine in the bandstand, acting as a type of love theme for the couple. In *Everyone Says I Love You*, Hyman adopts similar techniques. The title song is not actually sung until the end of the film, but Hyman anticipates this by introducing an instrumental version earlier on during D.J.'s (Natasha Lyonne) various voice-overs. Thus, anyone unfamiliar with the song will not necessarily know the significance of this music until later. (Hyman used a similar technique in *Zelig* with the "Leonard the Lizard Theme.") Many of the other songs also appear in different versions after they have been sung. On occasion, Hyman has slightly altered one or two of the song lyrics to suit the situation at hand, but apart from these minor tweaks the original lyrics to the songs have been retained and — despite their age — none of the songs seem out of place in the contemporary setting, which is a testament to their durability and timelessness.

## "Just You, Just Me"

*Written by Jesse Greer and Raymond Klages (1929). Performed by Edward Norton*

(Holden), Olivia Hayman (Skylar's voice), Vivian Cherry (Nurse), Diva Gray (Nanny), Arlene Martell, Helen Miles, Paul Evans, Jon Gordon (alto sax, in the salsa version only) and Dick Hyman and the New York Studio Players; also arranged and performed by Itzhak and Navah Perlman.

This song, sung as a duet between Holden (Edward Norton) and Skylar (Drew Barrymore), opens the film instead of the more customary black and white credits. Various shots of New York are then shown as people on the streets join in. The song then recurs several times throughout the film in a variety of guises: as a violin and piano duet at the soirée given by Steffi Dandridge (Goldie Hawn) to help the New York Philharmonic; as a salsa being played a the party in Venice when D.J. tells her father, Joe (Woody Allen), that she is going to marry a gondolier; and in an orchestral version near the end of the film when Holden turns up at the house for Halloween dressed as the Devil.

### "Everyone Says I Love You"

*Written by Harry Ruby and Bert Kalmar (1932). Performed by The Helen Miles Singers and Dick Hyman and the New York Studio Players.*

The title song appears directly after the "Just You, Just Me" opening sequence. An orchestral version is heard on four separate occasions during D.J.'s voice-overs, as she introduces her family. Later on, this version is being played at the Groucho Marx party, where Joe and Steffi (both dressed up as Groucho) are talking and drinking champagne by a Christmas tree. The vocal version is heard at the end of the film, as we see the main characters all dancing at the Groucho party during D.J.'s final voice-over, cutting to the end credits.

### "My Baby Just Cares for Me"

*Written by Walter Donaldson and Gus Kahn (1930). Performed by Edward Nor-*

*ton (Holden), Natasha Lyonne (D.J.), Edward Hibbert (Harry Winston Salesman), the Helen Miles Singers and Dick Hyman and the New York Studio Players.*

Sung and danced to in Harry Winston's jewelers by Holden, D.J. and everyone else in the shop, after Holden has chosen a ring for Skylar. A jazzy instrumental version is later used during the gangster/car chase sequence after a dumbfounded Skylar is driven off by Charles Ferry (Tim Roth) and his escaped convict friends. This instrumental version is reprised during the end credits.

### "Recurrence"

*Written by Dick Hyman. Arranged and conducted by Dick Hyman. Performed by Dick Hyman and the New York Studio Players.*

This brief orchestral piece (just over a minute long) is heard in full as Skylar is kissed by Charles Ferry on the balcony, just before he sings "If I Had You." However, the last few bars can be heard earlier as a brief introduction to Skylar singing, "I'm a Dreamer, Aren't We All?" thus anticipating her later association with Ferry.

### "I'm a Dreamer, Aren't We All?"

*Written by Ray Henderson, Buddy G. DeSylva and Lew Brown (1929). Performed by Olivia Hayman (Skylar's voice) and Dick Hyman and the New York Studio Players.*

Sung by Skylar in her bedroom, as she gets ready for her date with Holden. A piano version is heard in the background when the two are at the restaurant. The piano version reappears later in the film during D.J.'s voice-over about an "unexpected visitor," as we see shots of Central Park in fall. As with "Recurrence" above, this also hints at Skylar's relationship with Ferry.

## "Makin' Whoopee"

*Written by Walter Donaldson and Gus Kahn (1928). Performed by Timothy Jerome (X-Ray Room Doctor), Daisy Prince (Nurse), Linda Maurel-Sithole, Helen Miles (Nurse), Arlene Martell (Nurse), the Helen Miles Singers and Dick Hyman and the New York Studio Players.*

Sung and danced to in the hospital sequence by staff and patients. An orchestral version is heard afterwards when Steffi visits the prison.

## "Venetian Scenes"

*Written by Dick Hyman. Performed by Dominic Cortese (accordion) and the Dick Hyman Combo.*

Another brief orchestral piece heard as we see shots of Venice during D.J.'s voice-over about visiting her dad in August. This directly precedes Joe singing "I'm Thru with Love."

## "I'm Thru with Love"

*Written by Matt Malneck, Fud Livingston and Gus Kahn (1931). Performed by Woody Allen (Joe), Natalie Portman (Laura), Alan Alda (Bob), Edward Norton (Holden), Goldie Hawn (Steffi Dandridge) and Dick Hyman and the New York Studio Players.*

Sung by Joe when he is in Venice. The song reappears when it is briefly sung in sequence by Laura (Natalie Portman), Bob (Alan Alda) and Holden after various romantic upsets, eventually being parodied as the first line in the rap song, "No Lover, No Friend" (see below). Steffi also sings the song (a full version this time) near the end of the film when she is with Joe in Paris and they dance by the Seine (which is a direct quote from *An American in Paris*). Immediately after this, a solo violin starts a reprise of the melody as they sit by the river talking and eventually kiss. The orchestral section from this latter version is reprised during the end credits.

## "Just Say I Love Her" ("Dicitencello Vuie!")

*Adapted by Jack Val and Jimmy Dale with English lyrics by Mark Kalmanoff and Sam Ward (1950), after the Neapolitan song by Rodolfo Falvo and Enzo Fusco (1930). Performed by Dick Hyman (piano), Dominic Cortese (accordion) and the New York Studio Players.[18]*

An up-tempo version of this Neapolitan song (usually performed slowly by Italianate crooners such as Jerry Vale and Dean Martin) is used humorously during the scene where Joe "accidentally" attempts to bump into Von (Julia Roberts) while the two are jogging around the streets of Venice. Dick Hyman has arranged this piece in a style not dissimilar to that found in silent movies, and it perfectly fits the comedic shots of Joe following Von until the music ends at the point where the two do eventually bump into each other (literally). The track returns briefly as Joe starts reading the book on Tintoretto, cutting to the Scuola di San Rocco, where we see Von already at the museum and Joe just happens to turn up. It also reappears again a little later when they leave and sit by a canal, as Joe tell her he loves Mahler's Fourth Symphony.[19]

## "All My Life"

*Written by Sam H. Stept and Sidney D. Mitchell (1936). Performed by Julia Roberts (Von), Joe Wilder (trumpet), Derek Smith (piano) and Dick Hyman and the New York Studio Players.*

Sung by Von as she sits by a canal in Venice with Joe, continuing during the scene where Joe agrees to take a photo of some tourists and the flash explodes, ending as he brings her an African daisy. The song is then associated with these two characters and reappears in instrumental versions during their subsequent scenes: when they bump into each other on the stairs and kiss; after making love in

Venice (directly following on from "Enjoy Yourself"); when they are in Joe's garret in Paris; and finally when Von tells Joe that she is leaving him and going back to her husband. A brief quote also appears in the middle of the version of "I'm Thru with Love" heard at the point when Joe and Steffi talk about Von.

### "Cuddle Up a Little Closer"

*Written by Karl Hoschna and Otto Harbach (1908). Hindi translation by Sanjeev Ramabhadran. Performed by Billy Crudup (Ken), Sanjeev Ramabhadran (taxi driver's voice) and Dick Hyman and the New York Studio Players.*

Sung by Ken (Billy Crudup) in the taxi with D.J. The taxi driver then joins in, singing in Hindi. An orchestral version of the song is heard briefly when we see shots of a snow-covered New York, shortly before the family go to Paris for Christmas.

### "Looking at You"

*Written by Cole Porter (1929). Performed by Alan Alda (Bob) and Dick Hyman (piano) and the New York Studio Players.*

Sung by Bob, at the piano, to Steffi at her birthday party. During the song, we see various photos of the couple when they were younger; this is reminiscent of the scene in *Hannah and Her Sisters* when Hannah's father is playing "You Are Too Beautiful" on the piano.

### "If I Had You"

*Written by Jimmy Campbell, Reg Connelly and Ted Shapiro (1929). Performed by Tim Roth (Charles Ferry) and Dick Hyman and the New York Studio Players.*

Sung by Charles Ferry to Skylar on the balcony. The "fresh start" sentiment expressed in the lyrics proves to be false, as Ferry — having won Skylar over — returns immediately to his life of crime, beginning with a prison breakout.

### "Enjoy Yourself (It's Later Than You Think)"

*Written by Herb Magidson and Carl Sigman (1950). Performed by Patrick Cranshaw (Grandpa), the Helen Miles Singers and Dick Hyman and the New York Studio Players.*

After a brief quote from Chopin's famous funeral march (from Piano Sonata No. 2 in B flat minor, Op. 35), this song is sung by a ghostly Grandpa (Patrick Cranshaw) at Campbell's funeral parlor on Madison Avenue during his own service. He is then joined by various other phantoms, and they all sing and dance until we eventually segue into "All My Life" (see above). An instrumental version is heard during the end credits.

### "Satan Takes a Holiday"

*Written by Larry Clinton (1937). Performed by Dick Hyman and the New York Studio Players.*

An extract from this novelty item (about sixteen bars) is incorporated into the previous song as a kind of bridge. It can be heard just before and during the dance by the figure made from ashes. Dick Hyman remarks, "I selected it because it has some association in my recollection with dancing skeletons or some such macabre use in an animated cartoon."[20]

### "No Lover, No Friend (That's the End)"

*Written by Dick Hyman, Robert Walker, Devalle Hayes and Loris Holland. Performed by Robert Walker, Devalle Hayes and Loris Holland.*

Sung by three rap artists at a concert watched by D.J. The song mockingly begins with the line, "I'm through with love." Hyman's remarks on this song are enlightening: "It was of course Woody's idea to base a rap piece on 'I'm Thru with Love,' but I remember immediately rising to the occasion when he suggested it and declaiming the obscene first line. I wrote the basic lyrics but my collaborators, established rappers, finessed them and added certain elements, including a refrain, which became the title. A full-length version was recorded, but only the short length was needed, and Woody did not want to include it in the cast album, a decision which I concurred with."[21]

## "I Can't Believe That You're in Love with Me"

*Written by Clarence Gaskill and Jimmy McHugh (1926). Performed by Tim Roth (Charles Ferry), Olivia Hayman (Skylar's voice) and Dick Hyman and the New York Studio Players.*

The final few bars of this song are sung by Charles Ferry and Skylar, as they drive into the woods, where Charles is secretly awaiting a prison breakout. An orchestral version is then heard briefly as they walk from the car talking.

## "What a Little Moonlight Can Do"

*Written by Harry Woods (1934). Performed by Tommy John and the Dick Hyman Combo.*

## "Chinatown, My Chinatown"

*Written by Jean Schwartz and William Jerome (1910). Performed by Richard Cummings, Lindsey Canuel, Kristen Pettet and the Dick Hyman Combo.*

## "Cocktails for Two"

*Written by Sam Coslow and Arthur Johnston (1934). Performed by Patrick Lavery and the Dick Hyman Combo.*

## "Chiquita Banana"

*Written by Leonard McKenzie, Garth Montgomery and William Wirges (1944).*[22] *Performed by Christy Romano, Jonathan Giordano, Gabriel Millman and the Dick Hyman Combo.*

All four songs are briefly sung by children, appropriately dressed up, as they come to the Dandridge's apartment "trick or treating" during Halloween.

## "Mimi"

*Written by Richard Rodgers and Lorenz Hart (1932). Performed by Dick Hyman and the New York Studio Players.*

## "Louise"

*Written by Richard Whiting and Leo Robin (1929). Performed by Dick Hyman and the New York Studio Players.*

## "You Brought a New Kind of Love to Me"

*Written by Irving Kahal, Sammy Fain and Pierre Norman Conner (1930). Performed by Dick Hyman and the New York Studio Players.*

These three songs are heard in a brief medley during the Paris sequence. This is a mini-homage to Maurice Chevalier, with all the songs coming from three of his earliest films, thus providing an appropriate musical counterpart to the various shots of Paris, where the Dandridges are spending Christmas. "Mimi" (from the 1932 film *Love Me Tonight*) is heard as we see the Ritz; "Louise" (from the 1929 film *Innocents of Paris*, Chevalier's debut) as we see Scott looking through binoculars; and "You Brought a New Kind of Love to Me" (from the 1930 film, *The Big Pond* and also sung by the Marx Brothers in *Monkey Business* a year later when they were mimicking Chevalier) as Holden and Skylar are by the fountain kissing.

## "Hooray for Captain Spaulding"

*Written by Bert Kalmar and Harry Ruby (1928). Performed by the Helen Miles Singers and Dick Hyman and the New York Studio Players.*

Sung (in French) and danced to at the Groucho Ball in Paris by a cast all dressed in various Grouch Marx costumes.[23]

# Everything You Always Wanted to Know About Sex* (*but were afraid to ask) (1972)

*Original music composed and conducted by Mundell Lowe, with additional songs from the repertoire.*

For Allen's fourth film, jazz guitarist Mundell Lowe was hired to compose the score. Lowe is first and foremost a performer, who has worked with a number of eminent jazz musicians including Billie Holiday, Lester Young, Charlie Parker and Charles Mingus. In recent years, he has made several recordings with André Previn. Before *Everything You Always Wanted to Know About Sex*, Lowe had written scores for TV shows including *Wild, Wild West* and *Hawaii Five-O* and soundtracks to the films *Satan in High Heels* (1962), *A Time for Killing* (1967) and *Billy Jack* (1971), the last two being latter day B-movie Westerns.

Unlike films in the present day — which are often saturated with contemporary songs — soundtracks at this time could be sparse with long periods devoid of music, and this is particularly noticeable here. Heard today, the score is typical of the period in which it was written, despite the different times and styles we see in the film. Apart from the choice of song over the opening and end credits, Lowe was given *carte blanche* to compose as he wished for each of the seven segments. He viewed the segments as separate little films and composed what he thought appropriate for each. The most enduring music in the score is the jazz/lounge music heard in sections two and three. Here, Lowe is in his element and his jazz roots shine through. Much of the remainder is adequate for its purpose, but is nothing more than functional film music. Compared to the raw energy and lyricism found in the two earlier scores by Marvin Hamlisch — which still stand up well today — Lowe's score sounds a little dated to modern ears. Allen himself was not overly impressed with the music written for the soundtrack (see page 6) and, significantly, he did not employ a composer again for over twenty years.

In addition to Lowe's music, Irving Aaronson's 1928 recording of "Let's Misbehave" is used to bookend the film. (The same recording reappears twenty-two years later in *Bullets Over Broadway*). This is the first time Allen uses a pre-existent recording in one of his films[1] and, characteristically, he chooses a jazzy rendition of a song by Cole Porter, his favorite songwriter. Moreover, we are given a foretaste of how Allen would later use his record collection to provide music for his films. Allen has picked this song specifically for its risqué nature to reflect the film's sexual theme; choosing appropriate music in this way is something that Allen continues to develop in his later films.

### "Let's Misbehave"

*Written by Cole Porter (1927). Performed by Irving Aaronson and His Commanders (vocal refrain by Phil Saxe and Chorus) (1928).*

Opening and end credits, during shots of white rabbits.

## Segment 1: "Do Aphrodisiacs Work?"

There are two musical themes. The first is a Greensleeves-like piece played on recorder and lute, which reflects the medieval period. However, the other is somewhat dated "do be doo" music typical of the late 1960s and early 1970s.

## Segment 2: "What Is Sodomy?"

There is no music in this segment until Doctor Ross (Gene Wilder) and his wife have dinner, when we briefly hear some cocktail music played on the piano, which returns at the end. The most noticeable music is the jazz quartet piece heard when Ross takes the sheep to the hotel.

## Segment 3: "Why Do Some Women Have Trouble Reaching an Orgasm?"

This segment has more music in it than any other. The main theme is a big band number, which opens the segment and then returns every time Fabrizio (Woody Allen) and Gina (Louise Lasser) make love in public. The piece incorporates a number of guitar solos, which were played by Lowe himself, and also makes use of the then novel-sounding Hammond electronic organ, which Lowe liked and thought was the right sound; this was played by Dick Hyman, in what was his first involvement in a Woody Allen film.

## Segment 4: "Are Transvestites Homosexuals?"

The incidental music in this sketch is virtually all on piano and played in the style of a silent movie.

## Segment 5: "What Are Sex Perverts?"

Here, Lowe uses his experience in writing music for television by providing game show music for the pastiche TV show "What's My Perversion?" and the music for the Lancer commercial.

## Segment 6: "Are the Findings of Doctors and Clinics Who Do Sexual Research and Experiments Accurate?"

As Victor Shakapopulis (Woody Allen) and Helen Lacy (Heather MacRae) arrive at Doctor Bernardo's (John Carradine) mansion, we briefly hear the faint sounds of an organ, which is music typically associated with mad scientists. Apart from this, there is no music at all until the second part of the story after the explosion in the mansion. Then standard dramatic music is heard as the giant breast roams the countryside. There is also a brief love theme at the end.

## Segment 7: "What Happens During Ejaculation?"

Lowe did compose music for this segment, but Allen decided not to use it and left it scoreless. Two traditional songs are heard as follows: "Glory Hallelujah" is sung by the workmen as they try and raise an erection, and "The Red River Valley" is played on the harmonica by Woody Allen's sperm, as he awaits ejaculation.

## Hannah and Her Sisters (1986)

*Music and songs from the repertoire.*

In many ways, the score to *Hannah and Her Sisters* is the quintessential Woody Allen soundtrack, having all of the musical elements we have come to associate with a Woody Allen film. The multifaceted plot has an old-fashioned air, dealing with a variety of themes such as love, fidelity and hope, and the romantic nature of the drama is given added support by an equally romantic score. This comprises a number of timeless examples from the American songbook, including songs by some of Allen's favorite songwriters, such as Cole Porter, Jerome Kern and Rodgers and Hart. Several of these reflect many of the sentiments found in the film, and it is not coincidence that the soundtrack contains such songs as "I'm in Love Again," "I'm Old Fashioned" and "Isn't It Romantic?" Having played a significant role in Allen's previous three films, Dick Hyman is employed here to arrange and perform many of the songs found within the score. In addition, Allen utilizes a selection of classical music to enhance further the romantic spirit of the film. This marks the beginning of a trend where classical music — notably Bach — is used more pointedly in several of his films during the late 1980s; add to this some typical slices of jazz and swing and you have a score that is perhaps the most representative of all Allen's soundtracks.

We have seen in earlier films that Allen had been developing a method where the score plays an important role, rather than simply providing background music. With *Hannah*, new heights are reached in this respect; the use of music is more elaborate and the score is far richer in thematic development. Allen continues to use songs as a subtext to the narrative of the story, as seen in *Manhattan* and *Stardust Memories*. But in *Hannah*, this technique is further enhanced and, moreover, goes hand in hand with a sophisticated use of *leitmotif*, where not only music, but composers and performers as well, are specifically linked to certain characters. As Girgus remarks, "Different sequences and the characters within them have their own musical themes that play throughout the film, almost in a manner of silent movies, a similarity that seems especially appropriate when new titles on the screen are announced by new musical motifs. The music, therefore, proffers a method of continuity and development of both mood and tone as well as theme and characterization."[1]

Looking at some of the characters, we find that Puccini attends David (Sam Waterston), the opera lover, not just when he is at the Metropolitan Opera House with Holly (Dianne Wiest) watching *Manon Lescaut*, but also when we see a montage of his favorite New York buildings and when Holly is thinking about him in the back of his car. Also, the more manifest examples of jazz in the film are, not too surprisingly, associated with Allen's character, Mickey. Here, two Count Basie tracks are linked to his "The hypochondriac," "The anxiety of the man in the booth" and "The abyss" scenes, while Roy Eldridge's plaintive rendition of "If I Had You" appropriately accompanies his search for the meaning of life.

In other areas, musical themes are used with more subtlety and the associations are more complex. The film's theme song, as it were, is "Bewitched, Bothered and Bewildered," which appears throughout as a recurring motif. The title to this song is used to provide a subtext to various scenes and accompanies certain characters who are actually bewitched, bothered or bewildered: Lee (Barbara Hershey) is bewitched by the e.e. cummings poem she reads that Elliot (Michael Caine) has recommended; Hannah (Mia Farrow) is bothered by her parents' quarrel and her mother's drunkenness; and Elliot is bewildered by his feelings for both Lee and Hannah, which he confesses to his analyst — "For all my education, accomplishments, and so-called wisdom ... I can't fathom my own heart."[2] Moreover, the song title can also be seen as an epithet for the three sisters. As Carol Goodson remarks, "The three categories mentioned in the title of the song characterize the sisters' lives perfectly. Hannah is 'bewitched' in that she seems to have been born under a lucky star: like an enchanted princess, everything goes right for her; 'bothered' is Lee, the middle sister [sic] who is being pursued by Elliott [sic], Hannah's husband; and Holly, the youngest [sic], is 'bewildered,' the one who just cannot seem to get her life together."[3] This is also reflected in the music. As a foretoken, the song is heard first sung by the sisters' parents. Subsequently, it returns at crucial points in each of the sisters' lives: when Lee reads the e.e. cummings poem Elliot gives her (as mentioned before), which kindles their affair; when Hannah and Elliot finally reconcile their marriage; and during Holly's chance meeting with Mickey, which results in their new (and improved) relationship. Robert Lindner, who performed this song in *Hannah*, recounts his experiences of working on the film: "I was called to Mia Farrow's apartment in the Dakota Building where Woody was shooting some of the scenes and was introduced to Maureen O'Sullivan (Mia's mother) and Lloyd Nolan, who play the parents of the sisters. We then rehearse 'Bewitched' and I find a good key for their voices. They are sweet, polite and charming. When we shoot the scene, I play off-camera while Mr. Nolan pretends to be playing on screen as they sing. In addition to this, I 'wild-tracked' some solo renditions on a small console piano to use during scene changes or as background. Of these, Woody only ended up using my solo version of "Bewitched" which occurs several times throughout the film. Somewhat disappointingly, I was not credited in the film or on the subsequent soundtrack album."[4]

A good example of how musical themes are attached to certain elements of the plot can be seen in the way Bach and Harry James are used to accompany the affair between Lee and Elliot. The opening movement of Bach's Concerto for Two Violins in D Minor is heard as Lee thinks about Elliot in the cab on the way home from the first Thanksgiving dinner; this anticipates how important Bach's music will become in connection with their relationship. Bach's F Minor Harpsichord Concerto is then heard three times during the different stages of the affair: it is the piece that Lee plays for Elliot shortly before he takes the plunge and kisses her; it reappears when the two rent a hotel room for the first time; and finally, this music accompanies the "Autumn Chill" scene when Lee is thinking about how much fun she is having with Doug, her literature professor, a relationship that precipitates the end of her affair with Elliot. Running parallel to Bach are two songs performed by Harry James which accompany the affair in much the same way. "You Made Me Love You" is heard over the film's opening credits, presaging the first scene ("God, she's beautiful...") where Elliot struggles to contain his desire for Lee. The song returns when the two are enjoying "Afternoons" together dancing and drinking champagne. "I've Heard That Song Before" is used for the aforesaid opening scene and then later when Elliot contrives to bump into Lee outside her apartment. Notably, this song then returns during the last Thanksgiving party — after the affair has ended — in a mirror image of the film's opening.

Corresponding to the film's parallel and overlapping plot lines, certain songs are also used to accompany more than one set of characters. We have already seen how "Bewitched" has been associated with all of the principal players. Harry James's rendition of "You Made Me Love You" is another example. As seen above, it is originally used to reflect Elliot's inexorable desire for Lee. Later, it attends the unexpected romance between Holly and Mickey. Once again, the lyrics provide a subtext to the narrative — despite a disastrous first date, the two eventually fall in love. This unpredictable relationship is likewise accompanied by the song "I'm in Love Again," heard performed at the Café Carlyle by Bobby Short on the couple's aforementioned date. Ostensibly, this is just source music. However, the song is actually more relevant to the couple than we realize and is reprised significantly during the film's dénouement when the audience discovers that Holly and Mickey are now married and Holly is pregnant, thus bringing about the film's happy ending.

## "You Made Me Love You"

*Written by James V. Monaco and Joseph McCarthy (1913). Performed by Harry James and His Orchestra (1941).*

Opening credits. The song is also used when Elliot and Lee are dancing in the hotel room; when Mickey Sachs (Woody Allen) and Holly go to lunch and take a walk in Central Park; and then as we return to Mickey and Holly in the park after the flashback about Mickey's attempted suicide, cutting to "One Year Later" and the third Thanksgiving dinner.

## "I've Heard That Song Before"

*Written by Sammy Cahn and Jule Styne (1942). Performed by Harry James and His Orchestra (1942).*

This song is thematically linked to Elliot and Lee's characters. It is heard first right at the beginning of the film ("God, she's beautiful...") as Elliot thinks about Lee and how attracted to her he is, during shots of the first Thanksgiving dinner, cutting to the scene with Hannah and Holly in the kitchen when Holly wants to borrow money. It returns when Elliot manufactures a "chance meeting" with Lee outside her apartment, and is used again for the third Thanksgiving dinner in a scene which parallels the film's opening: Elliot is again looking at Lee and thinking about her, but now their affair is over and she is married to someone else.

## "Bewitched, Bothered and Bewildered"

*Written by Richard Rodgers and Lorenz Hart (1941). Performed by Robert Lindner (piano); also sung by Lloyd Nolan and Maureen O'Sullivan, accompanied by Robert Lindner (piano).*

An important song that permeates the film. It is heard first at the opening Thanksgiving dinner, sung by Evan (Lloyd Nolan) and Norma (Maureen O'Sullivan) at the piano. A piano version is heard when Elliot and Lee are in the bookstore and Lee later reads a poem by e.e. cummings in bed. This piano version returns briefly when Hannah is in a taxi going to see her parents after her mother has got drunk; during the "Summer in New York" scene when Elliot is with his analyst; and finally when Elliot and Hannah make up and kiss in bed, cutting to the scene where Mickey bumps into Holly at the record shop.

## "Just You, Just Me"

*Written by Jesse Greer and Raymond Klages (1929). Performed by Dick Hyman (piano).*

Played on the piano by Evan at the first Thanksgiving dinner as Hannah and Holly, and then April (Carrie Fisher) are talking in the dining room, while Elliot is flirting with Lee in one of the bedrooms. It is heard again at the second Thanksgiving dinner (directly following "Avalon" in the piano medley, see below) when Elliot and Hannah are arguing.

## "Where or When"

*Written by Richard Rodgers and Lorenz Hart (1937). Performer unknown (possibly Dick Hyman or Bernie Leighton).*

Played on the piano by Evan at the first Thanksgiving dinner as Hannah comes into the bedroom to find Elliot and Lee talking (directly following the first hearing of the previous song).

## Concerto for Two Violins in D Minor, BWV 1043, 1st movement: Vivace

*Written by Johann Sebastian Bach (1717). Performed by Georgi Badev and Stoika Milanova (soloists) and the Sofia Soloists Chamber Orchestra, conducted by Vassil Kazandjiev.*

"We all had a terrific time." Heard briefly as Lee is going home in a taxi and is wondering if Elliot has a crush on her.

## "Back to the Apple"

*Written by Frank Foster and Count Basie (1959). Performed by Count Basie and His Orchestra (1959).*

## "The Trot"

*Written by Benny Carter (1961). Performed by Count Basie and His Orchestra (1961).*

These two Count Basie tracks are exclusively linked to Woody Allen's character, Mickey. "Back to the Apple" is heard first as we are introduced to him as "The hypochondriac," when he is at work discussing his TV show with his crew, and during the shot of Norman (Tony Roberts), his ex-partner, in a car in California. The track reappears briefly when Mickey comes out of the Mount Sinai hospital elated, having been told he does not have cancer. "The Trot" is heard first when Mickey is walking down the street on his way to the doctor and during the subsequent ear tests. It reappears when we see "The anxiety of the man in the booth," as Mickey undergoes further ear tests at hospital.

## "I Remember You"

*Written by Victor Schertzinger and Johnny Mercer (1942). Performed by the Dave Brubeck Quartet: Dave Brubeck (piano), Paul Desmond (alto sax), Ron Crotty (bass) and Joe Dodge (drums) (live at the College of the Pacific, 1953).*

"The Stanislavski Catering Company in action." Background music during Holly and April's first catering job, where they meet David.

## Introduction to Act I from *Madam Butterfly*

*Written by Giacomo Puccini (1904). Performed by the Rome Opera Chorus and*

Orchestra, conducted by John Barbirolli (1966).[5]

A brief orchestral excerpt, which is heard twice: first as we see shots of David's favorite buildings in New York, and then again a little later when Holly is in the back of David's car thinking about her rivalry with April for David's affections.

### "Sola, perduta abbandonata" from Manon Lescaut

*Written by Giacomo Puccini (1893). Performed by Maria Chiara (Manon Lescaut) and the Orchestra of the Regio Theater, Turin, conducted by Angelo Campari.*

Being performed when Holly and David are at the Metropolitan Opera. Note how the apparent happiness in this scene is undercut by the opera aria, which translates to "Alone! Lost! Abandoned!" thus foreshadowing later events — Holly's date with David leads to nothing, and later he discards her for April.

### Harpsichord Concerto No. 5 in F Minor, BWV 1056, 2nd movement: Largo; 3rd movement: Presto

*Written by Johann Sebastian Bach (1742). Performed by Gustav Leonhardt and the Leonhardt Consort (1968).*

The beautiful slow movement from this concerto is also thematically linked to Elliot and Lee. It is heard first when Lee plays a record of it in her and Frederick's (Max von Sydow) apartment when Elliot is there with his client, Dusty Frye (Daniel Stern). The two are left alone and listen to the music, while making polite conversation. After thinking to himself that he should proceed cautiously, Elliot impulsively kisses her. At this point, they knock the record player and the needle jumps to the third movement. The faster music matches the now frantic scene, as Elliot confesses his love to Lee. The slow movement then recurs when Elliot and Lee meet in a hotel room and make love, continuing after the cut to Lee walking home in the rain; and when Lee is by the river ("Autumn Chill") deliberating over her relationships with Elliot and Doug.

### "You Are Too Beautiful"

*Written by Richard Rodgers and Lorenz Hart (1932). Performed by Derek Smith.*

Heard when Hannah is with her drunken mother and reminisces about her parents. Although giving the impression of being scored, it turns out that this song is actually being played by Evan on the piano.

### "If I Had You"

*Written by Jimmy Campbell, Reg Connelly and Ted Shapiro (1929). Performed by the Roy Eldridge Quartet: Roy Eldridge (trumpet), Gerald Wiggins (piano), Pierre Michelot (bass) and Kenny Clarke (drums) (1950).*

"The only absolute knowledge obtainable by man is that life is meaningless." Heard during Mickey's voice-over as he leaves Columbia University (which has a replica statue of Rodin's "The Thinker" outside) and walks by the river.

### "Slip into the Crowd"

*Written by Chris Barry and Pierre Major.[6] Performed by 39 Steps.*

Performed by the punk band when Mickey and Holly are on their first date.

### "I'm in Love Again"

*Written by Cole Porter (1924). Performed by Bobby Short (vocals and piano) with Beverly Peer (bass) and Rob Scott (drums); also performed by Dick Hyman or Bernie Leighton (solo piano).*

This song is being performed live at the Café Carlyle when Mickey and Holly are on their first date. A piano arrangement of this song is heard as Mickey walks home after the date. This latter version is significantly reprised at the end of the film (directly following "Isn't It Romantic?") when Mickey and Holly—now married—are standing at the mirror and she tells him she is pregnant, cutting to the end credits.

## "I'm Old Fashioned"

*Written by Jerome Kern and Johnny Mercer (1942). Sung by Dianne Wiest, accompanied by Bernie Leighton (piano).*

## "The Way You Look Tonight"

*Written by Jerome Kern and Dorothy Fields (1936). Sung by Carrie Fisher, accompanied by Bernie Leighton (piano).*

Both these songs are heard being sung at an audition, firstly by Holly, and then April. Note how the rivalry between these two is reflected in the fact that they both choose songs by Jerome Kern.

## "Gloria" from *Missa Secunda*

*Written by Hans Leo Hassler (1599).[7] Performed by the Choir of the Church of the Transfiguration, conducted by John Gordon Morris.*

Heard as we see a shot of "The Little Church Around the Corner" on East 29th Street covered in snow, cutting to the interior of the church and a congregation listening to the choir. The music continues during the following sequence where Mickey is given numerous books by the priest, cutting to Mickey looking at a statue of Jesus, before he goes back to his apartment to unload several religious artifacts, followed by a loaf of Wonder Bread and a jar of mayonnaise. Both the mass and the food are used to signify Mickey's attempted conversion from Judaism to Catholicism.

## "Freedonia Is Going to War" (from the soundtrack of *Duck Soup*)

*Written by Harry Ruby and Bert Kalmar (1933).[8] Performed by the Marx Brothers.*

An excerpt of this song is heard as Mickey is watching *Duck Soup* in the Metro Cinema on Broadway.

## "It Could Happen to You"

*Written by James van Heusen and Johnny Burke (1944). Performed by Dick Hyman (piano).*

## "Polkadots and Moonbeams"

*Written by James van Heusen and Johnny Burke (1939). Performed by Dick Hyman (piano).*

## "Avalon"

*Written by Vincent Rose, Al Jolson and Buddy G. DeSylva (1920). Performed by Dick Hyman (piano).*

All three songs (along with "Just You, Just Me," see above) are played by Evan on the piano as a medley at the second Thanksgiving dinner during the scenes where Hannah and Holly argue about Holly's book and Lee tells Elliot that their affair is over.

## "Isn't It Romantic?"

*Written by Richard Rodgers and Lorenz Hart (1932). Performed by Derek Smith.*

Played by Evan on the piano at the third Thanksgiving dinner as Holly arrives and we discover that she and Mickey are married (the song then segues into the piano version of "I'm in Love Again").

# Hollywood Ending (2002)

*Music and songs from the repertoire.*

The soundtrack to *Hollywood Ending* contains fewer songs than is usual for a Woody Allen film, as did *The Curse of the Jade Scorpion*; and in a similar fashion to this earlier film, it focuses on a handful of songs which are used repeatedly. Here, Allen centers his score on three recordings by Jackie Gleason and Bobby Hackett, and these form the nucleus of the soundtrack. The most predominant song is "Too Close for Comfort," which permeates the whole film. Once again, Allen provides a subtle subtext to the action on screen: the song's title aptly alludes to the precarious situation Val Waxman (Woody Allen) finds himself in when trying to direct a film blind without anybody knowing. The recording comes from the same session as two tracks used in *Alice*, where Jackie Gleason's orchestra is augmented with a jazz combo featuring a number of eminent musicians (see the section on *Alice*). The other two songs, "Poor Butterfly" and "Serenade in Blue," both feature Bobby Hackett, the first with his 1938 band and the other in his later role as soloist with Jackie Gleason's orchestra; Hackett was the star performer on Gleason's "Music for Lovers Only" album series during the 1950s. On the soundtrack, these two artists are both heard separately and are then brought together with the recording of "Serenade in Blue," and this link between the performers provides the score with a unity which is not immediately obvious.

"Serenade in Blue" acts as a love theme for Val and Ellie (Téa Leone), and is used by Allen on several levels. The lush mood music of Jackie Gleason gives the appropriate romantic sound (just as it did in *Alice* and *Celebrity*), while the unheard lyrics reflect the fond memories Val has for the happier times with his ex-wife, whom he still loves. Furthermore, on the second hearing of the song, when Val's sight returns, Allen synchronizes the song so that the melody that would normally go with the lyric "Once again your face comes back to me"[1] immediately precedes Val enthusing about how beautiful Ellie is now that he can see her again. Using this as an example, Allen makes the following comment on the difference music can make to a given scene: "If I showed scenes from a film before I scored them, they're lifeless, very often. Then you put the score in, and the same material suddenly comes to life. It's the difference between life and death in certain sequences. For example, in *Hollywood Ending* when I regain my eyesight, if I did that without music, it would have a twentieth of the effect."[2]

Given the film's title and its satirical look at the movie business, it is not too surprising to find Allen utilizing a couple of songs that make a direct reference to Hollywood itself. Typically, these songs come from Allen's favored musical period, in this case the 1930s, and also have a link with his beloved jazz — one performed by Bing Crosby, the other by Benny Goodman. Both songs are appropriately used either before or during the opening scenes involving the Hollywood producers.

In addition to the scored elements of the soundtrack, there are a number of songs that appear as source or background music, and again these mostly feature jazz musicians. Val plays a recording of Edmond Hall at the barbeque, while pianist Barbara Carroll has a cameo in the film. Carroll herself remarks, "That was great fun.... I've known Woody for years, but I've never worked with him before. But, since they filmed one scene of that movie in Bemelman's Bar at the Carlyle, where I was performing, I was included in the cast. I was only involved in it for one day's shooting, but it was great, great fun."[3] Carroll also states that she played three songs including "Softly, as in a Morning Sunrise." However, this song does not appear in the end credits. I have included it in this book for the sake of completeness, but it is hard to decipher exactly what is being played in the film owing to the more dominant dialogue and background noise, and it might be that this last song was edited out.

Characteristically, Allen makes a number of tongue-in-cheek, self-referential statements in the film. During his first meeting with the producers, when they are discussing the new film titled *The City That Never Sleeps*, he mentions hand-held cameras and black and white photography. Echoing the opening to *Manhattan* he says, "New York is a black and white town; it reeks of black and white, of old movies." As for the music for this new film, Allen's character typically shares the director's own musical tastes, and turns to Allen's favorite songwriter: "I see it all maybe with like a Cole Porter score." Allen also shows his disdain for modern music, as he did in *Hannah and Her Sisters*, by contrasting contemporary music—which he finds unpalatable—with his more conventional tastes. In *Hannah*, the punk band 39 Steps was juxtaposed with Bobby Short performing Cole Porter. In *Hollywood Ending*, Allen uses Val's reconciliation scene with his son—a green-haired metaller—to express his traditionalistic stance on music: "An electronic band where you rip off your shirt and eat a live rat is not music.... And don't call it a concert; Heifetz at Carnegie Hall is a concert!"

### "Going Hollywood" (from the soundtrack of *Going Hollywood*)

Written by Arthur Freed and Nacio Herb Brown (1933). Performed by Bing Crosby (1933).

Opening credits.

### "Hooray for Hollywood" (from the soundtrack of *Hollywood Hotel*)

Written by Richard Whiting and Johnny Mercer (1937). Performed by Benny Goodman and His Orchestra (1937).[4]

Heard briefly as we see Ellie, Hal Jaeger (Treat Williams) and Ed (George Hamilton) discussing the movie and Val Waxman's involvement.

### "It's Been So Long"

Written by Walter Donaldson and Harold Adamson (1936). Performed by Edmond Hall and His Swingtet (1944).

Heard during Val and Lori's (Debra Messing) barbeque.

### "No Moon at All"

Written by David Mann and Reed Evans (1947). Performed by Barbara Carroll.

### "Sweet and Lovely"

Written by Harry Tobias, Jules Lemare (né Charles N. Daniels) and Gus Arnheim (1931). Performed by Barbara Carroll.

### "Softly, as in a Morning Sunrise"

*Written by Sigmund Romberg and Oscar Hammerstein II (1928). Performed by Barbara Carroll.*

All being played by the pianist (Barbara Carroll) in Bemelman's Bar at the Carlyle Hotel. Val and Ellie meet here in order to talk about the new movie, but end up arguing about the break-up of their marriage.

### "Too Close for Comfort"

*Written by Jerry Block, Larry Holofcener and George David Weiss (1957). Performed by Jackie Gleason and His Orchestra, featuring Ruby Braff (trumpet), Buck Clayton (trumpet), Yank Lawson (trumpet), Buster Bailey (clarinet), Andy Fitzgerald (clarinet), Lawrence Brown (trombone), Claude Hopkins (piano), Al Caiola (guitar) and Milt Hinton (bass) (1960).*

This is the main piece of music used by Allen, and it appears no less than nine times throughout the film:

1) During the long sequence beginning with Ellie on her cell phone talking about Val's choice of cameraman and ending with some of the production crew in Central Park discussing the color scheme for the film.

2) As we see a cab pass the Balthazar restaurant where Ellie and Hal are meeting each other, ending as they bump into Val.

3) When Val and Lori are at the airport, cutting to a shot of Sharon Bates (Tiffani Thiessen) on set, fading as Val talks to *Esquire* journalist Andrea Ford (Jodie Markell).

4) During an Andrea Ford voice-over when Val is with his translator, Chau (Yu Lu), on the set and then bumps into Hal.

5) Briefly during another Andrea Ford voice-over about one of the actors, Sharon Bates, having a crush on Val.

6) When Ellie gets off the plane and arrives on the set, continuing as she speaks to Andrea Ford, ending as Val falls.

7) When a blind Val and Ellie are in Hal's hotel suite practicing walking around the room.

8) At the movie theater when the producers are reading the audience reviews.

9) During the end credits (following "Serenade in Blue").

### "Poor Butterfly"

*Written by Raymond Hubbell and John L. Golden (1916). Performed by Bobby Hackett and His Orchestra (1938).*

Heard during the first day of shooting, as we hear Andrea Ford's first voice-over, continuing as a blind Val arrives on the set. The track returns briefly later on the final day of shooting.

### "Serenade in Blue"

*Written by Harry Warren and Mack Gordon (1942). Performed by Jackie Gleason and His Orchestra (1956).*

This acts as the love theme for Val and Ellie. It is first heard after Ellie has put a blind Val to bed and they talk about old times. The track returns (during another Andrea Ford voice-over) when the two are having a drink and dining together (again at Bemelman's Bar), cutting to them sitting on a bench in Central Park when Val's sight comes back. The song is also heard at the end of the film when Val hears that his movie has had rave reviews in Paris. We then cut to the final scene where Val and Ellie are leaving to live in Paris; the music swells as they kiss before segueing into the end credits.

### "Descarga"

*Written by Chico O'Farrill (1957). Performed by Tito Puente (1991).*

Background music at the wrap party.

### "Grindhouse (A Go-Go)"

*Written by Ivan de Prune, Shauna Reynolds, Jay Yuenger and Rob Zombie (1992). Performed by White Zombie (1992).*

Being played on the stereo at Val's son Tony's (Mark Webber) apartment.

# *Husbands and Wives* (1992)

*Music and songs from the repertoire.*

Although not normally classed in the same group as *Interiors*, *September* and *Another Woman*, *Husbands and Wives* is nevertheless a bittersweet drama about disrupted relationships and disrupted lives, leaning more toward serious than comic. From a musical perspective, such films have prompted Allen to adapt his normal musical approach. After using "functional source music" in *September* and then scoring with classical music in *Another Woman*, Allen here returns, in principle, to the method he adopted during the 1970s when making *Annie Hall* and *Interiors*. With these films, Allen was under the influence of Bergman and was experimenting with the idea of having music employed purely diegetically. *Husbands and Wives* is without question the most musically barren film Allen has made since this time. There is actually less music here than in the forty-one minute long "Oedipus Wrecks," with the whole "score" comprised of source music, either found in the background at one type of party or another, or being performed at a concert.

Where Allen departs from the soundtracks to *Annie Hall* and *Interiors* is during the opening and end credits. Tellingly, he chooses Cole Porter's "What Is This Thing Called Love?" to frame the film, a song that poses the film's underlying question. Characteristically, Allen selects a specific recording: "In *Husbands and Wives* I use 'What Is This Thing Called Love?' A very good version of it. A very, very old version with Bubber Miley, a great black cornet player who played with Duke Ellington and Jelly Roll Morton."[1]

Despite the dearth of music in *Husbands and Wives*, the soundtrack can still be seen as a microcosm of a typical Woody Allen score, comprising jazz, classical music and songs from some of Allen's favorite songwriters, including Cole Porter, Jerome Kern and Irving Berlin.

### "What Is This Thing Called Love?"
*Written by Cole Porter (1929). Performed by Leo Reisman and His Orchestra, featuring Bubber Miley (cornet), Eddy Duchin (piano) and Lew Conrad (vocal) (1930).*

Opening and end credits (abridged both times).

### "West Coast Blues"
*Written by John L. "Wes" Montgomery (1960). Performed by Wes Montgomery (guitar), Tommy Flanagan (piano), Percy Heath (bass) and Albert Heath (drums) (1960).*

Heard twice when we see flashbacks of the first meeting of Gabe Roth (Woody Allen) and his future wife, Judy (Mia Farrow), during a party at the Hamptons.

### Symphony No. 9, 1st movement: Andante comodo
*Written by Gustav Mahler (1909). Performed by the Berlin Philharmonic Orchestra, conducted by Sir John Barbirolli (1964).*

A brief passage from the opening movement is heard while Sally (Judy Davis) and Michael (Liam Neeson) are at a concert on a date. The camera is pointed at the audience who are seemingly watching a performance of this symphony, although what we hear is a pre-existent recording.

### "That Old Feeling"
*Written by Lew Brown and Sammy Fain (1937). Performed by Gerry Mulligan (baritone and tenor sax), Stan Getz (tenor and baritone sax), Lou Levy (piano), Ray Brown (bass) and Stan Levey (drums).*

Being played at a party where Jack (Sydney Pollack) is told by some friends that Sally is seeing someone, continuing as Sam (Lysette Anthony) is having a heated discussion about astrology with some other guests before she and Jack leave arguing.

### "Top Hat, White Tie and Tails"
*Written by Irving Berlin (1935). Performed by Bernie Leighton (piano).*

Being played at Rain's (Juliette Lewis) 21st birthday party, as Gabe tells her parents that he has split up from his wife. Segues into...

### "Makin' Whoopee"
*Written by Walter Donaldson and Gus Kahn (1928). Performed by Bernie Leighton (piano).*

Heard as Rain opens a window to look closer at the thunderstorm and we see her parents in the kitchen talking about how they cannot believe that she is twenty-one. Segues into...

### "The Song Is You"
*Written by Jerome Kern and Oscar Hammerstein II (1932). Performed by Bernie Leighton (piano).*

Heard after the lights go out and Gabe and Rain are in the kitchen. He gives her a music box as a birthday present and they eventually kiss.

# *Interiors* (1978)

*Songs from the repertoire.*

*Interiors* sits between two of Allen's most beloved cinematic creations — *Annie Hall* and *Manhattan* — and is his first attempt at a serious drama. Drawing from Bergman and Chekhov, Allen did not feel that a score was appropriate for a film with such solemn themes, and there is less music here than in any other Woody Allen film to date. "Again, I was in that period, just coming off *Annie Hall*, where I still was not firm about the musical direction that I wanted to go in. So in *Annie Hall* I used no music and I didn't do that in *Interiors* either. At that point I was in a transitional phase from composed music to the recordings of 'my kind of music.' So I felt, as this picture is a serious picture, it didn't need any music. But there's ambience in it throughout anyway."[1]

The only music to be found in the film is source music being played (presumably on a record player) at Arthur (E.G. Marshall) and Pearl's (Maureen Stapleton) wedding. Although clearly diegetic, the music nevertheless has some function in the context of the film. Whereas lively jazz is often used by Allen to accompany slapstick or other comedic scenes, here it works to increase the tension. We see Pearl happily dancing, but this contrasts with the disapproving and resentful looks she gets from Joey (Mary Beth Hurt) and the look of despondency seen on the face of Renata (Diane Keaton). The loudness of the music emphasizes this contrast and the scene increasingly intensifies until Pearl breaks a vase, at which point Joey's feelings boil over as she shouts, "Jesus Christ! Be careful!"[2]

**"Keepin' Out of Mischief Now"**
*Written by Thomas "Fats" Waller and Andy Razaf (1932). Performed by Tommy Dorsey and His Orchestra (1935).*

**"Wolverine Blues"**
*Written by Ferdinand "Jelly Roll" Morton, Benjamin Spikes and John Spikes (1923).*

*Performed by the World's Greatest Jazz Band (1970).*

"Keepin' Out of Mischief Now" is heard first, as Arthur and Pearl dance together along with other guests at the wedding reception. This track ends and "Wolverine Blues" begins as we see a close up of a cheerless Renata, the few seconds of silence in between the two tracks emphasizing her unhappiness. The track continues as Pearl eventually dances on her own, ending as she knocks over the vase.

## *Love and Death* (1975)

*Music composed by Sergei Prokofiev,
with additional music from the repertoire.*

Having explored the future in *Sleeper*, Allen looked to the past for his next film, which is set in Russia during the early nineteenth century. Primarily, *Love and Death* is a parody on all things Russian, from the novels of Tolstoy and Dostoyevsky to the films of Sergei Eisenstein; Allen also draws from various other sources including Ingmar Bergman (*The Seventh Seal, Persona*), Charlie Chaplin (*Shoulder Arms, The Great Dictator*) and Bob Hope (*Monsieur Beaucaire*). In keeping with the Russian theme, Allen chooses music by the composer Sergei Prokofiev, who had provided scores for Eisenstein's last two films. Having used small extracts of classical music in some of his earlier films, Allen now provided a wholly classical score, with extended sequences scored to pre-existent recordings chosen by himself and editor Ralph Rosenblum. As with *Sleeper*, the film credits give no information as to what music actually appears in the film, stating only, "Music by S. Prokofiev." The three main sources are from *Lieutenant Kijé* (1933), *Alexander Nevsky* (1938) and the *Scythian Suite* (1916), with two brief appearances of the March from *The Love of Three Oranges* (1919). None of the performers are listed either, but with the end credits stating "Musical Recordings Courtesy of Vox/Turnabout Production and Phonogram Inc." it has been possible to identify some of the recordings used by Allen and Rosenblum, and those known have been given below. (See also note 4 to this chapter, and appendix 1.)

Allen had originally intended to use Stravinsky for the film, but Rosenblum persuaded him to use Prokofiev instead. In his book "*When the Shooting Stops...*" he remarks:

> The picture is special to me also because of the score. Woody proposed the music for *Love and Death* during our expedition

to Paris, suggesting that we back the film entirely with Stravinsky, a choice that seemed appropriate considering the Russian setting and the themes. When we started cutting, I listened to a lot of Stravinsky and found him too overpowering for the film. He was like a tidal wave, drowning every part of the picture he came in contact with. As an alternative, I introduced Woody to three compositions by Sergei Prokofieff. Prokofieff was a great composer of ballet, opera, and orchestral works, but, unlike Stravinsky, he had written film scores, too. *Love and Death* was scored with two pieces of music I had known and loved since my OWI [Office of War Information] years — "Lieutenant Kijé," from an old Soviet film of that name, "Alexander Nevsky," composed for the Eisenstein film — as well as a third piece, the "Scythian Suite." It was a heartwarming moment for me, the first time I sat through the screen credits and saw "Score by S. Prokofieff" [sic] — in part because of my fondness for the composer, but more because of my fondness for the director and the freedom he had given me to contribute to his work.[1]

Allen himself concurs, "Originally I wanted it to be Stravinsky. But I found that when I put Stravinsky behind the scenes, it made it unfunny. It was too heavy. And in addition to that — but this was not the reason — Stravinsky was very expensive to obtain and Prokofiev was not. But the real reason was that Stravinsky was far too heavy. Ralph Rosenblum, the editor, would say, 'Why don't we forget about Stravinsky? He's not working. Why don't we try Prokofiev?' And we did, and it was just fine. It lightened the whole mood, it was brilliant and gay, whereas Stravinsky was always strange and off-putting and disturbing."[2]

Whereas Prokofiev is certainly more melodic than Stravinsky and therefore more accessible, it should be pointed out that some of the music chosen is still quite stringent, particularly the movements from the *Scythian Suite*; interestingly, this work was composed while Prokofiev was under the influence of Stravinsky's *The Rite of Spring*. Nevertheless, the more discordant pieces suit the various frantic scenes that they accompany, and there is a good balance between these and more popular works such as *Lieutenant Kijé* and *The Love of Three Oranges*.

In addition to the music of Prokofiev, the film also includes source music by Beethoven, Mozart, Boccherini and Mendelssohn, as well as a traditional Russian folk song. (Contrary to what has been stated in some books, there is no music from Tchaikovsky's *The Sleeping Beauty* in this film.) This source music is historically accurate for the most part (Beethoven 1801, Mozart 1791, Boccherini 1771), with the exception of the Mendelssohn, which was composed in 1839, some twenty-seven years after the events depicted — sometime between the Battle of Austerlitz (1805) and Napoleon's campaign in Russia (1812).

All of the following compositions are by Sergei Prokofiev unless otherwise stated.

## *Lieutenant Kijé Suite*, Op. 60, 4th movement: Troika
*Performed by the Paris Philharmonic Orchestra, conducted by Jascha Horenstein (1955).*

This is one of Prokofiev's more famous works and the most memorable piece of music in the film. It is used for the opening credits and the closing scene where Boris Grushenko (Woody Allen) is dancing around trees with Death.[3] It is also heard several times within the film: when the brothers go off to war; throughout the slapstick scenes at the army training camp; and briefly during Boris and Sonja's (Diane Keaton) carriage journey via Minsk to the inn where they meet the Spanish nobles.

### *Alexander Nevsky*, Op. 78, 2nd movement: Song about Alexander Nevsky

This is another important piece that appears several times and, along with the "Troika," is used to frame the film. The piece is heard as the film begins and we see fast-moving clouds, continuing throughout Boris's voice-over where he introduces himself and his family. A little later, an extract from the "piu mosso" middle section is heard briefly when a young Boris is walking through the woods and meets Death. The music is not used again until near the end of the film when it is heard three times in quick succession: when the angel appears to Boris in his prison cell (briefly preceded by the solo cornet motif that occurs at the beginning and end of the *Lieutenant Kijé Suite*); for Boris's subsequent speech; and finally when Boris gives his concluding monologue before being taken away by Death.[4]

### *Scythian Suite*, Op. 20 (from *Ala et Lolly*), 1st movement: The Adoration of Veless and Ala

*Performed by the London Symphony Orchestra, conducted by Antal Dorati (1957).*

Heard first during Boris's bizarre dream where waiters come out of coffins and dance. It reappears later during the battle when Boris is in a cannon, before being fired and landing on the French generals' tent. A brief passage near the end of this movement is heard when we see a shot of Boris's feet as he goes back to kill Napoleon (James Tolkan), who is lying unconscious on the floor.

### "Akh, vy seni, moi seni"

*Traditional Russian folk song.*

Being played and danced to outside the Grushenkos' house when Boris introduces his brothers and then himself, as they each dance the *kazatsky*. The folk song is heard again during the scene after Boris and Countess Alexandrovna (Olga Georges-Picot) have made love.

### Violin Sonata No. 5 in F Major, Op. 24, "Spring," 1st movement: Allegro

*Written by Ludwig van Beethoven (1801).*

Being played by Sonja and an admirer at the Voskovec house, as they begin an affair.

### Overture from *The Magic Flute*, K. 620

*Written by Wolfgang Amadeus Mozart (1791).*

An extract from the Overture is heard during the opera scene where Boris and the Countess Alexandrovna exchange looks to one another from their respective boxes.

### *Scythian Suite*, Op. 20 (from *Ala et Lolly*), 2nd movement: The Enemy God and the Dance of the Spirits of Darkness

*Performed by the London Symphony Orchestra, conducted by Antal Dorati (1957).*

The opening to this movement is used four times: when Boris is marching to the battlefield; as Boris and Anton Inbedkov (Harold Gould) are walking ten paces during their duel; during the shot of Boris and Sonja's carriage traveling to see Napoleon; and finally when Boris is about to shoot Napoleon, but is beaten to it by an unknown assassin. In addition, the rapid triplet passage in the strings (which appears a little later in the movement) is heard briefly when Boris and Sonia decide that someone should go back and kill Napoleon.

### *Alexander Nevsky*, Op. 78, 5th movement: The Battle on Ice

Used during the main battle scene, and when Boris and Sonja make love the night before the duel. It is heard briefly later when Napoleon's invasion of Russia is announced.

### Piano Trio No. 1 in D Minor, Op. 49, 2nd movement: Andante con moto tranquillo

*Written by Felix Mendelssohn (1839).*

This is being played at the party where Boris again meets Countess Alexandrovna and they arrange a liaison. (Note the bad miming by the "musicians" in the background, where we see a double bass, but no piano!)

### *Lieutenant Kijé Suite*, Op. 60, 1st movement: The Birth of Kijé

*Performed by the Paris Philharmonic Orchestra, conducted by Jascha Horenstein (1955).*

Heard as Boris creeps up on Sonja while she is reading.

### *Lieutenant Kijé Suite*, Op. 60, 3rd movement: The Wedding of Kijé

*Performed by the Paris Philharmonic Orchestra, conducted by Jascha Horenstein (1955).*

Heard first as the recently married Boris and Sonja arrive in a carriage at their new home. It returns briefly later when Boris and Sonja are with Berdykov, the village idiot, shortly before Napoleon's invasion of Russia is announced.

### *Lieutenant Kijé Suite*, Op. 60, 2nd movement: Romance

*Performed by the Paris Philharmonic Orchestra, conducted by Jascha Horenstein (1955).*

Used during the scenes where Boris and Sonja begin married life in their new home, where Sonja makes food out of snow and they play music together. The end section is also used briefly when Boris attempts to hang himself.

### String Quintet in E Major, Op. 13 No. 5, 3rd movement: Minuet and Trio

*Written by Luigi Boccherini (1771).*

Being played at Napoleon's palace where Boris and Sonja are pretending to be Spanish nobles and Sonja has too much to drink. The Trio is then heard when Napoleon and his guests are sitting at the dinner table.

### *The Love of Three Oranges Suite*, Op. 33b, 3rd movement: March

The opening few bars of this famous march are used to announce Napoleon's entrance at the palace. The end section of the piece is heard later as Boris is taken to the firing squad and shot.

# *Manhattan* (1979)

*Music composed by George Gershwin, with additional music from the repertoire.*

Now ... to him ... no matter what the season was, this was still a town that existed in black and white and pulsated to the tunes of George Gershwin.[1]

The 1970s culminated with a film that many still regard as Allen's *magnum opus*, and the success of *Manhattan* can be attributed not least to its impressive score. Allen turned to his fellow Brooklynite George Gershwin to accompany his paean to the city he adores: "Gershwin's music captures the feeling of the city better than anyone else. Along with Cole Porter, he's my favorite composer."[2] After the musically sparse *Interiors*, the benefits that scoring can bring to a film are clearly demonstrated here as the music takes on a life of its own, harmonizing perfectly with the beautiful black and white images of New York City.

Normally, Allen's finding and adding music to a film would be done during the editing process. However, in this case Allen knew beforehand exactly what he wanted: "Sometimes I know in advance. When I made *Manhattan*, for example, I knew I was going to use this Gershwin music. There I filmed scenes that in themselves might not mean anything, but I knew that later, when I put music behind it, the combination would be good."[3] Most of the music was recorded especially for the film by the New York Philharmonic Orchestra. "I wanted to use scoring in *Manhattan*, because I wanted to use the Philharmonic and I had a certain sound in mind."[4] Although Allen's inspiration came from elsewhere: "I had been listening to Michael Tilson Thomas's recording of Gershwin overtures and I knew that would be a great back-up for the movie. And I knew it had to be Gershwin with strings."[5] Allen is referring to the CBS Masterworks LP of Gershwin overtures in arrangements by Don Rose, recorded in 1976 by Michael Tilson Thomas and the Buffalo Philharmonic Orchestra, and he had this in mind for the music when he was filming: "I was shooting scenes deliberately to put music that I knew beforehand. I played those records every single day as soon as I got up in the morning. I played them on the way to work, and listened to them over and over."[6]

Although ultimately the majority of the orchestral music used in the film was performed by the New York Philharmonic in arrangements by Tom Pierson, Allen's preconceived ideas and partiality for the Tilson Thomas recording affected the final score. After Pierson had finished his arrangements, Allen called him back to make certain amendments. "Woody had put some of those [Tilson Thomas] tracks against the film 'temporarily' before I was even hired. He grew fond of certain nuances between that music and the film. I was instructed to re-write some of the orchestrations, take out some of the highs, and get a little closer to Woody's pre-selected temporary score. I realize now that it was Broadway Gershwin that Woody loved. I was thrown off by the fact that they had booked the New York Philharmonic before I was involved. I prepared by studying Gershwin's own orchestration to *An American in Paris*. But if you look at Woody's later scores — Dick Hyman's work — you can understand Woody's taste."[7]

It is no surprise then that the majority of the songs chosen for the film come from the overtures to the shows featured on the Tilson Thomas LP, namely *Oh Kay!*, *Funny Face*, *Girl Crazy*, *Strike Up the Band* and *Of Thee I Sing*. In the end Allen even replaced some of Pierson's arrangements that had been written for the film for those by Don Rose from the LP. "Woody missed the temporary recordings that he had put against the film in the early editing before I even came on the scene. Later, he paid for the rights to use a few of those recordings in the film."[8] And with hindsight, Allen feels that he should have kept to his original conception. "I used a little of Tilson Thomas, certain cuts. If I were doing the movie over, I would use the whole album by Tilson Thomas and just have the New York Philharmonic play the Rhapsody."[9] The "certain cuts" that Allen refers to are "Someone to Watch Over Me," "He Loves and She Loves," and "But Not for Me." On the soundtrack album, however, Tom Pierson's original arrangements were retained, including two additional songs, "Blue, Blue, Blue" and "Bronco Busters," which were eventually cut from the film.

Besides the orchestral arrangements, *Manhattan* also includes a number of Gershwin songs performed by smaller forces not given in the end credits. Tom Pierson had a hand in two of these: "The small group versions of 'Mine' and 'Love Is Here to Stay' were 'arranged' by me in the sense that I provided the melody and the chords from which the players improvised, which is typical for jazz small groups."[10] The lovely performance of "Love Is Here to Stay," in a style not dissimilar to Django Reinhardt's Quintette du Hot Club de France, is one of the highlights of the score. The pianist on these two recordings was Dick Hyman, who here makes his first substantial contribution to a Woody Allen film. In addition to playing in the above ensemble, Hyman arranges and performs two other songs, which are also heard in orchestral versions by Tom Pierson, namely "Sweet and Low-Down" and "Embraceable You." While "Mine" and "Love Is Here to Stay" both appear on the soundtrack album, these latter two Hyman arrangements are sadly missing. One other song, "Let's Call the Whole Thing Off," performed by tenor sax and rhythm section, is also heard in the film; however, neither Tom Pierson nor Dick Hyman recall being involved in this recording, and the performers remain unknown.

In the score to *Manhattan*, specific songs have been chosen to supply a subtext to the narrative of the story. Allen had touched upon this technique in *Sleeper*, where he used a few of the songs to reflect what we see on screen, but here the process is developed further. All of the songs in *Manhattan* are performed instrumentally, but most of them are so familiar that the lyrics — or at least the titles — would be known to much of the audience. Allen therefore provides a "subliminal commentary" whereby "the Gershwin songs in *Manhattan* comment so aptly on the action ('Someone to Watch Over Me' for the night when Isaac finds himself falling for the abrasive intellectual played by Diane Keaton, 'But Not for Me' in his final encounter with the schoolgirl Tracy)" that they have a "profound effect on the film."[11] Maurice Yacowar makes the interesting statement that "the tunes over the scenes between Tracy and Isaac are direct expressions of love. Behind their first intimate scene in his apartment, 'Our Love is Here to Stay' undercuts Isaac's detachment from her. Over their ride through Central Park we hear 'He Loves and She Loves,' which is reprised when Isaac's list of life's rewards concludes with Tracy's face. When he finds her in the apartment lobby, about to leave for London, his sense of her remoteness is suggested visually in the intervening door, a bar across its glass, and musically by the song, 'They're Writing Songs of Love, But Not for Me.' On the other hand, the music in Isaac's scenes with Mary are [sic] ominous: 'Let's Call the Whole Thing Off' at the MoMA reception; 'Someone to Watch Over Me' when they take her dog, 'a penis substitute,' for a walk." He concludes, "In these ironic references, the songs establish a setting which either expresses or undercuts the attitude of the characters. The musical setting is analogous to Allen's use of Manhattan as the symbolic setting of his film."[12] This musical dichotomy between Tracy (Mariel Hemingway) and Mary (Diane Keaton) correlates to Douglas Brode's observations about Tracy being "lit with brightness," while Mary "is kept in dark clothing and moves through shadows."[13] Yacowar's statement highlights an important element of the film. However, there is one section in *Manhattan* where Allen's character, Isaac, and Mary are accompanied by more positive love songs. As we are taken through the developing stages of their affair, we hear in order, "I've Got a Crush on You" at the beginning of the relationship; "Do, Do, Do (What You've Done, Done Done Before)" as they kiss for the second time; "'S Wonderful" as they make love for the first time (afterwards Mary even says, "That was wonderful") and "Embraceable You" as the relationship is established.

Other musical references found in the film include Louis Armstrong's "Potato Head Blues" and the second movement of Mozart's "Jupiter" Symphony (No. 41 in C Major), both of which appear on Isaac/Allen's "why is life worth living?" list (note that the "Jupiter" Symphony was used in *Annie Hall*, albeit the fourth movement). It would seem that Allen uses this list, recited near the end of the film, to counterbalance Yale (Michael Murphy) and Mary's "Academy of the Over-rated" heard near the beginning, where they disparage the likes of Gustav Mahler, F. Scott Fitzgerald and Ingmar Bergman (all of whom Allen admires). Mozart is mentioned here too as Isaac irately retorts, "Hey, what about Mozart? You guys don't wanna leave out Mozart — I mean, while you're trashing people."[14] After this sarcastic remark, Allen makes a point of commending Mozart later in the film: in addition to the "Jupiter" Symphony's inclusion on Isaac's life-affirming list, the same four characters also attend a concert where Mozart's Symphony No. 40 in G Minor is being performed.

## *Rhapsody in Blue*

*Written by George Gershwin (1924). Orchestrated by Ferde Grofé. Performed by Paul Jacobs (piano) and the New York Philharmonic Orchestra, conducted by Zubin Mehta.*

> It opens, spectacularly, with a montage of cityscapes cut to the swelling rhythms of Gershwin's "Rhapsody in Blue" ... the opening kaleidoscope is a tribute to the city's vitality and diversity, a visual bouquet to Woody's beloved hometown. And a gorgeous piece of film making, the crowning touch to his first decade as a director.[15]

Heard during the famous opening to the film where a series of black and white images of New York City are shown, beginning with a shot of the Empire State and Chrysler buildings at dawn/dusk. The various views of New York continue to flash on and off the screen as Isaac attempts to dictate the opening lines for a new novel. As Isaac's voice-over ends, the music reaches a crescendo and the montage culminates in a firework display over the Manhattan skyline.[16] The beautiful slow section of the work is used in the final scene where Isaac tries to dissuade Tracy from going to London ("I don't want that thing I like about you to change"). It continues to the end of the film, where Allen reprises some of the opening shots of New York at dawn/dusk (again beginning with the Empire State and Chrysler buildings, the film's first image) before cutting to the end credits. In this way, Allen correlates the film's opening and closing scenes not only in content, but also provides a subtle musical parallel as well.

### "Mine" (from the show *Let 'Em Eat Cake*)

*Written by George and Ira Gershwin (1933). Performed by Dick Hyman (piano), Milt Hinton (bass) and Eric Cohen (drums).*

Heard during the opening scene in Elaine's restaurant, where we are introduced to Isaac, his girlfriend Tracy, and his friends Yale and Emily (Anne Byrne), who are talking and having a drink.

### "Love Is Here to Stay" (from the film *The Goldwyn Follies*)

*Written by George and Ira Gershwin (1937). Performed by Lewis Eley (violin), Dick Hyman (piano), Brian Koonin (guitar), Milt Hinton (bass) and Eric Cohen (drums).*

Heard as we see Tracy in Isaac's apartment as he walks down a spiral staircase. The track continues through the whole scene as they talk about their relationship and he tells her she can't stay over.

### "Let's Call the Whole Thing Off" (from the film *Shall We Dance?*)

*Written by George and Ira Gershwin (1937).*

Background music being played at the reception in support of the Equal Rights Amendment at the Museum of Modern Art's Sculpture Gallery, where Isaac meets Mary for a second time.

### "Someone to Watch Over Me" (from the show *Oh Kay!*)

*Written by George and Ira Gershwin (1926). Arranged by Don Rose. Performed by the Buffalo Philharmonic Orchestra, conducted by Michael Tilson Thomas (1976).*

Heard when Isaac and Mary go for a walk at night with Mary's dog, cutting to the three of them in an all-night diner. The track returns when they leave with their takeaway food and sit on a bench by the 59th Street (Queensboro) bridge until dawn. This iconic shot, which was used on the movie poster, is one of Woody Allen's — and cinema's — most resonant movie images.

### "Love Is Sweeping the Country" (from the show *Of Thee I Sing*)

*Written by George and Ira Gershwin (1931). Adapted and arranged by Tom Pierson. Performed by the New York Philharmonic Orchestra, conducted by Zubin Mehta.*

Heard as Isaac and his son, Willie (Damion Scheller), are dribbling a basketball down the street. The track continues as they stand in front of the FAO Schwarz toy shop window looking at toy boats. The music fades as the scene shifts to the Russian Tea Room.

### "He Loves and She Loves" (from the show *Funny Face*)

*Written by George and Ira Gershwin (1927). Arranged by Don Rose. Performed by the Buffalo Philharmonic Orchestra, conducted by Michael Tilson Thomas (1976).*

This song can be viewed as Isaac and Tracy's love theme. It is heard first when the two take a buggy ride through Central Park at night. The song then returns significantly near the end of the film at the point when Isaac thinks of Tracy's face after asking himself the question, "Why is life worth living?" The track builds to a crescendo as he finds the harmonica she bought him and then tries to phone her, before finally deciding to go out and try and catch her before she leaves for London. The music then segues into "Strike Up the Band" (see below).

## "Sweet and Low-Down" (from the show *Tip-Toes*)

*Written by George and Ira Gershwin (1925). Adapted and arranged by Tom Pierson. Performed by the New York Philharmonic Orchestra, conducted by Zubin Mehta; also performed by Dick Hyman (piano).*

The brief orchestral version of this is used during the scene where Isaac is moving apartments and the movers mishandle his things. A piano version is also used later in the film when Isaac is alone in his apartment after Mary has decided to go back to Yale. This track continues as we see Isaac typing his novel and he and Willie carving pumpkins and playing football with the "Divorced Fathers and Sons All Stars" in Central Park.

## "I've Got a Crush on You" (from the show *Strike Up the Band*)

*Written by George and Ira Gershwin (1930). Adapted and arranged by Tom Pierson. Performed by the New York Philharmonic Orchestra, conducted by Zubin Mehta.*

Heard as Isaac and Mary come out of the Cinema Studio having seen Hiroshi Inagaki's *Chushingura* (1962) and Alexander Dovzhenko's *Earth* (1930). The track fades as we see them back in Mary's apartment.

## "Do, Do, Do" (from the show *Oh Kay!*)

*Written by George and Ira Gershwin (1926). Adapted and arranged by Tom Pierson. Performed by the New York Philharmonic Orchestra, conducted by Zubin Mehta.*

Described by Ira Gershwin himself as "a catchy song about a kiss,"[17] Allen aptly chooses this song to accompany the scene where he kisses Mary for the second time. The song continues as the couple visit the Whitney Museum and then take a taxi back from a restaurant in Brooklyn, continuing as they kiss again and Mary turns out the light.

## "'S Wonderful" (from the show *Funny Face*)

*Written by George and Ira Gershwin (1927). Adapted and arranged by Tom Pierson. Performed by the New York Philharmonic Orchestra, conducted by Zubin Mehta.*

Heard during the scenes where Isaac and Mary go for a drive in the country and are walking by a waterfall, cutting to them in bed after making love. Mary says, "That was wonderful."

## "Embraceable You" (from the show *Girl Crazy*)

*Written by George and Ira Gershwin (1930). Adapted and arranged by Tom Pierson. Performed by the New York Philharmonic Orchestra, conducted by Zubin Mehta; also performed by Dick Hyman (piano), Milt Hinton (bass) and Eric Cohen (drums).*

A charming trio version of this is used when Isaac and Mary are dancing, continuing as they go for a boat trip on the Central Park lake and then look in the shop window at Zabar's. The orchestral version is heard during the end credits.

## Symphony No. 40 in G Minor, K. 550, 1st movement: Molto allegro

*Written by Wolfgang Amadeus Mozart (1788).*[18]

We hear the opening movement of this symphony being performed at a concert attended by Isaac, Mary, Yale and Emily. The camera pauses on Isaac and Mary, who are uncomfortable owing to their recent affair. One might simply expect to hear the famous opening to this symphony in this situation. But Allen deliberately uses the development section

84 / *Manhattan Murder Mystery* (1993)

here — which is by nature more unsettling owing to the rapid key changes — because it better reflects the characters' uneasiness.

### "Oh, Lady, Be Good!" (from the show *Lady, Be Good!*)

*Written by George and Ira Gershwin (1924). Adapted and arranged by Tom Pierson. Performed by the New York Philharmonic Orchestra, conducted by Zubin Mehta.*

Heard during the scene where Yale drives Emily, Isaac and Mary in his new Porsche over the Tappan Zee Bridge to Nyack. The track continues as Mary buys Isaac a framed picture which he throws away when she's not looking, ending as they see copies of Jill's (Meryl Streep) new book in a shop window.

The song's title is used by Allen to reflect his ongoing concerns about his ex-wife's book, titled *Marriage, Divorce and Selfhood*, which contains material he would prefer not to be made public. The song actually ends on an ominous minor chord, which anticipates the following scene in which the characters read extracts from the book.

### "Land of the Gay Caballero" (from the show *Girl Crazy*)

*Written by George and Ira Gershwin (1930). Adapted and arranged by Tom Pierson. Performed by the New York Philharmonic Orchestra, conducted by Zubin Mehta.*

We hear this after Mary has told Isaac that she is still in love with Yale and Isaac marches round to the university to confront Yale.

### "Strike Up the Band" (from the show *Strike Up the Band*)

*Written by George and Ira Gershwin (1930). Adapted and arranged by Tom Pierson. Performed by the New York Philharmonic Orchestra, conducted by Zubin Mehta.*

Following on directly from the second hearing of "He Loves and She Loves," this is heard at the climax of the film when Isaac runs down Second Avenue, past Gramercy Park, to Tracy's apartment building. The music segues into "But Not for Me" (below).

### "But Not for Me" (from the show *Girl Crazy*)

*Written by George and Ira Gershwin (1930). Arranged by Don Rose. Performed by the Buffalo Philharmonic Orchestra, conducted by Michael Tilson Thomas (1976).*

Heard as Isaac sees Tracy in the lobby of her apartment building with the porter and they look at each other through the door, fading after Isaac walks through the door to talk to her.

This song, heard at the end of the film, counterbalances "Love Is Here to Stay," heard at the beginning. The earlier song is positive about the relationship between Isaac and Tracy, but by the final scene the tone has changed and Allen's use of "But Not for Me" here aptly accompanies *Manhattan*'s ambiguous ending.

# *Manhattan Murder Mystery* (1993)

*Music and songs from the repertoire.*

Following on from the visceral *Husbands and Wives*, *Manhattan Murder Mystery* was a piece of light relief for Allen. "I feel it's an unambitious undertaking. I feel it's a trivial picture, but fun for me. It's sort of like giving myself a little personal reward. Just an indulgence. It's something that I've always wanted to do. I just felt I had done — I don't know, twenty-two, twenty-three pictures — and I just wanted to take part of a year and do this little thing for fun. Like a little dessert or something. Not a real meal."[1] The enjoyment Allen had making the film can be seen in the way he incorporates many of his pet likes (and dislikes) into the script. This is, of course, something that Allen does in many of his films, but here it is even more evident. Shot mostly in his preferred weather — rain or overcast — the film includes references to sport (New York Rangers), classic films (*Double Indemnity* and *The Lady from Shanghai*) and musicals (*Guys and Dolls*). Equally, the happy and light-hearted nature of the film is also reflected in the score, which typically draws on a mixture of jazz and American standards.

With his two previous films, Allen had chosen to adapt his musical approach to suit the type of film he was making. In *Manhattan Murder Mystery*, there are no such restrictions and Allen simply chooses music he enjoys, reflecting the fun he had making the movie. This is apparent right from the outset: over the opening credits, cutting to an aerial shot of New York at night, Bobby Short is heard singing "I Happen to Like New York," written by Allen's favorite songwriter, Cole Porter. Echoing the celebrated opening to *Manhattan*, Allen again brings together the music he loves with the city he adores.

As a counterbalance, Allen also uses music to highlight certain dislikes. One of the funniest moments in the film occurs when Larry (Woody Allen) and Carol (Diane Keaton) go to the opera to see *The Flying Dutchman*. Allen uses this event to make a couple of anti–Wagner jokes combined with his customary scorn for Nazis. As Larry leaves the opera early he quips, "I can't listen to that much Wagner, ya know? I start to get the urge to conquer Poland." It is worth noting that Allen selects a suitable extract from the opera, one which occurs near the beginning of the first act. If one includes ten minutes for the overture, Larry only stays for about twenty-five minutes. The inclusion of music that Allen is averse to in order to point up his musical distastes can also be seen in other films, notably *Hannah and Her Sisters* and *Hollywood Ending*.

Much of the music in *Manhattan Murder Mystery* is background or source music, coming from some form of show, or from a film, or is being played in a restaurant. As a result, the few examples of scoring that are present stand out, and the highlights in the score involve the scenes where Allen makes use of Benny Goodman's "Sing, Sing, Sing" (previously heard in "Oedipus Wrecks") and the stylistically similar "The Big Noise from Winnetka." The latter was a hit record for Bob Crosby's orchestra in 1938 and features a remarkable duet between bassist Bob Haggart and drummer Ray Bauduc. Both these tracks begin with pulsating drums — which Allen uses to spell danger — and are equally good examples of how upbeat, rhythmically driven music can enhance a comedic sequence with little or no dialogue (as discussed earlier in the introduction). During his interview with Melvyn Bragg for *The South Bank Show* in 1994, Allen was asked what Goodman's "Sing, Sing, Sing" was giving us during the scene when Larry and Carol follow the killer over the Hudson River to New Jersey. Allen replied, "Something frantic and exciting. And with a slightly sinister quality to it, in addition to a hot quality to it. The tempo of it is very, very exciting and it's not just the speed, but the character of the piece of music."[2]

### "I Happen to Like New York"

*Written by Cole Porter (1930). Performed by Bobby Short (vocals and piano), Beverly Peer (bass) and Richard Sheridan (drums) (live at the Café Carlyle, 1973).*

Opening credits and aerial shot of New York City.

### "The Best Things in Life Are Free"

*Written by Ray Henderson, Buddy G. DeSylva and Lew Brown (1927). Performed by Erroll Garner (piano), Eddie Calhoun (bass) and Kelly Martin (drums) (1961).*

Heard when Larry and Carol meet Sy (Ron Rifkin) and Marilyn (Joy Behar) in a market.

### "The Hallway" (from the soundtrack of *Double Indemnity*)

*Written by Miklós Rózsa (1944).*

Heard briefly while Larry and Carol are in the cinema watching Billy Wilder's classic *film noir*.

### "Wie oft in Meeres tiefsten Schlund" from *The Flying Dutchman*

*Written by Richard Wagner (1841). Performed by Hans Hotter and the Orchestra of the Munich State Opera, conducted by Clemens Krauss.*

Heard briefly while Larry and Carol are at the opera and we see Larry leaving early.

### "Take Five"

*Written by Paul Desmond (1959). Performed by the Dave Brubeck Quartet: Dave Brubeck (piano), Paul Desmond (alto sax), Eugene Wright (bass) and Joe Morello (drums) (1959).*

Background music heard in Elaine's restaurant, where Larry and Carol are discussing the supposed death of Mrs. House (Lynn Cohen) with Sy, Marilyn and Ted (Alan Alda).

### "I'm in the Mood for Love"

*Written by Jimmy McHugh and Dorothy Fields (1935). Performed by Erroll Garner (piano), John Simmons (bass) and Shadow Wilson (drums) (1951).*

Heard when Carol and Ted are looking at a location for a restaurant.

### "The Big Noise from Winnetka"

*Written by Bob Haggart, Ray Bauduc, Gil Rodin and Bob Crosby (1938). Performed by Bob Haggart (bass and whistling) and Ray Bauduc (drums) (1938).*[3]

Used to good effect during the sequence where Carol steals a copy of Mr. House's (Jerry Adler) key and sneaks into his apartment.

### "Out of Nowhere"

*Written by John Green and Edward Heyman (1931). Performed by Coleman Hawkins and His All-Star Jam Band (including Benny Carter and Django Reinhardt) (1937).*

Heard first when Carol meets Ted outside the hotel and they stake out Helen Moss's (Melanie Norris) apartment, returning a little later just before she comes out and they follow her to Mr. House's old movie theater. It returns at the end of the film as Ted and Marcia (Angelica Huston) are walking down the street talking about celebrating, cutting to Larry and Carol walking back to their apartment building, leading into the end credits.

### "Have You Met Miss Jones?"

*Written by Richard Rodgers and Lorenz*

Hart (1937). *Performed by Art Tatum (piano), Ben Webster (tenor sax), Red Callender (bass) and Bill Douglass (drums) (1956).*

Heard first when Larry and Carol meet their son, Nick (Zach Braff), in the hotel foyer and then again when Carol and Ted are at the wine tasting and Carol sees Mrs. House on a bus. It returns a little later when Carol takes Ted back to where she saw Mrs. House and they walk to the end of the bus terminal.

### "Guys and Dolls Overture"

*Written by Frank Loesser (1950). Performed by the New Broadway Cast.*

Heard briefly while Larry and Carol are in the theater.

### "Sing, Sing, Sing (with a Swing)"

*Written by Louis Prima (1936). Performed by Benny Goodman and His Orchestra (1937).*

Used for the scene where Larry and Carol follow Mr. House over the Hudson River to the factory in New Jersey, where he disposes of Mrs. House's body. The track returns later when Larry meets Mr. House outside the movie theater to exchange Mrs. House's body for Carol.

### "Misty"

*Written by Erroll Garner (1954). Performed by Erroll Garner (piano), Wyatt Ruther (bass) and Eugene "Fats" Heard (drums) (1954).*

Background music at Vincent's restaurant in New Jersey, where Larry, Carol, Ted and Marcia are discussing the murder.

### Incidental music from *The Lady from Shanghai*

*Written by Heinz Roemheld (1948).*[4]

Orsen Welles's *film noir* is being shown in Mr. House's cinema as Larry goes there to rescue Carol. The music accompanying the film is heard as the famous hall of mirrors scene is simultaneously imitated behind the movie screen by Larry, Mr. House and Mrs. Dalton (Marge Redmond). Mrs. Dalton walks with a cane like Everett Sloane's character, Bannister, and Allen even borrows dialogue from the film.

# *Match Point* (2005)

*Music from the repertoire.*

With *Match Point*, Allen returns to the genre of serious drama, abandoning his beloved New York to make his first film in England. Characteristically, he chooses pre-existent recordings for the soundtrack rather than an especially composed score. But instead of the usual array of jazz and American standards, Allen opts for classical music, which, as we have seen in films such as *Another Woman, Crimes and Misdemeanors* and *Shadows and Fog*, he sometimes prefers when the subject matter is non-comical. Allen explains, "In this movie I knew I couldn't use the music I usually use — because I generally use Cole Porter and Irving Berlin and George Gershwin, and here that was really inappropriate for the movie. And I was testing things, and I thought: I should really test an opera piece, because at least there's a connection in the movie — in the movie the family goes to the opera. And I tried it, and the second I put the opera piece in, it looked good. And so I started using opera for the entire movie ... there's all this blood and intensity in the story, so I used opera."[1] In his earlier films with classical scores (*Love and Death*, *A Midsummer Night's Sex Comedy* and *Shadows and Fog*), Allen had chosen music from one specific composer; in *Match Point*, however, he uses a variety of composers, selecting various operatic extracts from the 19th century. Verdi predominates, but there are also contributions from Donizetti, Bizet, Gomes and Rossini. Notably, the majority of the extracts chosen feature the legendary tenor Enrico Caruso, in historic recordings that date as far back as 1904, and these form the backbone of the score.

To highlight the basic themes expressed in the film, a number of appropriate arias and duets have been selected to underscore certain scenes or reflect the feelings of the characters. Echoing the film's tagline — "Passion. Temptation. Obsession." — Allen remarks, "The story is operatic; it deals with the kinds of things that opera is so often about: love and lust, passion and jealousy, betrayal and tragedy ... and, of course, the confluence of fate and luck."[2] Central to the story is the passionate, but illicit, relationship between Chris Wilton (Jonathan Rhys Meyers) and Nola Rice (Scarlett Johansson), and these characters are thematically linked by music that reflects many of these emotions. The evocative "Mi par d'udir ancora," for example, gives emphasis to the themes of passion and temptation. In the opera *The Pearl Fishers*, this aria is sung by Nadir, who is unable to resist the allure of Leila, a beautiful priestess, despite an oath with his rival, Zurga, not to pursue her. Allen thus provides a subtle insight into Chris's feelings as he waits for Nola to come out of her audition, just prior to the scene where the two indulge in a flirtatious exchange. Donizetti's poignant *Romanza*, "Una furtiva lagrima," also plays an important role in the score. Appearing over the opening and closing credits, it is used by Allen to frame the film, and occurs at two key points in the story (see below). Interestingly, each time this aria is heard, it starts from the second verse. It would seem that Allen begins here deliberately, partly so that Chris's inexorable desire for Nola can be posited from the outset, echoed in the words, "To feel for just one moment the throbbing of her beautiful heart!"; and partly because it allows Allen to play out the remainder of the aria for the film's end credits.[3] Significantly, the final words we hear Caruso sing as the film concludes provide a telling coda to the story: "Si può morir d'amore" (I could die of love). Both these arias come from Caruso's early 1904 session for Victor; they share a slow, lilting 6/8 rhythm and minor key tonality and this, combined with the age of the recordings, transmits a sinister atmosphere that permeates the film.

Understandably, several commentators have compared *Match Point* to *Crimes and Misdemeanors*, as both films share a murder plot where the duplicitous perpetrator goes unpunished. In the earlier film, Allen used music to heighten the scenes immediately before and after the actual killing, employing Schubert's last string quartet to good effect. In contrast, he approaches *Match Point* differently by scoring the whole sequence (a lengthy nine minutes) where Chris carries out the murders of both Nola and her neighbor, Mrs.

Eastby (Margaret Tyzack). The music Allen chooses here is Act II, Scene 5 from Verdi's *Otello*, and during the course of this duet Otello succumbs to murderous thoughts after the seeds of jealousy have been sown by Jago. It is interesting to note that the "Piu lento" segment (thirteen bars) has been cut to allow for the more animated and dramatic "Allegro agitato" section to be heard just prior to Nola's murder. Moreover, this cut allows for the words, "All my fond love, thus do I blow to heaven," to be sung at the point that Chris shoots Nola.

Other observations regarding excerpts that comment on the film's narrative have been given under their respective titles below.

### "Una furtiva lagrima" from *L'Elisir d'amore*

*Written by Gaetano Donizetti (1832). Performed by Enrico Caruso (tenor) with an unknown pianist (1904).*

Opening credits and Chris Wilton's subsequent narration, as we see a slow motion shot of a tennis ball hitting the top of the net. The aria then reappears twice at significant points within the film: when Chris seeks out Nola at Tate Modern and attempts to rekindle their affair; and later when he is lying in bed contemplating Nola's murder. Finally, the aria returns for the closing scene, as the camera pauses on Chris's face, cutting to the end credits.

### "Un dì felice, eterea" from *La Traviata*[4]

*Written by Giuseppe Verdi (1853). Performed by Alan Oke (tenor) and Tim Lole (piano).*

Being performed at the Royal Opera House[5] where Chris has been invited to join the Hewetts in their box.

In *La Traviata*, Alfredo sings this to Violetta, telling her that he has loved her since the first time he saw her. Reversing gender, this aria is used to reflect Chloe's (Emily Mortimer) obvious attraction toward Chris when she meets him for the first time.

### "Mal reggendo all'aspro assalto" from *Il Trovatore*

*Written by Giuseppe Verdi (1853). Performed by Enrico Caruso (tenor) and the Victor Orchestra (1910).*[6]

Heard when Chris is walking around the Hewetts' country house at the dinner party.

### "Mia piccirella" from *Salvator Rosa*

*Written by Antonio Carlos Gomes (1874). Performed by Enrico Caruso (tenor) with the Victor Orchestra (1919).*

Heard when Chris and Chloe meet up prior to going to the cinema (we see shots of the Saatchi Gallery, the Houses of Parliament and Buckingham Palace). It returns shortly afterwards when the two are making love in Chris's apartment, and then again later when we see them getting married, cutting to their new apartment on the Thames.

In *Salvator Rosa*, this song is especially composed by Gennariello to use when seducing women, and thus acts as a fitting accompaniment for the mutual seduction that occurs between Chris and Chloe, culminating in their eventual marriage.

### "Mi par d'udir ancora" from *The Pearl Fishers*

*Written by Georges Bizet (1863). Performed by Enrico Caruso (tenor) and an unknown pianist (1904).*

Heard when Chris is waiting for Nola to come out of her audition. It continues as she arrives and they decide to go for a drink. The aria returns later when Chris and Nola are together in her apartment and he is putting oil on her back, fading as the shot of snow falling outside through the window cuts to the Hewetts' garden in summer.

### "Gualtier Malde! ... Caro nome" from *Rigoletto*

*Written by Giuseppe Verdi (1851). Performed by Mary Hegarty (soprano) and Tim Lole (piano).*

Being performed at the Royal Opera House when Tom gets a phone call for Nola, who goes outside to take the call. Chris follows Nola and expresses his continued desire for her, but is rejected.

This aria is heard immediately after Chris and Nola's fervent lovemaking scene in the rain, and the words "Dearest name, which made my heart throb for the first time," reinforce the imagery found in "Una furtiva lagrima." It is ironic that, as the soprano sings of the pleasures of love, Nola tells Chris that their recent infidelity was a mistake.

### Valse from Act I ("Che è ciò?") from *La Traviata*

*Written by Giuseppe Verdi (1853).[7] Performed by Tim Lole (piano).*

Background music heard at the dinner party where Eleanor Hewett (Penelope Wilton) gets drunk and asks Chris and Chloe when they are getting married. It continues as Chris walks downstairs and sees Tom and Nola making love. In *La Traviata*, this waltz, which is also heard as background music to a party, immediately precedes the duet "Un di felice, eterea," heard earlier in the film.

### "Arresta ... Quali sguardi" from *William Tell*

*Written by Gioacchino Rossini (1829). Performed by Janez Lotrič (tenor) and Igor Morozov (baritone) with the Slovak Radio Symphony Orchestra, conducted by Johannes Wildner (1995).*

Heard briefly as we see a distant shot of the Hewetts' box at the Royal Opera House, where Chris can be seen kissing Chloe.

In the context of the narrative, this excerpt appears just after Chris decides not to tell Nola that the cruise has been cancelled, and it is now clear that Chris is in a dilemma. The specific extract we hear begins with the words "We want to be free," which can be seen as reflecting Chris's feelings at this point in the story.

### "Desdemona rea!" from *Otello*

*Written by Giuseppe Verdi (1887). Performed by Janez Lotrič (tenor) and Igor Morozov (baritone) with the Slovak Radio Symphony Orchestra, conducted by Johannes Wildner (1995).*

Heard as Chris goes to Nola's apartment and throughout the whole of the following "murder scene," ending as Chris and Chloe walk downstairs to the cloakroom at the Palace Theater, where they have gone to see *The Woman in White*.

### "I Believe My Heart" from *The Woman in White*

*Written by Andrew Lloyd Webber and David Zippel (2004). Performed by Martin Crewes, taken from the original cast recording, conducted by Stephen Brooker.[8]*

Heard briefly when Chris and Chloe are watching *The Woman in White*.

### "O figli, o figli miei! ... Ah, la paterna mano" from *Macbeth*

*Written by Giuseppe Verdi (1847). Performed by Enrico Caruso (tenor) with an unknown orchestra, conducted by Walter Rogers (1916).*

Heard when Chris goes to the Thames to throw the jewels and drugs into the river. "Ah, la paterna mano" begins just as the film cuts to Chris at the police station.

# *Melinda and Melinda* (2004)

*Music and songs from the repertoire.*

Harking back to *Crimes and Misdemeanors*, *Melinda and Melinda* combines two distinct storylines, one tragic and the other comic. In a similar manner to the earlier film, Allen selects classical music (in this case Stravinsky, Bach and Bartók) to accompany the serious drama, while jazz (Duke Ellington and Erroll Garner) is chosen to complement the romantic comedy. As we have seen, these two types of music pervade Allen's films. "Jazz is a big thing with me. My favorite kinds of music are jazz and classical. It's a very big passion of mine, to play it. I'm an amateur musician and I love everything about it. I was obsessed with jazz when I was fifteen years old and I know a lot about it because I've loved it so much. I've listened to so much and read so much about it and played it a lot. And I find in my movies, I like my old personal feelings to inform the movie, and so it's jazz and classical."[1] The film's duality is immediately pronounced over the opening credits, where Allen uniquely juxtaposes two pieces of music — Stravinsky and Ellington — instead of using one. This sets the scene for the rest of the film, which subsequently alternates between drama and comedy, with the two styles of music thematically linked to the interwoven storylines.

Allen's choice of classical music is interesting. On the one hand, he uses Johann Sebastian Bach, who has featured in a number of previous films; and as before, Bach is used as an example of a composer enjoyed by the wealthy and sophisticated classes. (Many of the characters in the film complain of being poor, but this is belied by their opulent New York apartments.) On the other, the film includes music by two twentieth century composers — Stravinsky and Bartók — which is more unusual. Allen had considered using Stravinsky in *Love and Death*, but found that the music was "unfunny" and "far too heavy." "Stravinsky was always strange and off-putting and disturbing," he told Stig Björkman.[2] It would seem that Allen called this to mind when scoring *Melinda and Melinda*, as these "disturbing" qualities are a fitting accompaniment to the tragic storyline. Allen's choice of Bartók also demonstrates that he was looking for a more austere sound world for the dramatic aspects of the film. Bartók, like Stravinsky, can be a difficult composer to listen to, and his string quartets are among some of his more demanding works. This said, the two movements that Allen selects are each the most approachable from the respective compositions. The "Arioso" from Stravinsky's *Concerto in D*, with its lilting melodic line, is far less stringent than the outer movements.[3] Likewise, the pizzicato movement from Bartók's Fourth Quartet is the easiest on the ear; the other four movements are far more dissonant and severe. It would seem then that, although Allen has deliberately selected discordant classical music to accompany the serious facets of the film, he is still mindful of the public's limits; while Stravinsky and Bartók are more aurally challenging than his regular mainstream fare, he has stopped short of subjecting his audience to music that might be too taxing. It should also be pointed out that when Allen chooses music of this sort it is always purposefully. In earlier films where he has used equally astringent compositions, such as Prokofiev's *Scythian Suite* in *Love and Death* and Varèse's *Ecuatorial* in *Another Woman*, the works have been chosen specifically to underscore dramatic scenes or sequences of a disturbing nature. In a similar manner to this, Stravinsky and Bartók have been utilized in *Melinda and Melinda* to reflect Melinda's (Radha Mitchell) neurotic and unbalanced character.

The tragic story is accompanied exclusively by classical music except for the dinner party sequence, where Allen turns once more to a familiar repertoire of American popular songs. Long-time musical collaborator, Dick Hyman, is yet again employed to arrange and perform these songs, which he does in much the same way as he did for the Thanksgiving parties in *Hannah and Her Sisters*— there is even a four-song medley as there was in the earlier film. (More unusually, Hyman also turns his hand to performing Bach.) During this sequence, we are introduced to the pianist-composer character played by Chiwetel Ejiofor, who has the implausible name of Ellis Moonsong. Drolly, Allen includes two songs with "moon" in the title ("Moonglow" and "No Moon at All"), which anticipate Ellis's later appearance when we see him performing Bach at the piano.[4] Furthermore, the other song Ellis plays, "Darn That Dream," can be seen as foreshadowing the doomed affair he has with Melinda. From Melinda's perspective, the lyrics (which also mention the word "moon") aptly predict the abandonment she will experience later, when, having been successfully wooed by the smooth-talking Ellis, she is discarded for Laurel (Chloé Sevigny).

The recordings by Duke Ellington and Erroll Garner that Allen has selected for the comic storyline provide an agreeable contrast to the starkness of the Stravinsky and Bartók. Three of the five songs chosen have appeared in earlier films: "Take the 'A' Train" (*Radio Days*), "The Best Things in Life Are Free" (*Manhattan Murder Mystery*) and "Will You Still Be Mine?" (*Alice* and *Celebrity*). As usual, we find examples of Allen's favored technique of using songs as a subtext to the film's narrative. "Somebody Stole My Gal" is playing during the episode with Greg (Josh Brolin), and the title is used by Allen to reflect Hobie's (Will Ferrell) feelings: he is now in love with Melinda and sees Greg as a threat. Also, near the end of the film when Hobie is with Stacey (Vinessa Shaw) in his apartment, he plays "Will You Still Be Mine?" which is the question he is asking himself, as Stacey, who begins to think about her previous boyfriend, becomes increasingly less ardent.

With several of the characters in the film having musical associations, it is unsurprising to find a number of musical references in the dialogue, and these are often linked to the music found in the score. In the tragic story, we find the characters listening to and commenting on both Stravinsky and Bartók. Laurel plays Bach with Ellis and cries when she hears Mahler's Second Symphony. Ellis boasts about his operas and would like to be another Verdi or Puccini. And typically, Allen even cites Cole Porter: when Melinda is telling Hobie about her chance meeting with Billy (Daniel Sunjata), she quotes a line from the song "Just One of Those

Things," which Allen has used in two previous films (*Stardust Memories* and *Radio Days*).

## Concerto in D for String Orchestra, 2nd movement: Arioso: Andantino
*Written by Igor Stravinsky (1946). Performed by the English Chamber Orchestra, conducted by Colin Davis (1962).*

First part of the opening credits. This piece is the main theme for the tragic Melinda and appears regularly. After the opening credits, it is heard again as Max (Larry Pine) says, "I see this lone figure" as the film cuts to Melinda approaching Lee and Laurel's apartment. The film then moves inside where Lee and Laurel are having a dinner party, and the music becomes the piece being played on the stereo. This music then returns when the tragic Melinda is at Belmont watching the races. The music continues through the succeeding sequence where Melinda is at the piano in Ellis's apartment and Melinda, Ellis, Lee (Jonny Lee Miller) and Laurel are seen coming out of a concert of Mahler's Second Symphony at the New York Town Hall. We briefly cut to Max (who has been narrating these events), who states that Melinda has fallen in love with Ellis. The music then stops when Melinda, who is talking to Ellis in his apartment, says, "I killed him!" Finally, this piece is heard as the tragic Melinda story concludes, when she attempts to commit suicide at Ellis's apartment.

## "Take the 'A' Train"
*Written by Billy Strayhorn (1939). Performed by Duke Ellington and His Orchestra (1941).*

This piece acts as a counterbalance for the Stravinsky and is the main theme for the comic Melinda storyline. It is heard phased in after the Stravinsky during the opening credits, continuing into the opening scene as we see a shot of the Bistrot Café Bar in the rain. It then returns a little later as Sy (Wallace Shawn) begins the "comic" Melinda story and the film cuts to Susan (Amanda Peet) and Hobie's dinner party. The music continues throughout the whole scene, stopping as Susan meets Melinda in the hallway. The piece is heard in full during the end credits.

## Partita No. 3 in A Minor, BWV 827, 1st movement: Fantasia
*Written by Johann Sebastian Bach (1726). Performed by András Schiff (1983).*

Played at Lee and Laurel's dinner party. This is the piece that Laurel asks Lee to turn down, and as he gets up, he recounts how Laurel cried while listening to Mahler's Second Symphony.

## "Will You Still Be Mine?"
*Written by Matt Dennis and Thomas M. Adair (1940). Performed by Erroll Garner (piano), Wyatt Ruther (bass) and Eugene "Fats" Heard (drums) (1953).*

Heard first at Susan and Hobie's dinner party as Hobie is serving sea bass, continuing during Melinda's dramatic entrance. The song then returns near the end of the film when Hobie is with Stacey in his apartment. He says, "Maybe a little jazz," and plays this just before Stacey says, "I'm going out the window."

## "The Best Things in Life Are Free"
*Written by Ray Henderson, Buddy G. DeSylva and Lew Brown (1927). Performed by Erroll Garner (piano), Eddie Calhoun (bass) and Kelly Martin (drums) (1961).*

Heard first at Hobie and Susan's dinner party when the guests are all listening to Melinda's life story. It returns when Melinda and Hobie are in the hospital and then at the end of the film as Hobie tells Melinda that he is in love with her. The scene then cuts back to the Bistrot, and the song continues as Sy and his friends bring the film to a close.

### "In a Mellotone"[5]

*Written by Duke Ellington (1940). Performed by Duke Ellington and His Orchestra (live at Carnegie Hall, 1946).*

Hear briefly on two occasions when Hobie and Walt (Steve Carell) take Melinda to Belmont to watch horseracing.

### "Darn That Dream"

*Written by James van Heusen and Eddie DeLange (1939). Performed by Dick Hyman (piano).*

The first song heard at Cassie's (Brooke Smith) dinner party. Segues into...

### "Moonglow"

*Written by Will Hudson, Eddie DeLange and Irving Mills (1934). Performed by Dick Hyman (piano).*

Heard while Lee and Cassie are talking in the kitchen. Segues into...

### "No Moon at All"

*Written by David Mann and Reed Evans (1947). Performed by Dick Hyman (piano).*

This is heard as Melinda is talking to the dentist. (It transpires that this, and the two previous songs, are all being played by Ellis at the piano, who remains unseen until he plays the Bach Prelude below.)

### Prelude No. 2 in C Minor, BWV 847, from *The Well-tempered Clavier*

*Written by Johann Sebastian Bach (1722). Arranged and performed by Dick Hyman (piano).*

Following the previous scene, this is played by Ellis on the piano. Cassie persuades Laurel to play as well, and she sits down next to Ellis, joins him briefly (Hyman simulates three hands through overdubbing), and then takes over the keyboard as a soloist. (The miming here is particularly poor by both actors, who hardly move their arms, but this is because the scene was shot before the music had even been selected.)

### "Love Me"

*Written by Victor Young and Ned Washington (1932). Performed by Dick Hyman (piano).*

Following the previous scene, this is heard (presumably played by Laurel off-camera) as Melinda and Ellis are at the bar talking.

### "Memories of You"

*Written by Eubie Blake and Andy Razaf (1930). Performed by Dick Hyman (piano).*

Following the previous scene, this is heard (again presumably played by Laurel off-camera) as Melinda and Ellis continue talking and he tells her about the two operas he has written.

### "Somebody Stole My Gal"

*Written by Leo Wood (1918). Performed by Erroll Garner (piano), Eddie Calhoun (bass), and Kelly Martin (drums) (1961).*

Heard as Greg drives Melinda, Hobie and Susan to the Hamptons. It returns a little later when he drives them back, continuing as Melinda asks Greg if he wants to come in for a drink.

### String Quartet No. 4, 4th movement: Allegretto pizzicato

*Written by Béla Bartók (1928). Performed by the Shanghai Quartet.*

Heard as we see a shot of the Shanghai Quartet performing this in a recording studio. The music then returns when Melinda goes round to Ellis's apartment and finds him there with Laurel. In this latter scene, the jump-cuts combined with the quartet's pizzicato are deftly used by Allen to mirror Melinda's overanxious state, as she correctly suspects that Ellis and Laurel are having an affair.

## "I Let a Song Go Out of My Heart"

*Written by Duke Ellington, Irving Mills, Henry Nemo and John Redmond (1938). Performed by Duke Ellington and His Orchestra (1938).*

Heard as Hobie goes to a shop and buys Melinda a deco pin. While in the shop he finds a lamp and makes a wish. The song continues as Hobie walks back to his apartment and catches Susan in bed with Steve (David Aaron Baker).

## "Don't Get Around Much Anymore"

*Written by Duke Ellington and Bob Russell (1942). Performed by Dick Hyman (piano).*

Acting as a counterpart for the Bach Prelude, this song is played by Melinda on a piano she comes across in the street. This instigates a meeting with Billy (the corresponding pianist-composer character in the comic story) who happens to be walking past. He joins her at the piano and the two play together. (As with the Bach above, Hyman again simulates three hands by overdubbing.)

## "Come On"

*Written by James Harris III, Terry Lewis, James Wright and Barry White. Performed by Barry White (1995).*

Being played in Melinda's apartment when Hobie goes to listen in on her and Billy. It continues as his robe gets caught in the door.

## Cat Scream (from the soundtrack of *The Black Cat*)

*Written by Heinz Roemheld (1934).*

## Symphony No. 7 in A Major, Op. 92[6]

*Written by Ludwig van Beethoven (1812). Arranged by Heinz Roemheld from the 1934 film* The Black Cat.

Incidental music from the film watched by Hobie and Stacey, who are on a double date with Melinda and Billy. The Beethoven can be heard as the film cuts from the film to a shot of Hobie and Stacey.

## "Comin' at Ya"

*Written by Bhooka and T-Bone. Performed by Soul Avengerz, featuring Shena (vocal).*

Being played at the club where Hobie and Stacey are dancing.

## "Big Eternity"

*Written by Adam Hamilton. Performed by Adam Hamilton.*

Following on from the previous scene, this is heard as Hobie and Stacey are talking about politics and sex, before deciding to go back to Hobie's apartment.

# *A Midsummer Night's Sex Comedy* (1982)

*Music composed by Felix Mendelssohn,
with additional music from the repertoire.*

Described by Allen as a "small intermezzo with a few laughs,"[1] *A Midsummer Night's Sex Comedy* is one of his more light-hearted films, made quickly when he had some spare time on his hands. "I finished the script of *Zelig*, and while they were budgeting it and doing all the preproduction work, I had nothing to do and I was at home and I thought, 'Wouldn't it be fun to do just some little tiny summer picture?' And I wrote the script in two weeks. Just this simple story, like a-day-in-the-country for fun."[2] Inspired by both Shakespeare's *A Midsummer Night's Dream* and Bergman's *Smiles of a Summer Night* (1955), Allen's film is a delightful, farce-like comedy of manners set at the turn of the century in upstate New York. For the musical accompaniment, Allen turned once again to the classical repertoire — as he had done with his earlier period piece *Love and Death*— choosing the lyricism of Mendelssohn to complement the pastoral atmosphere. "I knew all the Mendelssohn music and that was the kind of mood I was thinking of. Just light prettiness."[3] Having composed music for Shakespeare's *A Midsummer Night's Dream*, Mendelssohn was a natural choice. Allen uses three movements from his "Incidental Music," Op. 61, as well as the earlier *A Midsummer Night's Dream Overture*, Op. 21, and supplements these with movements from three of Mendelssohn's other orchestral works.

As with several of his films, Allen uses the music to score a series of extended sequences, where there is little or no dialogue. Much of the film is set outdoors and Allen deliberately accentuates the natural beauty of the countryside. "We talked a lot about the coloring. We wanted to film during the most beautiful days in the country that you could think of. We just made it as lovely as we could. And everything was subsumed into that. We made sure that the light was perfect all the time and that the sun was at the exact right place. Finally, by the end of the season we were painting all the leaves green."[4] Gordon Willis's stunning photography is one of the film's highlights, and this is greatly enhanced by the enchanting Mendelssohn score. The marriage of music and cinematography is perhaps best seen in the dawn sequence near the beginning of the film, where the lively second movement of the Scottish Symphony — in the pastoral key of F major — accompanies various shots of flora and fauna. This sequence can be seen as a rural counterpart to the celebrated opening to *Manhattan*. New York's skyscrapers and urban streets are replaced with idyllic woods and meadows; butterflies, ladybugs and deer take the place of bustling city dwellers. And indeed this was Allen's intention. "I wanted to do for the country what I'd done for New York in *Manhattan*. I wanted to show it in all its beauty."[5] The contrast between the two films is nicely summed up in the following comparison by Douglas Brode:

> *AMSNSC* is in many ways the inverse of his masterpiece *Manhattan*. The country film is shot in glorious color, whereas, that city film was done in muted black and white; the country film is set against the ecstatic sounds of Mendelssohn's classic compositions, while the city film was accompanied by the jazz-drenched compositions of Gershwin. Moreover, the city film, generally accepted by critics and audiences alike as Woody's valentine to the Big Apple, was nonetheless described by him as a depiction of New York City as "a metaphor for everything wrong with our culture." In comparison *AMSNSC* is an attempt to do the opposite, to make a subject he has consistently criticized (the country) and show its good points, its enchantments, its magic.[6]

Besides Mendelssohn, we hear three items by other composers (none of which are included in the end credits) in the form of source music when Leopold (José Ferrer) sings to the other members of the party. The pastoral imagery in Schubert's *Die schöne Müllerin* is in keeping with the film, particularly the repeated references to "the brook," the place where Allen's characters attempt to have their clandestine meetings. Schumann's *Dichterliebe* is also appropriate. This song cycle deals with the anguish of unrequited love, and the extract we hear is sung at the point where Maxwell (Tony Roberts), tormented by Ariel's (Mia Farrow) rejections, attempts to woo her through the window. In addition to Schubert and Schumann (note that Bergman also used Schumann in *Smiles of a Summer Night*), Leopold sings Albert Hay Mallotte's setting of "The Lord's Prayer," which is used to good effect as a counterpoint to Adrian's (Mary Steenburgen) abortive attempt to make love to Andrew (Woody Allen). It should be mentioned that, if the film is set around 1910 as Allen himself asserts,[7] then the inclusion of this piece is not historically accurate, as it was published in 1935.

All of the following compositions are by Felix Mendelssohn unless otherwise stated.

### *A Midsummer Night's Dream* (Incidental Music), Op. 61: Wedding March

*Performed by the Philadelphia Orchestra, conducted by Eugene Ormandy (1977).*

Opening credits, anticipating the marriage of Leopold and Ariel.

### Symphony No. 3 in A Minor, Op. 56, "Scottish," 2nd movement: Vivace non troppo

*Performed by the New York Philharmonic Orchestra, conducted by Leonard Bernstein (1964).*

Heard during the beautifully constructed dawn sequence (see above for a more detailed description).

### Violin Concerto in E Minor, Op. 64, 3rd movement: Allegro molto vivace

*Performed by Stoika Milanova and the TVR Symphony Orchestra, conducted by Vassil Stefanov.*

Heard during the picnic sequence, starting with a shot of the brook and continuing as we see the characters participating in various activities in the countryside. The music fades as Ariel takes a photograph of Andrew, and then returns later when Maxwell eats a mushroom and feigns illness in order to be alone with Ariel.

### *A Midsummer Night's Dream* (Incidental Music), Op. 61: Scherzo

*Performed by the Philadelphia Orchestra, conducted by Eugene Ormandy (1977).*

Heard first as we see Andrew setting the table for dinner in the garden. The music continues during the subsequent sequence where the characters are seemingly getting ready for dinner (taking baths, etc.), but in reality are secretly preparing to have clandestine meetings: Maxwell sneaks out to the brook to meet Ariel; Leopold sneaks out to the brook to meet Dulcy (Julie Hagerty) and Andrew makes various attempts to get Ariel's attention. After a brief break the music returns as we see Maxwell by the brook, cutting to Ariel in her room as Andrew hovers outside her window on his flying bicycle trying to persuade her to meet Maxwell and not marry Leopold. It continues as Andrew and Ariel both fly to the brook, stopping as Maxwell and Leopold see each other. The music is heard a third time later, when Leopold chases Andrew through the woods with a bow and arrow, but accidentally shoots Maxwell instead.

### Piano Concerto No. 2 in D Minor, Op. 40, 2nd movement: Adagio, molto sostenuto

Performed by the Columbia Symphony Orchestra, conducted by Eugene Ormandy (1959).[8]

This beautiful slow movement is heard briefly on three occasions. (Note that Allen only uses the main theme stated by the orchestra near the beginning of the movement, omitting the brief piano introduction and fading before the piano re-enters.) It appears first when Andrew and Ariel are walking by the brook reminiscing; the music becomes louder as they kiss, cutting to a shot of an owl, the moon and then Dulcy sitting up in bed reading the *Katzenjammer Kids*. This piece then returns when we see the silhouette of Andrew and Ariel together, and again near the end of the film after Andrew and Adrian have reconciled their marriage by making love in the barn.

### *Die schöne Müllerin*, D. 795, No. 2, "Wohin?"

Written by Franz Schubert (1823). Sung by José Ferrer.

We hear the end of this being sung by Leopold after dinner, accompanied by Adrian at the piano.

### *Dichterliebe*, Op. 48, No. 7, "Ich grolle nicht"

Written by Robert Schumann (1840). Sung by José Ferrer.

Continuing from the previous scene, Leopold then sings this as Maxwell, sitting outside on the porch, talks to Ariel through the window in an attempt to persuade her to meet him and reconsider her marriage to Leopold.

### "The Lord's Prayer"

Written by Albert Hay Malotte (1935). Sung by José Ferrer.

Continuing from the previous scene, Ariel now accompanies Leopold, as Adrian takes Andrew into the kitchen and tries to make love with him.

### *A Midsummer Night's Dream* (Incidental Music), Op. 61: Intermezzo

Performed by the Philadelphia Orchestra, conducted by Eugene Ormandy (1977).

Heard as we see Ariel and then Dulcy in bed, continuing as Maxwell and Ariel both sneak out to meet each other, stopping as Andrew turns up at the brook first and tells Maxwell that he is in love with Ariel as well.

### *A Midsummer Night's Dream* Overture, Op. 21

Performed by the Philadelphia Orchestra, conducted by Eugene Ormandy (1977).

Heard at the end of the film as the "spirit ball" explodes and Leopold's spirit emerges. He announces that the woods are indeed enchanted, before flying into them, followed by the other characters, cutting to the end credits.

# *Mighty Aphrodite* (1995)

*Music and songs from the repertoire.*

With *Mighty Aphrodite* Allen presents a typical modern day tale about Upper East Side Manhattanites, but draws on the mechanics of Greek theater — by using a traditional Greek chorus — to provide a backdrop to the story. In classical plays, the chorus consisted of a company of actors who commented on the action, either by speaking or singing in unison. The leader of the chorus interacted with the characters in the play, and spoke for the general population — the play's public opinion. The whole chorus tried to stay in rhythm with each other so they could be viewed as one entity, although occasionally certain members would take minor roles to bring news which impacts on the story. Essentially, Allen's chorus in *Mighty Aphrodite* functions in this way, but it is used more as a comic conceit, regularly adding humor to the plot.

Musically, the chorus follows its traditional role quite closely, but the music has been updated to make it more accessible to modern ears. In the film, the chorus sings two songs which are relevant to the storyline, and although these are not in unison, the first, "You Do Something to Me," is sung *a cappella*, which similarly conveys the chorus's unity. The other song, "When You're Smiling," also begins with just the chorus, but then develops into a full-blown jazz number. (Note that during the rousing ending, the chorus renounces its unanimity and succumbs to self-expression, with the various members each dancing and pantomiming to the song individually.) These arrangements were made by Allen's long-time collaborator, Dick Hyman, who, having worked on Allen's previous film *Bullets Over Broadway*, was here asked to swap the Broadway chorus for a Greek chorus.

The Greek theme is emphasized further in the score. Allen includes two pieces of bouzouki music performed by Vassilis Tsitsanis and George Zambetas respectively, two of Greece's most famous exponents in this field. Allen uses Tsitsanis's own composition "Neo Minore" over the opening credits in order to set the scene from the outset. (Allen then establishes the film's true location by immediately following this with Rodgers and Hart's "Manhattan.") Apart from this, *Mighty Aphrodite* has a score that is typical Woody Allen, comprising the customary mixture of jazz and popular song. However, it should be noted that most of the music employed is more modern than usual. Only the recording of "When Your Lover Has Gone" by Ambrose predates 1950, with all of the remaining music emanating from the 1950s and 1960s. This is uncharacteristic, of course; Allen himself has stated a number of times that the music he likes most — and thus the music he usually employs in his films — comes from the first half of the century. Having said this, these "modern" jazz pieces are still mainstream and accessible, and the majority of the songs interpreted come from the 1920s and 1930s.

As is typical, a number of the song titles reflect what is happening on screen. The aforementioned "You Do Something to Me" is heard as Linda Ash (Mira Sorvino) and Kevin (Michael Rapaport) go on their date, and the lyrics befit the two dim-witted characters who are seemingly the perfect match for each other. Also, after Lenny Weinrib (Woody Allen) and his wife, Amanda (Helena Bonham Carter), separate we hear in succession, "I Hadn't Anyone Till You" and "When Your Lover Has Gone." But perhaps the most notable use of music to provide a subtext to the action on screen is "I've Found a New Baby," which is heard while Lenny is at the adoption agency. This scene, with its upbeat Dixieland jazz and Allen's semi-slapstick fumblings, is a delightful throwback to earlier comedies such as *Sleeper*.

## Mighty Aphrodite (1995)

### "Neo Minore"
*Written and performed by Vassilis Tsitsanis (bouzouki).*

Opening credits and opening scene at the Greek theater, stopping as the Greek Chorus speaks.

### "Manhattan"
*Written by Richard Rodgers and Lorenz Hart (1925). Performed by Carmen Cavallaro (piano).*

Background music in the restaurant where Lenny and Amanda are discussing having children with Bud (Steven Randazzo) and his wife.

### "Penthouse Serenade (When We're Alone)"
*Written by Will Jason and Val Burton (1931). Performed by Erroll Garner (piano), John Simmons (bass) and Shadow Wilson (drums) (1950).*

Heard during the sequence where Lenny and Amanda are with their newly adopted son, Max, who we see gradually get older as time passes. The sequence includes shots of Amanda with her parents and Max; Lenny and Max playing basketball and Lenny and Max unpacking.

### "I've Found a New Baby"
*Written by Jack Palmer and Spencer Williams (1926). Performed by Wilbur de Paris (trombone), Sidney de Paris (trumpet), Omer Simeon (clarinet), Don Kirkpatrick (piano), Eddie Gibbs (banjo), Nat Woodley (bass) and Zutty Singleton (drums) (1953).*

Heard when Lenny sneaks back into the adoption agency office to try and find out the name of Max's real mother. The track continues through the subsequent scenes where Lenny discusses his actions with the Greek Chorus Leader (F. Murray Abraham), cutting to a shot of his car and the Greek Chorus stating that he is traveling to Pennsylvania to find Max's real mother.

### "Take Five"
*Written by Paul Desmond (1959). Performed by the Dave Brubeck Quartet: Dave Brubeck (piano), Paul Desmond (alto sax), Eugene Wright (bass) and Joe Morello (drums) (1959).*

Heard as Lenny and Amanda are driving to visit Jerry Bender (Peter Weller) and during the following scenes in his house. After a brief break, the track returns when Lenny is on the phone and is talking to Cassandra (Danielle Ferland), and then again when Lenny and Amanda are driving home.

### "The 'In' Crowd"
*Written by Billy Page (1964). Performed by the Ramsey Lewis Trio (live at the Bohemian Caverns in Washington, D.C., 1964).*

Heard when Lenny knocks on Linda's door, continuing as they talk and Lenny is shown around her apartment.

### "Li'l Darlin'"
*Written by Neal Hefti (1957). Performed by the Count Basie Orchestra (1957).*

Immediately following the previous song. This is heard as Lenny and Linda continue talking and she gradually comes on to him, but gets upset and eventually kicks him out. The song returns briefly later when Lenny and Linda are walking back to her apartment after the two have been to the horse races.

### "Walking My Baby Back Home"
*Written by Fred E. Ahlert and Roy Turk (1931). Performed by Dick Hyman (piano).*

Being played by a pianist (it is not Dick Hyman on screen) at the anniversary party. Hyman states that the piece was arranged in a "generic New York party" style.

### "Horos Tou Sakena"

Written by Stavros Xarhakos. Performed by George Zambetas (bouzouki).

Heard briefly as Lenny and the Greek Chorus listen to Cassandra as she warns of danger, cutting to Lenny on the phone.

### "Whispering"

Written by Richard Coburn, Vincent Rose, and John Schonberger (1919). Performed by the Benny Goodman Swing Quintet: Benny Goodman (clarinet), Russ Freeman (piano), Turk Van Lake (guitar), George Duvivier (bass) and Shelly Manne (drums) (1958).[1]

Heard as Lenny helps Linda prepare for her date with Kevin. The track is reprised in full during the end credits.

### "You Do Something to Me"

Written by Cole Porter (1929). Arranged by Dick Hyman. Performed by the Dick Hyman Chorus.

Sung *a cappella* by the Greek Chorus as Linda and Kevin go on their first date.

### "I Hadn't Anyone Till You"

Written by Ray Noble (1938). Performed by Erroll Garner (piano), Eddie Calhoun (bass) and Kelly Martin (drums) (1961).

Heard briefly as we see Lenny sitting in a bar and Amanda at the apartment after she has told him she is leaving him for Jerry Bender, cutting to Lenny bumping into Kevin.

### "When Your Lover Has Gone"

Written by Einar A. Swan (1931). Performed by Bert Ambrose and His Orchestra (1931).

Heard as Lenny and Linda kiss. The music continues through the subsequent scenes where Amanda realizes she is not happy about leaving Lenny and the two eventually kiss and make up, through to the *deus ex machina* ending where Linda meets a helicopter pilot named Donny (Bray Poor).

### "Welcome to Our World of Toys" (aka "FAO Schwarz Clock Tower Song")

Written and performed by Bobby Gosh.

Being played on the clock tower in the FAO Schwarz toyshop where Lenny bumps into Linda and her baby daughter.

### "When You're Smiling"

Written by Larry Shay, Mark Fisher and Joe Goodwin (1928). Performed by the Dick Hyman Chorus and Orchestra, featuring Kenny Davern (clarinet), Randy Sandke (trumpet), John Froske (trumpet) and Ted Sommer (drums).

Sung and danced to by the Greek Chorus during the film's end sequence where we see various "happy ending" shots of the principal characters.

# "Oedipus Wrecks" (from *New York Stories*) (1989)

*Music and songs from the repertoire.*

"Oedipus Wrecks" is Allen's contribution to the three-part anthology *New York Stories*, the other two thirds being supplied by Martin Scorsese and Francis Ford Coppola. After two serious films in a row, Allen returns to pure comedy, producing a charming miniature that "contains almost every Allen theme in crystallized comedic form."[1] As the pun in the film's title suggests, the main premise concerns a challenging mother-son relationship, in this case between Sheldon Mills (Woody Allen) and Sadie Millstein (Mae Questel), his emasculating *yenta*. At the beginning of the film, Sheldon tells his analyst, "I'm fifty years old. I'm a partner in a big law firm, ya know, I'm very successful. And I still haven't resolved my relationship with my mother." Interestingly, the idea for the story actually came from one of Allen's jazz heroes: "The truth of the matter is that I was sitting in this room one day, and I was listening to a Sidney Bechet record, and I was looking out into the sky, and I thought to myself, 'Gee, I miss him so much. It would be so dramatic and so fantastic, if I could see a huge figure of him playing up there. That big brown face he had with his soprano saxophone.' His music was so beautiful, and I could almost visualize him out there playing. That image stuck with me. And I thought, 'Wouldn't it be funny, if it was my mother, and she would be such a nag....' But how would I get her up there? Then I got the idea of taking her to a magic show. She disappears and reappears in the sky."[2]

Despite its brevity (forty-one minutes), "Oedipus Wrecks" still includes a fair amount of music (more than *Husbands and Wives*, for example), and many of Allen's typical musical techniques are still present, although in a condensed form. To reflect the maternal theme of the film, Allen employs two songs that are particularly appropriate. When Sheldon has a dream that his mother has died, but she still criticizes his driving from her coffin, Allen sardonically uses the novelty song "M-O-T-H-E-R (A Word That Means the World to Me)." In a way, this joke foreshadows events in the actual film: even though his mother has "departed," she still manages to tell him what to do.[3] The second mother-related song used by Allen is "I Want a Girl (Just Like the Girl That Married Dear Old Dad)." Heard over the opening and closing credits, as well as appearing throughout the film, this song can be seen as the movie's main theme, and essentially sums up the principal storyline. The psychological implications within this song are evident. Wernblad sees it as "grossly Freudian,"[4] while James Fuld remarks, "The title is 'merely the living out neurotically of an unresolved Oedipus complex.'"[5] It is hard to believe then that this song—which is so apposite—was not Allen's first choice. As Eric Lax recalls, "One day he stood by the turntable in the editing room, trying to find a piece of piano music to replace Frankie Carle's 'If You Were the Only Girl in the World,' which he was unable to use because the rights to it were not available. Beside him was a stack of twenty or so records that he has pulled out from the shelves that store several hundred albums, mainly music from the 1920s through the early 1950s. He repeatedly picked up and dropped the arm into the groove of a possible replacement from Erroll Garner, Earl 'Fatha' Hines, and George Shearing, among others, but to no avail. He found one 'too baroque,' another 'too sweet,' a third 'like a cocktail bar.' He wanted 'a piece of the right age, not too old, not Fats Waller. I want a straightforward melody,' he said as he put on another record."[6]

As seen in other films, especially *Hannah and Her Sisters*, certain songs or performers are associated with particular characters. Sheldon's relationship with Treva (Julie Kavner) is linked to Jerome Kern's classic "All the Things You Are," which acts as a love theme. This song is played by Treva on the piano shortly after the two have met. Later, when Treva cooks Sheldon dinner, the background music is "June in January," a typical "I'm in love with you" song performed in a lush orchestration by David Rose. Significantly, Allen then merges these two musical facets together by using David Rose's romantic rendition of "All the Things You Are" for the film's dénouement. As Sheldon is unwrapping a piece of leftover chicken given to him by Treva, he comes to realize the true object of his heart's desire, and at this point, the music swells to a rousing climax.

In contrast to the romantic elements of the score, Allen also provides a number of delightfully funny scenes, which he accompanies with his usual assortment of jazz. Despite the abovementioned inspiration from Sidney Bechet, none of his recordings are included in the score; however, Allen does use two tracks by Wilbur de Paris, a musician who played with Bechet in the 1940s and '50s. De Paris's remarkable interpretation of Ketèlbey's "In a Persian Market," with Eddie Gibbs's distinctive banjo introduction, is used to good effect during the magic show, and its Eastern flavor reflects fittingly the mystical nature of the scene. Interestingly, Allen also refers to this piece in his 1981 play *The Floating Light Bulb*. The character, Paul Pollack, plays a record of the work (presumably in its original orchestral form) during the scene in which he performs for Jerry Wexler, and later at the end of the play, when he retreats to his room to practice magic tricks.[7] Clearly then, Allen feels that this composition, with its exotic tone, is the ideal accompaniment for magical situations. This is emphasized further by the fact that Allen later reuses the Wilbur de Paris recording in *The Curse of the Jade Scorpion*, when his character is under the power of hypnosis.[8]

Without doubt, the highlight of the score, and arguably the funniest moment in the film, is when Benny Goodman's classic recording of "Sing, Sing, Sing" is used to accompany the visit of Sheldon's mother and his Aunt Ceil (Jessie Keosian) to his office. As Spignesi rightly points out, "The choice of this song is inspired."[9] Eric Lax was with Allen during some the editing of "Oedipus Wrecks" and describes how the use of this track came about: "That day he had the idea of putting Gene Krupa's [sic] 'Sing, Sing, Sing' behind his character's watching in horror as his mother and aunt make an unannounced visit to his law office. The beating of the tom-tom signals trouble when his secretary interrupts a meeting with the head of the firm to tell him of the visit, and then Benny Goodman's clarinet swings up as the scene cuts to the long hallway where the two little old ladies wearing *Cats* buttons march inexorably toward him. 'Ominous,' Woody said, red-faced with laughter as he watched it with the music for the first time."[10] This Goodman recording becomes a favorite of Allen's and is subsequently used in *Manhattan Murder Mystery* and *Deconstructing Harry*. Indeed, Allen must have been pleased with the music used in "Oedipus Wrecks," as five of the eight songs — and four of the exact same recordings — were to be used again in later films.

## "I Want a Girl (Just Like the Girl That Married Dear Old Dad)"

## "Oedipus Wrecks" (from *New York Stories*) (1989)

*Written by Harry von Tilzer and William Dillon (1911). Performed by Frankie Carle (piano); also performed by Bernie Leighton (piano).*

With its title having an obvious reference to the film's main theme, it is not surprising that this song appears several times. It is used for the opening credits and then reappears at significant points throughout the film involving Sheldon's mother, Sadie: when Sheldon takes Lisa (Mia Farrow) to meet his mother; when Sheldon is at work after Sadie has disappeared (this is a slower version played on the piano by Bernie Leighton); when Sheldon visits his private eye and he tells him to drop the case; and finally at the end when Sadie shows Treva photos of Sheldon as a boy, cutting to the end credits.

### "M-O-T-H-E-R (A Word That Means the World to Me)"

*Written by Theodore Morse and Howard Johnson (1915). Performed by Bernie Leighton (piano).*

Heard briefly when Sheldon has a dream that his mother has died.

### "Sing, Sing, Sing (with a Swing)"

*Written by Louis Prima (1936). Performed by Benny Goodman and His Orchestra (1937).*

Heard as Sheldon's mother and his Aunt Ceil visit him at work (see above for a more detailed description).

### "In a Persian Market"

*Written by Albert Ketèlbey (1920). Performed by Wilbur de Paris (trombone), Sidney de Paris (trumpet), Omer Simeon (clarinet), Don Kirkpatrick (piano), Eddie Gibbs (banjo), Nat Woodley (bass) and Zutty Singleton (drums) (1953).*

This jazz version of Ketèlbey's light music classic is used during the magic show scenes, as the magician first appears and then again during the "Great Chinese Box Illusion" when Sadie disappears. The track is reprised later in the film during the scenes where Sheldon and Treva are doing strange rituals and reading tarot cards, and ends as they visit Sadie's apartment.

### "I'll Be Seeing You"

*Written by Sammy Fain and Irving Kahal (1938). Performed by Liberace (piano).*

Heard as a sad and concerned Sheldon is comforted by Lisa. They kiss and the scene cuts to them in bed after making love. This track works on two levels: its sad/romantic quality is appropriate to the scene, but it is also subtly telling us that Sheldon will be seeing his mother again soon, although perhaps not where he may have expected.

### "I've Found a New Baby"

*Written by Jack Palmer and Spencer Williams (1926). Performed by Wilbur de Paris (trombone), Sidney de Paris (trumpet), Omer Simeon (clarinet), Don Kirkpatrick (piano), Eddie Gibbs (banjo), Nat Woodley (bass) and Zutty Singleton (drums) (1953).*

Heard as Sheldon is hounded by the press on his way to work, continuing as the film cuts to Sheldon attempting suicide by sticking his wet finger into a lamp socket. Note how Allen skillfully uses Wilbur de Paris's trombone introduction to create tension as Sheldon tentatively tries to sneak past the reporters, the music then changing to upbeat Dixieland as he is chased through the streets.

### "All the Things You Are"

*Written by Jerome Kern and Oscar Hammerstein II (1939). Performed by Bernie Leighton (piano); also performed by David Rose and His Orchestra.*

Played on the piano by Treva in Sadie's apartment. The track continues during the subsequent scenes where we see a doll of Sheldon's mother and Sheldon being picked on by workmen. (Note how the song begins as source music but then develops into scoring as it continues over other scenes.) The song is reprised at the end of the film (in the orchestral version) when Sheldon is leaving Treva's apartment and again a little later after he has read Lisa's letter and unwraps a piece of chicken; it continues in the next scene where he announces to his mother that Treva is his new fiancée.

### "June in January"
*Written by Ralph Rainger and Leo Robin (1934). Performed by David Rose and His Orchestra.*

Heard as Sheldon and Treva are having dinner at her apartment.

## *Play It Again, Sam* (1972)
*Original music composed by Billy Goldenberg, with additional music and songs from the repertoire.*

Originally a play, the film version of *Play It Again, Sam* was not actually directed by Allen, but by Herbert Ross, who would go on to direct a number of films based on plays by Neil Simon, such as *The Sunshine Boys* (1975) and *California Suite* (1978). According to Ross, Allen did not want to direct the film because "he felt that as a play it was too structured and therefore he didn't direct it for the stage. He wanted it that way for the film."[1] However, as Bendazzi points out, "Allen's mark is very clear. The subject, the screenplay and the interpretation bear his signature, and the cast is made up of friends and colleagues, with whom he had played the same script in the theater for a year and a half."[2] Unlike *The Front* (1975) and later films in which Allen has been involved only as an actor, such as *Scenes from a Mall* (1991) and *Picking Up the Pieces* (2000), *Play It Again, Sam* is rightly deemed a "Woody Allen film," and has therefore been included in this book.

For the soundtrack, Billy Goldenberg was employed to provide original music. Like both Allen and Ross, Goldenberg originates from Brooklyn. He has worked primarily for television, writing music for numerous TV shows including *Alias Smith and Jones*, *Colombo* and *Kojak*, to name only a few of the more famous. It is likely that Goldenberg was Ross's choice as composer on the film, as the two collaborated again the following year on *The Last of Sheila* (1973). Allen was at this time already beginning to dislike the process of using a composer and it is probable that he had no input in this respect.

As director, Ross naturally made modifications in order to adapt the story for the screen, and there are some significant changes between the play and the film. The most important of these is the expanded role given to *Casablanca*, the film from which Allen takes the famous misquote for his title. The play begins with Allen's character, Allan Felix, watching *The Maltese Falcon* and ends with Allan talking about *The African Queen* in what is basically a tribute to Humphrey Bogart. In the film, however, Ross leaves out several of the references to other films and focuses on *Casablanca*. As Brode points out, "this

Bogart classic is only fleetingly referred to in Woody's play, *Sam*, but in the film version, it is the framing device which opens and closes the picture."[3] Indeed, the director's ingenious notion to bookend *Play It Again, Sam* with *Casablanca* improves the plot considerably, and results in "a deeply satisfying adaptation."[4] Ross himself remarks, "It was my idea to do the Bogart/*Casablanca* opening. Woody liked that ... from that came the opening sequence under the titles and the idea to paraphrase the last sequence of *Casablanca* shot by shot. I wanted to have that last scene in our picture play in the same style as the last scene in *Casablanca*."[5]

This change not only alters the tone of the story, but also impacts on the soundtrack, and as a consequence, the film incorporates original music written for *Casablanca* by Max Steiner. Not only is this heard during the opening scene when Allan Felix is watching *Casablanca* in the movie theater, but it is also used effectively during the film's end sequence when Ross pays homage to the famous airport ending. As stated above, Ross reconstructs this scene shot for shot, and this allows the opportunity for Steiner's "Airport Finale" cue to be fitted against Ross's version, thus adding further emphasis to the film's climax. In addition, Goldenberg is able to utilize *Casablanca*'s "theme song," "As Time Goes By," as Steiner had done in the earlier film. This standard had actually been written by Herman Hupfeld for the now forgotten musical *Everybody's Welcome* in 1931, but was rejuvenated by its inclusion in *Casablanca*, after which it became highly successful, appearing on the *Hit Parade* radio program for twenty-one straight weeks in 1943. As well as being highlighted in *Casablanca* and *Play It Again, Sam*, the song has appeared in a number of other films, notably *What's Up Doc?* (released the same year as *Play It Again, Sam*) and *Sleepless in Seattle* (1993).

Apart from the musical links with *Casablanca*, Goldenberg's score is primarily centered on one main theme, which pervades the film throughout and appears in an assortment of styles (see below). The score also contains two pop songs written for the disco sequence; the title for the song, "It's the Same Sad Story All Over Again," may have been chosen by Goldenberg and lyrist Graeme Kronsberg deliberately to reflect Allan's continued failure to attract women. In addition, there are a number of musical parodies to accompany various references, such as Italian cinema, *Easy Rider* (1969) and other Bogart films like *The Maltese Falcon* (1941).

*Play It Again, Sam* also includes "Blues for Allan Felix," a piece especially composed and recorded for the film by Oscar Peterson. This is the earliest example of jazz to appear in a Woody Allen film.

## Incidental Music from *Casablanca*
*Written Max Steiner (1942).*

The dramatic incidental music composed by Max Steiner (incorporating "As Time Goes By" and "Les Marseillaise") can be heard at the beginning of the film, as Allan Felix (Woody Allen) is watching the end of *Casablanca* in a cinema. This scene is then mirrored at the end, and Steiner's "Airport Finale" music returns as the propellers start up on the plane, continuing through the final scene at the airport.

## "As Time Goes By"
*Written by Herman Hupfeld (1931). Incor-*

porated into the score; also performed by Dooley Wilson (1942).

The song is heard first integrated into Max Steiner's incidental music (see above), as Allan is watching *Casablanca*. We then hear a frantic piano version when Allan and Linda (Diane Keaton) kiss for the first time in his apartment, cutting to them in bed under a poster of *Across the Pacific* after making love. Goldenberg also hints at the song within the dramatic music used when Allan is in a taxi cab thinking about how he will end his affair with Linda. Finally, Dooley Wilson's recording is heard briefly at the end of the film as Allan walks off into the fog at the airport; Goldenberg adds a lush string accompaniment, which eventually takes over before the film concludes with a plaintive piano version of the song.

## "Les Marseillaise"
*Written by Claude Rouget de Lisle (1792).*

Incorporated into Max Steiner's incidental music to *Casablanca* (see above).

## Theme from "Play It Again, Sam"
*Written by Billy Goldenberg.*

Goldenberg's infectious main theme appears throughout the film in a number of different guises:

1) A slow, sultry saxophone version is heard when Allan impersonates Bogart and imagines what his date with Sharon (Jennifer Salt) will be like.
2) A jaunty version is heard when Allan gets into a cab previously used by dope-smoking hippies.
3) A slow piano version is heard when Allan, Linda and Dick (Tony Roberts) are driving back in the rain, cutting to Allan and then Linda back in their apartments thinking about each other.
4) The jaunty version returns as a happy Allan is walking home, is attacked by a dog and then pushes a man reading a newspaper off the edge of the Golden Gate Bridge.
5) The theme is finally heard incorporated into the dramatic music near the end of the film, when Allan is following Linda into the airport.

## "Blues for Allan Felix"
*Written by Oscar Peterson (1972). Performed by the Oscar Peterson Trio (1972).*

An LP of this is put on the record player to set the scene before Sharon arrives and is heard throughout the subsequent scene. Just prior to this Allan asks Linda, "Do I go with Oscar Peterson or Bartók's String Quartet Number Five?" to which Linda replies, "Why don't you play your Oscar Peterson and leave Bartók out so that everybody can see it?"[6]

## "It's the Same Sad Story All Over Again"
*Written by Billy Goldenberg and Graeme Kronsberg (1972).*

This is being played at the disco where Allan and Linda are having a drink and Allan is watching a blonde girl (Susanne Zenor) dancing.

## "Easy Lovin'"
*Written by Billy Goldenberg and Graeme Kronsberg (1972).*

Following the previous song, this is being played when Allan attempts to chat up the blonde girl on the dance floor.

# The Purple Rose of Cairo (1985)

*Original music composed by Dick Hyman
with additional songs from the repertoire.*

The *Purple Rose of Cairo* retraces similar territory covered in Allen's short story "The Kugelmass Episode" and his play (and later film) *Play It Again, Sam*: once again the boundaries between the real and the unreal are blurred as the main protagonist interacts with a fictional character. From a movie aspect, this interaction is purely imaginary in *Play It Again, Sam*, as Humphrey Bogart appears only in the mind of Allan Felix. But in *Purple Rose*, Allen enters the realm of out-and-out fantasy by having the movie star literally come down off the screen into the real world and affect everyone with whom he comes into contact. It is clear that *Purple Rose* had an influence on later filmmakers, as there have been a number of films since which have involved characters stepping in and out of the screen, for example, *Ladre di saponette* (*The Icicle Thief*, 1989), *Last Action Hero* (1993) and *Pleasantville* (1998). As for Allen's own inspiration, several commentators have pointed towards Buster Keaton's *Sherlock Jr.* (1924) as being his major stimulus for the film. But this is something he vehemently denies:

> Let me explain this: it was in no remote way an inspiration. I had seen *Sherlock Jr.* years ago.... I think Buster Keaton made very, very brilliant films, but he's not my favorite. This thing about entering the screen was a much later afterthought. I wrote a story based on only this: that a woman's dream man comes off the screen and she's in love with him, and then the real actor comes along and she's forced to choose between reality and fantasy. And of course one can't choose fantasy, because that can lead to madness, so one has to choose reality. And when you choose reality, you get hurt. It's as simple as that. All the rest was just stuff that came up as I was writing. I saw the Buster Keaton film maybe 25 years ago. It had nothing to do with my story. The whole thrust of the idea was different. Her entering the screen was an afterthought really.[1]

The title *The Purple Rose of Cairo* refers to both Allen's film and the inner film which Cecilia (Mia Farrow), the central character, becomes transfixed with at her local movie theater, the Jewel. This film-within-a-film is a pastiche on the popular RKO society comedies of the 1930s. "It was like one of those films I saw as a kid, what I called 'champagne comedies'—those comedies from the 1930s and 1940s with all those romantic people who wore tuxedos and went to big nightclubs and lived in penthouses and drank champagne all the time."[2] The films of Fred Astaire and Ginger Rogers were perhaps the epitome of these "champagne comedies," and Allen highlights this by showing a clip of *Top Hat* (1935) at the end of the film. Moreover, the song that Astaire sings is "Cheek to Cheek," and the lyrics are used by Allen to reflect Cecilia's need for escapism from the harsh realities of her drab life during the Depression—she seems to find happiness when watching movies. To emphasize this further, Allen also plays the song over the opening credits and, more significantly, during the opening of the film; Astaire sings about being in heaven just at the point where we see a close up of Cecilia looking longingly at the new movie poster at the Jewel. As McCann remarks, "The song, the theme, the thought, frame the movie; it is its leitmotif, its principle of hope. Astaire's distinctive vocal, never sounding strong enough to cope with the music yet always succeeding despite itself, captures the fragility that seems so noticeable in Cecilia."[3] He goes on to say, "Astaire's arc-lit RKO heaven is a haven in a heartless world, a gentle place where Cecilia is temporarily transported; more accurately, this is 'heaven' to her, the only heaven her heart can hold onto."[4]

Having worked closely with Allen on his two previous films, Dick Hyman was now offered the chance to compose a complete original score for the first time. As the film is set in the 1930s, and contains within it a contemporaneous high society comedy, Hyman is given the opportunity to compose music on two levels. For the main film, he has written an appropriately jazz-tinged score, rich in melodic content, which befits perfectly the atmosphere and sentiment of the film. Hyman combines jazzy upbeat numbers such as "New Show at the Jewel" and "Hollywood Fun" with more lyrical pieces like "Carousel Memories" and "The Theme from *The Purple Rose of Cairo*" (also known as "Cecilia's Choice"). The latter of these is an especially tender melody, tinted with a melancholic air, which depicts Cecilia's sad predicament. For many of these arrangements, Hyman successfully emulates the style of Guy Lombardo and His Royal Canadians.[5]

For the film-within-the-film, Hyman once again displays his skill at providing authentic-sounding period music. Just as Allen and Gordon Willis were able to imitate convincingly the films from the 1930s, Hyman is able to fabricate music from that era in the same fashion. During the scene in the night club we hear a swing band arrangement of the inner film's title music, "Try It On for Size," which is followed by the song, "One Day at a Time." In *Zelig*, Hyman had aped the songs of the 1920s; here he turns his hand to the type of song that accompanied the musical comedies of the 1930s. Although Hyman had no particular model in mind, the song's minor key inflection is reminiscent of Irving Berlin's "Let's Face the Music and Dance," which was written for the 1936 Astaire and Rogers film *Follow the Fleet*. In addition, Hyman's score includes some realistic incidental music, notably during the "Night Club Montage" sequence. Here, "Try It On for Size" is heard again, this time in a variety of styles reflecting the different clubs that Cecilia and Tom Baxter (Jeff Daniels) go to during their night out on the town. This use of montage to illustrate the passing of time within a few minutes was a device typical of films of this period, and Hyman's accompanying music is especially fitting. As the couple returns to the Manhattan apartment, the music changes to "Penthouse Mood," and here Hyman parodies the romantic, pseudo–Rachmaninov–like scores of the time, something he had done before with "The Changing Man Concerto" in *Zelig*. Hyman's title for this piece was suggested to him by the 1931 Val Burton and Will Jason song, "Penthouse Serenade."

It is also worth noting that certain cues can be found in both the inner and outer films; just as certain characters interplay between the two films, so does some of the music. "Well I Am Impressed!" for instance, is originally heard as incidental music for the inner film, its title being taken from the first line Tom speaks when he arrives in Manhattan. However, this theme is later used by Hyman in the outer film, when Gil is waiting for Cecilia outside her house. This is just one example of Hyman developing his thematic material to create unity within the score as a whole. Other examples include the numerous variants of "Try It On for Size," the use of "One Day at a Time" for the "In the Tomb of Osiris" cue, and the way in which "Penthouse Mood" hints at "Carousel Memories." Furthermore, "Well I Am Impressed!" shares the same schottische-like opening rhythmic figure as "Penny Pitching." The former theme is more upbeat and its jauntiness reflects Tom's sanguine character; on the other hand, Monk's (Danny Aiello) unpleasantness is mirrored in the brooding, minor key melody of "Penny Pitching." With Cecilia as the link, there is an interrelationship between these two diametrically opposed characters, which the composer reflects in the two themes associated with them.

The following titles are taken from the soundtrack album, but have been placed in the order in which they appear in the film; all are composed and conducted by Dick Hyman unless otherwise stated.

### "Cheek to Cheek" (from the soundtrack of *Top Hat*)

*Written by Irving Berlin (1935). Sung by Fred Astaire with Leo Reisman and His Orchestra (1935).*

Opening credits, continuing into the opening scene where Cecilia is outside the Jewel Theater daydreaming. The music stops abruptly when a letter is dropped by a workman, nearly hitting her and thus bringing her back to reality. We hear the song again at the end of the film, when *Top Hat* is being shown at the Jewel. Cecilia realizes that Gil is not coming to meet her and so sits down to watch the film, thus retreating into the dream world she was in at the beginning.

### "Penny Pitching"

Heard first as we see Monk pitching pennies with his buddies shortly before Cecilia arrives. The track returns when Monk is doing the same thing later and is told that Cecilia has been seen at the "Dine and Dance" with another man, cutting to Cecilia bringing Gil Shepherd (Jeff Daniels) to see Tom.

### "New Show at the Jewel"
*Featuring Urbie Green (trombone).*

This jolly theme (reminiscent of "Five Foot Two, Eyes of Blue") is, as you might expect, primarily associated with the Jewel Theater. It is heard first as we see a shot of the movie house, shortly before various people including Cecilia buy tickets for the new film, continuing as Cecilia buys popcorn and takes her seat. A slow version (with trombone solo) is heard as Cecilia closes the door on an unfaithful Monk and starts packing in an effort to leave him. The original version then returns as we see Cecilia walking the streets with her suitcase. The track continues as she looks longingly at the now shut Jewel Theater, before we briefly see Emma (Dianne Wiest) and her co-prostitute about to enter a tavern, thus prompting Cecilia to return home. The track is also heard later when the press are outside the Jewel covering Tom's disappearance, amid moviegoers leaving. The track is reprised in full during the end credits.

### "The Film within the Film"

1) Opening Titles ("Try It On for Size")

## 2) In the Tomb of Osiris ("One Day at a Time")

*Featuring Romeo Penque (English horn).*

Heard on the soundtrack to the inner film that is showing at the Jewel. After the opening titles, the film cuts to a scene in Egypt, where we are introduced to the Tom Baxter character. The melody of "One Day at a Time" is incorporated into the incidental music. The opening titles are heard later as Cecilia repeatedly sees the film.

## "Try It On for Size"

*Arrangement for Swing Band. Featuring Mel Davis (trumpet).*

A jazzed up version of the opening titles theme being performed at the nightclub shortly before the six "on screen" characters arrive and are seated. This version is heard again later at the same point in the film, but this time with the addition of Cecilia, who has entered the picture.

## "One Day at a Time"

*Sung by Karen Akers.*

Performed at the club by Kitty Haines (Karen Akers). The song is not actually heard complete, but in two different extracts. The verse and first two lines are heard the first time we see the inner film, when Tom is enamored by Kitty Haines. Later, when Cecilia has joined the characters on screen, we hear the song sung again, this time from the middle to the end.

## "Well, I Am Impressed!"

This cue has two distinct sections. The first is a sprightly theme heard when Cecilia takes her sister (Stephanie Farrow) to see the film. This music underscores the scene in the inner film where Tom Baxter has just arrived in Manhattan, and is then heard again each time we see this scene repeated (at different points) as Cecilia keeps going back to watch the film. It also appears when Gil Shepherd is waiting for Cecilia outside her house and then again a little later as they walk off, continuing as the film cuts to the scene where Tom meets Emma. The second section is a fast-moving chase number, which is heard first after Tom has left the screen and he and Cecilia run out of the cinema, continuing during the ensuing mayhem. Subsequently, Hyman uses this music for animated scenes that involve Tom: when he and Cecilia run off without paying from the "Dine and Dance" and when he fights with Monk in the church.

## "Carousel Memories"

*Performed by Dick Hyman (piano).*[6]

This exquisite melody can be seen as the love theme for Cecilia and Tom. It is heard exclusively during the scenes when the two are at the amusement park, the one significant exception being at the end of the film when Cecilia realizes that she has been abandoned by Gil and her thoughts turn to Tom. We then dissolve into a shot of Gil on the plane, whose expression suggests that he has at least some guilt and regret for his actions.

## "I'd Rather Be Sleeping"

Being played at the "Dine and Dance" as Cecilia and Tom dance together, "cheek to cheek."

## "Hollywood Fun"

This is heard first at the Hollywood party where Gil Shepherd is being interviewed, continuing as he is told that Tom Baxter has come down off the screen. The track then returns two times: when Gil and the producer, Raoul Hirsh (Alexander Cohen), visit the Jewel and talk to the characters on screen; and during the sequence where Cecilia and Tom go to the soup kitchen and eventually end up in a church. The track is reprised in full during the end credits.

### "Laughing Every Morning"

Being played at the "Dine and Dance" where Cecilia and Tom are drinking champagne, continuing as Tom attempts to pay the check with false money, segueing into the "Well, I Am Impressed!" chase music as they run off without paying.

### "Emma's Place"
*Performed by Dick Hyman (piano).*

This ragtime piece is heard during the scene where Tom is at the brothel. Apart from indulging his love of ragtime, Hyman is making a subtle reference here. He has composed the music deliberately in the manner of Jelly Roll Morton, who began his career playing in New Orleans bordellos, as did a number of other ragtime exponents, including Scott Joplin, Tom Turpin and Eubie Blake.[7]

### "Alabamy Bound"
*Written by Ray Henderson, Buddy G. DeSylva and Bud Green (1924). Featuring Cynthia Sayer (ukulele).*

### "I Love My Baby, My Baby Loves Me"
*Written by Harry Warren and Bud Green (1926). Featuring Cynthia Sayer (ukulele).*

Both sung by Gil Shepherd and accompanied by Cecilia on the ukulele in the music store (Mia Farrow does a convincing job of miming the chords). After they have both performed "Alabamy Bound," the music store assistant instigates the second song by playing it on the piano and the others join in.

### "Theme from *The Purple Rose of Cairo* (Cecilia's Choice)"
*Featuring Dick Hyman (piano).*

This plaintive theme is heard first as Cecilia and Gil kiss in the music store. It then returns in three different versions near the end of the film. A heart-rending solo piano version accompanies the scene where Cecilia chooses Gil over Tom (hence the subtitle), leaving Tom to return to the movie screen. The theme then immediately becomes livelier as we see Cecilia running home to pack. After a brief break, a slightly different rendering of the theme is heard as Cecilia leaves Monk to meet Gil outside the cinema. Even though these last two versions are more upbeat, thus giving the impression that a "happy ending" is just round the corner, the inherent sadness of the melody tells us that this will not be the case.

### "Night Club Montage"
1) "Try It On for Size"
2) "Penthouse Mood"

*Featuring Eugene Anthony (tap dancer).*

"Try It On for Size" is heard (in various different styles) as Cecilia (now in the film on screen) and Tom go out on the town. "Penthouse Mood" follows as Cecilia and Tom return to the apartment alone and kiss, before being interrupted by Gil, who is watching them from inside the Jewel.

# Radio Days (1987)

*Music and songs from the repertoire, with original music by Dick Hyman.*

Radio Days is Woody Allen's wistful look back at the golden age of radio during the 1930s and '40s. Throughout the film, we hear an assemblage of popular songs and jazz, forming a continuous musical backdrop to which Allen adds anecdotes from his childhood. The initial inspiration for the film stemmed from Allen's own reminiscences about specific songs, which brought to mind particular events. "It originated from an idea that I wanted to pick out a group of songs that were meaningful to me, and each one of those songs suggested a memory. Then this idea started to evolve: how important radio was to me when I was growing up and how important and glamorous it seemed to everyone."[1] The music from this period made an indelible imprint on Allen's consciousness as a child, and *Radio Days* is his attempt at capturing the nostalgic feeling he has for an era when big band music and the songs of Cole Porter were the pop music of the day.

As Allen's script developed, he added more scenes and consequentially more music. "When I started to write the memories of the songs, I got inspiration for other scenes and sequences which could strengthen and support these memories. If I had done *Radio Days* faithfully, I would have done about 25 different songs and described what comes into my mind when I hear them."[2] Although by the time the film was completed it included more than forty songs (more than any other Woody Allen film to date, including musically oriented films like *Everyone Says I love You* and *Sweet and Lowdown*), Allen still adheres to his original idea to some extent. At one point in the film Joe/Allen remarks, "To this day, there are certain songs that — no matter where I am — the minute I hear them, I get instant memory flashes." Beginning with "The Donkey Serenade" and ending with "If You Are but a Dream," Joe/Allen recalls a number of songs which have a special meaning for him when he was growing up. "I would think back to those songs I heard when I was young, the Carmen Miranda song ['South American Way'], for instance. And I remembered how my cousin used to dance to that music all the time and pantomime to it and put on a fancy hat. So, in a way, I reconstructed this, or rather my feeling for this. You know, those songs did have memories for me. They were real songs with real memories. And I don't know if I attached the exact, correct memory to the song. But they were real memories of mine, and some of them were quite accurate."[3]

Several of the songs chosen would also have a deeper meaning for numerous other people who lived through this period. Songs such as "I Don't Want to Walk Without You," "The White Cliffs of Dover," "Paper Doll," "Frenesi," "Pistol Packin' Mama," "They're Either Too Young or Too Old," and especially "You'd Be So Nice to Come Home To" were particularly popular during the war years. Indeed, the latter of these — a ballad written by Cole Porter in 1942 — became something of an anthem for servicemen posted abroad during World War II, and Allen was clearly mindful of this when choosing a song for Diane

Keaton's cameo. "That was an important song from my childhood as well. It was an important song during the war. And I wanted to make sure, since Diane was making one little appearance in the picture, that the song was potent."[4]

As with virtually all of his films, Allen uses music purposefully in *Radio Days*. However, as his main premise was to include songs from a certain period that sparked off certain memories, he was restricted when selecting which songs to use; consequently, this film has fewer instances of music being used as a subtext to the narrative. Nevertheless, there are still a few delightful examples where an appropriate song has been chosen to enhance what we see on screen; for instance, "Dancing in the Dark," when the two burglars are fumbling around with flashlights; "You and I," when Joe recalls an early romantic encounter with a girl; and "I'm Getting Sentimental Over You," when Aunt Bea (Dianne Wiest) consoles her boyfriend, who is crying over his lost fiancé, Leonard! Furthermore, Allen uses music to fuse together the film's various episodes, often having the music overlap both the scenes at the radio station and the scenes at the family's home, thus linking the two contrasting worlds of the radio stars and the average listener.

Although a large majority of songs used in the film were taken from the repertoire, Allen also continued his association with Dick Hyman, who is credited as musical supervisor. "The only thing I needed from Dick was a couple of arrangements of the songs. And I wanted him to create the music for the pretend commercials and things like that. But basically the songs were songs that I chose from my childhood. Songs that were significant to me."[5]

Original music by Hyman includes the "Re-Lax Jingle" and a number of "Radio Show Themes" which are heard briefly during the various radio shows that appear throughout the film, including "The Masked Avenger," "Uncle Walt Squirrel Rangers' Club Song," "Bill Kern's Sports Show" and "The Court of Human Emotions."

Of Hyman's various arrangements, the one for Kurt Weill's "September Song" is the most outstanding, and significantly Allen uses this melody to frame the film. "That was a major song. Many people consider that the best American popular song ever written. And it may well be.... It was a very dominating song when I was younger. One heard it interpreted by everybody all the time."[6] Although we hear an instrumental version, many people would be familiar with Maxwell Anderson's plaintive lyrics. Allen thus makes use of the song's pensive quality to create an aura of nostalgia that enhances the key opening and closing narrations where he reflects on his childhood memories. Carol Goodson even goes as far as to say that, "*heard* in a subliminal sense, these lyrics serve as an effective subtext for the scene; they inform us that we are about to hear the reminiscences of a person at least middle-aged, nostalgic about the past, who realizes that life is inexorably drawing to a close. In the time left, this person wants to be sure to keep treasured memories alive, and to remain mentally and emotionally in the company of the long-dead people from childhood, who are, in many ways, more real and important than people of the present. Furthermore, the song lyrics allow Allen to convey ideas which would seem too sentimental and embarrassing if actually verbalized."[7] These retrospective feelings are complemented by Hyman's beautiful arrangement, which, after the piano opening, stresses the nostalgic mood with its muted trumpet and solo violin. Sadly, only an extract of this arrangement was used in the film. As Hyman remarks, "A complete performance was recorded, but Woody only required the beginning. Since the original intent was for nightclub background music, an exact length of this cue did not need to be computed, and it was simply faded out as required for its different uses. Unfortunately, the soundtrack album used only those commercially released phonograph records which were also a part of the score."[8]

A number of commentators have remarked upon the similarities between *Radio Days* and Fellini's *Amarcord*.[9] But while Allen admits that *Amarcord* is one of his favorite films and that *Radio Days* shares with it a plotless structure, he denies any inspiration from Fellini.[10] Likewise, it should be noted that, unlike in *Stardust Memories* and *Alice*, there are no musical parallels between Allen's soundtrack and Nino Rota's score. As Schwartz points out, "*Radio Days* most significantly departs from *Amarcord* in its use of music as a dominant presence in each scene and as a structuring device, and perhaps this is why Allen does not emphasize the movies' similarities."[11]

## "The Flight of the Bumble Bee" (from *The Tale of Tsar Saltan*)

*Written by Nikolai Rimsky-Korsakov (1899). Performed by Harry James and His Orchestra (1941).*

Opening credits. (Note how the music is perfectly timed to the duration of the credits and how the main theme begins at the point that the film title is seen on the screen.)

## "Dancing in the Dark"

*Written by Arthur Schwartz and Howard Dietz (1931).*

## "Chinatown, My Chinatown"

*Written by Jean Schwartz and William Jerome (1910).*

## "The Sailor's Hornpipe" (aka "Jack's the Lad")

*Traditional.*[12]

All three are played by the radio orchestra to one of the burglars over the telephone as part of the "Guess That Tune" quiz show. "The Sailor's Hornpipe" is heard again briefly when, the next day, a truck arrives to deliver the prizes to the Needleman's house.

## "Let's All Sing Like the Birdies Sing"

*Written by Roger Hargreaves, Stanley J. Damerell and Tolchard Evans (1932).*

Being sung by a child star on a radio advert for cereal.

## "September Song"

*Written by Kurt Weill and Maxwell Anderson (1938). Arranged by Dick Hyman. Performed by Dick Hyman (piano) and studio musicians.*

This lovely arrangement is heard as the "story proper" unfolds. As the narrator (Woody Allen) begins to recount his childhood, we see stormy shots of Rockaway and then Joe's mother (Julie Kavner) listening to "Breakfast with Irene and Roger." The song reappears when Joe (Seth Green) and his friends are on the beach talking about which pin-ups they like, continuing as Joe sees a German submarine off the coast. It then returns at the end of the film during Allen's final narration, leading into the end credits.

## "Body and Soul"

*Written by John Green, Edward Heyman,*

*Robert Sour and Frank Eyton (1930). Performed by Benny Goodman (clarinet), Teddy Wilson (piano) and Gene Krupa (drums) (1935).*

This jazz standard is heard first when the narrator introduces himself and his family.[13] It is used later when we see a shot of a rollercoaster just before Joe is on his way to school and when Joe and his parents meet the 14-year-old whiz-kid at the zoo.

### "In the Mood"

*Written by Joe Garland and Andy Razaf (1939). Performed by Glenn Miller and His Orchestra (1939).*

Being played on the radio when Aunt Bea is dancing around the room. The track continues into the next scene at Joe's school.

### "I Double Dare You"

*Written by Jimmy Eaton and Terry Shand (1937). Performed by Larry Clinton and His Orchestra (1938).*

On the radio as Aunt Bea prepares for her date with Sidney Manulis (Andrew Clark).

### "You're Getting to Be a Habit with Me"

*Written by Harry Warren and Al Dubin (1932). Performed by Lee Erwin.*

Being performed on the organ at the roller skating rink where Bea is on her date with Sidney Manulis.

### "La Cumparsita"

*Written by Gerardo Matos Rodriguez (1917). Performed by the Castilians (1951).*

This famous tango is played briefly on the car radio after Bea and Sidney Manulis's car runs out of gas when driving home from their date. The track is interrupted suddenly by news that Martians have invaded earth. (This is a reference to Orsen Welles's infamous radio production of H.G. Wells's *War of the Worlds*, broadcast on October 30, 1938.)

### "The Carioca"

*Written by Vincent Youmans, Gus Kahn and Edward Eliscu (1933).*

### "Tico-Tico"

*Written by Zequinha Abreu, Aloysio Oliveira and Erwin Drake (1944). Sung by Denise Dumont.*

### "Begin the Beguine"

*Written by Cole Porter (1935).*

All three of these Latinesque songs are being performed at the King Cole Room nightclub by the resident orchestra, where Tito Puente appears as the bandleader. The three songs follow on from each other as the narrator recounts an inside story about radio stars, Roger (David Warrilow) and Irene (Julie Kurnitz), and Roger's affair with Sally White (Mia Farrow), which eventually leads to the two having a tryst on the roof.

### "Opus One"

*Written by Sy Oliver (1944). Performed by Tommy Dorsey and His Orchestra (1944).*

Being played loudly on the neighbors' radio while the family is talking about fasting. Segues into...

### "Frenesi"

*Written by Alberto Dominguez, Ray Charles and S.K. Russell (1939). Performed by Artie Shaw and His Orchestra (1940).[14]*

Heard as the family awaits Abe's (Josh Mostel) return, continuing during the Mrs. Silverman anecdote and as Abe eventually comes back from the neighbors and experiences chest pains.

### "All or Nothing at All"

*Written by Jack Lawrence and Arthur Altman (1939). Arranged by Dick Hyman. Sung by Todd Field.*

Being performed by a crooner and listened to by numerous swooning girls including Joe's cousin, Ruthie (Joy Newman). This is clearly a parody of Frank Sinatra, who recorded this song with Harry James in 1939.

## "The Donkey Serenade"

*Written by Herbert Stothart, Rudolf Friml, Bob Wright and Chet Forrest (1937). Performed by Allan Jones (1937).*

Heard while Aunt Bea is sitting on the steps outside the house.

## "You and I"

*Written by Meredith Willson (1941). Performed by Tommy Dorsey and His Orchestra (1941).*¹⁵

Heard while Joe is under the boardwalk, kissing Evelyn Goorwitz (Rebecca Nickels) persistently.

## "Paper Doll"

*Written by Johnny S. Black (1915). Performed by the Mills Brothers (1942).*

On the radio during Joe's parents' wedding anniversary.

## "Pistol Packin' Mama"

*Written by Al Dexter (1942). Performed by Bing Crosby and the Andrews Sisters (1943).*¹⁶

Heard while Joe builds a snowman outside the school.

## "South American Way"

*Written by Al Dubin and Jimmy McHugh (1939). Performed by Carmen Miranda (1939).*

On the radio, being danced and mimed to by Ruthie in front of the mirror. The song is reprised in full during the end credits.

## "Mairzy Doats"

*Written by Milton Drake, Al Hoffman and Jerry Livingston (1943). Performed by the Merry Macs (1944).*

Heard as we see Abe eating fish, continuing during the Mr. Zipsky anecdote.

## "If You Are but a Dream"

*Written by Moe Jaffe, Jack Fulton and Nat Bonx (1941). Performed by Frank Sinatra (1944).*

Heard when Joe, Aunt Bea and her current boyfriend go to the Radio City Music Hall to see *The Philadelphia Story*.

## "If I Didn't Care"

*Written by Jack Lawrence (1939). Performed by the Ink Spots (1939).*

Heard as Sally witnesses the shooting of club owner, Mr. Davis, by Rocco (Danny Aiello).

## "Schlof, mein Kind"

*Traditional Yiddish folksong (more often spelt "Schlaf, mein Kind"). Performed by Emil Decameron and His Orchestra (1959).*

Background music to a radio adaptation of a Chekhov play, in which Sally gets a part. The play is interrupted by the announcement that Pearl Harbor has been bombed.¹⁷

## "I Don't Want to Walk Without You"

*Written by Frank Loesser and Jule Styne (1942). Arranged by Dick Hyman. Sung by Mia Farrow, accompanied by Ken Levinsky.*

Sung by Sally to the troops during a USO (United Service Organizations) concert.

## "Remember Pearl Harbor"

*Written by Sammy Kaye and Don Reid (1941). Performed by Sammy Kaye and His Orchestra (1941).*

Heard while Joe is collecting scrap iron, continuing during the Biff Baxter radio show.

### "Babalu"

Written by Margarita Lecuona and S.K. Russell (English lyric) (1941). Performed by Richard Hayes (vocal) with Xavier Cugat and His Orchestra (1952).

Heard when Joe and his friends see a woman dancing in front of the mirror in her underwear through her bedroom window. The track is briefly reprised when she turns out to be Miss Gordon (Sydney A. Blake), their substitute teacher.

### "They're Either Too Young or Too Old"

Written by Frank Loesser and Arthur Schwartz (1943). Sung by Kitty Carlyle.

Sung on a radio advert for tea. The song continues as the film cuts to Bea painting on nylons. Segues into...

### "That Old Feeling"

Written by Lew Brown and Sammy Fain (1937). Performed by Guy Lombardo and His Orchestra (1937).

The scene continues as Bea and Joe's mother begin talking about men and marriage.

### "The White Cliffs of Dover"

Written by Walter Kent and Nat Burton (1941). Performed by Glenn Miller and His Orchestra (1941).

On the radio as Joe's mother and father discuss names for the new baby.

### "Goodbye"

Written by Gordon Jenkins (1935). Performed by Benny Goodman and His Orchestra (1935).

On the radio when there is an air raid drill, continuing into the subsequent scene where Joe's parents look at the search lights before going to bed.

### "I'm Gettin' Sentimental Over You"

Written by George Bassman and Ned Washington (1932). Performed by Tommy Dorsey and His Orchestra (1935).

Joe is awoken by this being played on the radio as Aunt Bea brings home Fred (Robert Joy) after a date. It continues during the following scene in the kitchen, where Fred breaks down and cries.

### "Re-Lax Jingle"

Written and arranged by Dick Hyman (1987). Sung by Mia Farrow, accompanied by Phil Bodner (clarinet), Derek Smith (piano), Dave Carey (vibraphone), Adam Romoff (bass) and Ted Sommer (drums).

Radio advert for a laxative sung by Sally.

### "Lullaby of Broadway"

Written by Harry Warren and Al Dubin (1935). Performed by Richard Himber and His Ritz-Carlton Orchestra 1935).

Heard as Sally's new show, Sally White's "Gay White Way," is introduced. The song continues as the scene cuts to Abe and Aunt Ceil (Renée Lippen) getting ready for bed when Abe breaks the radio by thumping it.

### "American Patrol"

Written by Frank W. Meacham (1885). Performed by Glenn Miller and His Orchestra (1942).

Heard as Joe is picking up the radio from the repair shop and gets a taxi, which turns out to be driven by his father (Michael Tucker).

### "Take the 'A' Train"

Written by Billy Strayhorn (1939). Performed by Duke Ellington and His Orchestra (1941).

Heard at the hospital after the baby has been born. It is heard again shortly afterwards during the scenes where Joe is taken to Manhattan and a radio show by Aunt Bea and Sy (Richard Portnow), her latest boyfriend.

**"You'll Never Know"**

*Written by Harry Warren and Mack Gordon (1943). Performed by Jane Jarvis (piano), Barbara Gallo (bass) and Liz Vochecowizc (drums).*

Being played by a trio at the Dance Palace, where Joe watches Aunt Bea and Sy dancing.

**"One, Two, Three, Kick"**

*Written by Xavier Cugat and Al Stillman (1939). Performed by Xavier Cugat and His Waldorf-Astoria Orchestra (1939).*

Being played on the radio when the family does the conga around the house, while Joe is being chased by his father.

**"Just One of Those Things"**

*Written by Cole Porter (1935).*

Being played at the King Cole Room where Sally is with the Masked Avenger (Wallace Shawn), cutting to a scene at the house, where the family are listening to the same song on the radio.

**"You'd Be So Nice to Come Home To"**

*Written by Cole Porter (1942). Arranged by Artie Butler. Sung by Diane Keaton, accompanied by Artie Butler (credited as band leader).*

Sung by radio singer (Diane Keaton) during the New Year's Eve broadcast.

**"Night and Day"**

*Written by Cole Porter (1932).*

Being played at the King Cole Room on New Year's Eve where Sally is dining with other radio stars including the Masked Avenger.

**"Auld Lang Syne"**

*Traditional.*[18]

Played by the orchestra at the King Cole Room after counting down to the New Year.

## *September* (1987)

*Songs from the repertoire.*

With *September*, Allen harks back to *Annie Hall* and *Interiors* by using music sparingly and by having it come only from a discernable source. Indeed, a notable feature of Allen's more serious films is the decrease in the amount of scoring he uses, something that is particularly evident in other dramas such as *Crimes and Misdemeanors* and *Husbands and Wives*. However, by the late 1980s we can see how Allen's adeptness at adding music has become more developed. In these later films, situations are introduced where characters either perform or play recordings of music, or are attending a function where music is heard in the background. Moreover, the songs we hear are usually relatable to the plot or the specific scene they accompany. We have seen how Allen has scored his films with songs that provide a subtext to the storyline, but here he achieves this with more subtlety; although the music is technically diegetic, it transcends its purely ornamental purpose and effectively becomes scoring in another form.

This sophisticated use of source music is clearly demonstrated in *September*. All of the songs we hear either come from an LP or are played on the piano. However, unlike *Interiors*, Allen manages to fill the film with music, and in fact provides a skillfully constructed soundtrack that subtly complements the spoken and unspoken emotions of the characters. Even though *September* is not regarded as one of Allen's best films, from a musical perspective it does provide one of the finest examples of the director using song lyrics as a subtext to the narrative. Reflecting the prevailing themes of desire and lost or unrequited love, the songs he has chosen mirror the feelings and frustrations of the film's six main characters.

Musically, the play-like structure of the film can be compared to an opera. "On a Slow Boat to China" functions as an overture — music that sets the scene and is heard again later. This song, which also promulgates the "desire theme" that pervades the film, is followed by four distinct "acts." During the opening "act," we are introduced to the characters, and here the music is less dominant. Nonetheless, the unheard lyrics to the two songs being played on the record player — "Out of Nowhere" and "Just One More Chance" — reflect Lane's (Mia Farrow) feelings regarding her relationship with Peter (Sam Waterston). The two had a short-lived affair, but even though his interest in her has waned, Lane still hopes that they can get back together.

During the second "act" the characters are getting ready for a dinner party, and here the "desire theme" predominates. In the same way that Elliot bought Lee an LP of Bach in *Hannah and Her Sisters* as a romantic preamble, Peter has bought Stephanie (Dianne Wiest) an Art Tatum and Ben Webster Quartet recording with the same objective. From this LP, the song "My Ideal" is playing as Peter corners Stephanie and reveals his feelings towards her. This song is the foremost piece of music in the film and is used not only to accompany Peter's attempted seduction, but also to reflect the longing — and uncertainty — that most of the other characters have about finding the object of their desire.

Art Tatum and Ben Webster are abruptly cut off as a storm brings about a power failure in the house. This ushers in the third "act," where Stephanie plays the piano by candlelight. Under the supposed security of half-darkness, the characters now reveal their various feelings for one another. Here Allen skillfully uses a medley of apt love songs to provide a musical commentary throughout.

Tatum and Webster return to the fore for the final "act." As the power comes back on, "My Ideal" starts up on the record player. We then cut to the next day and "Night and Day" from the same album is heard. This song continues the "desire theme" and is particularly relevant to Peter's "hungry yearning" for Stephanie, and significantly it is heard just before the two kiss. Allen concludes with a full rendition of "My Ideal" and the doubt inherent in the song reaffirms the character's "unfulfilled dreams and unfulfilled passions."[1]

In addition to the music we hear, Allen typically articulates his own musical tastes through his characters, and the "score" is frequently supplemented with references to music in the dialogue, notably jazz and American standards. Benny Goodman, the Coon-Sanders Nighthawks Orchestra and Prokofiev are all mentioned. Diane (Elaine Strich) repeatedly comments on the Art Tatum/

Ben Webster record: "I love all the music from that era." "That music is fabulous. I used to go to Harlem to listen to music like that." And when Peter approaches Stephanie at the piano, the first thing he says to her is, "I love those old songs."

### "On a Slow Boat to China"

*Written by Frank Loesser (1948). Performed by Bernie Leighton (piano).*

Opening credits, going into the first scene where Stephanie and Howard (Denholm Elliot) are practicing French. The same version is also heard later when Stephanie plays a selection of songs on the piano after the power failure in the house (see below).

### "Out of Nowhere"

*Written by John Green and Edward Heyman (1931). Performed by Bert Ambrose and His Orchestra (1931).*

### "Just One More Chance"

*Written by Sam Coslow and Arthur Johnston (1931). Performed by Bert Ambrose and His Orchestra (1931).*

An Ambrose LP is being played, and these two tracks are heard in succession as Diane and Peter are playing backgammon and Stephanie is playing pool with Howard. "Just One More Chance" can (just about) be heard as Lane talks about selling the house through to the scene where she and Peter talk about her mother.

### "My Ideal"

*Written by Richard Whiting, Newell Chase and Leo Robin (1930). Performed by Art Tatum (piano), Ben Webster (tenor sax), Red Callender (bass) and Bill Douglass (drums) (1956).*

An Art Tatum and Ben Webster LP is put on the record player by Stephanie (out of shot) and this song is heard as the party starts, being danced to by Diane and Lloyd (Jack Warden). Diane remarks, "What is that record, it's terrific!"[2] The track continues as Peter tells Stephanie how he feels about her, then the storm outside causes the power to go off. The song can be heard briefly when the electricity comes back on later, as the LP starts up again. The next morning, the same LP is put on the record player again by Stephanie as she makes a cup of tea, and the song is heard in full during the final scene where Stephanie tries to convince Lane that "it's gonna be OK." The camera then slowly pans to the right before cutting to the end credits.

### "What'll I Do?"

*Written by Irving Berlin (1924). Performed by Bernie Leighton (piano).*

The first in a series of songs played on the piano by Stephanie by candlelight after the power failure. The camera pans left and we see both Peter and then Howard before cutting to Diane at the Ouija board.

This song reflects both Stephanie's and Howard's uncertainty. Stephanie is not entirely happy with her marriage and is tempted by Peter's advances; this is emphasized by a shot of Peter as she begins to play the piano. The brief glimpse of Howard tells us that he too is not sure what to do. He is apprehensive about confessing his love to Lane, and this song is heard shortly before he eventually does so.

### "On a Slow Boat to China"

*Written by Frank Loesser (1948). Performed by Bernie Leighton (piano).*

Continuing from the previous scene, Diane is still at the Ouija board drinking vodka. The song continues as the film cuts to Howard and Lane on the porch and Howard tells her how he feels about her.

This is an important song in the film,

which underscores the various strands of desire between the characters: Howard's feelings toward Lane, Lane's feelings toward Peter and Peter's feelings toward Stephanie. All of these characters would like to be alone with the objects of their desire, to increase their chances of success without the interference of the others.

## "Who?"

*Written by Jerome Kern, Otto Harbach and Oscar Hammerstein II (1925). Performed by Bernie Leighton (piano).*

Continuing from the previous scene, this song — with its sentiment about unrequited love — is heard at the point where Lane rejects Howard, and continues over to Lloyd and Peter playing pool.

## "I'm Confessin' (That I Love You)"

*Written by Doc Daugherty, Ellis Reynolds and Al J. Neiburg (1930). Performed by Bernie Leighton (piano).*

Continuing from the previous scene, this song is heard as Peter asks Lloyd about working on the atomic bomb.

Significantly, we hear this played on the piano just after Howard has confessed to Lane that he loves her and during the scene when Lloyd tells Peter how much he loves Diane.

## "Moonglow"

*Written by Will Hudson, Eddie DeLange and Irving Mills (1934). Performed by Bernie Leighton (piano).*

Continuing from the previous scene, this song is heard shortly before we see Howard smoking on the porch, cutting back to Diane at the Ouija board, where she is talking about Lane to her dead husband, Richard.

## "When Day Is Done"

*Written by Robert Katscher and Buddy G. DeSylva (English lyric) (1926). Performed by Bernie Leighton (piano).*

After a break in the piano playing (due to the scene where Peter confesses his desire for Stephanie), this track is heard as Lloyd goes upstairs with a candle, cutting to Lane making coffee in the kitchen before Peter comes in and they talk about their relationship. The music initially gives the impression of being scored for this sequence, but it transpires that this is also being played on the piano by Stephanie. She stops as the electricity comes back on and the Art Tatum/Ben Webster LP starts up.

The song is used on two levels. It appears just prior to the power coming back on, and its title tells us that this "act" is ending: the storm has passed and we see Lloyd going to bed and Peter announces to Lane that he is about to leave. Additionally, the song reflects Lane's feelings toward Peter and is heard during their scene in the kitchen when Lane asks, "What happened to us?" Their relationship is over and although Lane still has hope, deep down she realizes that she has lost him.

## "Night and Day"

*Written by Cole Porter (1932). Performed by Art Tatum (piano), Ben Webster (tenor sax), Red Callender (bass) and Bill Douglass (drums) (1956).*

Being played on the record player during the scene where prospective buyers are viewing the house. Significantly, the song ends just before Peter shows up at the house, and Allen subtly uses the theme of "longing" and "yearning" to reflect the feelings that Peter and Stephanie share, anticipating their passionate kiss.

# *Shadows and Fog* (1992)

*Music composed by Kurt Weill, with additional songs from the repertoire.*

Based on his 1975 play *Death*, *Shadows and Fog* is Woody Allen's homage to German expressionist films of the 1920s and 1930s. "When I think of shadows and fog and menacing figures and being out in the night, I tend to think back to those German masters who worked so frequently with that kind of atmosphere."[1] In particular, the murder mystery plot and chiaroscuro cinematography recall such silent classics as F.W. Murnau's *Sunrise* (1927), Robert Wiene's *The Cabinet of Dr. Caligari* (1920) and especially Fritz Lang's *M* (1931). Although the film was unsuccessful at the box office, Allen nevertheless enjoyed the experience. "I had the fun for six months of doing an expressionistic film all on a set. I enjoyed showing mysterious streets with dramatic lighting and having dark shadows peek around corners and people getting strangled and Kurt Weill music in the background."[2]

Kurt Weill's music is particularly suitable for the tone of the film and does much to enhance the atmosphere. It is hard to believe, therefore, that Allen actually considered using music by Grieg. "In *Shadows and Fog* I didn't know what I was going to do for music. I looked at some classical music, but that was too ponderous. I looked at some Edvard Grieg at one point, and I couldn't get what I wanted. Then, after the film was finished, I played a piece of Kurt Weill and it seemed very good. And I played another and another, and then it took shape and we did the whole picture with it. It just seemed to fit in perfectly."[3] That Allen considered Grieg is somewhat surprising for a film of this kind, but it is possible that he was influenced by Fritz Lang's use of "In the Hall of the Mountain King" from *Peer Gynt* in *M*.[4] Lang's *M*—which also concerns the search for a maniacal killer within a city gripped with fear and paranoia—was filmed in Berlin, and although the city is deliberately unnamed in *Shadows and Fog*, Allen may have had Berlin in mind when choosing the music.[5] All of the Weill pieces selected were written during the period when he was still in Berlin—the Canadian Chamber Ensemble's version of "The Cannon Song" even comes from their 1982 album *Music from Berlin in the 1920s*—and the three Jack Hylton recordings that also figure in the film are all German songs which appear on the LP *Hits from Berlin, 1927–31*. Although Weill's music predominates, it should be pointed out that the song "When Day Is Done" also features heavily in the score. This song was previously used by Allen in *September*, where the (unheard) lyrics about lost love reflected the film's narrative. Here the imagery of the (again unheard) lyrics, which refer to "shadows," "night" and "twilight," subliminally enhance the sullen atmosphere. To add further to the ambience of the film, Allen also chose mostly historic recordings: "We used period material. We found lots of recordings. We sent our guy out, and he brought back everything he could find."[6] (For more details on these recordings, see the notes below and appendix 1.)

## *Kleine Dreigroschenmusik* (Little Threepenny Music), 6th movement: "The Cannon Song"

*Written by Kurt Weill and Bertolt Brecht (1929). Performed by the Canadian Chamber Ensemble, conducted by Raffi Armenian (1980); also performed by the London Sinfonietta, conducted by David Atherton (1975).*

This track and the following song, "When Day Is Done," form the two major pieces of music in the film. "The Cannon Song" occurs several times, usually during dramatic moments, with the faster London Sinfonietta recording being used for the more animated scenes.

1) Opening credits, continuing into the opening scene where we first see the killer (Michael Kirby) committing murder.

2) When Irmy (Mia Farrow) storms round to Marie's (Madonna) and catches Clown (John Malkovich) flirting with her.

3) When the clairvoyant, Spiro (Charles Cragin), arrives and sniffs Max (Woody Allen) before Max blows pepper in the mob's faces and runs away.

4) When Max flees the brothel as the mob arrive, continuing as he bumps into Simon Carr (Wallace Shawn), his rival colleague, cutting to a shot of the killer at the circus where Clown and Irmy are with the baby.

5) The final hearing occurs during the climax of the film when the killer approaches Max and Armstead the Magician (Kenneth Mars) and they avoid his clutches by hiding in a mirror, eventually trapping him.

## "When Day Is Done"

*Written by Robert Katscher and Buddy G. DeSylva (English lyric) (1926).[7] Performed by Jack Hylton and His Orchestra (1927).*

This song appears on several occasions throughout the film:

1) First, as we see a shot of the circus and are introduced to Irmy and Clown (the Wurlitzer organ adds to the circus atmosphere).

2) When Clown is walking outside and meets Marie and she invites him in, continuing as they flirt with each other, before being suddenly interrupted by "The Cannon Song," as Irmy arrives (see above).

3) When the students arrive at the brothel and Student Jack (John Cusack) sees Irmy and offers her increasing amounts of money to sleep with him.

4) Just after the killer has murdered the doctor (Donald Pleasence) and the camera moves up to show the window of the backroom where Student Jack and Irmy have just had sex.

5) Near the end of the film when Irmy goes out to get some water and the killer creeps up on her, continuing as she is warned by Max, who confronts the killer, but then runs off. It fades as Max stumbles upon Armstead the Magician.

6) During the end credits, when it is heard in full.

## "Ja, ja, die Frau'n sind meine schwache Seite"

*Written by Austin Egen and Kurt Schwabach (1928). Performed by Jack Hylton and His Orchestra (1928).*

Heard briefly in the brothel when Irmy is brought there by a prostitute (Lily Tomlin). Note that this song is particularly appropriate to a brothel, the English translation being, "Yes, Yes, Women Are My Greatest Weakness."

## *Die sieben Todsünden* (The Seven Deadly Sins), 1st movement: Prologue

*Written by Kurt Weill and Bertolt Brecht (1933). Orchestra conducted by Wilhelm Brückner-Rüggeberg (1956).[8]*

This brief extract is used twice, both times involving Max and Irmy as they walk through the streets. We hear it first during the scene after the two have met and are looking for a hotel. It returns a little later when they are walking down some steps, after Max's fiancée, Eve (Kate Nelligan), has sent them away.

**"Alabama Song" (from *Mahagonny Songspeil*)**
*Written by Kurt Weill and Bertolt Brecht (1927). Performed by Marek Weber and His Orchestra (1928).*

The verse of this song (in an instrumental version) is heard briefly as a coach drives past and we see Clown searching for Irmy and shouting her name.

**"When the White Lilacs Bloom Again" ("Wenn de Weiße Flieder Blüht")**
*Written by Franz Doelle and Fritz Rotter (1929). Performed by Jack Hylton and His Orchestra (1929).*

Heard briefly in the brothel as Max turns up, being pursued by the mob. It returns a little later when Max takes Jodie Foster's prostitute to bed, continuing as Student Jack talks to Lily Tomlin's prostitute.

***Kleine Dreigroschenmusik*** **(Little Threepenny Music),[9] 2nd movement: "Moritat von Mackie Messer" (aka "Mack the Knife")**
*Written by Kurt Weill and Bertolt Brecht (1929). Performed by the Berlin Staatsoper, conducted by Otto Klemperer (1931).*

Heard at the end of the film when Max and Irmy are saying goodbye and Max asks, "Why would I want to join the circus?" It continues as Max decides to become the Magician's assistant and the Magician makes them both disappear, cutting to the end credits.

# *Sleeper* (1973)

*Music and songs from the repertoire.*

"Woody Allen takes a nostalgic look at the future," the tagline to Allen's fifth film, appropriately sums up its two prominent stylistic themes, the film being at one and the same time a homage to the silent film era and a playful parody on the science fiction genre. Drawing on the slapstick methods of Buster Keaton, Charlie Chaplin and Harold Lloyd, Allen for the first time combines his verbal wit with a more visual and physical comedic style. Set in the year 2173, *Sleeper* amalgamates aspects of *A Brave New World* and *1984* with films such as *Metropolis* (1927), *A Clockwork Orange* (1971) and *2001: A Space Odyssey* (1968)—Allen even uses the voice of Douglas Rain, who had provided the voice for Hal in Kubrick's 1968 classic. Musically, *Sleeper* was Allen's first film in which he did not employ someone to write the music. After *Everything You Always Wanted to Know About Sex*, he had been disillusioned with the process of using a composer and decided instead to supply the music for the film himself, turning to his beloved New Orleans jazz. (Note that this is the first Woody Allen film to have the now familiar black and white opening titles accompanied by jazz.) The anachronistic Dixieland score adds to the nostalgic element and acts as a foil to the futuristic setting. As Brode remarks,

"The paradox principle, as well as the ability to use a soundtrack of a film to contrapuntal effect, is brilliantly employed. Here, the music is the meaning. The improvisational charms of Dixieland jazz aurally represent the opposite of the sterile 'perfection' that's been achieved in the visual scheme of the futureworld."[1]

Allen's choice of music was atypical. Science fiction films at that time, for example *The Andromeda Strain* (1971), *Westworld* (1973), *Soylent Green* (1973) and *The Fantastic Planet* (1973), tended to use electronic or eerie orchestral music. But Allen went for a completely different approach, deciding instead to help propel the film's fast-paced comic tempo by providing an upbeat Dixieland accompaniment. "I didn't know what kind of music to use. And then I thought, since it was the future, I wasn't going to use any futuristic music, as that's unpleasant and strange to listen to. And since it was a slapstick movie, I wanted to use that kind of music."[2] Allen then adds credence to the score by having his character in the film play the clarinet in a jazz band named the Ragtime Rascals. Nevertheless, some commentators at the time missed the point and criticized Allen for his choice of music. He responded, "It would have been old-time and obvious and not inventive to use the same silly science fiction music used by everyone for *Sleeper*. Also it was the music one heard in old, silent comedies which *Sleeper* was modeled after. It was the most perfect music possible and did everything I wanted it to do."[3]

Interestingly, the credits for this film only state, "Music by Woody Allen with the Preservation Hall Jazz Band and the New Orleans Funeral and Ragtime Orchestra." As none of the actual songs, music or the people who wrote them are acknowledged in the credits, it would be easy to suppose that Allen actually wrote the music for the film himself, rather than just performing it. Indeed, certain books do give this impression by simply having "Music by Woody Allen" in their filmographies. Some commentators go even further: Benayoun states, "He himself also composed the music for *Sleeper*";[4] Bendazzi comments that "the music is composed and performed by Woody Allen himself";[5] while Fox remarks that "Woody duly opted for a combination of jazz standards and originals."[6] However, excluding source music, the score actually consists entirely of Dixieland/Tin Pan Alley standards, mostly written during the 1920s. As Allen himself points out, "It was classical New Orleans jazz. I listened to a whole lot of New Orleans music from which I chose. I gave myself a library."[7]

Indeed, the score contains several bulwarks of the traditional jazz repertoire such as "Tain't Nobody's Biz-Ness If I Do," "Wolverine Blues," "Canal Street Blues," "San," and "Till We Meet Again," as well as a couple of songs which have a special affiliation to the Preservation Hall Jazz Band itself, namely "Joe Avery" and "Ice Cream." The latter was also a favorite of the clarinetist George Lewis, who had played with the band at the end of his career. Lewis is one of Allen's idols, as Tom Sancton observes: "Woody models his own playing on Lewis' and speaks of him with a reverence he accords to only a handful of his cultural heroes, including Willie Mays, Groucho Marx and Swedish filmmaker Ingmar Bergman. 'He was a great, great artist on the clarinet,' enthuses Woody. 'He had that sort of sweet, soulful, just beautiful, beautiful sound.'"[8] In *Rolling Stone*, Allen commented, "George Lewis is without a doubt the greatest clarinet player that ever lived. Black, illiterate, untaught, the man was just a genius."[9] Lewis's influence on Allen's playing can be heard clearly throughout the film's score. Prime examples include "Till We Meet Again," which is reminiscent of Lewis's 1956 recording with Dick Oxtot's Traditional Jazz Quartet, and the aforementioned "Ice Cream," which bears a striking resemblance to Lewis's 1953 recording with Avery "Kid" Howard (but without the vocals), including an identical piano introduction. (See also appendix 1.)

Allen's original intention was to record all of the tracks with the Preservation Hall Jazz Band, an authentic New Orleans band with whom he had already played at the historic 1970 jazz festival in Congo Square. "We contacted Preservation Hall and said we wanted to record the band there and that I would be playing the clarinet. And it was all worked out. It was fine with them. And it was fun to play with the old guys."[10] The band's line-up at that time comprised of Percy Humphrey (trumpet), Jim Robinson (trombone), Emanuel Sayles (banjo), James "Sing" Miller (piano), Chester Zardis (bass) and Josiah "Cie" Frazier (drums), with Allan Jaffe (the Preservation Hall's founder) occasionally playing tuba on some numbers. Allen fitted in well, as Percy Humphrey remarked at the time: "He has a wonderful ear. He did what you should do when you sit with another man's band. He played along with what we played. He didn't try to be a celebrity."[11] After the sessions, Allen was congratulated by Albert Burbank, arguably the foremost New Orleans–style clarinetist at the time, and was also paid a compliment by the then eighty-three-year-old trombonist, Jim Robinson, which would have especially pleased Allen:

> "Did anyone ever tell you you sound like my old friend George Lewis?" he asked Woody at the end of the set.
> "What's your name again?"
> "Woody," he mumbled.
> "Willard? You're real good, Willard."[12]

With many of the scenes involving music being chase sequences or otherwise slapstick in nature, it was important for Allen to get just the right tempo; as previously mentioned in the introduction, comedy invariably requires upbeat music in order to obtain the desired effect. However, some of the tracks originally recorded with the Preservation Hall Jazz Band were too slow for this purpose. As a result, certain tunes were re-recorded with Allen's own band, the New Orleans Funeral and Ragtime Orchestra. "I went to New Orleans and played with the Preservation Hall Jazz Band. And we brought home all the tracks and put them in. And—correctly—the New Orleans band, the authentic ones, play at slower tempos. And these slower tempos were killing us. So I was only able to use a few songs I recorded in New Orleans. I had to record with my own band in New York, from Michael's Pub, to get some of those same songs but at rousing tempos, because otherwise the scenes were dying."[13] Allen's own band at this time consisted of occasional co-writer Marshall Brickman (banjo); John Bucher (cornet); husband and wife Dick and Barbara Dreiwitz (trombone and tuba); Dick Miller (piano) and Jay Duke (drums). In the end, only a handful of the Preservation Hall Jazz Band's tracks were used in the film. Whether playing in New Orleans or with his own band back in New York, this was the part of the film making process that Allen enjoyed most: "The most fun I had on the movie was playing the score."[14]

## "Tain't Nobody's Biz-Ness If I Do"

*Written by Porter Grainger and Everett Robbins (1922). Performed by Woody Allen (clarinet) and the New Orleans Funeral and Ragtime Orchestra.*

Opening credits.

## "Yes, Sir, That's My Baby"

*Written by Walter Donaldson and Gus Kahn (1925). Performed by Woody Allen (clarinet) and the New Orleans Funeral and Ragtime Orchestra.*

Heard just after Miles Monroe (Woody Allen) has been revived and is in a wheelchair, continuing as the doctors try to get him into a car and then eventually drive off to Dr. Melik's (Mary Gregory) house. The track returns briefly when Luna (Diane Keaton) and Erno (John Beck) kidnap a brainwashed Miles from his apartment. Note that in both cases the song title alludes to Miles's child-like behavior.

## "Wolverine Blues"

*Written by Ferdinand "Jelly Roll" Morton, Benjamin Spikes and John Spikes (1923). Performed by Dick Miller (piano).*

Heard as Dr. Melik tells Miles where — and when — he is and what has happened to him.

## "Canal Street Blues"

*Written by Joseph "King" Oliver (1923). Performed by Woody Allen (clarinet) and the New Orleans Funeral and Ragtime Orchestra.*

Heard during the sequence where Miles is escaping the security police, having been told by the doctors to find the Aries Project. We see Miles climbing out of the window using a ladder; trying to work a car; and then eventually eluding the security police by using a flying pack, which gets stuck in a tree; the piece ends as he gets into a robot delivery truck. The track returns later when Luna is lowering Miles out of a window on a piece of tape so he can steal operating gowns.

## "And the Glory of the Lord shall be revealed" from *Messiah*

*Written by George Frideric Handel (1742).*

The last few bars of this chorus are heard as accompaniment to the Leader saying goodnight on television.

## "Ice Cream (I Scream, You Scream, We All Scream For)"

*Written by Howard Johnson, Billy Moll and Robert King (1927). Performed by Woody Allen (clarinet) and the New Orleans Funeral and Ragtime Orchestra.*

Heard as Miles tries to escape from the robot repair shop, continuing as he attacks a security guard with a bleu cheese, tells Luna who he is and, as she screams, absconds with her into the woods. The track returns when we see Miles shooting the Leader's nose with a "bang" gun and running off. It continues through to the final scene where Miles and Luna are sitting in a car, having escaped.

## "Joe Avery"[15]

*Performed by Woody Allen (clarinet) and the Preservation Hall Jazz Band.*

Heard as Miles goes to look for food and steals a giant banana and a piece of celery, before being chased back into the woods. The opening of the piece is heard later when Miles and Luna go to steal operating gowns, using a phony thumb to get past security.

**"San"**
Written by Lindsey McPhail and Walter Michels (1920). Performed by Woody Allen (clarinet) and the New Orleans Funeral and Ragtime Orchestra.

Heard as the security police catch up with Miles and Luna by the river, continuing as they fend off the police and eventually escape with the aid of Miles's inflated "hydrovac" suit. Note the quote of "Yankee Doodle."

**"Smiles"**
Written by Lee S. Roberts and J. Will Callahan (1917). Performed by Woody Allen (clarinet) and the Preservation Hall Jazz Band.

Heard as Luna is taking a bath, cutting to Miles shaving in front of the "Gyro-mirror." (This scene is reminiscent of Chaplin shaving to Brahms's Hungarian Dance No. 5 in *The Great Dictator*.)

In European TV releases of the film, the above scene is replaced with the following:

**Piano Sonata No. 17 in D Minor, Op. 31 No. 2, "Tempest" 1st movement: Largo — Allegro**
Written by Ludwig van Beethoven (1802).

Miles plays this on a tape player and then eats his food in time to the music in front of an amused Luna. It continues as Miles performs magic tricks, ending as his arm catches fire.

**"A Pretty Girl Is Like a Melody"**
Written by Irving Berlin (1919). Performed by Woody Allen (clarinet) and the Preservation Hall Jazz Band.

Heard as we see Miles's colleague, Rainer Krebs (Chris Forbes) — a pretty girl — with an orb and then Miles with a giant orb, cutting to Luna — another pretty girl — waking up in the woods, continuing as she attempts to shoot a bow and arrow and then swing from a tree, before being abducted by Erno. The song returns a little later after Miles's confession, continuing as we see Erno giving instructions to the rebels and Miles coming out of McDonald's.

**"Till We Meet Again"**
Written by Richard Whiting and Raymond B. Egan (1918). Performed by Woody Allen (clarinet) and the Preservation Hall Jazz Band.

In New Orleans jazz, this song is traditionally played at the end of a concert, and Allen adopts this idea by using it at the end of the film. The song is heard faintly in the background during the final scene between Miles and Luna, and then gets louder as the film cuts to the end credits.

## *Small Time Crooks* (2000)

*Music and songs from the repertoire.*

With *Small Time Crooks* Allen returns to the combination of crime and comedy seen previously in *Take the Money and Run*, *Manhattan Murder Mystery* and *Bullets Over Broadway*. The film is primarily an unpretentious, light-hearted caper movie, in which Allen "chucks off his fabled angst and returns in spirit to those wide-eyed days of yesteryear, before Chekhov, Kafka and Bergman invaded his creative imagination."[1] As Allen himself remarks, "*Small Time Crooks* was fun for me to do. It was an old idea of mine that was lying around for years that I also felt was funny, or charming at least, but trivial. It was one of those films that has a good premise to it and if I can work it out, fine, but in the end it's never going to be *Rashomon*."[2]

The film highlights the cultural differences between high society and the lower classes, and points up the fact that, although one may be wealthy, it does not necessarily follow that one also has good taste; Frenchy (Tracey Ullman) herself remarks, "Class is something you can't fake and you can't buy." Allen primarily plays for laughs, however, and only touches on these issues. Nevertheless, it is clear that he was mindful of them when choosing the music for the film. Although he still includes some examples of his preferred jazz and American standards, the score has a greater emphasis on music associated with the upper classes, including numerous songs by society dance king Lester Lanin, and several pieces of classical music, both of which are used to reflect the sophisticated world of the social elite. The "money can't buy you happiness, but it helps" theme is nicely illustrated from the outset. Allen, in typical fashion, provides an especially fitting song to frame the film using Harry Warren's "With Plenty of Money and You" over the opening and closing titles. This song, from *Gold Diggers of 1937*, sets the scene and acts as the ideal prelude and postlude.

We have seen in a number of earlier films (in particular, *Hannah and Her Sisters*) that Allen often uses certain pieces of music to accompany specific characters. In *Small Time Crooks*, Allen uses a similar technique, this time to underline the contrast in class between the film's main protagonists and the well-to-do with whom they find themselves rubbing shoulders. Ray (Woody Allen) and his cronies, a bunch of cerebrally challenged ne'er-do-wells, are drolly accompanied by Benny Goodman and Harry James. The lively swing numbers we hear provide just the right amount of comedic pace to complement the scenes involving Ray and his gang's exploits. In addition, these big band numbers accompany the scenes when Ray, now seeking consolation in the company of his dim-witted cousin May Sloane (Elaine May), enjoys the simpler things: baseball, Chinese food in front of old movies (à la *Manhattan* and *Crimes and Misdemeanors*) and playing cards with his buddies.

In marked contrast to this, Frenchy is taken to galleries, concerts and chic restaurants by her cultural guru, David Grant (Hugh Grant), a suave art dealer. David is accompanied by the smooth sounds of Carmen Cavallaro, with "Cocktails for Two," in particular, aptly capturing his debonair character and their new "relationship." Furthermore, David is also associated with classical music, which also highlights the class division. As with earlier films such as *Another Woman* and *Crimes and Misdemeanors*, Allen uses classical music to reflect culture and sophistication. Thus, when David proceeds to edify Frenchy, we see them attend a series of recitals.[3] Note how the serious nature of Bach's cello music, used with such effectiveness in *Another Woman*, is here undercut by Allen's cellular phone joke. Allen also sends up modern music by including an audio collage composition by Scott Marshall, during which Ray falls asleep. Marshall was especially commissioned by Sweetland Productions to compose this work for inclusion in the film.

Music is used to emphasize further the cultural gulf between the Winklers and the well-to-do at the two dinner party sequences — one at Ray and Frenchy's, who are now part of the nouveau riche after the overnight success of the Sunset Cookies; the other at Chi Chi Potter's (Elaine Stritch), a wealthy socialite and patron of the arts. In a vain attempt at being classy, Ray and Frenchy play a Strauss waltz, which can be regarded as populist classical music. Moreover, the Winklers also play "Tequila" at the same party, a song which is invariably included on "party hits" compilations more associated with "low brow" than "high brow." This is a particularly atypical track for an Allen score (which he even reprises for the end credits) and it is clear that its inclusion is designed to illustrate the Winklers' lack of culture. Significantly, we hear it as Ray tells his guests distasteful jokes and shortly before Frenchy overhears some of her guests saying that she is "the definition of bad taste."

"Tequila" contrasts wonderfully with the music of Lester Lanin heard at Chi Chi Potter's party later in the film. Lanin, known as "The Musical Maharajah of High Society," is famous for providing a variety of musical styles for the *haut monde*. We are given a foretaste of this style of music when Frenchy and David are walking into the bar during the intermission of a concert. Allen then uses six tracks in succession throughout the film's "third act" during Ray's bungled attempts to steal Chi Chi Potter's necklace. Note that the first of these is Steve Allen's "This Could Be the Start of Something Big," a title which reflects Ray's vain hopes of being a successful thief.

## "With Plenty of Money and You"

*Written by Harry Warren and Al Dubin (1936). Performed by Hal Kemp and His Orchestra (1936).*

Opening credits and opening scene where Ray is watching the bank behind a newspaper, continuing as he buys chocolates before going back to his apartment. The track returns at the end of the film when Ray and Frenchy, now broke, decide to pawn the Duke of Windsor cigarette case (which Frenchy lifted from David's safe) and move to Florida with the money.

## "Stompin' at the Savoy"

*Written by Edgar Sampson, Benny Goodman, Chic Webb and Andy Razaf (1934). Performed by Benny Goodman and His Orchestra (1935).*

This is heard first when the gang drive up to Benny Borkowshi's (Jon Lovitz) apartment and Ray knocks on his door with flowers. The track then recurs several times throughout the film: when the gang meet Benny outside his apartment block and in the subsequent scenes where they are buying timber and dynamite; during the shot of a long line outside the cookie shop; briefly when officer Ken Deloach (Brian Markinson) suggests a franchise and the film jumps ahead one year; outside Ray and Frenchy's apartment block as Frenchy leaves for Europe, while Ray spends time with May at the baseball ground and watching TV; and finally when Ray is casing Chi Chi Potter's apartment.

## "Could It Be?"

*Written by Stephen Lang. Performed by Stephen Lang.*

Faintly heard coming from the television while Frenchy is watching the *Lives of the Rich and Famous* TV show.

## "Music Makers"

*Written by Harry James and Don Raye*

(1941). Performed by Harry James and His Orchestra (1941).

Another track that occurs several times throughout the film. It is heard first when the gang are working on the tunnel, as the cookie shop begins to get busy. It then returns on three occasions: when Ray fakes illness to play cards with the gang (note that this immediately follows the Henry James/Harry James mix-up joke); during a later shot of the gang playing cards; and then when Ray bumps into May outside Ruby Foo's Chinese restaurant on Broadway.

### Voices of Spring (Frühlingsstimmen), Op. 410

*Written by Johann Strauss II (1883). Performed by the Vienna State Opera Orchestra, conducted by Jascha Horenstein (1962).*

This famous waltz is heard as Ray is walking down the stairs at the dinner party, continuing as the quests arrive and are shown around.

### "Tequila"

*Written by Chuck Rio (1958). Performed by the Champs (1958).*

Heard during the scenes at the dinner party where Ray is telling jokes. After the second of these, it continues as Frenchy overhears some of her guests talking about her bad taste. The song is reprised in full during the end credits.

### "Cocktails for Two"

*Written by Sam Coslow and Arthur Johnston (1934). Performed by Carmen Cavallaro (piano).*

Heard briefly on two occasions: first when we see a shot of David's apartment block and then later when Frenchy meets David outside his apartment block to go to the jewelers.

### "The Modern Dance"

*Written by Scott Marshall. Performed by Judith Cohen, Carol Genetti and Scott Marshall.*

A contemporary theater piece watched by Frenchy, Ray (asleep) and David.

### Prelude in B Minor, Op. 32, No. 10

*Written by Sergei Rachmaninov (1910). Performed by Ruth Laredo.*

Played at a recital attended by Frenchy and David.

### "Mountain Greenery"

*Written by Richard Rodgers and Lorenz Hart (1926). Performed by Lester Lanin.*

Heard as Frenchy and David are walking into the bar at the interval.

### "Fascination"

*Written by Filippo D. Marchetti and Dick Manning (1904). Performed by Carmen Cavallaro (piano).*

Heard during the intermission while Frenchy and David are sitting down and she gives him the Duke of Windsor cigarette case.

### Cello Suite No. 2 in D Minor, BWV 1008, 4th movement: Sarabande

*Written by Johann Sebastian Bach (1721). Performed by Jesse Levy.*

Played at a recital attended by Frenchy and David, when Frenchy's cell phone rings.

### "Zelda's Theme"

*Written by André Previn (1964). Performed by Perez Prado.*

Heard, briefly, as Ray checks out Chi Chi Potter's safe.

### "This Could Be the Start of Something Big"

*Written by Steven Allen (1954). Performed by Lester Lanin.*

The first in a series of Lester Lanin

tracks being played at Chi Chi's party; this is heard as Ray tries to sneak upstairs to steal the necklace.

### "Lester Lanin Cha Cha"

*Written by Lester Lanin. Performed by Lester Lanin.*

Heard as Ray goes upstairs and bumps into a waitress, knocking over her tray.

### "Just in Time"

*Written by Betty Comden, Benny Green and Jule Styne (1956). Performed by Lester Lanin.*

Heard as May goes upstairs to warn Ray that Chi Chi is looking for him.

### "Old Devil Moon"

*Written by Burton Lane and E.Y. Harburg (1947). Performed by Lester Lanin.*

Heard as Chi Chi goes upstairs to get the photos.

### "The Hukilau Song"

*Written by Jack Owens (1948). Performed by Lester Lanin.*

Heard as Chi Chi goes to get the doctor and Ray gets the necklaces mixed up.

### "Steady, Steady"

*Written by Ronald Graham and Milton Schafer (1962). Performed by Lester Lanin.*

Heard as Chi Chi and the doctor come upstairs to examine May, continuing until Ray and May leave.

## *Stardust Memories* (1980)

*Music and songs from the repertoire, with original music by Dick Hyman.*

Following on from the acclaimed *Manhattan*, Allen's next film caused something of a stir for fans and critics alike. Being seen as autobiographical, his audience felt offended by Allen's portrayal of sycophantic fans, while critics panned the film for being self-indulgent and a flagrant imitation of Fellini's *Otto e mezzo* (1963). Allen has denied that the character of Sandy Bates was based on his own persona and has stressed that the film was purely fictional. True or not, one thing for certain is that, throughout his films, many of Allen's characters do possess the same cultural tastes as the director — cinema, literature, sports and music. And in *Stardust Memories*, Sandy Bates clearly shares Allen's love of jazz, something that is manifestly reflected in the score. In the film, Sandy is seen playing records by Django Reinhardt and Louis Armstrong, and when the new studio heads try to change the ending to his latest movie, his characters end up in "jazz heaven" instead of a garbage dump. One studio head states, "I thought you'd like it, Sandy. You love jazz." It is not surprising, then, that the soundtrack to *Stardust Memories* is replete with numerous jazz standards, performed by a number of jazz's leading exponents — Louis Armstrong, Sidney Bechet, Count Basie, Lester Young, Chick Webb and Django Reinhardt.

Despite Allen playing down any influence from Federico Fellini, *Stardust Memories* does have certain aspects that resemble the Italian director's *Otto e mezzo*.[1] Musically, however, the films are, for the most part, dissimilar. Fellini uses regular collaborator Nino Rota to supply an original soundtrack, whereas Allen's score predominantly consists of a selection of pre-existent recordings.[2] However, while Brode's statement that *Stardust Memories* is "accompanied by tinny music that sounds suspiciously like Nino Rota" is erroneous,[3] there are some musical parallels between Allen's film and *Otto e mezzo*. It is apparent that Allen was conscious of the way music was used in Fellini's film and, taking certain musical elements, translated them into his own American, jazz-oriented idiom. For instance, Allen chooses a somewhat curious recording by Sidney Bechet; is it coincidence that this is a rumba, a dance which also features in *Otto e mezzo*? Moreover, in Fellini's film there is a sequence beginning with a close-up of a cabaret singer performing "Gigolette" from Lehár's *La danza della libellule*. This is shortly followed by a magical mind-reading act, accompanied by Rota's "L'illusionista," which eventually leads to one of Guido's childhood flashbacks ("Asa nisi masa"). In *Stardust Memories*, Allen includes a scene which condenses the same combination of themes — music, magic and memories of childhood. In the scene when Sandy goes to a roadside bar for a drink with Jack (John Rothman) and Daisy (Jessica Harper), Allen too has a close-up of a cabaret singer, here performing "Brazil" — a samba which equates to Lehár's tango — and this is immediately followed by Sandy experiencing a flashback-like hallucination where he sees himself on stage as the child illusionist, "The Amazing Sandy." (The trick we see here is the "floating light bulb," which becomes the title of Allen's play written the following year.) Allen typically chooses Dixieland music for this scene, but his choice of the exotic "Palesteena" is significant: when choosing music to accompany magic scenes Allen often turns to Eastern-flavored music, as seen later in his use of "In a Persian Market" ("Oedipus Wrecks" and *The Curse of the Jade Scorpion*) and "Limehouse Blues" (*Alice*).

The soundtrack to *Stardust Memories* marks a watershed for Allen. In addition to jazz, it also includes other musical elements that we have come to expect from a Woody Allen film. Classical music, Cole Porter, big band and Dick Hyman are all combined for the first time, anticipating the scores to several of Allen's subsequent films. Up to this point, Allen had been experimenting, to a large extent, with a number of different ways of using music in his films. With *Stardust Memories* he annunciates many of the musical styles and techniques that are now an integral part of his scores. Most significantly, this is the first film in which Allen applies the now customary method of using a variety of appropriate songs and music from the repertoire to accompany particular scenes. Allen adopts a similar approach to that found in *Sleeper*, *Love and Death* and *Manhattan*, but now draws on various pre-existent recordings instead of music recorded expressly for the film and/or from one specific composer. In addition, this is the first film in which Dick Hyman contributes original music; Allen and Hyman develop a regular and fruitful working relationship from this point on, as we shall see in later films.

Most of *Stardust Memories* actually takes place in Sandy Bates's imagination.

As Allen points out, "He is in his apartment in the beginning of the movie, and his housekeeper brings in this dead rabbit. And he looks at this dead thing and it reminds him of his own mortality. And then the rest of the film takes place in his mind."[4] This fantasy world, comprising a mixture of dream sequences and flashbacks, is reflected in Allen's choice of music. As with *Manhattan*, Allen continues to use certain songs to provide a subtext to the action on screen, but also introduces the technique of associating certain songs or performers with specific characters. "If Dreams Come True," for example, is exclusively used for the scenes with Isobel (Marie-Christine Barrault). One could also argue that the song's title alludes to the film's supposed "happy ending." Likewise, both the Django Reinhardt tracks in the film are linked to Dorrie's (Charlotte Rampling) character. We see Dorrie for the first time immediately after Sandy has put a recording of "I'll See You in My Dreams" on the record player, as he imagines her in the room with him. Later, "Body and Soul" is heard when we see the two enjoying happier times.

Conversely, the difficulties Sandy had in his relationship with Dorrie are sardonically commented upon by the Cole Porter songs "Easy to Love" and "It Was Just One of Those Things." Regarding "Easy to Love," Neil Sinyard makes an interesting, deeper observation:

> The song, "Easy to Love" is heard over the soundtrack during part of the film's haunting finale, which mixes fantasy, death, a grudging premiere and the director alone in a deserted cinema. The context gives the familiar tune an angle of irony — far removed from the unmodulated nostalgia of the soundtrack for *Manhattan*— particularly as people have been watching a film that is hard even to like. "Easy to Love" might refer to Woody Allen's uneasy reassessment of his lovable screen persona which he feels has been accepted a little too smugly, a smugness which this film is concerned to rebuke. Above all, the melody makes one think. For if there is a consistent refrain in his films, it is that, in Woody Allen, love is never easy.[5]

Without a doubt, the most important song in the film is "Stardust," which provides the source for Allen's film title. Near the end of the film, Louis Armstrong's 1930 recording of Hoagy Carmichael's classic accompanies the most outstanding and beautiful scene in the movie. As Sandy searches for something to give his life meaning, he recalls:

> It was one of those great spring days. It was Sunday, and you knew summer would be coming soon. I remember, that morning Dorrie and I had gone for a walk in the park. We came back to the apartment. We were just sort of sitting around. And ... I put on a record of Louis Armstrong, which is music that I grew up loving. It was very, very pretty, and ... I happened to glance over, and I saw Dorrie sitting there. And I remember thinking to myself ... how terrific she was, and how much I loved her. And, I don't know ... I guess it was the combination of everything ... the sound of that music, and the breeze and how beautiful Dorrie looked to me. And for one brief moment, everything just seemed to come together perfectly, and I felt happy. Almost indestructible in a way. It's funny that that simple little moment of contact moved me in a very, very profound way.[6]

This scene is timed so that Sandy's voice-over is heard during the instrumental introduction to the song — Armstrong's trumpet solo begins at the point

136 / *Stardust Memories* (1980)

that Sandy begins to reminisce about Dorrie. As he finishes, Armstrong's vocal enters while the camera stays focused on Dorrie. Sandy's feelings of longing and lost love, but also the memory of a happier time, are all captured in Mitchell Parish's plaintive lyrics. The most memorable moment in the movie, then, takes its lead from Allen's previous film, *Manhattan*: "at the end, we are left with the reiteration of Ike Davis' list; two good reasons for being alive, Louis Armstrong and a woman's face."[7]

Allen also includes a number of other musical references: Beethoven is listed as one of the world's great losses when Sandy worries that the universe is gradually breaking down; when Daisy buys Sandy a flute (which is reminiscent of Tracy buying Isaac a harmonica in *Manhattan*), he asks if it will play the Mozart Flute Concerto; and when Sandy is trying to impress Daisy he tells her his one classical music joke, which he puts in every single picture, but invariably cuts out: "I don't know much about classical music. For years I thought the Goldberg Variations were something Mr. and Mrs. Goldberg tried on their wedding night."[8]

### "Tropical Mood — Rhumba" (aka "Diane")[9]

*Traditional. Performed by The Haitian Orchestra: Kenneth Roane (trumpet), Sidney Bechet (clarinet), Willie "The Lion" Smith (piano), Olin Alderhold (bass) and Leo Warney (drums) (1939).*

Opening credits. The track is reprised later in the film when Sandy and Daisy come across a group of UFO enthusiasts having a party as they await the appearance of flying saucers.

### "I'll See You in My Dreams"

*Written by Isham Jones and Gus Kahn (1924). Performed by Django Reinhardt (lead guitar), Pierre Baro Ferret (guitar) and Emmanuel Soudieux (bass) (1939).*

Played on Sandy's stereo. Shortly after, he thinks of Dorrie and imagines her with him in the room.

### "Tickle Toe"

*Written by Lester Young (1940). Performed by Count Basie and His Orchestra, featuring Lester Young (tenor saxophone) (1940).*

Heard as Sandy looks at the dead rabbit in his kitchen, cutting to the scene where he arrives outside the Hotel Stardust and is confronted by numerous fans.

### "Three Little Words"

*Written by Bert Kalmar and Harry Ruby (1930). Arranged by Kirk Nurock. Sung by Judith Roberts with the Jazz Heaven Orchestra, featuring Joe Wilder (trumpet), Earl Shendell (clarinet), Arvell Shaw (trombone), Hank Jones (piano) and Richie Pratt (drums).*

Song and dance routine being performed in one of Sandy's films shown at the retrospective.

### "Brazil" (aka "Aquarela do Brasil")

*Written by Ary Barroso and S.K. Russell (English lyric) (1939). Sung by Marie Lane.*

Heard as we see a car shot after Sandy, Daisy and Jack decide go to for a drink at a roadside bar. It turns out that the song is being sung at the bar by a cabaret singer and continues as the three talk.

### "Palesteena"

*Written by Con Conrad and J. Russell Robinson (1920). Performed by the Original Dixieland Jazz Band (1920).*

Heard during "The Amazing Sandy" flashback, when Sandy (as a child) does magic tricks and his mother, analyst and others talk about him. The track is reprised later when Sandy shows Daisy a magic trick by elevating her in front of the UFO enthusiasts. The song is also heard briefly when Sandy is chasing the aliens through the woods.

## "Body and Soul"
*Written by John Green, Edward Heyman, Robert Sour and Frank Eyton (1930). Performed by Django Reinhardt and the Quintette du Hot Club de France (1937).*

Heard as Sandy and Dorrie kiss under an umbrella in the rain. This turns out to be a scene from one of Sandy's films, as does the following clip when Dorrie slaps Sandy too hard. The track continues as the film cuts to Sandy's apartment where the two are together making spaghetti, and then a bird flies in. The song is reprised in full during the end credits.

## *Night on Bald Mountain*
*Written by Modest Mussorgsky (1867). Performed by the Vienna State Opera Orchestra, conducted by Vladimir Golschmann (1960).*

Used twice in scenes from Sandy's films; firstly, when Sidney Pinklestein's hostility has escaped and is being pursued through the woods; and secondly, when Sandy's character is in a laboratory with Tony (Tony Roberts), planning to put Doris's brain into Rita's body.

## "If Dreams Come True"
*Written by Irving Mills, Edgar Sampson and Benny Goodman (1934). Performed by Chick Webb's Savoy Orchestra (1934).*

This is used during the scenes involving Sandy and Isobel. It is heard first as Sandy sees Isobel approaching from a distance and continues as she and Sandy talk while being constantly interrupted by fans, cutting into the following scene where Sandy bumps into Daisy. It is heard again when Sandy takes Isobel to the station to meet her kids and then finally at the end of the film when Sandy follows Isobel to the station and tries to persuade her not to leave, eventually succeeding as they kiss. This then becomes the end of Sandy's most recent film.

## "Hebrew School Rag"
*Written and performed by Dick Hyman (piano).*

Heard briefly as Sandy's sister (Anne de Salvo) and Isobel are looking at old photos of Sandy, continuing as we flashback to a play Sandy appeared in at Hebrew school.

## "One O'Clock Jump"
*Written by Count Basie (1937). Performed by the Jazz Heaven Orchestra.*

Performed by the Jazz Heaven Orchestra during the re-cut ending to Sandy's latest film.

## "Easy to Love"
*Written by Cole Porter (1936). Performed by Dick Hyman (piano).*

This is heard first when Sandy and Tony are talking and drinking at an outside bar, as couples dance in the background. (The song segues into "Just One of Those Things"; see below.) It reappears at the end of the film, as the last members of the audience leave the auditorium and Sandy comes back to pick up his sunglasses, ending as the film ends.

## "Just One of Those Things"
*Written by Cole Porter (1935). Performed by Dick Hyman (piano).*

This is linked to the previous Cole Porter song. It directly follows "Easy to Love" in the scene where Sandy and Tony are in an outside bar and begin talking about Dorrie and the time she had a camera, cutting to a flashback of her taking pictures of pipes. The track is heard again near the end (this time preceding "Easy to Love") as the audience and actors are leaving the auditorium, commenting on Sandy's film.

### "Sugar (That Sugar Baby of Mine)"

Written by Maceo Pinkard, Sidney D. Mitchell and Edna Alexander (1928).

Played by a solo trumpeter in the background as Sandy and Isobel bump into Jack and Daisy outside an open-walled bar.

### Incidental music from *Ladri di Biciclette*

Written by Alessandro Cicognini (1948).[10]

Heard faintly on the soundtrack to De Sica's classic film, watched by Sandy and Daisy.

### "Sweet Georgia Brown"

Written by Maceo Pinkard, Ben Bernie and Kenneth Casey (1925).

Being played by a rehearsal pianist as dancers practice in the background while Sandy is trying to reassure Dorrie about her part in his film.

### "Moonlight Serenade"

Written by Glenn Miller (1939). Performed by Glenn Miller and His Orchestra (1939).

Heard just as the aliens leave and we see shots of hot air balloons. The track continues as Sandy and Daisy watch the balloons land and eventually kiss just as other characters arrive, ending as Sandy gets shot.

### "Stardust"

Written by Hoagy Carmichael and Mitchell Parish (1928). Performed by Louis Armstrong and His Orchestra (1931).

Heard as Sandy is talking to the audience, having just received an award. He talks about Dorrie and the film flashbacks to the two together in his apartment, where the track becomes the record he has put on the record player (see above for a more detailed description). It continues through the subsequent scenes with the critical audience, and when Sandy and Isobel are in the hospital.

# *Sweet and Lowdown* (1999)

*Music and songs from the repertoire, with original music by Dick Hyman.*

As we have seen, jazz themes have provided a backdrop to a number of Allen's earlier films — *Zelig*, *Radio Days*, *Bullets Over Broadway*. With *Sweet and Lowdown*, Allen now brings his beloved jazz to the fore, in what is described as "a beautifully colorful period piece set in the 1930s about the adventures of a wild and eccentric jazz guitar genius played by Sean Penn, who experiences a number of hilarious and harrowing events as he clashes with lovers, musicians and gangsters."[1] The story concerns Emmet Ray, a fictional jazz guitarist who was considered second only to the great Django Reinhardt. Although imaginary, Ray's character resembles a composite of several real-life jazz artists, some of whom exhibited sublime virtuosity in their art but chaotic, comical foibles in their personal lives.[2] Allen presents a screen biography in the same "mockumentary" style as *Take the Money and Run* and *Zelig*, with the story basically made up of a series of anecdotes told by real life (and occasionally bogus) jazz aficionados. The talking heads comprise Nat Hentoff (journalist and jazz historian), Douglas McGrath (filmmaker and jazz enthusiast), Ben Duncan (disc jockey, WFAD-FM), A.J. Pickman (author of *Swing Guitars: American Perspective Series*), Sally Jillian (author of *Guitar Kings*) and Woody Allen himself.

As with his musical *Everyone Says I Love You*, Allen had wanted to make this type of film for some time: "I've been dying to make a jazz movie over the years. To make a jazz movie is an expensive proposition and I'm usually used to making inexpensive films. This to me was more expensive than usual. This time we had the money and did it and it was fun to do. I mean to work for almost a year or eight months or so on a project that involves all that music[—]it was like making *Everyone Says I Love You*. And here I had such a great time making the movie as well because it's not like making a movie about, say, an investment banker which is not too much fun."[3] In fact, the story is actually based on a much earlier project of Allen's, as Lax points out: "*Sweet and Lowdown* is a lighter and much reworked version of *The Jazz Baby*, a script Woody wrote more than thirty years ago. His first version of the story of a self-destructive jazz guitar genius named Emmet Ray is so unrelievably bleak that he realized he would have to inject some spirit if the film had any chance of working."[4]

The title for *Sweet and Lowdown* was inspired by Gershwin's song of the same name, a "portmanteau phrase, arrived at from 'sweet and low' and 'lowdown.'"[5] But as Allen points out, it was primarily chosen to reflect the duality between the two main protagonists: "There were phrases that I was trying to get for the picture. The first one I thought of was "Sweet and Hot" which is a jazz phrase, and I felt it characterized the two characters in the picture. But I felt "Sweet and Lowdown" was even better. "Sweet and Lowdown" was a musical phrase, idiomatic, and she [Hattie] was sweet and he [Emmet] was lowdown."[6]

Dick Hyman, Allen's long-time musical collaborator, is once again heavily involved. In addition to conducting and occasionally playing, he has made a series of period arrangements which lovingly recreate the sound of the swing era. Most of the songs are jazz standards, but the score also includes two original compositions especially written for the film. Hyman has assembled an all-star line-up of contemporary jazz musicians. At the forefront is Howard Alden, who Owen Cordle in *Jazz Times* says "may be the best guitarist of his generation." Alden has worked with an impressive list of jazz musicians, including Woody Herman, Benny Carter, Mel Powell, Bud Freeman and Dizzy Gillespie. According to Alden, "Dick called me and asked, 'Howard, can you play like Django Reinhardt?' I laughingly said, 'Yes, sure, of course. Who can't?' I told him I'd try. Originally, I thought I was getting called for just a couple of days recording. But the producer wanted me working with Sean so it turned the project into six months, rather than two days."[7] Eventually Alden was chosen to perform all of Emmet Ray's guitar solos which Sean Penn mimes. According to the *Sweet and Lowdown* official Web site, "Penn, who has never played the guitar, learned the hyper-dexterous fingering for some thirty virtuoso jazz songs."[8] Alden himself remarks, "Sean is great to work with.... He had never played guitar before and I don't think he had really had any concept or experience with jazz. But he got into it right away and by the end of the first four months, I had him playing a few tunes and, more important for his role, was that he was an incredibly good observationist. He picked up on how to really look natural playing the guitar and to look like he knew what he was doing. He picked up mannerisms from me that I didn't even know I had."[9]

Alden is joined by fellow guitarist Bucky Pizzerelli (who has performed with Benny Goodman, Frank Sinatra, Skitch Henderson, Doc Severinson, Mitch Miller, Les Paul and Stéphane Grappelli), Kelly Friesen (bass), Ted Sommer (drums) and Ken Peplowski. Peplowski was one of the most gifted clarinetists to emerge in the 1990s and was a member of Benny Goodman's last band; he has also recorded with Mel Torme, Peggy Lee, Rosemary Clooney and Charlie Byrd, and is a frequent collaborator with Alden.[10] These five make up the Emmet Ray Hot Quintet, which is clearly modeled on Reinhardt's famous Quintette du Hot Club de France. However, as there is no equivalent for Stéphane Grappelli's violin, the group has more in common with Reinhardt's later quintet, which he formed after the outbreak of the Second World War, with Hubert Rostaing's clarinet replacing Grappelli.

Django Reinhardt is, in fact, a central character in *Sweet and Lowdown*; although he only appears very briefly, his presence haunts Ray throughout the whole film. Ray idolizes him out of all proportion; he cries every time he hears his music and faints every time he sees him. Ray repeatedly refers to Reinhardt, mostly notably when he is boasting about his own ability: "I'm the greatest guitar player in the world. Except maybe this gypsy." But even here he cannot quite bring himself to be dishonest and so refers to him in a derogatory manner. To accentuate the shadow that Reinhardt casts over Ray, Allen and Hyman have produced a score that incorporates a number of Reinhardt's original recordings. These have been placed at significant points: it is Reinhardt, not Ray (Alden), that we hear over the opening credits, thus announcing his importance from the outset; when we do hear Emmet perform for the first time, he quotes "Mystery Pacific," one of Reinhardt's original compositions; and when Emmet plays a recording to Blanche (Uma Thurman) it is Reinhardt's "Liebestraum No. 3," not one of his own recordings. The score also includes other tracks that are particularly associated with Reinhardt. With Ray being in awe of "this gypsy in France," it is, of course, natural for him to perform the same works, and it is no surprise to find that the large majority of the songs played by Ray's group have been recorded by Reinhardt. The score even includes a trio version (two guitars and bass) of "I'll See You in My Dreams," which corresponds to Reinhardt's classic 1939 recording, used previously by Allen in *Stardust Memories*.

In addition to Hyman's original compositions and arrangements, the score includes a number of pre-existent jazz recordings. Even though the film is centered around one specific musician and his band, with much of the music in the film coming naturally from them, Allen still manages to incorporate some fine examples of scoring, and utilizes a host of eminent musicians from the period. Some of these recordings are used by Allen in the customary way, for example, over the opening credits or accompanying traveling shots ("Clarinet Marmalade" and "Indiana"). But he also illustrates how a particularly appropriate piece of music can be used to enhance a scene with no dialogue, and add to the comedic visual effect. Notable examples include Bunny Berigan's sublime rendition of "Caravan," where Allen uses the desert imagery to complement Hattie's (Samantha Morton) Hollywood filming of *The Tomb of the Mummy*; Sidney Bechet's reefer song, "Viper Mad," when Ray indulges in pot smoking; and the hold-up/car chase sequence accompanied by Henry Busse's delightful "Hot Lips," which reminds one of the Keystone Cops. It should also be mentioned that, in addition to the references to Django Reinhardt, the score includes a track by Eddie Lang, another notable jazz guitarist from the 1920s and '30s.

These original period recordings, together with Hyman's deft arrangements, combine to produce a score that succeeds in evoking the atmosphere of the 1930s and provides the perfect accompaniment to Allen's jazz-age fable. Even though the film is replete with music, *Sweet and Lowdown* is not a musical in the traditional sense, as Allen points out: "There's a lot of music in it, but to me a 'musical' is always a classic musical. You know, *My Fair Lady* or *Meet Me in St Louis*."[11] But music is nevertheless at the heart of the film. "Throughout it all, the music adds to the film's humor and pathos.... In the end, the movie is permeated not only by music, but by the spirit of jazz."[12]

## "When Day Is Done"
*Written by Robert Katscher and Buddy G. DeSylva (English lyric) (1926). Performed by Django Reinhardt and the Quintette du Hot Club de France (1937).*

Opening credits. The track is timed so that the introduction ends and the main theme begins at the point when the film title comes onto the screen.

## "Clarinet Marmalade"
*Written by Larry Shields and Henry W. Ragas (1918). Performed by Ted Lewis's Orchestra (1928).*

Heard as the film cuts to the roadside joint in Chicago where Emmet Ray (Sean Penn) is supposed to be performing. It is heard again a little later when Emmet is driving from the pool hall to the club.

## "Speak to Me of Love" ("Parlez-Moi d'Amour")
*Written by Jean Lenoir and Bruce Siever (English lyric) (1930). Arranged by Howard Alden and Dick Hyman. Performed by Howard Alden (solo guitar).*

The first piece performed solo by Emmet when he finally arrives at the club.

## "Mystery Pacific"
*Written by Django Reinhardt and Stéphane Grappelli (1937). Performed by Howard Alden (solo guitar), Bucky Pizzerelli (rhythm guitar) and Kelly Friesen (bass).*

## "Limehouse Blues"
*Written by Philip Braham and Douglas Furber (1922). Performed by Howard Alden (solo guitar), Bucky Pizzerelli (rhythm guitar) and Kelly Friesen (bass).*

Following on from "Speak to Me of Love," these pieces are performed next at the club by Emmet with his band now joining in. It was Howard Alden's idea to use the imitation train sound from "Mystery Pacific" as a brief introduction.

## "It Don't Mean a Thing (If It Ain't Got That Swing)"
*Written by Duke Ellington and Irving*

*Mills (1932). Performed by Howard Alden (solo guitar), Byron Stripling (trumpet), Joe Wilder (trumpet), Ken Peplowski (clarinet), Jerome Richardson (saxophone), Chuck Wilson (saxophone), Joel Helleny (trombone), Dick Hyman (piano), Kelly Friesen (bass) and Ted Sommer (drums).*

A very brief extract of this track (over six minutes in: 6:21 on the soundtrack album) is being played during the jam session in the back room of the black musicians' house in Chicago that Emmet is visiting. We hear the track properly later during the scenes where Emmet falls through the roof and inadvertently lands on some counterfeiters, continuing through the scenes where Emmet brings Hattie presents in his new car and takes her out to a restaurant.

### "Out of Nowhere"

*Written by John Green and Edward Heyman (1931). Performed by Dick Hyman (piano).*

Heard during the same jam session as "It Don't Mean a Thing." It is being played on the piano in the back room, while Emmet talks about Django Reinhardt and himself in the kitchen.

### "I'll See You in My Dreams"

*Written by Isham Jones and Gus Kahn (1924). Performed by Howard Alden (solo guitar), Bucky Pizzerelli (rhythm guitar) and Kelly Friesen (bass).*

Heard first when Emmet has a large crescent moon made for him, which he plans to use for a dramatic entrance at his next gig. The song is heard again later as one of the first three tracks Emmet records in the studio for the RCA Victor label. It is repeated in full during the end credits.

### "Sweet Georgia Brown"

*Written by Maceo Pinkard, Ben Bernie and Kenneth Casey (1925). Performed by Howard Alden (solo guitar), Bucky Pizzerelli (rhythm guitar), Ken Peplowski (clarinet), Kelly Friesen (bass) and Ted Sommer (drums).*

Played at the gig where Emmet attempts to make his entrance on the crescent moon he had specially made.

### "Avalon"

*Written by Vincent Rose, Al Jolson and Buddy G. DeSylva (1920). Performed by Coleman Hawkins with Michel Warlop and His Orchestra (1935).*[13]

Heard while Emmet and Billy Shields (Brian Markinson) are looking to pick up girls on the boardwalk at a New Jersey resort.

### "After You've Gone"

*Written by Henry Creamer and Turner Layton (1918). Performed by Joe Venuti, Eddie Lang and Their All-Star Orchestra, featuring Benny Goodman (clarinet) and Jack Teagarden (trombone and vocals) (1931).*

Heard a little later during the scenes where Emmet and Billy are with Hattie and Gracie (Kaili Vernoff) and rent a riverboat, continuing through the following scenes at the resort.

### "I'm Forever Blowing Bubbles"

*Written by Jean Kenbrovin and John William Kellette (pseudonyms for James Kendis, James Brockman and Nat Vincent) (1919). Arranged by Howard Alden and Dick Hyman. Performed by Howard Alden (solo guitar).*

Played solo by Emmet after he and Hattie have made love. Before playing it, Emmet asks Hattie what her favorite song is, but then quickly realizes that she cannot answer and so plays this. Hattie is taken by the song, and it then becomes "their song," recurring throughout the film. It is played by Emmet when Hattie is changing the car wheel and when Emmet opens Hattie's birthday card. Most significantly, it is heard twice at the end of the film after Emmet has lost Hattie. He plays it when he is with Ellie (Gretchen Mol) at the railway tracks, interrupting "Sweet Sue, Just You" as he begins to think of Hattie. The song is then repeated as Emmet finally shows some emotion by smashing his guitar against a lamppost and crying. It continues as A.J. Pickman and Woody Allen comment on how, after this, Emmet Ray's playing improved and was equal to that of Django Reinhardt, before he faded into obscurity.

## "S-H-I-N-E"
*Written by Ford Dabney, Cecil Mack and Lew Brown (1924). Performed by Howard Alden (solo guitar), Bucky Pizzerelli (rhythm guitar), Ken Peplowski (clarinet), Kelly Friesen (bass) and Ted Sommer (drums).*

Played at the club by Emmet and his quintet, while Hattie watches as she eats desserts. It continues through the following scenes where Emmet takes Hattie out to watch trains, choose clothes and watch him play pool. The track is repeated in full during the end credits.

## "There'll Be Some Changes Made"
*Written by Billy Higgins and W. Benton Overstreet (1921). Performed by Howard Alden (solo guitar), Bucky Pizzerelli (rhythm guitar), Ken Peplowski (clarinet), Kelly Friesen (bass) and Ted Sommer (drums).*

Being played by Emmet and his quintet during another gig at the club, as Emmet is approached by a woman with jet black hair.

## "Viper Mad" (aka "Pleasure Mad")
*Written by Sidney Bechet and Clarence Williams (1924).[14] Performed by Sidney Bechet and Noble Sissle's Swingsters, featuring O'Neil Spencer (vocal/drums) (1938).*

Heard after the gig when Emmet flirts with other girls at the club and is handed a reefer by the woman who approached him earlier, cutting to a shot of an unhappy Hattie before Emmet wakes up out of town.

## "Indiana (Back Home Again In)"
*Written by Ballard MacDonald and James F. Hanley (1917). Arranged by Glenn Miller. Performed by Red Nichols and His Five Pennies, featuring Benny Goodman (clarinet), Jack Teagarden and Glenn Miller (trombones) (1929).*

Heard briefly while Emmet, Hattie and Billy are driving to Hollywood. (The music stops before we hear a precocious solo by the then–19-year-old Benny Goodman.)

## "Aloha Oe" (aka "Farewell to Thee")
*Written by Queen Lili'Uokalani (1878). Performed by Dick Monday.*

Played on a saw at the talent contest.

## "Abide with Me"
*Written by William H. Monk and Henry F. Lyte (1861). Performed by Mary Stout.*

Sung at the talent contest.

## "Twelfth Street Rag"
*Written by Euday L. Bowman (1914). Arranged and performed by Howard Alden (solo guitar).*

Played by Emmet at the talent contest.

## "All of Me"
*Written by Gerald Marks and Seymour B. Simons (1931). Performed by Carol Woods (vocal), Howard Alden (solo guitar), Bucky Pizzerelli (rhythm guitar), Ken Peplowski (clarinet), Kelly Friesen (bass) and Ted Sommer (drums).*

## "The Peanut Vendor"
*Written by Moises Simons, L. Wolfe Gilbert and Marion Sunshine (1931). Performed by Carol Woods (vocal), Howard Alden (solo guitar), Bucky Pizzerelli (rhythm guitar),*

144 / *Sweet and Lowdown* (1999)

Ken Peplowski (clarinet), Kelly Friesen (bass) and Ted Sommer (drums).

A mixture of the two songs (mostly "All of Me" with "The Peanut Vendor" used as an interpolation) performed at the Hollywood filming.

### "Caravan"

Written by Duke Ellington, Juan Tizol and Irving Mills (1937). Performed by Bunny Berigan and His Orchestra (1937).

Heard during the scenes where Hattie is in make-up and filming repeated takes of the film *The Tomb of the Mummy*, where she is kissed by William Weston (Fred Goehner). The track continues as Woody Allen relays the events.

### "Old Fashioned Love"

Written by James P. Johnson and Cecil Mack (1923). Performed by Howard Alden (solo guitar), Byron Stripling (trumpet), Joe Wilder (trumpet), Ken Peplowski (clarinet), Jerome Richardson (saxophone), Chuck Wilson (saxophone), Joel Helleny (trombone), Dick Hyman (piano), Kelly Friesen (bass) and Ted Sommer (drums).

A Dixieland arrangement of this is being played at the club while Emmet and his band are backstage and someone tells Emmet that Django Reinhardt is in the audience.

### "Just a Gigolo"

Written by Leonello Casucci, Julius Brammer and Irving Caesar (English lyric) (1930). Performed by Howard Alden (solo guitar), Bucky Pizzerelli (rhythm guitar), Ken Peplowski (clarinet), Kelly Friesen (bass) and Ted Sommer (drums).

Played by Emmet's quintet outside at a party.

### "Nevertheless (I'm in Love with You)"

Written by Bert Kalmar and Harry Ruby (1931). Performed by Bert Ambrose and His Orchestra (1931).

Heard while Emmet, at the same party, steals a box and is caught by Blanche Williams.

### "3:00 AM Blues"

Written by Dick Hyman. Performed by Howard Alden (solo guitar), Byron Stripling (trumpet), Joe Wilder (trumpet), Ken Peplowski (clarinet), Jerome Richardson (saxophone), Chuck Wilson (saxophone), Joel Helleny (trombone), Dick Hyman (piano), Kelly Friesen (bass) and Ted Sommer (drums).

Back in the black musicians' house in Chicago, this is being played in the back room while Emmet and Blanche talk and eat chili. Emmet then joins in the jam session.

### "Liebestraum No. 3"

Written by Franz Liszt (1850). Performed by Django Reinhardt and the Quintette du Hot Club de France (1937).

A recording of this is playing on the record player when Emmet is with Blanche in his apartment. It continues during the succeeding scenes when they get married and when they are in the pool room.

### "Since My Best Gal Turned Me Down"

Written by Ray Ludwig and Howdy Quicksell (1927). Performed by Bix Beiderbecke and His Gang: Bix Beiderbecke (cornet), Bill Rank (trombone), Don Murray (clarinet), Adrian Rollini (bass saxophone), Frank Signorelli (piano) and Chauncey Morehouse (drums) (1927).

Heard first when Blanche comes into the club to persuade the owner, Mr. Bedloe (Brad Garrett), to give Emmett his job back. While waiting, she meets Bedloe's bodyguard, Al Torrio (Anthony LaPaglia) and they flirt with each other. It returns briefly later when Blanche and Torrio go into the back room together, drawing the curtain behind them.

## "Wrap Your Troubles in Dreams (and Dream Your Troubles Away)"

*Written by Harry Harris, Ted Koehler and Billy Moll (1931). Performed by Howard Alden (solo guitar), Bucky Pizzerelli (rhythm guitar) and Kelly Friesen (bass).*

Being played by Emmet and his band while Blanche watches, asking herself why she is bored with her husband. The track continues into the succeeding scene in the pool hall.

## "Hot Lips"

*Written by Henry Busse, Harry Lange and Lou Davis (1922). Performed by Henry Busse and His Orchestra (1934).*

Heard when Emmet secretly follows Blanche as she meets Al Torrio and sneaks into the back of their car. It returns when they pull up at the gas station, continuing during the hold up and car chase. The track is repeated for all of the alternative gas station scenes.

## "You Were Meant for Me"

*Written by Nacio Herb Brown and Arthur Freed (1929).*

The title of this song is sung briefly by Emmet to the police as he gets out of the bullet-ridden car after it has been crashed by the two hold-up guys. As he emerges with his gun in his hand, looking decidedly guilty, he says, "I'm Emmet Ray. I'm the greatest guitar player in the world. Except maybe this gypsy. Perhaps you've heard my recording of 'You Were Meant for Me,' RCA Victor — *You were meant for me...*"

It is interesting to note that on the information card shown before the film starts, there is a list of six songs that Emmet Ray recorded for RCA Victor, but this is not one of them. The six given are: "I'll See You in My Dreams," "My Melancholy Baby," "I'm Forever Blowing Bubbles," "Exactly Like You," "Unfaithful Woman" and "Dancing in the Dark."

## "Unfaithful Woman"

*Written by Dick Hyman. Performed by Howard Alden (solo guitar), Bucky Pizzerelli (rhythm guitar) Ken Peplowski (clarinet), Kelly Friesen (bass) and Ted Sommer (drums).*

Played at the New Jersey recording sessions. The song is presented as an original composition by Ray, and reflects his feelings after Blanche's infidelity.

## "Lulu's Back in Town"

*Written by Harry Warren and Al Dubin (1935). Performed by Dick Hyman (piano), Kelly Friesen (bass) and Ted Sommer (drums).*

Being played in the bar (the scene was shot in Chumley's in New York) where Emmet is talking to Ellie, before he takes her to watch trains.

## "Sweet Sue, Just You"

*Written by Victor Young and Will J. Harris (1928). Arranged by Howard Alden and Dick Hyman. Performed by Howard Alden (solo guitar).*

Played solo by Emmet when he is with Ellie at the railway tracks. He stops in the middle and, as his thoughts turn to Hattie, plays "I'm Forever Blowing Bubbles" instead, which induces his emotional outburst.

# Take the Money and Run (1969)

*Original music composed by Marvin Hamlisch.*

Described as "the first unadulterated 'Woody' movie,"[1] *Take the Money and Run* is unquestionably Woody Allen's first film "proper," with Allen not only writing the screenplay (with Mickey Rose), but directing and starring as well. "That's really where I feel my career in films began. Before that it was all reasons not to go into the cinema."[2] Likewise, it is also the first film in which Allen had to make a decision about what music would be used. Following the current trends, he chose to employ a composer, and at the suggestion of producer Jack Grossberg, Marvin Hamlisch was brought in to provide an original score. Prior to this, Hamlisch had only scored *The Swimmer* (1968), starring Burt Lancaster. The composer had been studying at college at the same time as working on the film, and the combination had given him an ulcer. Having only recently left the hospital when he got the call to score Woody Allen's film, he thought to himself, "There's no way I'm going to get myself into this kind of mess again. I've got to finish school and live up to the promise I gave my father once and for all. I made my decision. A Woody Allen film? Me, Marvin Hamlisch? Of course I said yes."[3]

Hamlisch's score is primarily based on two principal themes — the main title music and a plaintive waltz — both of which permeate the film in varying forms. The waltz is heard first at the beginning of a long pre-titles sequence and then recurs later in the film, often to reflect Virgil's pitiful life. The main theme appears as dramatic title music over the opening and closing credits, but is also transformed into a love theme for Virgil (Woody Allen) and Louise (Janet Margolin). Both these themes display Hamlisch's innate gift for lyricism, something he would display more fully later in his career. In addition, the film's mock-documentary format presented a number of opportunities for the composer to ape various musical styles, which suited Hamlisch's ability to compose music in a variety of genres. Supplementing the two main themes mentioned above, Hamlisch also includes a Sousa-like march, klezmer music, 1950s "montage music," jazz and Keystone Cop–like chase numbers. (This "mockumentary" format foreshadowed Allen's later film *Zelig*, in which Dick Hyman composed a score which also draws on a wide range of musical styles, several of which are similar to those heard in *Take the Money and Run*.)

According to Ralph Rosenblum — who was brought in to help Allen with the editing — Hamlisch and the director were "two emotionally opposite men" and had certain difficulties working together. "His collaboration with Woody, as important as it was for the picture, was not easy for Marvin, whose expressiveness turned melodramatic alongside Allen's unswerving calm."[4] Hamlisch himself remarks, "Woody was very quiet when I met him. He was quiet when I worked for him. He was quiet when I recorded the music for *Take the Money and Run* and then on *Bananas*. He hardly said a word to me unless he didn't like something I wrote. The only difficulty I had with our relationship was trying to tell when he was happy or unhappy, because he never really communicated with me."⁵ Nevertheless, Hamlisch produced an effective score which complemented Allen's comedic style. As Lax points out, "Comedy demands accompaniment and the music is a great, almost subconscious part of *Take the Money and Run*."⁶ And despite his inexperience, Hamlisch's talent impressed Rosenblum: "Of all the composers I've worked with, and there have been many, for composers often work directly with editors, none compares to Hamlisch in knowledge and ability. His mind is so free and so quick to make connections that if he accepts your intent, he can write a new piece of music in virtually any style in an astonishingly short time."⁷

Hamlisch's skill in this respect proved useful, as, with Rosenblum's involvement, it was necessary to re-enlist the composer to rewrite certain sections of the score. One scene in particular required a drastic change. "When I did *Take the Money and Run*, there's the scene where I come home and I'm in the bathroom, dressing to go on a date with Janet Margolin. Marvin Hamlisch, under my direction, did a too slow Chaplinesque thing, this kind of melancholy thing. And it was—*death*!"⁸ In order to inject some life into the scene, Rosenblum made an important suggestion: "I realized that what made it maudlin instead of funny was the mournful music that accompanied the wordless scene. I laid in a piece of upbeat Eubie Blake ragtime in its place, and the effect was magical."⁹ In Allen's interview with Melvyn Bragg for *The South Bank Show* in 1994, the director has a similar recollection: "The editor who I was working with put a Eubie Blake tune behind it—real fast and up-piano. And it just transformed it miraculously; there wasn't a frame of that scene re-cut in any way."¹⁰ From the above accounts, it would be easy to suppose that the accompaniment heard in the finished film is Eubie Blake; however, this is not the case. Both Allen and Rosenblum correctly recall using a Eubie Blake piece to edit the scene, but then Hamlisch was requested to compose new music in a similar style to the Eubie Blake recording.¹¹ The end result had the desired effect. "The whole thing just came to life. I was suddenly just bouncing along. It made all the difference in the world."¹²

Another change required Hamlisch to construct a re-working of Quincy Jones's "Soul Bossa Nova." As Rosenblum recalls, "The important thing about Marvin was that he could grasp immediately the kind of music we needed in order to transform the tone of the scene, and unfailingly provided it. A typical example was the escape from the chain gang.... I replaced the chase music that originally accompanied the bicycle shot with a piece of Quincy Jones bossa nova. Hamlisch immediately liked and understood the alteration and wrote an original piece of bossa nova that took the joke all the way to its completion. For other scenes, we simply told him what tone we were looking for, and he composed impeccably appropriate music."¹³

It is clear then that Rosenblum's input on the film was considerable. "Probably seventy-five percent of the movie that was released is from my first edit, but what Ralph did was the difference between living and dying. My version was sure death. I edited it but I didn't make it alive. Ralph made it breathe. I feel he saved me on that picture."[14] Moreover, Rosenblum also had an important impact on Allen. One significant technique that Rosenblum introduced to the fledgling director was the editing of scenes with music. As we have seen, Rosenblum would play records behind scenes to give Allen the general idea of what was required and would then get Hamlisch to write what was necessary. This technique proved highly influential, and can be seen as having a seminal effect on how Allen would use music in his later films.[1]

## *Zelig* (1983)

*Music composed and adapted by Dick Hyman, with additional music and songs from the repertoire.*

After nearly ten years of providing recorded music for his films, Allen decided to employ a composer to write most of the score for his next film, *Zelig*, a pseudo-documentary about a fictional 1920s *cause célèbre* who, like a human chameleon, has the ability to change his appearance to look like those around him. *Zelig* is the first in a triptych of films in which Dick Hyman plays a key role as composer, pianist and arranger. Here, Hyman was brought in to provide a score, recreating the sounds of the Jazz Age where original music — composed in the styles of that era — blends seamlessly with genuine period pieces. Having written a small piano piece for *Stardust Memories*, Hyman is now given the opportunity to expand in a field in which he excels. "Dick Hyman is a wonderful jazz musician and composer and arranger who lives in New York. He's a brilliant pianist. And whenever I need special things, I contact him. Here I needed special songs written and special arrangements for the chameleon thing and he did that. He composed the music. *Zelig* was a movie where I needed special compositions and special documentary music, and he did that. He's got the same feel that I have. He's basically jazz-orientated. He likes and knows all the kinds of songs that I like. When I need the kind of songs that Cole Porter would write or the kind of jazz arrangements that Paul Whiteman or Jelly Roll Morton would do, Dick Hyman knows that code."[1]

The remarkable score for *Zelig* is arguably Dick Hyman's finest to date, and certainly his best for a Woody Allen film, outshining even the lyrical *The Purple Rose of Cairo*. Hyman composed and wrote lyrics for five authentic-sounding period songs: "Doin' the Chameleon," "Chameleon Days," "Leonard the Lizard," "You Have Such Reptile Eyes" and "You May Be Six People, but I Love You." Of these, the latter three were based on titles given to him by Allen himself. As well as these songs, he supplies dramatic music to accompany the narrator's voice-overs and many of the ersatz Hearst Metrotone and Pathe newsreels. In order to accompany Zelig's various transformations and add flavor to the various settings and events seen in the film (a Communist march, a Parisian music hall, a Spanish bullfight and Nazi Germany), Hyman skillfully provides an assortment of nationalistic-like miniatures, and also incorporates a number of apt quotations from popular pieces by other composers. Furthermore, the first few notes of "Leonard the Lizard" are used as a recurring motif, appearing in various guises, which the composer cleverly assimilates into the fabric of the score. This motif actually antedates the song within the chronology of the story, and so the audience is not aware of its significance until further on in the film.

Hyman's score is complemented with a selection of some of the most popular songs of the time. These include "Charleston," "Runnin' Wild," "I Love My Baby, My Baby Loves Me," "Five Foot Two, Eyes of Blue" and "I'm Sittin' on Top of the World," all of which encapsulate the era perfectly. Perhaps it is a little surprising that Allen did not include anything by Cole Porter; however, he is mentioned. Allen asked a number of real life "talking heads" to be in the film, and one of these was Ada Smith, better known as Bricktop. In the 1920s, Bricktop's was a popular Paris nightclub, which was frequented by Cole Porter. In her interview she states, "Cole Porter was fascinated by Leonard. He once wrote a line in a song, 'You're the Tops, You're Leonard Zelig,' but then he couldn't find anything to rhyme with 'Zelig.'"[2]

The songs are performed either in recordings by original contemporary artists (Guy Lombardo and Ben Bernie), or have been arranged and performed by Dick Hyman with various studio orchestras. Several singers were deliberately brought in to impersonate some of the leading performers of the day — Al Jolson, Helen Kane, Fanny Brice — and these performances enhance further the "realism" of the film. In addition, there are a number of recordings by the Charleston City All-Stars (made not in the 1920s but in the 1950s on Enoch Light's "Grand Award" label), which by chance also featured Dick Hyman. "Woody Allen often works with specific records in mind during the editing process. Before I began to score *Zelig*, he had discovered several items in a long-out-of-print album dating back to the 1950s. These performances, by a group known as the Charleston City All-Stars, expressed to him the right relationship of music and image in certain scenes, and are now embodied in the *Zelig* score. By a strange coincidence, and with the inscrutable working of destiny and my personal *karma*, I was the All-Stars' piano player."[3]

Dick Hyman has kindly provided me with the titles of his original compositions and arrangements for the score to *Zelig*. These have been incorporated within the following list of songs and music, thus giving a comprehensive overview to all of the music in the film. All compositions are by Dick Hyman unless otherwise stated and are performed by him with a variety of studio musicians.

### "Charleston"

*Written by James P. Johnson and Cecil Mack (1923). Featuring Bernie Leighton (piano).*

Heard over the opening Jazz Age sequence. The narrator (Patrick Horgan) states that the year is 1928, and we see various shots from the period, including a party at a Long Island estate, where F. Scott Fitzgerald is writing in his notebook. He mentions Leonard Zelig (Woody Allen) a man who appears to have changed from an aristocrat with an upper class Boston accent to a Democrat speaking with the kitchen help.

### "Leonard the Lizard" Motif

A somber version is heard as a coda to the "Charleston." This motif subsequently permeates the score, often appearing in cues with other titles; some, but not all, are mentioned below.

### "The Ballpark Theme"

Heard during the Hearst Metrotone newsreel reporting on a "strange new player" at the New York Yankees' training camp. Note how Hyman paraphrases the well-known "Take Me Out to the Ball Game," a song written in 1908 by Jack Norworth and Albert von Tilzer, which is traditionally sung at baseball games.

### "Chicago (That Toddlin' Town)"

*Written by Fred Fisher (1922). Featuring Mel Davis (cornet).*

Heard briefly when we see shots of a speakeasy on the south side of Chicago, where Zelig changes into a gangster and a jazz musician. The hand we see rapping on the door of the speakeasy is cleverly synchronized with the solo drum introduction to the song.

### "Sleuthing in Chinatown"

Heard as the New York police investigate Zelig's disappearance. The track returns a little later when they eventually find a "Chinese" Zelig in Chinatown.

### "Vesti la giubba" from *Pagliacci*

*Written by Ruggiero Leoncavallo (1892).*

This celebrated aria from Leoncavallo's one act opera is quoted briefly as we see a photograph of Zelig as Canio in *Pagliacci* (taken from the famous photograph of Enrico Caruso).

### "Ukrainian Joys"

*Featuring Mel Davis (trumpet) and Vince Giordano (tuba).*

A typically Jewish melody heard as the film looks at Zelig's background, including a scene where his father appears in an Orthodox version of *A Midsummer Night's Dream*.

### "Leonard the Lizard" Motif

Heard as Eudora Fletcher (Mia Farrow) arranges a series of experiments and invites the skeptical staff at Manhattan Hospital to observe Zelig transform into a psychiatrist, a Frenchman and a Chinese person. The music continues as a series of newspaper clippings are seen.

### "Hot Off the Presses" (Includes "Leonard the Lizard" Motif)

Heard as fresh stories about Zelig roll off the presses, continuing as the doctors claim to have the situation in hand.

### "Coffin"

This cue begins with a funereal dirge, heard briefly as we see pallbearers carrying Dr. Birsky's (Paul Nevens) coffin, after he has died of a brain tumor. The music then changes as we see Eudora Fletcher walking up the steps to the hospital, continuing as more experiments are carried out, one of which turns Zelig's legs upside down and reversed. We then see news stands selling papers, as the press and public hang on every bit of news.

### "Art Card Music for New York City"

*Original newsreel music or from a stock music library.*

Heard as a newsreel begins, stating, "Hospital Patient Astonishes Medical World."

### "Who Says Women Are Just Good for Sewing?"

Following on from the previous Art Card, this is heard as we see Zelig undergoing further experiments, during which he becomes obese and black. This music is reprised later in the film.

### "Leonard the Lizard" Motif

Heard as newspaper articles headline with stories about a "Human Chameleon."

### "Hot Off the Presses" (Includes "Leonard the Lizard" Motif)

This music returns as we see shots of New York's theater district. The narrator comments, "Overnight, Leonard Zelig has become the topic of conversation everywhere."

### "Doin' the Chameleon"

*Sung by Bernie Knee, Steve Clayton and Tony Wells.*

The first of Dick Hyman's period songs is a foxtrot, composed in the style of the Rhythm Boys, a popular male vocal trio who performed with Paul Whiteman's orchestra during the late 1920s, and featured a young Bing Crosby. It is heard during the sequence where the dance craze sweeps the nation. We see various shots of people dancing to it in clubs and speakeasies and a man with a "Don Brown Dance Studio" sandwich board advertising the latest dance steps to "The Charleston" and "The Chameleon." It continues as Zelig undergoes more experiments, eventually turning into a Scotsman.[4] The song is reprised in full during the end credits.

### "L'Internationale"

*Written by Eugène Pottier and Pierre Degeyter (1871/1888).*

This anthem, written in Paris in 1871, has become strongly associated with leftist movements and Communism, particularly in Russia, where it was the official anthem of the Soviet Union between 1917 and 1944. Like "Die Fahne Hoch" (see below), it is frequently used in films and has appeared in, among others, *Doctor Zhivago* (1965), *Amarcord* (1973) and *Reds* (1981). In *Zelig* we hear it briefly as we see shots of marching Communists.

### "Ku Klux Klan"

Ominous music used to accompany scenes of Ku Klux Klan members marching down the street and gathering around a burning cross.

### "A New Twist"

Heard as Zelig is escorted out of the hospital by his half-sister, Ruth (Mary Louise Wilson), who takes him into her custody.

### "Runnin' Wild"

*Written by Arthur Harrington Gibbs, Joe Grey and Leo Wood (1922). Performed by the Charleston City All-Stars, featuring Dick Hyman (piano) and Bobby Byrne (trombone) (1958).*

Heard during the sequence where Zelig is exhibited as "The Phenomenon of the Ages" by his half sister and her "dubious-looking lover," Martin Geist (Sol Lomita). Crowds of people line the roads to glimpse Zelig as he is displayed as a freak.

### "The Changing Man Concerto"

*Featuring Bernie Leighton (piano) and Dick Hyman (piano). Note that both these pianists played at different points of the recording of this work.*

*The Changing Man* is the title of the film within the film, a 1935 biopic of Zelig's life, parodying Warner Brothers' historical/biographical movies of the thirties such as *The Story of Louis Pasteur* (1935) and *The Life of Emil Zola* (1936). We see two clips, the first when Eudora Fletcher is concerned about the custody of Zelig; the second during the Munich Rally where Eudora is waving to Zelig and they are eventually reunited. The music apes the romantic, Rachmaninov-like mini concertos used in a number of films at this time, which culminated in the 1940s with works such as Richard Addinsell's *Warsaw Concerto*.

### "Chameleon Days"

*Performed by Mae Questel (impersonating Helen Kane).[5]*

Heard during shots of various Zelig novelties and endorsements. We then see a fake HMV Victor 78rpm record label, which notes the song as a foxtrot composed by Farrell and Garris with the vocal by Helen Kane (Hyman deftly includes her trademark "boop boop de doop" in his parody) accompanied by Phil Sable and His Orchestra. The song is reprised in full during the end credits.

This song is the first in a sequence of four songs about Zelig, which accompany a montage of fabricated sheet music covers unfolding one after the other.

### "You May Be Six People, but I Love You"

*Sung by Bernie Knee.*

The fictitious sheet music cover states, "From the show 'Freshman Follies,' words by Norman Gaines and music by Harvey Rosten."

### "Leonard the Lizard"

*Sung by Bernie Knee, Steve Clayton and Tony Wells.*

The fictitious sheet music cover states, "Words and music by Al Koenig [a reference to Woody Allen's real name, Allen Koenigsberg], writer of 'Sweethearts and You,' from the picture 'Hearts of the City.'"

Having previously heard the opening motif of this song on numerous occasions, we now hear an extract of the song itself.

### "You Have Such Reptile Eyes"

*Sung by Rosemarie Jun.*

The fictitious sheet music cover states, "Music by Chester Kelly, writer of 'Love Dream Days,' words by Matt Harris. Sung by Corrine Mackay. A George Rogers Production."

### "Endless Exhibitions" ("Leonard the Lizard" Motif)

Heard as we see a shot of a New York street with a theater marquee in the foreground advertising Leonard Zelig, and underneath his name, that of Eddie Cantor. The music continues as Zelig is seen with Clara Bow in Hollywood, with Jack Dempsey and with both Calvin Coolidge and Herbert Hoover.

### "Ça C'est Paris" (aka "Paree!" with English words by Leo Robin)

*Written by José Padilla, Charles Jacques, Leopold di Lima and Lucien Boyer (1926).*

A brief quotation of this song (made famous by the flamboyant French singer Mistinguett) is heard as the film cuts to Paris and we see three men looking at a poster advertising "L'Homme Caméléon." Segues into...

### "La Mattchiche" (aka "La Sorella" and "La Maxixe")

*Written by Charles Borel-Clerc (1905).*

This famous French song-cum-march was the signature piece of the café-concert singer Felix Mayol and typified "Gay Paree" in the early part of the twentieth century; so much so, that Gershwin quoted the first few bars of the tune in his *An American in Paris*. It is heard during the scene where Zelig is on stage in Paris and turns into a Rabbi. Segues into...

### "Doin' the Chameleon" (Reprise)

An exotic version of the song is danced to by Joséphine Baker at the Folies Bergère.

### "I've Got a Feeling I'm Falling"

*Written by Harry Link, Thomas "Fats" Waller and Billy Rose (1929). Sung by Roz Harris (impersonating Fanny Brice) with Dick Hyman (piano).*

Sung by (a dubbed) Fanny Brice with

her husband, Billy Rose, as she serenades Zelig atop Westbury Hotel. In the final "A" section of the song, "Mr. Zelig" is inserted in place of "Mr. Parson"; the footage conveniently cuts to a shot of Zelig at this point.

## "Leonard's Fandango"

Heard as the film cuts to Spain, where Zelig has been booked for the summer. Segues into...

## "España Cañi"

*Written by Pascual Marquina Narro (1925). Featuring Tony Mottola (guitar).*

This famous *paso doble* is quoted during the bullfight scene with Martinez (Dimitri Vassilopoulos).

## "Five Foot Two, Eyes of Blue"

*Written Ray Henderson, Samuel M. Lewis and Joe Young (1925). Featuring Bernie Leighton (piano).*

Heard during the news sequence where Zelig is still missing; fresh scandals and eventually the Wall Street Crash overshadow his disappearance.

## Hearst Metrotone News — Huge Turnout Greets Pope Pius

*Original newsreel music or from a stock music library.*

## "Return from the Vatican" ("Leonard the Lizard" Motif)

Following on from the previous scene, this is heard as we see a shot of an ocean liner carrying Zelig back across the Atlantic to New York.

## "Thinking About Bix"[6]

*Featuring Dick Hyman (piano).*

This is heard when we see a shot of Eudora Fletcher's country home where the "White Room Sessions" will take place. It then returns a little later during the sessions when Eudora Fletcher is writing in her journal. The first version is with orchestra, the second with piano and orchestra.

## "You May Be Six People, but I Love You"

*Featuring Phil Bodner (flute).*

A sad quotation of the opening melody of this song is heard briefly as we see a shot of a frustrated Eudora Fletcher smoking.

## "Ain't We Got Fun?"

*Written by Richard Whiting, Gus Kahn and Raymond B. Egan (1921). Performed by the Charleston City All-Stars (1957).*

Heard as Eudora Fletcher and her fiancé spend some hours off relaxing on Broadway and then at a nightclub, where she is "struck by a brilliant and innovative plan that will create a major breakthrough in the case."

## "Thinking About Bix"/"You May Be Six People, but I Love You"

Heard just before Zelig succumbs to being hypnotized.

## "A Sailboat in the Moonlight"

*Written by Carmen Lombardo and John Jacob Loeb (1917). Original recording performed by Guy Lombardo and His Royal Canadians (1937).*

This song is used as a love theme for Zelig and Eudora Fletcher. It is heard first after Zelig has been cured, during the sequence where they begin to enjoy spending time together — sitting on a bench, walking the dog and cleaning the car. It reappears a little later when we see Eudora Fletcher thinking about her relationship with Zelig. It continues as we see various stills of the two together, as they visit Eudora's sister, and as Zelig gives his opinion on a number of topics, including baseball, music and Mussolini.

## "Chameleon Cured By Woman Doctor"[7]

Art card music for Hearst Metrotone Newsreel.

### "Who Says Women Are Just Good for Sewing" (Reprise)

Heard during the newsreel which reports on how Eudora Fletcher cured Zelig with the help of her cousin, Paul Deghuee (John Rothman), and how the couple have "become fast friends in the process."

### "On to City Hall"

As the newsreel continues, the music changes to a march-like piece, as we see a shot of a motorcade and then the town's newest celebrities are given the key to the city.

### "Luncheon at the Waldorf"

The newsreel then cuts to the Waldorf-Astoria, where Eudora Fletcher is being honored by fellow scientists.

### "Anchors Aweigh"

*Written by Capt. Alfred H. Miles, U.S.N. (Ret.) and Charles A. Zimmermann (1907).*

The trio section from this famous march (the official U.S. Navy song) is quoted briefly at the end of the newsreel, as we see Eudora Fletcher christening a ship.

### "I Love My Baby, My Baby Loves Me"

*Written by Harry Warren and Bud Green (1926). Performed by the Charleston City All-Stars (1957).*

Background music during the Pathe newsreel sequence at San Simeon, where we see Zelig and Eudora Fletcher socializing with various celebrities. The song is reprised in full during the end credits.

### "I'm Sitting on Top of the World"

*Written by Ray Henderson, Samuel M. Lewis and Joe Young (1925). Sung by Norman Brooks (impersonating Al Jolson).*

Heard during the "Zelig on the go" sequence. Zelig is in Atlantic City with Miss America contestants; at a boxing gym and then in Times Square with a shy Eudora Fletcher. As with "I've Got a Feeling I'm Falling," above, Hyman again inserts a new lyric in place of the original in order to make reference to Zelig.

### "Sunny Side Up"

*Written by Ray Henderson, Buddy G. De-Sylva and Lew Brown (1929). Performed by the Charleston City All-Stars (1957).*

Heard during the sequence where Zelig and Eudora Fletcher are on a boat, playing tennis and dancing, as the narrator states that they have fallen in love and have wedding plans.

### "The Roof Fell In" ("Leonard the Lizard" Motif)

Heard as a show girl named Lita Fox (Deborah Rush) announces that she is married to Zelig.

### "Shifting Public Opinion" (Includes "Leonard the Lizard" Motif)

Heard as Zelig is seen with his attorneys and as Lita Fox is portrayed as an abandoned woman. The music increases in intensity as the scandal breaks and another woman, Helen Gray (Jeanine Jackson), steps forward claiming that Zelig is the father of her twins.

### "Leonard the Lizard" Motif ("Hot Off the Presses")

A dramatic version of this is heard as the film cuts to a mob scene in front of a courthouse and we then see Zelig in court. After Zelig's announcement, the music becomes more frantic as Zelig is branded a criminal, fading as the scene shifts to the insignia poster of the Holy Family Christian Association.

### "Three in One"
*Featuring Phil Bodner (clarinet).*

This cue incorporates three separate sections:

1) "Throughout the humiliating ordeal...." Zelig and Eurora Fletcher are seen outside a courtroom with two lawyers, cutting to shots of city streets and traffic.

2) Greek music is heard as Zelig begins to turn Greek in the midst of a meal with Eudora Fletcher at a Greek restaurant.

3) "Public clamor...." A loud blare of music is heard as Zelig vanishes on the eve of his sentencing. The music changes as the film cuts to a close-up of a political cartoon, a busy newsroom and then the driveway of Eudora Fletcher's house.

### "Coffee Cup" (Includes "Leonard the Lizard" Motif)

"My sister was just shattered." Dramatic music as they search for Zelig, ending as he is apparently spotted as a member of a mariachi band.

### "A Sailboat in the Moonlight" (Reprise)

Heard as we see Eudora Fletcher sitting on a bench drinking coffee outside her country house, thinking about Zelig.

### Universal Newspaper Newsreel — National Socialists on the Rise

*Original newsreel music or from a stock music library.*

### "Sailing for Europe"

A brief introduction to the following piece. Segues into...

### "Die Fahne Hoch" ("Raise the Flag High," aka "Horst Wessel Lied")

*Written by Horst Wessel (1927).*

Heard during footage of Adolf Hitler just prior to the Munich Rally scene. This German song was adopted by the Nazi Party as its official anthem and is frequently used in films and television.

### "The Changing Man Concerto" (Reprise)

(See above.)

### UFA Films/Ton-Woch Newsreel Art Card

*Original newsreel music or from a stock music library.*

### "Escape from Germany"

### "America the Beautiful"

*Written by Samuel A. Ward and Katherine Lee Bates (1882).*

In his book *Piano Pro*, Dick Hyman himself describes this scene in the film:

> My own favorite cue appears toward the end of *Zelig*. We witness the hero (Woody Allen) and Eudora Fletcher (Mia Farrow) escaping from Nazi Germany in a tiny biplane, all of the Luftwaffe in hot pursuit. I called on buried memories of the music for a Flash Gordon serial I saw as a kid, brass blaring portentously under the action, and captured the comicstrip hokiness of the scene. Although a film composer almost always accepts the length of a specific scene as a given, I asked Sandy Morse [the film editor] to extend the escape-from-Germany footage with more of the stock shots of Leonard and Eudora's plane flying triumphantly, although upside-down, across the Atlantic. A few seconds more were needed to complete a grand phrase of "America the Beautiful," orchestrated in as stirring a manner as possible.[8]

Note how Hyman includes the "Leonard the Lizard" motif in the final chord.

### "Zelig Returns to Big Reception"

Art card music for Hearst Metrotone Newsreel.

### "Leonard and Eudora on Parade"

Heard as we return to the film's opening shot of a parade on Fifth Avenue, where Zelig and Eudora Fletcher are welcomed back to New York by cheering crowds.

### "March for a Total Psychotic"

Heard briefly as we see crowds of people being held back by police, cutting to a snowstorm of swirling tickertape.

### "I'll Get By"

*Written by Fred E. Alhert and Roy Turk (1928). Original recording performed by the Ben Bernie Orchestra (1928).*

Heard as Zelig and Eudora Fletcher get married and we see various home movie shots, before cutting to the end credits.

Allen concludes with a song in which the lyrics and sentiment are particularly appropriate to the narrative of the story, and this sentiment is echoed in the narrator's final voice-over where he quotes F. Scott Fitzgerald: "In the end, it was, after all, not the approbation of many but the love of one woman that changed his life."[9]

# Appendix 1: Soundtracks on Record or CD

As with the main body of the book, each film covered is given below in alphabetical order. The tracks are listed as they appear on the albums (so there may be some errors), but I have omitted composer and performer information, as this can be found elsewhere. Certain tracks on some of the compilations have different performers or are different recordings and these have been pointed out. If there is no soundtrack available, I have made suggestions as to where many of the recordings can be found. This also applies to tracks that have been left off a given soundtrack album. Most of this music is now available on CD, but some of the references below pertain to LPs.

## Music from Individual Films

### *Alice* (1990)

No soundtrack album.
Jackie Gleason's "Limehouse Blues" and "Breezin' Along with the Breeze" can both be found (along with "Too Close for Comfort" from *Hollywood Ending*) on the excellent *Jackie Gleason Presents Lazy, Lively Love* LP released in 1961 (Capitol W1439). "I Remember You" is on *Music, Martinis and Memories* which, combined with *Tawny*, has been re-released onto one CD by Koch (Collector's Choice CCM 01682), while "Moonlight Becomes You" appears on both *Lush Moods* (Pair PAI 1069) and *Shangri-La* (Pair PAI 1176). However, both tracks can be found on *For Lovers Only*, a three-disc CD boxed set released by CEMA Special Markets in 1993 (S23-17759). Paul Weston's "I Dream Too Much" is on *The Columbia Album of Jerome Kern* (Sony Music AK 47861). Ambrose's rendition of "Limehouse Blues" appears on the *Woody's Winners* compilation (two-disc version, see below). Artie Shaw's "Moonglow" can be found on *Woody Allen, More Movie Music* (see below). The Castilians' "La Cumparsita" is more difficult to find, but does feature on a 10" LP titled *Valentino*, a collection of tangos inspired by the movie *Valentino: The Lives and Loves of Valentino* (Decca DL-5347). Erroll Garner's "Caravan" and "Will You Still Be Mine?" were originally included on the LP sometimes incorrectly titled *At the Piano* (CL 535). This album has since been re-released on CD (combined with Garner's *Soliloquy* LP) as part of the CBS Jazz Piano Collection (CBS 465631 2). Note that "Lullaby of Birdland" (used in *Celebrity*) and "Will You Still Be Mine?" (used in *Celebrity* and *Melinda and Melinda*) are also on this CD, as well as being included on the respective soundtrack albums for the other films (see

below). Garner's "The Way You Look Tonight" (which is also used in *Deconstructing Harry*) can be found on *Body and Soul* (COL 467916 2), along with "I'm in the Mood for Love," which appears in *Manhattan Murder Mystery*. Wayne King's "Alice Blue Gown" is on his *Waltzes You Saved for Me* album (RCA Victor LPM-1186). The trio version of Thelonious Monk's "Darn That Dream" is on *The Unique Thelonious Monk* (Riverside/Original Jazz Classics OJCCD 064-2), *not* on *Monk's Dream*, as implied by the film. "Southern Comfort" by the Firehouse Five Plus Two can be found on the double CD release *The Firehouse Five Plus Two Story* (Good Time Jazz 2GTJCD-22055-2), which brings together the three volumes previously released on separate LPs. "Flight of the Foo Birds" is on the classic *The Complete Atomic Basie* (Roulette Jazz 7243 8 28635 2 6), which also includes "Li'l Darlin'," used in *Mighty Aphrodite*. Liberace's medley "O Tannenbaum/We Wish You a Merry Christmas" can be found on *A Liberace Christmas*, re-released on CD in 1995 (Universal Special Products 31146).

## Annie Hall (1977)

No soundtrack album.

Tommy Dorsey's rendition of "By the Sleepy Lagoon" can be found on *An Introduction to Tommy Dorsey—His Best Recordings 1928–1942* (Best of Jazz 4029). The Christmas medley performed by the Do-Re-Mi Children's Chorus is available on *Christmas Sing-A-Longs* (MCA Special Products 112111). Tim Weisberg's cover of Savoy Brown's "A Hard Way to Go" originally appeared on his debut album, *Tim Weisberg*, released in 1971 on A&M Records, but has more recently been included on his CD album *Undercover* (Fahrenheit Records 9602).

## Another Woman (1988)

No soundtrack album.

The recording of Satie's *Gymnopédie No. 1*, by the Orchestre de la Société des Concerts du Conservatoire conducted by Louis Auriacombe, originates from the 1967 LP released on EMI (EAC-40124), which also included *Gymnopédie No. 3, Parade* and *Relâche*. This LP was released a year later in the USA on Angel (S-36486), and it is likely that Allen used a copy of this for the film. These recordings of the two Debussy-orchestrated *Gymnopédies* can now be found on CD, appearing on *Les Inspirations insolites d'Erik Satie* (EMI 7243 5 85189 2 4). Note that both the LP and the CD have inverted Nos. 1 and 3, as referred to in the section on *Another Woman*. Dave Brubeck's "Perdido" is on *Jazz at Oberlin* (Original Jazz Classics OJC20 046-2). Jim Hall's "You'd Be So Nice to Come Home To" is on his classic *Concierto* album (Sony 65132). Both "A Fine Romance" and "Make Believe" by Erroll Garner can be found on *The Music of Gershwin and Kern* re-released (together with *Magician*) on Telarc (CD 83337). Bernstein's recording of Mahler's 4th Symphony with the New York Philharmonic has been transferred to CD by Sony (SMK 60733). Both "On the Sunny Side of the Street" and "Smiles" by the Teddy Wilson Trio can be found on *I Got Rhythm* (Verve POCJ-2586). The Bach Cello Sonatas, performed by Mischa Maisky and Martha Argerich, are on Deutsche Grammophon (415 471-2). Frankie Carle's "Roses of Picardy" is included on the 10" LP release *Roses in Rhythm* (Columbia CL6032). If this proves difficult to find, or you prefer a CD, then the track can also be found on *Big Band Dancing: For Dancers Only/Dancing with the Stars*, a 2002 reissue of two LPs on one CD (Collectables CCL 0007473). Bach's Suite for Unaccompanied Cello, performed by Yo-Yo Ma, is on Sony/CBS Masterworks (37867).

## Anything Else (2003)

No soundtrack album.

The three Billie Holiday tracks are easily available on a number of recordings, although I would recommend *Teddy Wilson: Of Thee I Swing* (HEP CD 1020), which includes both "Easy to Love" and "The Way You Look Tonight," and *Teddy Wilson: Blue Mood* (HEP CD 1035), which contains not only "I Can't Believe That You're in Love with Me," but also "Honeysuckle Rose" from Wilson's quartet session with Harry James and Red Norvo. "Easy to Love" can also be found on the *Woody's Winners* compilation (two-disc version, see below). The two Lester Young/Oscar Peterson tracks ("I Can't Get Started" and "There Will Never Be Another You") are both on *Lester Young with the Oscar Peterson Trio* (Verve 521 451-2). Wes Montgomery's "Gone with the Wind" can be found on *The Incredible Jazz Guitar of Wes Montgomery* (Riverside/Original Jazz Classics OJCCD-036-2), which also includes "West Coast Blues," used in *Husbands and Wives*.

### *Bananas* (1971)

No soundtrack album.

### *Broadway Danny Rose* (1984)

No soundtrack album.

The actual recordings used in the film of Nick Apollo Forte's two songs, "Agita" and "My Bambina," are not available. However, both of these songs (as well as "All of Me" and "You're Nobody Until Somebody Loves You") can be found on *Live at the Sands and More!* This is a rare CD produced by Nick Apollo Forte himself and released on Fan Records in 2001.

### *Bullets Over Broadway* (1994)

"Music from the Motion Picture" released on CD in 1994 on Sony Classical (SK 66822).

1. Toot, Toot, Tootsie! (Goodbye)
2. That Jungle Jamboree
3. Singin' the Blues (Till My Daddy Comes Home)
4. Poor Butterfly
5. Crazy Rhythm
6. At the Jazz Band Ball
7. Lazy River
8. Who?
9. Let's Misbehave
10. You've Got to See Mamma Ev'ry Night (or You Can't See Mamma at All)
11. You Took Advantage of Me
12. Nagasaki
13. When the Red, Red Robin Comes Bob, Bob Bobbin' Along
14. That Certain Feeling
15. Make Believe
16. Thou Swell

This CD includes all of the songs we hear in the film, with the exception of "Ma (He's Makin' Eyes at Me)," which is heard only very briefly.

### *Celebrity* (1998)

"Music from the Motion Picture Soundtrack" released on CD in 1998 (Milan 74321 64071).

1. You Oughta Be in Pictures
2. Kumbayah
3. Fascination
4. I Got Rhythm
5. Will You Still Be Mine?
6. Lullaby of Birdland
7. On a Slow Boat to China
8. Cocktails for Two
9. Soon
10. For All We Know

At less than 35 minutes this is the shortest Woody Allen soundtrack album to date, and one wonders why the insignificant 46 seconds of "Kumbayah" was included when a number of other tracks — "Tangerine," "That Old Feeling," "Did I Remember (To Tell You I Adore You)?" and Beethoven's Symphony No. 5 — were omitted. The exclusion of "Did I Remember" is particularly surprising since it appears prominently in the film, as well as during the end credits. This song can be found, however, on two compilations: *Woody Allen's Movie Music* and *Woody's Winners* (see below). Dave Brubeck's "Tangerine" can be found on *The Essential Dave Brubeck* (Columbia COL 510594-2). "That Old Feeling" (which also appears in *Husbands and Wives*) is on *Getz Meets Mulligan in Hi-Fi* (Verve 849 392-2). The recording of Beethoven's Symphony No. 5 by the Royal Philharmonic Orchestra, conducted by Rene Leibowitz in 1961, has been re-issued on CD by Chesky Records (CD 017).

### *Crimes and Misdemeanors* (1989)

No soundtrack album.

Both "All I Do Is Dream of You" and Coleman Hawkins's "Sweet Georgia Brown" are on *Woody Allen Film Music* released on the Soundtrack Factory in 2003 (SFCD 44413). For the latter, however, I would recommend buying *Django Reinhardt All Star Sessions* (Capitol Jazz Records 31577), which also includes "Out of Nowhere" (used in both *Manhattan Murder Mystery* and *Deconstructing Harry*) and "Avalon" (used in *Sweet and Lowdown*). The Juilliard Quartet's performance of Schubert's String Quartet No. 15 in G major was originally released on LP by Sony (CBS M 35827). This has since been released on Juilliard Quartet 50th Anniversary, volume 3 (Sony SMK62707). The opening movement is on the *Woody Allen Classics* compilation (see below). Alicia de Larrocha's recording of Bach's English Suite No. 2 can be found on an LP of various Bach pieces recorded in 1972 (London Records CS6748). See "Oedipus Wrecks" (below) for Liberace's "I'll Be Seeing You."

### The Curse of the Jade Scorpion (2001)

"The Music Inspired by Woody Allen's *Hollywood Ending* and *The Curse of the Jade Scorpion*," released on the Soundtrack Factory in 2002 (SFCD33571). This joint soundtrack album (see below) contains a selection of music from the two mentioned films on one CD. The six tracks from *The Curse of the Jade Scorpion* are:

1. Sophisticated Lady
2. Flatbush Flanagan
3. Sunrise Serenade
4. Two Sleepy People
5. Tuxedo Junction
6. How High the Moon

Of these only "Sophisticated Lady," "Flatbush Flanagan" and "Sunrise Serenade" are actually the same recordings as those used in the film. "Two Sleepy People" is here performed by Hoagy Carmichael and Ella Logan; the Earl Hines recording used in the film can be found on *The Jazz Greats Play Frank Loesser* (Prestige PRCD-24193-2). "Tuxedo Junction" and "How High the Moon" are not the arrangements by Dick Hyman made especially for the film, but are performed by Glenn Miller and Benny Goodman, respectively. The one absent track is Wilbur de Paris's "In a Persian Market," which is on the soundtrack album to *New York Stories* (see below).

### Deconstructing Harry (1997)

No soundtrack album.

Three of the tracks ("Out of Nowhere," "She's Funny That Way" and "Sing, Sing, Sing") can be found on the *More Movie Music* compilation (see below). "Twisted" by Annie Ross is on *Woody Allen Film Music*, the 2003 Soundtrack Factory compilation (see below). The famous "The Girl from Ipanema" can be found easily, but I would recommend the classic *Getz/Gilberto* (Verve 521414-2). Glen Dickson's "Waiting" is on the Shirim Klezmer Orchestra's 1993 album *Naftule's Dream* (Northeastern Records NR-5014). Art Tatum and Ben Webster's "All the Things You Are" is on *The Tatum Group Masterpieces*, vol. 8 (Original Jazz Classics/ Pablo PACD20 431-2). Erroll Garner's "The Way You Look Tonight" (also used in *Alice*) is on *Body and Soul* (COL 467916 2). The 1938 recording of "Rosalie" by Carroll Gibbons and the Savoy Hotel Orpheans can be found on *A Cole Porter Collection* (Jass Records J-CD 632).

### Everyone Says I Love You (1996)

"Original soundtrack recording" released on CD in 1997 on RCA Victor (09026 68756 2).

1. Just You, Just Me
2. My Baby Just Cares for Me
3. Recurrence/I'm a Dreamer
4. Makin' Whoopee
5. Venetian Scenes/I'm Thru with Love
6. All My Life
7. Just You, Just Me (Salsa Version)
8. Cuddle Up a Little Closer
9. Lookin' at You
10. Recurrence/If I Had You
11. Enjoy Yourself (It's Later Than You Think)
12. Chiquita Banana
13. Hooray for Captain Spaulding
14. I'm Thru with Love
15. Everyone Says I Love You

Being a musical, it is understandable that most of the album is taken up with the songs sung by the cast. However, with the length of the CD at only just over forty-four minutes, it is a shame that "Just Say I Love Her" and the instrumental versions of the title song and "Enjoy Yourself" are not included.

## *Everything You Always Wanted to Know About Sex* (1972)

No soundtrack album.

The exact same recording of "Let's Misbehave," used for the opening and end credits, can be found on the soundtrack to *Bullets Over Broadway* (see above).

## *Hannah and Her Sisters* (1986)

"A selection of music from the motion picture" released on LP (MCA-6190) and cassette (MCAC-6190) in 1987 on MCA Records.

**Side One**

1. You Made Me Love You
2. I've Heard That Song Before
3. Bewitched
4. Piano Medley: It Could Happen to You, Polkadots and Moonbeams, Avalon, Just You, Just Me
5. Concerto for Harpsichord in F Minor — 2nd Movement*

**Side Two**

1. Back to the Apple
2. I'm in Love Again
3. You Are Too Beautiful
4. If I Had You
5. Isn't It Romantic?

This release covers most of the principal music found in the film. The time limit offered by an LP accounts for some of the omissions, although it is a shame they could not squeeze in the delightful piano versions of "Where or When," "I'm in Love Again" and, in particular, "Bewitched." Other absentees from the soundtrack album include Count Basie's "The Trot," which can be found on "The Entertainers" compilation (see below); "I Remember You" by the Dave Brubeck Quartet, which is on *Jazz at the College of the Pacific* (Original Jazz Classics OJCCD-047-2) and Puccini's *Madam Butterfly* performed by the Rome Opera Chorus and Orchestra with Barbirolli, which has been re-released on EMI as part of their "Great Recordings of the Century" series (CMS769654). For those wanting the actual recording of the Bach F Minor Harpsichord Concerto heard in the film, this can be obtained on a 3 CD boxed set of all of Bach's harpsichord concerti performed by Gustav Leonhardt and the Leonhardt Consort (Teldec 4509-97452-2). "Slip into the Crowd" by 39 Steps was performed live to camera, but the band did issue a 12" EP shortly after the release of the film which includes this song (Gate Records GAEP 3.00001 E).

## *Hollywood Ending* (2002)

"The Music Inspired by Woody Allen's *Hollywood Ending* and *The Curse of the Jade Scorpion*," released on the Soundtrack Factory in 2002 (SFCD33571). This joint soundtrack album (see above) contains a selection of music from the two mentioned films on one CD. The eight tracks from *Hollywood Ending* are:

1. Going Hollywood
2. It's Been So Long
3. Hooray for Hollywood
4. Poor Butterfly
5. No Moon at All
6. Sweet and Lovely
7. Too Close for Comfort
8. Serenade in Blue

As with *The Curse of the Jade Scorpion*, only half of the songs are those versions used in the film. "No Moon at All" and "Sweet and Lovely" are performed by Nat King Cole and the George Shearing Trio, respectively, not by Barbara Carroll. "Too Close for Comfort" is not the version found on *Jackie Gleason Presents Lazy, Lively Love* (Capitol W 1439), but is by the Zoot Sims Quartet. "Serenade in Blue" is here performed by Glenn Miller, not Jackie Gleason; Gleason's recording can be found on *Body and Soul*, a double play album released

---

*"This version does not appear in the film." The LP cover gives the performers as George Malcolm and Simon Preston (harpsichords) with the Menuhin Festival Orchestra, conducted by Yehudi Menuhin.

on Pair Records containing two LPs on one CD.

## *Husbands and Wives* (1992)

No soundtrack album.

The 1930 recording of "What Is This Thing Called Love?" can be found on *Anything Goes, The Songs of Cole Porter* (ASV CD AJA 5331). Wes Montgomery's "West Coast Blues" can be found on *The Incredible Jazz Guitar of Wes Montgomery* (Riverside/Original Jazz Classics OJCCD-036-2), which also includes "Gone with the Wind," used in *Anything Else*. Barbirolli's 1964 recording of Mahler's 9th Symphony with the Berlin Philharmonic for EMI is available on CD (CDM 77 63115 2). "That Old Feeling" (which also appears in *Celebrity*) is on *Getz Meets Mulligan in Hi-Fi* (Verve 849 392-2). Sadly, Bernie Leighton's three piano arrangements of Berlin, Donaldson and Kern are unavailable.

## *Interiors* (1978)

No soundtrack album.

"Keepin' Out of Mischief Now" can be found on both "The Entertainers" and *Movie Music* compilations (see below). "Wolverine Blues" by the World's Greatest Jazz Band of Yank Lawson and Bob Haggart is on the second LP they recorded in 1970 for Project 3, titled *Extra! The World's Greatest Jazz Band* (PR 5039 SD).

## *Love and Death* (1975)

No soundtrack album.

All of the Prokofiev works used in the film are readily available. For those wanting some of the actual recordings used, Jascha Horenstein's 1955 Vox recording of the *Lieutenant Kijé Suite* with the Paris Philharmonic Orchestra has been re-released on Vox Legends (VOX2 7810), while the 1957 recording of the *Scythian Suite*, performed by the London Symphony Orchestra with Antal Dorati, has also found its way onto CD (Mercury Living Presence 432 753-2). The *Woody Allen Classics* compilation (see below) includes four of the more popular extracts from *Love and Death*—the "Troika" and "Kijé's Wedding" from the *Lieutenant Kijé Suite*, "Song about Alexander Nevsky" from *Alexander Nevsky*, and the "March" from *The Love of Three Oranges Suite*—but these are by different performers than those used in the film.

## *Manhattan* (1979)

"Music from the Woody Allen film including selections from the original soundtrack," originally released on LP (JS 36020) in 1979 on CBS. The soundtrack has since been released on CD (MK 36020).

1. Rhapsody in Blue
2. Land of the Gay Caballero
3. Someone to Watch Over Me
4. I've Got a Crush on You
5. Do, Do, Do
6. Mine
7. He Loves and She Loves
8. Bronco Busters
9. Oh, Lady, Be Good!
10. 'S Wonderful
11. Love Is Here to Stay
12. Sweet and Low-Down
13. Blue, Blue, Blue
14. Embraceable You
15. He Loves and She Loves
16. Love Is Sweeping the Country and Land of the Gay Caballero
17. Strike Up the Band
18. But Not for Me

There are a few differences between the music used in the film and that which is found on the soundtrack. In the film, three of the song arrangements are by Don Rose and performed by the Buffalo Symphony Orchestra, conducted by Michael Tilson Thomas, but on the soundtrack, all of the songs are performed by the New York Philharmonic Orchestra, conducted by Zubin Mehta in Tom Pierson's original arrangements. (See *Manhattan* section for more details.) In the film, the soloist on *Rhapsody in Blue* is Paul Jacobs; on the soundtrack, it is Gary Graffman. The version we hear of "Let's Call the Whole Thing Off," the trio version of "Embraceable You" and the piano version of "Sweet and Low-Down" do not feature on the soundtrack album. However, there are two songs, "Bronco Busters" and "Blue, Blue, Blue," that do appear on the soundtrack album, but are not actually used in the film.

## Manhattan Murder Mystery (1993)

No soundtrack album.
Several of the songs found on this soundtrack ("I'm in the Mood for Love," "Out of Nowhere," "The Big Noise from Winnetka" and "Sing, Sing, Sing") can be found on one or more of the various compilation CDs below. "I Happen to Like New York" is on *Bobby Short: Live at the Café Carlyle*, released on Atlantic Records in 1974; this double LP comprises twenty-four songs recorded in December 1973. "Have You Met Miss Jones?" by Art Tatum and Ben Webster is on *The Tatum Group Masterpieces,* vol. 8 (Original Jazz Classics/Pablo PACD20 431-2). Erroll Garner's "The Best Things in Life Are Free" is on *Close-up in Swing/A New Kind of Love* (Telarc CD 83383), but can also be found on the soundtrack album for *Melinda and Melinda*. "Misty" can be easily found on numerous Garner compilations. Dave Brubeck's "Take Five" originates from the classic *Time Out* album (Columbia/Legacy CK 65122), but also appears on the soundtrack to *Mighty Aphrodite* (see below).

## Match Point (2005)

"Original Motion Picture Soundtrack" released on Milan Entertainment Inc. in 2005 (5101 11693-2).

1. Mal reggendo all'aspro assalto
2. Un di felice, eterea
3. Mia piccirella
4. Gualtier Malde! ... Caro nome
5. Mi par d'udir ancora
6. Arresta ... Quali sguardi!
7. O figli, o figli miei!
8. Desdemona rea!
9. Una furtiva lagrima

The CD includes all of the pre-existent recordings used in the film, with the exception of "I Believe My Heart" from *The Woman in White*. Of the three items of source music, the "Valse" from *La Traviata* is also omitted, while the two arias heard accompanied by Tim Lole have been replaced with recordings from the 1990s taken from the Naxos label. The love duet "Un dì felice, eterea" from *La Traviata* is here performed by soprano Monika Krause, and tenor Yordi Ramiro (not baritone Georg Tichy, as stated on the cover); while "Gualtier Malde! ... Caro nome" from *Rigoletto* is performed by soprano Alida Ferrarini.

## Melinda and Melinda (2004)

"Original Motion Picture Soundtrack" released on Milan Entertainment Inc. in 2005 (M2-36106).

1. Take the "A" Train
2. The Best Things in Life Are Free
3. Somebody Stole My Gal
4. I Let a Song Go Out of My Heart
5. Medley — Memories of You/Moonglow/No Moon at All/Darn That Dream
6. Concerto in D for String Orchestra: 2. Arioso: Andantino (Stravinsky)*
7. String Quartet No. 4 (Bartók)
8. Prelude No. 2 Well Tempered Clavier (Bach)
9. Love Me
10. Don't Get Around Much Anymore
11. In a Mellow Tone [sic]
12. Will You Still Be Mine?

The album contains nearly all of the music heard in the film, the only omission being Bach's "Fantasia" from Partita No. 3 performed by András Schiff, which is on his recording of all six of Bach's Partitas (Decca 411 732-2).

## A Midsummer Night's Sex Comedy (1982)

"Music from the Woody Allen film including selections from the original soundtrack" released on LP (73673) and cassette (40-73673) in 1982 on CBS.

**Side One**

Incidental music to *A Midsummer Night's Dream.*
I — Overture

*The CD also includes the third movement, which is not used in the film.

II — Scherzo
III — Nocturne [not used in the film]
IV — Intermezzo
V — Wedding March

**Side Two**

Symphony No. 3 in A Minor, "Scottish"
*Second Movement— Vivace non troppo*
Concerto No. 2 in D Minor for Piano and Orchestra, Op. 40
*Second Movement— Adagio*
Concerto in E Minor for Violin and Orchestra, Op. 64
*Third Movement— Allegro molto vivace*

This album contains all of the music heard in the film, but only some of the actual recordings used. Here, the extracts from *A Midsummer Night's Dream* are performed by the Cleveland Orchestra conducted by George Szell, but the film uses a recording by the Philadelphia Orchestra conducted by Eugene Ormandy originally released on LP in 1977 (RCA Red Seal RL 12084) and later transferred to CD (RCD1-2084). The Violin Concerto is here performed by Isaac Stern and the Boston Symphony, whereas the film version is by Stoika Milanova and the TVR Symphony Orchestra. Symphony No. 3 and the Piano Concerto No. 2 are the same recordings as those heard in the film. But with the latter the album repeats the error found in the film's end credits, giving the Philadelphia Orchestra instead of the Columbia Symphony Orchestra, again with no mention of Rudolf Serkin. The Cleveland Orchestra/George Szell performances of the "Scherzo" and "Intermezzo" from *A Midsummer Night's Dream* also appear on the *Woody Allen Classics* compilation (see below), along with a different recording of the second movement from Symphony No. 3.

## *Mighty Aphrodite* (1995)

"Music from the Motion Picture" released on CD in 1995 on Sony Classical (SK 62253).

1. Neo Minore
2. Horos Tou Sakena
3. I've Found a New Baby
4. Whispering
5. Manhattan

6. When Your Lover Has Gone
7. Li'l Darlin'
8. Take Five
9. Penthouse Serenade (When We're Alone)
10. I Hadn't Anyone Till You
11. The "In" Crowd
12. You Do Something to Me
13. When You're Smiling

This CD includes all of the songs we hear in the film, except Dick Hyman's performance of "Walking My Baby Back Home."

## *New York Stories* (1989)

"Original motion picture soundtrack" released on LP (9 60 857-1), cassette (9 60 87-4) and CD (9 60 857-2) in 1989 on Elektra Musician.

**Side One**

*Francis Ford Coppola's "Life Without Zoe"*

1. People Will Talk
2. Back to School
3. Twinkle Twinkle
4. Zoe

*Woody Allen's "Oedipus Wrecks"*

5. I Want a Girl (Just Like the Girl That Married Dear Old Dad)
6. In a Persian Market

**Side Two**

1. All the Things You Are
2. I've Found a New Baby

*Martin Scorsese's "Life Lessons"*

3. A Whiter Shade of Pale
4. Sex Kick
5. What Is This Thing Called Love?
6. Like a Rolling Stone

The album includes only four songs from each of the three segments, and so space is obviously limited. The tracks from "Oedipus Wrecks" are the main ones used in the film, although it is a shame that "Sing, Sing, Sing" was not included. One bonus though is the non–Woody Allen track that could so easily be a Woody Allen track, i.e. Django Reinhardt's 1947 recording of Cole Porter's "What

Is This Thing Called Love?" used by Scorsese in *Life Lessons*. "Sing, Sing, Sing" is on both the compilations *Woody's Winners* and *More Movie Music* (see below). David Rose's somewhat bombastic arrangement of "All the Things You Are" is on the album *Beautiful Music to Love By* (MGM E3067), while his rendition of "June and January" is on *Songs of the Fabulous Thirties* (Kapp KXL-5004). The instrumental version of Liberace's "I'll Be Seeing You" appears on *As Time Goes By* (Universal/MCA 22088).

## *Play It Again, Sam* (1972)

"Original dialogue and music soundtrack recording" released in 1972 on Paramount Records (PAS 1004).

### Side One

1. Bogart — That's Strictly in the Movies *(Music: "As Time Goes By")*
2. Don't Take it Personal
3. Dames Are Shimple
4. She Wanted to Swing
5. A Date for Allen
6. What About Sharon?
7. You Ashamed to Sweat?
8. I Love the Rain *(Music: "Blues for Allan Felix")*
9. Bogart Fantasy

### Side Two

1. Blues for Allan Felix
2. One Two, One Two *(Music: "Easy Lovin'")*
3. How'd It Go with Julie?
4. Homosexual Panic
5. Allan, Did You Say You Loved Me?
6. "Slide"
7. Casablanca Revisited *(Music: "As Time Goes By")*

This album is mostly dialogue (with an annoying laugh track added) and each track is given a title corresponding to a line in the film. However, the music appears at different times than it does in the film and is invariably heard underneath dialogue. As a result, the only separate musical track is Oscar Peterson's "Blues for Allan Felix" at the beginning of side two, but as this is unavailable elsewhere, the album is worth getting for this alone.

## *The Purple Rose of Cairo* (1985)

"Original motion picture soundtrack" released in 1985 on MCA Records (MCA-6139).

### Side One

1. Theme from *The Purple Rose of Cairo* (Cecilia's Choice)
2. One Day at a Time
3. Hollywood Fun
4. Penny Pitching
5. The Film within the Film
    a) Opening Titles (Try It On for Size)
    b) In the Tomb of Osiris (One Day at a Time)
6. Carousel Memories
7. New Show at the Jewel
8. Night Club Montage
    a) Try It On for Size
    b) Penthouse Mood
9. Alabamy Bound
10. Medley for Trombone Soloist
    a) Theme from *The Purple Rose of Cairo* (Cecilia's Choice)
    b) New Show at the Jewel

### Side Two

1. Cheek to Cheek (Main Title)
2. Laughing Every Morning
3. I'd Rather Be Sleeping
4. Try It On for Size
    a) Arrangement for Three Pianos
    b) Arrangement for Swing Band
5. Well, I Am Impressed
6. Theme from *The Purple Rose of Cairo* (Cecilia's Choice)
7. Emma's Place
8. Dreams of the Nile

The LP covers all of the music found in the film — but in fuller versions — and has, in addition, a number of tracks that were recorded for the film but not used. These include two cues that comprise "Medley for Trombone Soloist," a three-piano version of "Try It On for Size" (with Dick Hyman playing all three pianos!) and "Dreams of the Nile." In addition, Hyman has recorded a solo piano version of "Carousel Memories" on the album *Live from Toronto's Café des Copains* (Music and Arts Programs of America CD 4622).

## Radio Days (1987)

"Selections from the Original Soundtrack of the Motion Picture," released on LP (3017-1-N) and CD (3017-2-N) in 1987 on RCA.
1. In the Mood
2. I Double Dare You
3. Opus One
4. Frenesi
5. The Donkey Serenade
6. Body and Soul
7. You and I
8. Remember Pearl Harbor
9. That Old Feeling
10. The White Cliffs of Dover
11. Goodbye
12. I'm Gettin' Sentimental Over You
13. Lullaby of Broadway
14. American Patrol
15. Take the "A" Train
16. One, Two, Three, Kick

The soundtrack to *Radio Days* only includes previously released recordings and none of the original material recorded specifically for the film. As a result, Dick Hyman's beautiful arrangement of "September Song," arguably the foremost song in the film, is unfortunately unavailable. (See the section on *Radio Days* for Dick Hyman's comments on the recording of this song.) Apart from this, the album offers a fair representation of the pre-existent recordings we hear, but with three notable omissions, namely "The Flight of the Bumble Bee" by Harry James, which is used over the opening credits, "If You Are but a Dream" by Frank Sinatra, and Carmen Miranda's "South American Way." This latter song is used for one of the funniest scenes in the film and again during the end credits; Allen himself even mentions this song when speaking about *Radio Days* to Stig Björkman (see the section on *Radio Days*). However, these songs can be found on "The Entertainers" compilation (see below). In addition, two other songs that are not on the original soundtrack album—"If I Didn't Care" by the Ink Spots and "Pistol Packin' Mama" by Bing Crosby and the Andrews Sisters — appear on the *Woody's Winners* compilation (two-disc version, see below).

## September (1987)

No soundtrack album.

"Just One More Chance" by Ambrose and His Orchestra is on the Vocalion CD *Just Once More Chance* (CDEA 6031), while "Out of Nowhere" is, at the time of writing, only available on LP (*Ambrose and His Orchestra* on Monmouth-Evergreen Records MES/7032). *The Tatum Group Masterpieces*, vol. 8 (Original Jazz Classics/Pablo PACD 20 431-2) contains both "My Ideal" and "Night and Day" by Art Tatum and Ben Webster, and "My Ideal" is also on "The Entertainers" compilation (see below). Unfortunately, the Bernie Leighton piano pieces are unavailable.

## Shadows and Fog (1992)

No soundtrack album.

The film uses two versions of "The Cannon Song" from *Kleine Dreigroschenmusik* (Little Threepenny Music), Weill's suite from *The Threepenny Opera*. The Canadian Chamber Ensemble's version is on their LP titled *Music from Berlin in the 1920s*, recorded in 1982 for CBC Enterprises (SM5010). The London Sinfonietta's 1975 recording can be found on Deutsche Grammophon (DG Double 459 442-2). Both these recordings will, of course, also include "Moritat von Mackie von Messer," as it is part of the same suite, but in the film Allen opts for a much older recording from 1931 performed by the Berlin Staatsoper, conducted by Otto Klemperer, and this can be found on *The Collector's The Threepenny Opera* (VAI Audio 1193). These two extracts can also be found on the CD *Woody Allen Classics*, but the recordings are by the London Symphony Orchestra, conducted by Michael Tilson Thomas (see below). The 1956 Lotte Lenya recording of *The Seven Deadly Sins* is on CBS Records Masterworks (MPK 45 886). The 1928 recording of "Alabama Song" by Marek Weber can be found on *O Moon of Alabama: Historic Recordings 1928–1944* (Capriccio 10347). All three Jack Hylton songs are on the LP *Hits from Berlin 1927–31*, which was released in 1979 as part of EMI's Retrospective Series (World Records/EMI SH 308).

## Sleeper (1973)

No soundtrack album.

As there is little to no chance of the soundtrack for this film ever being released, perhaps the closest one can get is to obtain recordings of the same songs by performers associated with either the Preservation Hall Jazz Band or some of Allen's clarinet playing idols such as George Lewis, Jimmie Noone, Johnny Dodds and Albert Burbank. I have compiled a list below of most of the songs used in *Sleeper*, with a selection of recordings approaching what we hear in the film.

### "Tain't Nobody's Biz-Ness If I Do"

Fats Waller's 1922 solo piano version (available on *Fats Waller 1922–26* Chronological Classics 664) is more in keeping tempo-wise with the film version, which opens with a piano introduction. Those wanting a band version may prefer George Lewis with the Original Zenith Brass Band on *George Lewis of New Orleans* (Original Jazz Classics OJCCD 1739-2), but this is more marching band than jazz.

### "Yes Sir, That's My Baby"

The Crescent City Joymakers' 1965 recording of this song on *Climax Rag* (Delmark DE 233) is probably the closest one can get to the version heard in the film, although it is understandably slower. Percy Humphrey's band had a number of musicians who also appeared in the Preservation Hall Jazz Band that Allen played with for the recording of *Sleeper*'s soundtrack. As well as Humphrey (trumpet) it also included Albert Burbank (clarinet), Jim Robinson (trombone) and Cie Frazier (drums).

### "Wolverine Blues"

The classic recording of this Jelly Roll Morton standard is, naturally enough, by Morton himself, performed in 1927 in a trio version with Johnny Dodds (clarinet) and Baby Dodds (drums).* Good versions for solo piano include Morton's older solo recording from 1923 (Retrieval RTR79002) and the much more recent recording by John Arpin on *Kings of Ragtime* (Pro Arte CDD 487).

### "Canal Street Blues"

There are, of course, several classic recordings of this jazz standard, notably the 1923 recording by King Oliver, featuring Johnny Dodds on clarinet. However, Allen's version in the film has a much faster pace, and the recording that best matches this is the 1943 live performance by George Lewis and His New Orleans Stompers on the album *Concert!* (Blue Note 1208), which includes a piano introduction identical to that heard in the film.

### "Ice Cream (I Scream, You Scream, We All Scream For)"

The Preservation Hall Jazz Band has recorded this number several times, as has George Lewis. Discounting the vocals, Lewis's 1953 recording with Avery "Kid" Howard on the album *Jazz Funeral in New Orleans* (Tradition TCD 1049) is remarkably similar to the film version, again with an identical piano introduction.

### "Joe Avery"

There are two recordings by the Preservation Hall Jazz Band that have similar personnel to that with which Allen played in 1973: one in 1964 on *Sweet Emma and Her Preservation Hall Jazz Band* (Preservation Hall Recordings 12) with Percy Humphrey, Jim Robinson, Emanuel Sayles, Cie Frazier and Allan Jaffe; and one in 1977 on *Preservation Hall Jazz Band: New Orleans, Volume I* (CBS MK 34549) with Percy Humphrey, Sing Miller, Cie Frazier and Allan Jaffe.

### "San"

There are a number of recordings of this Dixieland favorite, including an excellent rendition by Jimmie Noone with his Apex Orchestra in 1930.* But the 1965 recording with Percy Humphrey and the Crescent City Joymakers comes closest (*Climax Rag*, as above); it even includes the "Yankee Doodle" quote heard in the film version.

---

*Recordings with an asterisk featured in Allen's playlist on the BBC's Jazz File program he presented between December 2001 and February 2002.

### "Smiles" and "Till We Meet Again"*

Both these songs were recorded by George Lewis in 1957 with Dick Oxtot's Traditional Jazz Quartet. There are striking similarities stylistically between Lewis's and Allen's playing, and here we have the perfect examples of how Allen was influenced by Lewis's style. These songs were originally released on *George Lewis Jam Sessions* (Storyville STCD 6019), but if this proves difficult to find, they also appear on *Rare Cuts—Well Done, Volume 8 "Great Clarinet Players"* (Jazz Crusade JCCD 3109).

### *Small Time Crooks* (2000)

No soundtrack album.

Hal Kemp's "With Plenty of Money and You" can be found on *The Best of Hal Kemp and His Orchestra* (Sony Collectors' Choice Music CCM 125-2). Benny Goodman's "Stompin' at the Savoy" appears on the *Woody's Winners* compilation (two-disc version, see below). Harry James's "Music Makers" can be found on *I've Heard That Song Before* on Jasmine (JASCD 375). Johann Strauss's *Voices of Spring* recorded by the Vienna State Opera Orchestra is on *Strauss Waltzes, Volume II: The Return of Horenstein* (Chesky Records CD095). "Tequila" by the Champs is seemingly on every album available by this band. Carmen Cavallaro's "Cocktails for Two" can be found on the soundtrack to *Celebrity* (see above), while Cavallaro's "Fascination" is on *The Best of Carmen Cavallaro* (MCA UICY-1543). "Zelda's Theme" by Perez Prado can be found on *Ultra Lounge—Vol. 9: Cha-Cha De Amor* (Capitol C21S-37595). Most of the Lester Lanin songs used in the film are collected together on *Best of the Big Bands—Lester Lanin* (Sony Legacy 46149), while the only absentee, "Mountain Greenery," can be found on *Twistin' in the High Society/More Twistin' in the High Society* (Collectables 6466).

### *Stardust Memories* (1980)

No official soundtrack album was released at the time, but a German CD of the soundtrack has since become available on Bella Musica (BM-CD 31.4041); no date is given.

1. Stardust
2. Body and Soul
3. Tickle Toe
4. Palesteena
5. Tropical Mood Meringue [sic]
6. Moonlight Serenade
7. I'll See You in My Dreams
8. Three Little Words
9. If Dreams Come True
10. Fantasy

Although the quality of the CD is poor, it will still be of interest to collectors and is worth owning, as some of the recordings from the film (e.g. "Palesteena" and "Tropical Mood — Rhumba") are hard to come by. The track listing perpetuates the Sidney Bechet error found on the film's end credits (i.e. "Tropical Mood Meringue," *not* "Tropical Mood — Rhumba") and includes a version of "Three Little Words" by Duke Ellington, which does not appear in the film. There is also a track titled "Fantasy" which is just a badly stuck together medley of previously heard songs.

### *Sweet and Lowdown* (1999)

"Music from the Motion Picture" released on Sony Classical (SK 89019) in 1999.

1. I'll See You in My Dreams
2. Caravan
3. Sweet Georgia Brown
4. Unfaithful Woman
5. Viper Mad
6. Wrap Your Troubles in Dreams (and Dream Your Troubles Away)
7. Old Fashioned Love
8. Limehouse Blues / Mystery Pacific
9. Just a Gigolo
10. 3:00 AM Blues
11. All of Me / The Peanut Vendor
12. It Don't Mean a Thing (If It Ain't Got That Swing)
13. Shine
14. I'm Forever Blowing Bubbles
15. There'll Be Some Changes Made

As with *Radio Days*, there is a wealth of music in this film, and so not all of it makes it onto the soundtrack album. With the film's music showcasing Howard Alden, most of the tracks feature him in one combination or another, usually involving the Dick Hyman Group. While there are also two period recordings in "Viper Mad" and "Caravan," with the length of CD less than sixty minutes, there was room for some more of the non–Alden jazz tracks to be included. Django's "When Day Is Done," "Avalon" and "Liebestraum No. 3" can be found easily on one or more of the numerous collections that exist of Reinhardt's recordings, but I would recommend *Django Reinhardt: The Classic Early Recordings in Chronological Order.* This is a bargain-priced five CD collection (on JSP CD901), which includes the three recordings above as well as "Body and Soul" from *Stardust Memories* and a host of other excellent tracks. "When Day Is Done" can also be found on *Woody Allen Film Music*, the 2003 Soundtrack Factory compilation (see below). Ted Lewis's "Clarinet Marmalade" is on *Is Everybody Happy?* (ASV CD AJA 5273). Henry Busse's "Hot Lips" can be found on *Here's That Band Again! Themes from the Big Bands, Volume 3 1934–1947* (Naxos Jazz Legends 8.120619). "After You've Gone" by Joe Venuti, Eddie Lang and Their All-Star Orchestra and "Indiana (Back Home Again In)" by Red Nichols and His Five Pennies both appear on the *Woody's Winners* compilation (the latter on the two-disc version, see below). Alternatively, one can also find these songs on *B.G. & Big Tea in NYC* (Decca Jazz GRD 609), as Benny Goodman and Jack Teagarden feature in both groups. "Since My Best Gal Turned Me Down" can be found on a number of Bix Beiderbecke compilations, but I would recommend *Bix Beiderbecke Vol. II: At the Jazz Band Ball* (Columbia 460825-2).

## Take the Money and Run (1969)

No soundtrack album.

## Zelig (1983)

No soundtrack album.

Recordings of Dick Hyman's original songs are unavailable, but the sheet music can be found in his book *Dick Hyman: Piano Pro* (Ekay Music Inc., 1992). The four songs performed by the Charleston City All-Stars can be found on the various *Roaring 20s* volumes released by Grand Award between 1956 and 1958. Most of these were subsequently re-released in stereo. Guy Lombardo's "A Sailboat in the Moonlight" is on *The Band Played On* (ASV CD AJA 5406).

## Compilations

### Soundtrack Music from Woody Allen's Movies

Released on "The Entertainers" label originally on LP in 1988 (ENT LP 13.057) and later transferred onto CD in 1990 (CD 0275). The tracks marked * were added to the CD release.

1. My Ideal (*September*)
2. You Made Me Love You (*Hannah and Her Sisters*)
3. I've Heard That Song Before (*Hannah and Her Sisters*)
4. The Trot (*Hannah and Her Sisters*)
5. Rhapsody in Blue (fragment) (*Manhattan*)
6. Keepin' Out of Mischief Now (*Interiors*)
7. The Flight of the Bumble Bee (*Radio Days*)
8. Body and Soul (*Radio Days*)*
9. In the Mood (*Radio Days*)
10. Begin the Beguine (*Radio Days*)
11. Opus One (*Radio Days*)
12. Goodbye (*Radio Days*)
13. If You Are but a Dream (*Radio Days*)*
14. September Song (*Radio Days*)
15. I'm Gettin' Sentimental Over You (*Radio Days*)*
16. American Patrol (*Radio Days*)*
17. Take the "A" Train (*Radio Days*)
18. South American Way (*Radio Days*)
19. Stardust (*Stardust Memories*)
20. If Dreams Come True (*Stardust Memories*)*
21. I'll See You in My Dreams (*Stardust Memories*)
22. Wedding March (fragment) (*A Midsummer Night's Sex Comedy*)
23. As Time Goes By (*Play It Again, Sam*)

This was the first Woody Allen soundtrack compilation and, as a bargain priced CD with over seventy minutes of music, it serves as a good introduction to Allen's film music. Being originally released on LP in 1988 it is limited to the earlier films and does draw heavily from *Radio Days* (about half the album) although it includes three tracks from the film that are not — but perhaps should have been — on the official *Radio Days* soundtrack ("The Flight of the Bumble Bee," "If You Are but a Dream" and "South American Way"). Note also that the version of "September Song" by Harry James is not the version used in the film (see section on *Radio Days*). In addition, Count Basie's "The Trot" is a welcome inclusion, as it does not feature on the *Hannah and Her Sisters* soundtrack album. The fragments of *Rhapsody in Blue* and Mendelssohn's "Wedding March" (performed by different orchestras than those in the respective films) are too brief, however, to be of any real value.

## Woody Allen Classics

Released on Sony in 1993 (SK 53549).

1. *Little Threepenny Music*: Cannon Song
2. *Little Threepenny Music*: The Ballad of Mack the Knife
3. String Quartet in G Major, Op. 161, D. 887: Allegro molto moderato
4. *Gymnopédie No. 3* [This is actually no.1; see section on *Another Woman*]
5. Cello Sonata No. 2 in D Major, BWV 1028: Allegro
6. Harpsichord Concerto No. 5 in F Minor, BWV 1056: Largo
7. Sola, perduta, abbandonata (from *Manon Lescaut*)
8. *A Midsummer Night's Dream*, Op. 61: Scherzo
9. *A Midsummer Night's Dream*, Op. 61: Intermezzo
10. Symphony No. 3 in A Minor, Op. 56, "Scottish": Vivace non troppo
11. *Rhapsody in Blue*
12. *Lieutenant Kijé*— Symphonic Suite, Op. 60: Troika
13. *Lieutenant Kijé*—Symphonic Suite, Op. 60: Kijé's Wedding
14. *Alexander Nevsky*, Op. 78: Song about Alexander Nevsky
15. *The Love of Three Oranges Suite*: March

At 73:25 this is a generous collection of some of the most memorable pieces of classical music used by Allen, covering the period from *Love and Death* to *Shadows and Fog*. As this CD has been released on Sony it is limited to recordings available on their labels, and therefore virtually all of the recordings included are different than those actually used in each respective film. The one exception is the Juilliard Quartet's 1974 performance of Schubert's last string quartet. Note that the Graffman recording of *Rhapsody in Blue* is identical to that on the *Manhattan* soundtrack album, but this is not the version heard in film (see *Manhattan* above).

## Woody's Winners

Released on Castle Pie in 2000 (PIESD 239).

1. Frenesi (*Radio Days*)
2. Stardust (*Stardust Memories*)
3. Big Noise from Winnetka (*Manhattan Murder Mystery*)
4. Whispering (*Mighty Aphrodite*)
5. Take the "A" Train (*Radio Days*)
6. If You Are but a Dream (*Radio Days*)
7. I'm Getting' Sentimental Over You (*Radio Days*)
8. Cheek to Cheek (*The Purple Rose of Cairo*)
9. Tickle Toe (*Stardust Memories*)
10. I've Heard That Song Before (*Hannah and Her Sisters*)
11. After You've Gone (*Sweet and Lowdown*)
12. Body and Soul (*Stardust Memories*)
13. Did I Remember (To Tell You I Adore You)? (*Celebrity*)
14. In the Mood (*Radio Days*)
15. You Made Me Love You (I Didn't Want to Do It) (*Hannah and Her Sisters*)
16. The White Cliffs of Dover (*Radio Days*)
17. If Dreams Come True (*Stardust Memories*)
18. Lullaby of Broadway (*Radio Days*)
19. Sing, Sing, Sing (with a Swing) (*New York Stories*)
20. Goodbye (*Radio Days*)

Despite the name (filched from Woody

Herman's 1965 Columbia album), this is arguably one of the best compilations available. It includes three tracks that do not appear on the original soundtrack albums: "Sing, Sing, Sing" (listed as from *New York Stories*, but also in *Manhattan Murder Mystery* and *Deconstructing Harry*), "After You've Gone" (from *Sweet and Lowdown*) and "Did I Remember?" (from *Celebrity*). In addition, there are two tracks from *Stardust Memories* ("Body and Soul" and "Tickle Toe") that do not feature on the earlier "The Entertainers" collection and the excellent "The Big Noise from Winnetka" from *Manhattan Murder Mystery*. On the down side, the album still has too many tracks — eight in all — from *Radio Days*. Note that the recording of "Whispering" is not the same as the one heard in the film, although this is still by Benny Goodman, the one here is the 1936 quartet version, not the 1958 quintet version found on the *Mighty Aphrodite* soundtrack album.

## Woody Allen's Movie Music

Released on the Soundtrack Factory in 2001 (SFCD33559).

1. As Time Goes By (*Play It Again, Sam*)
2. Keepin' Out of Mischief Now (*Interiors*)
3. Stardust (*Stardust Memories*)
4. If Dreams Come True (*Stardust Memories*)
5. I'll See You in My Dreams (*Stardust Memories*)
6. You Made Me Love You (*Hannah and Her Sisters*)
7. I've Heard That Song Before (*Hannah and Her Sisters*)
8. The Flight of the Bumble Bee (*Radio Days*)
9. September Song (*Radio Days*)
10. Body and Soul (*Radio Days*)
11. In the Mood (*Radio Days*)
12. Begin the Beguine (*Radio Days*)
13. Opus One (*Radio Days*)
14. If You Are but a Dream (*Radio Days*)
15. Goodbye (*Radio Days*)
16. I'm Gettin' Sentimental Over You (*Radio Days*)
17. American Patrol (*Radio Days*)
18. Take the "A" Train (*Radio Days*)
19. South American Way (*Radio Days*)
20. I'm in the Mood for Love (*Manhattan Murder Mystery*)
21. The Big Noise from Winnetka (*Manhattan Murder Mystery*)
22. Toot, Toot, Tootsie! (Goodbye) (*Bullets Over Broadway*)
23. Singin' the Blues (Till My Daddy Comes Home) (*Bullets Over Broadway*)
24. Did I Remember (To Tell You I Adore You)? (*Celebrity*)
25. Cocktails for Two (*Celebrity*)
26. Rhapsody in Blue (fragment) (*Manhattan*)

This release is almost identical to "The Entertainers" compilation above, which is a little disappointing considering that it was released thirteen years later and could have included tracks from a wider range of films. If you already own a copy of "The Entertainers" release, you may well balk at buying another CD with twenty of its twenty-six tracks the same (including twelve from *Radio Days*). Of the six "new" recordings, three can be found on the original soundtracks (*Bullets Over Broadway* and *Celebrity*) and both "The Big Noise from Winnetka" and "Did I Remember?" are on *Woody's Winners*, which leaves Erroll Garner's "I'm in the Mood for Love" as the only track which has not appeared before.

## Woody Allen: More Movie Music

Released on the Soundtrack Factory in 2002 (SFCD33569).

1. Tickle Toe (*Stardust Memories*)
2. Body and Soul (*Stardust Memories*)
3. Frenesi (*Radio Days*)
4. Moonglow (*Alice*)
5. Alabama Song (*Shadows and Fog*)
6. Sing, Sing, Sing (with a Swing) (*Manhattan Murder Mystery*)
7. That Jungle Jamboree (*Bullets Over Broadway*)
8. At the Jazz Band Ball (*Bullets Over Broadway*)
9. Whispering (*Mighty Aphrodite*)

172 / Appendix 1

10. Penthouse Serenade (When We're Alone) (*Mighty Aphrodite*)
11. Out of Nowhere (*Deconstructing Harry*)
12. She's Funny That Way (*Deconstructing Harry*)
13. Truckin' (*Celebrity*)
14. Caravan (*Sweet and Lowdown*)
15. Sophisticated Lady (*The Curse of the Jade Scorpion*)
16. Sunrise Serenade (*The Curse of the Jade Scorpion*)

While there is still a bit of overlap with *Woody's Winners*, and still a number of tracks that can be found on the original soundtrack albums, this release does make up for the previous Soundtrack Factory album; it is also the first compilation not to be dominated by *Radio Days*. The CD mostly concentrates on the films from the 1990s, with the high points being the two tracks from *Deconstructing Harry*, including the classic "Out of Nowhere," and "Moonglow" from *Alice* (at last, something from *Alice*!). The most disappointing aspect of the CD is the inclusion of a number of recordings that are not actually the same as those heard in the film. These include "Whispering" (repeating the error found on *Woody's Winners*, see above), "Sophisticated Lady" (again this is by the same artist, Duke Ellington, but is not the 1940 Columbia recording used in the film) and "Alabama Song" (a vocal version by Lotte Lenya is included rather than the instrumental version by Marek Weber). Oddly, the album also includes a recording of "Truckin'" by the Mills Blue Rhythm Band. However, this is a recording of the Rube Bloom and Ted Koehler song with the same title written in 1935, not the Grateful Dead song from 1970 heard in the film.

## Woody Allen Film Music

A double CD released on the Soundtrack Factory in 2003 (SFCD44413).

### CD 1

#### Alice
1. Limehouse Blues
2. Caravan* [actual recording used in *Sweet and Lowdown*]
3. Moonlight Becomes You
4. Alice Blue Gown
5. Darn That Dream
6. Will You Still Be Mine?

#### Bullets Over Broadway
7. Make Believe
8. Lazy River
9. Poor Butterfly*
10. Let's Misbehave*
11. You Took Advantage of Me
12. Who?*
13. Thou Swell
14. Nagasaki

#### Celebrity
15. Tangerine
16. I Got Rhythm*
17. Lullaby of Birdland

#### Crimes and Misdemeanors
18. Rosalie
19. Taking a Chance on Love
20. I Know That You Know
21. Dancing on the Ceiling
22. Sweet Georgia Brown*
23. All I Do Is Dream of You*

### CD 2

#### Deconstructing Harry
1. Twisted*
2. All the Things You Are
3. The Way You Look Tonight
4. Christopher Columbus
5. Dream a Little Dream of Me

#### Mighty Aphrodite
6. I've Found a New Baby*
7. Manhattan*
8. When Your Lover Has Gone*
9. Walkin' My Baby Back Home
10. You Do Something to Me
11. I Hadn't Anyone Till You
12. When You're Smiling

#### The Purple Rose of Cairo
13. Cheek to Cheek*
14. Alabamy Bound

#### Sweet and Lowdown
15. When Day Is Done*

16. Clarinet Marmalade
17. Mystery Pacific
18. Limehouse Blues
19. It Don't Mean a Thing (If It Ain't Got That Swing)
20. I'll See You in My Dreams
21. Avalon
22. After You've Gone*
23. There'll Be Some Changes Made

This double CD comprises forty-six tracks and covers films mostly made in the 1990s. However, only fourteen of these (marked *) are actual recordings used by Woody Allen, and many of these have already appeared on the original soundtrack albums for several of the films: three from *Bullets Over Broadway*; two from *Mighty Aphrodite* and one each from *The Purple Rose of Cairo* and *Celebrity*. Furthermore, with Joe Venuti and Eddie Lang's rendition of "After You've Gone" and a CD version of "Cheek to Cheek" having already featured on *Woody's Winners*, this leaves only four actual recordings used by Woody Allen that have not appeared before. These are "Sweet Georgia Brown" by the Coleman Hawkins All Star Jam Band, "All I Do Is Dream of You" from *Singin' in the Rain* (both *Crimes and Misdemeanors*), "Twisted" by Annie Ross (*Deconstructing Harry*) and "When Day Is Done" by Django Reinhardt (*Sweet and Lowdown*). The album also contains a number of errors. The recording of "Caravan" under the section on *Alice* is given incorrectly as being performed by Duke Ellington. This is in fact Bunny Berigan's classic 1937 version, which *does* feature in *Sweet and Lowdown*. Unwittingly, the compilers have included a genuine Woody Allen track, but have listed it under a different film with the wrong performer. Furthermore, although "The Way You Look Tonight" is performed by Erroll Garner on this CD, the version here is Garner's 1949 Atlantic recording, not the Columbia recording he made two years later, which Allen uses in both *Alice* and *Deconstructing Harry*. It should also be pointed out that the inclusion of "Christopher Columbus" is not strictly accurate since this tune is only quoted within "Sing, Sing, Sing" and not actually heard as a separate song.

Having said all of this, it is nevertheless commendable that the Soundtrack Factory is at least attempting to produce CDs of Allen's film music. This is still an enjoyable compilation, with a wide range of fine jazz recordings, even if most of them are not the actual ones chosen by Woody Allen.

## Woody's Winners

In 2006, Castle Pie re-released this album as a two-disc set (PDSCD 640). The first disc is identical to the original CD cited above. The second disc comprises the following tracks:

1. Stompin' at the Savoy (*Small Time Crooks*)
2. Pistol Packin' Mama (*Radio Days*)
3. Out of Nowhere (*Manhattan Murder Mystery*)
4. If I Had You (*Hannah and Her Sisters*)
5. Easy to Love (*Anything Else*)
6. Singin' the Blues (Till My Daddy Comes Home) (*Bullets Over Broadway*)
7. Opus One (*Radio Days*)
8. I Got Rhythm (*Celebrity*)
9. Limehouse Blues (*Alice*)
10. They're Either Too Young or Too Old (*Radio Days*)
11. If I Didn't Care (*Radio Days*)
12. Flatbush Flanagan (*The Curse of the Jade Scorpion*)
13. Twisted (*Deconstructing Harry*)
14. I Can't Get Started (*Anything Else*)
15. South American Way (*Radio Days*)
16. Moonglow (*Alice*)
17. Poor Butterfly (*Hollywood Ending*)
18. Indiana (Back Home Again In) (*Sweet and Lowdown*)
19. In a Mellotone (*Melinda and Melinda*)
20. Christopher Columbus (*Deconstructing Harry*)

This update now includes songs from later films. Of the twenty tracks listed, most have already appeared on previous compilations and/or the original soundtrack album to the respective film. There are, in fact, only six recordings used by Allen that have not appeared before: "Stompin' at the Savoy" by Benny Goodman (*Small Time Crooks*); "Easy to Love" by Billie Holiday (*Anything Else*);

"Limehouse Blues" by Ambrose and His Orchestra (*Alice*); "Indiana" by Red Nichols (*Sweet and Lowdown*) and two songs from *Radio Days*, namely "Pistol Packin' Mama" and "If I Didn't Care." Note that the album includes five songs that are not the same recordings used by Allen ("If I Had You," "They're Either Too Young or Too Old," "I Got Rhythm," "I Can't Get Started" and "In a Mellotone") as well as the erroneous "Christopher Columbus" (see above).

# APPENDIX 2: MOST POPULAR SONGWRITERS

As one can see from the following list, Woody Allen has used music by some of the greatest songwriters from the first half of the century. As already mentioned, he has a predilection for Cole Porter, and he, along with Allen's other favorite songwriters — Gershwin, Kern, and Rodgers and Hart — appear most frequently.

## Irving Berlin

A Pretty Girl Is Like a Melody (*Sleeper*)
Cheek to Cheek (*The Purple Rose of Cairo*)
This Year's Kisses (*Crimes and Misdemeanors*)
Top Hat, White Tie and Tails (*Husbands and Wives*)
What'll I Do? (*September*)

## Buddy G. DeSylva

Alabamy Bound (*The Purple Rose of Cairo*)
Avalon (*Hannah and Her Sisters* and *Sweet and Lowdown*)
The Best Things in Life Are Free (*Manhattan Murder Mystery* and *Melinda and Melinda*)
I'm a Dreamer, Aren't We All? (*Everyone Says I Love You*)
Sunny Side Up (*Zelig*)
When Day Is Done (*September*, *Shadows and Fog* and *Sweet and Lowdown*)

## Walter Donaldson

Did I Remember (To Tell You I Adore You)? (*Celebrity*)
It's Been So Long (*Hollywood Ending*)
Makin' Whoopee (*Husbands and Wives* and *Everyone Says I Love You*)
My Baby Just Cares for Me (*Everyone Says I Love You*)
Yes, Sir, That's My Baby (*Sleeper*)

## Dorothy Fields

A Fine Romance (*Another Woman*)
I Dream Too Much (*Alice*)
I'm in the Mood for Love (*Manhattan Murder Mystery*)
Lovely to Look At (*Another Woman*)
On the Sunny Side of the Street (*Another Woman*)
The Way You Look Tonight (*Hannah and Her Sisters*, *Alice*, *Deconstructing Harry* and *Anything Else*)

## George Gershwin

But Not for Me (*Manhattan*)
Do, Do, Do (*Manhattan*)
Embraceable You (*Manhattan*)
He Loves and She Loves (*Manhattan*)
I Got Rhythm (*Celebrity*)
I've Got a Crush on You (*Manhattan*)
Land of the Gay Caballero (*Manhattan*)
Let's Call the Whole Thing Off (*Manhattan*)
Love Is Here to Stay (*Manhattan*)
Love Is Sweeping the Country (*Manhattan*)
Mine (*Manhattan*)
Oh, Lady, Be Good! (*Manhattan*)
'S Wonderful (*Manhattan*)
Someone to Watch Over Me (*Manhattan*)
Soon (*Celebrity*)
Strike Up the Band (*Manhattan*)

Sweet and Low-Down (*Manhattan*)
That Certain Feeling (*Bullets Over Broadway*)

## Ray Henderson

Alabamy Bound (*The Purple Rose of Cairo*)
The Best Things in Life Are Free (*Manhattan Murder Mystery* and *Melinda and Melinda*)
Five Feet Two, Eyes of Blue (*Zelig*)
I'm a Dreamer, Aren't We All? (*Everyone Says I Love You*)
I'm Sitting on Top of the World (*Zelig*)
Sunny Side Up (*Zelig*)

## Gus Kahn

Ain't We Got Fun? (*Zelig*)
The Carioca (*Radio Days*)
Dream a Little Dream of Me (*Deconstructing Harry*)
I'll See You in My Dreams (*Stardust Memories* and *Sweet and Lowdown*)
I'm Thru with Love (*Everyone Says I Love You*)
It Had to Be You (*Annie Hall*)
Makin' Whoopee (*Husbands and Wives* and *Everyone Says I Love You*)
My Baby Just Cares for Me (*Everyone Says I Love You*)
Toot, Toot Tootsie! (Goodbye) (*Zelig*)
Yes, Sir, That's My Baby (*Sleeper*)

## Jerome Kern

A Fine Romance (*Another Woman*)
All the Things You Are ("Oedipus Wrecks" and *Deconstructing Harry*)
I Dream Too Much (*Alice*)
I'm Old Fashioned (*Hannah and Her Sisters*)
Lovely to Look At (*Another Woman*)
Make Believe (*Another Woman* and *Bullets Over Broadway*)
The Song Is You (*Husbands and Wives*)
The Way You Look Tonight (*Hannah and Her Sisters*, *Alice*, *Deconstructing Harry* and *Anything Else*)
Who? (*September* and *Bullets Over Broadway*)

## Frank Loesser

Guys and Dolls Overture (*Manhattan Murder Mystery*)
I Don't Want to Walk Without You (*Radio Days*)
I've Got You (*Crimes and Misdemeanors*)
Murder He Says (*Crimes and Misdemeanors*)
On a Slow Boat to China (*September* and *Celebrity*)
They're Either Too Young or Too Old (*Radio Days*)
Two Sleepy People (*The Curse of the Jade Scorpion*)

## Jimmy McHugh

I Can't Believe That You're in Love with Me (*Everyone Says I Love You* and *Anything Else*)
I'm in the Mood for Love (*Manhattan Murder Mystery*)
Lovely to Look At (*Another Woman*)
Murder He Says (*Crimes and Misdemeanors*)
On the Sunny Side of the Street (*Another Woman*)
South American Way (*Radio Days*)

## Cole Porter

All of You (*Broadway Danny Rose*)
Begin the Beguine (*Broadway Danny Rose* and *Radio Days*)
Easy to Love (*Stardust Memories* and *Anything Else*)
I Happen to Like New York (*Manhattan Murder Mystery*)
I'm in Love Again (*Hannah and Her Sisters*)
Just One of Those Things (*Stardust Memories* and *Radio Days*)
Let's Misbehave (*Everything You Always Wanted to Know About Sex* and *Bullets Over Broadway*)
Looking at You (*Everyone Says I Love You*)
Night and Day (*Radio Days* and *September*)
Rosalie (*Crimes and Misdemeanors* and *Deconstructing Harry*)
What Is This Thing Called Love? (*Husbands and Wives*)
You Do Something to Me (*Mighty Aphrodite*)
You'd Be So Nice to Come Home To (*Radio Days* and *Another Woman*)

## Rodgers and Hart

Thou Swell (*Bullets Over Broadway*)

You Took Advantage of Me (*Bullets Over Broadway*)
I Could Write a Book (*Deconstructing Harry*)
Mimi (*Everyone Says I Love You*)
Bewitched, Bothered and Bewildered (*Hannah and Her Sisters*)
Isn't It Romantic? (*Hannah and Her Sisters*)
Where or When (*Hannah and Her Sisters*)
You Are Too Beautiful (*Hannah and Her Sisters*)
Have You Met Miss Jones? (*Manhattan Murder Mystery*)
Manhattan (*Mighty Aphrodite*)
Mountain Greenery (*Small Time Crooks*)
Dancing on the Ceiling (*Crimes and Misdemeanors*)

### Ruby and Kalmar

Everyone Says I Love You (*Everyone Says I Love You*)
Hooray for Captain Spaulding (*Everyone Says I Love You*)
Nevertheless (I'm in Love with You) (*Sweet and Lowdown*)
Three Little Words (*Stardust Memories*)
Freedonia Is Going to War (*Hannah and Her Sisters*)

### Harry Warren

I Love My Baby, My Baby Loves Me (*Zelig* and *The Purple Rose of Cairo*)
Lullaby of Broadway (*Radio Days*)
Lulu's Back in Town (*Sweet and Lowdown*)
Nagasaki (*Bullets Over Broadway*)
Serenade in Blue (*Hollywood Ending*)
There Will Never Be Another You (*Anything Else*)
With Plenty of Money and You (*Small Time Crooks*)
You'll Never Know (*Radio Days*)
You're Getting to Be a Habit with Me (*Radio Days*)

### Richard Whiting

Ain't We Got Fun? (*Zelig*)
Breezin' Along with the Breeze (*Alice*)
Hooray For Hollywood (*Hollywood Ending*)
Louise (*Everyone Says I Love You*)
My Ideal (*September*)
She's Funny That Way (*Deconstructing Harry*)
Till We Meet Again (*Sleeper*)

# Appendix 3: Most Popular Performers

Corresponding to his customary practice of using a stable of certain actors repeatedly, Allen also tends to include music from particular musicians on a regular basis. Below is a list of the most popular performers used by Woody Allen in his films, including the tracks performed and the films in which they appear. I have omitted names that have appeared many times but in only one film, for instance, Lester Lanin (*Small Time Crooks*) and artists who have recorded specifically for a particular film, for example, Howard Alden (*Sweet and Lowdown*). Of the musicians given below (but see note on Dick Hyman), the unsung Bernie Leighton appears more than any other, playing the piano on no fewer than 22 songs. He is closely followed by Erroll Garner, whose recordings have appeared 17 times (including repetitions) in the same number of years (from 1988, *Another Woman*, to 2004, *Melinda and Melinda*).

### Bert Ambrose

Just One More Chance (*September*)
Limehouse Blues (*Alice*)

Nevertheless (I'm in Love with You) (*Sweet and Lowdown*)
Out of Nowhere (*September*)
When Your Lover Has Gone (*Mighty Aphrodite*)

## Count Basie

Back to the Apple (*Hannah and Her Sisters*)
Flight of the Foo Birds (*Alice*)
Li'l Darlin (*Mighty Aphrodite*)
Tickle Toe (*Stardust Memories*)
The Trot (*Hannah and Her Sisters*)

## Dave Brubeck Quartet

I Remember You (*Hannah and Her Sisters*)
Perdido (*Another Woman*)
Take Five (*Manhattan Murder Mystery* and *Mighty Aphrodite*)
Tangerine (*Celebrity*)

## Tommy Dorsey

By the Sleepy Lagoon (*Annie Hall*)
I'm Gettin' Sentimental Over You (*Radio Days*)
Keepin' Out of Mischief Now (*Interiors*)
Opus One (*Radio Days*)
You and I (*Radio Days*)

## Duke Ellington

I Let a Song Go Out of My Heart (*Melinda and Melinda*)
In a Mellotone (*Melinda and Melinda*)
Take the "A" Train (*Radio Days* and *Melinda and Melinda*)
That Jungle Jamboree (*Bullets Over Broadway*)

## Erroll Garner

A Fine Romance (*Another Woman*)
The Best Things in Life Are Free (*Manhattan Murder Mystery* and *Melinda and Melinda*)
Caravan (*Alice*)
I Hadn't Anyone Till You (*Mighty Aphrodite*)
I'm in the Mood for Love (*Manhattan Murder Mystery*)
Lullaby of Birdland (*Celebrity*)
Make Believe (*Another Woman*)
Misty (*Manhattan Murder Mystery*)
Penthouse Serenade (When We're Alone) (*Mighty Aphrodite*)

She's Funny That Way (*Deconstructing Harry*)
Somebody Stole My Gal (*Melinda and Melinda*)
The Way You Look Tonight (*Alice* and *Deconstructing Harry*)
Will You Still Be Mine? (*Alice*, *Celebrity* and *Melinda and Melinda*)

## Jackie Gleason

Breezin' Along with the Breeze (*Alice*)
I Remember You (*Alice*)
Limehouse Blues (*Alice*)
Moonlight Becomes You (*Alice*)
On a Slow Boat to China (*Celebrity*)
Serenade in Blue (*Hollywood Ending*)
Too Close for Comfort (*Hollywood Ending*)

## Benny Goodman

Body and Soul (*Radio Days*)
Goodbye (*Radio Days*)
Hooray for Hollywood (*Hollywood Ending*)
Sing, Sing, Sing (with a Swing) ("Oedipus Wrecks," *Manhattan Murder Mystery* and *Deconstructing Harry*)
Stompin' at the Savoy (*Small Time Crooks*)
Whispering (*Mighty Aphrodite*)

## Billie Holiday

Did I Remember (to Tell You I Adore You)? (*Celebrity*)
Easy to Love (*Anything Else*)
I Can't Believe That You're in Love with Me (*Anything Else*)
The Way You Look Tonight (*Anything Else*)

## Dick Hyman

The volume of work Hyman has performed in Allen's films (playing on more than 80 songs) is too large to list here.

## Harry James

Flatbush Flanagan (*The Curse of the Jade Scorpion*)
The Flight of the Bumble Bee (*Radio Days*)
I've Heard That Song Before (*Hannah and Her Sisters*)
You Made Me Love You (*Hannah and Her Sisters*)
Music Makers (*Small Time Crooks*)

## Bernie Leighton

All the Things You Are ("Oedipus Wrecks")
The Bilbao Song (*Another Woman*)
The Changing Man Concerto (*Zelig*)
Charleston (*Zelig*)
Dancing on the Ceiling (*Crimes and Misdemeanors*)
Great Day (*Crimes and Misdemeanors*)
Five Foot Two, Eyes of Blue (*Zelig*)
I Know That You Know (*Crimes and Misdemeanors*)
I Want a Girl (Just Like the Girl That Married Dear Old Dad) ("Oedipus Wrecks")
I'm Confessin' (That I Love You) (*September*)
I'm Old Fashioned (*Hannah and Her Sisters*)
Lovely to Look At (*Another Woman*)
Makin' Whoopee (*Husbands and Wives*)
Moonglow (*September*)
M-O-T-H-E-R (A Word That Means the World to Me) ("Oedipus Wrecks")
On a Slow Boat to China (*September*)
The Song Is You (*Husbands and Wives*)
Top Hat, White Tie and Tails (*Husbands and Wives*)
The Way You Look Tonight (*Hannah and Her Sisters*)
What'll I Do? (*September*)
When Day Is Done (*September*)
Who? (*September*)

## Glenn Miller

American Patrol (*Radio Days*)
In the Mood (*Radio Days*)
Moonlight Serenade (*Stardust Memories*)
Sunrise Serenade (*The Curse of the Jade Scorpion*)
The White Cliffs of Dover (*Radio Days*)

## Django Reinhardt

Avalon (*Sweet and Lowdown*)
Body and Soul (*Stardust Memories*)
I'll See You in My Dreams (*Stardust Memories*)
Liebestraum No. 3 (*Sweet and Lowdown*)
Out of Nowhere (*Manhattan Murder Mystery* and *Deconstructing Harry*)
Sweet Georgia Brown (*Crimes and Misdemeanors*)
When Day Is Done (*Sweet and Lowdown*)

## Art Tatum and Ben Webster Quartet

All the Things You Are (*Deconstructing Harry*)
Have You Met Miss Jones? (*Manhattan Murder Mystery*)
My Ideal (*September*)
Night and Day (*September*)

# APPENDIX 4: MOST POPULAR SONGS AND JAZZ

Below is a list of songs or jazz tracks that Woody Allen has used more than once. "Out of Nowhere" and "The Way You Look Tonight" are the most frequently used songs (four times), while Benny Goodman's "Sing, Sing, Sing" and Erroll Garner's "Will You Still Be Mine?" are the most popular recordings (three times). Not surprisingly, Cole Porter is the predominant songwriter (seven songs). An asterisk indicates that the same recording of the song was used for multiple films.

All the Things You Are ("Oedipus Wrecks" and *Deconstructing Harry*)
Avalon (*Hannah and Her Sisters* and *Sweet and Lowdown*)
Begin the Beguine (*Broadway Danny Rose* and *Radio Days*)
The Best Things in Life Are Free (*Manhattan Murder Mystery* and *Melinda and Melinda*)*

## Most Popular Songs and Jazz / 179

Body and Soul (*Stardust Memories* and *Radio Days*)
Caravan (*Alice* and *Sweet and Lowdown*)
Chinatown, My Chinatown (*Radio Days* and *Everyone Says I Love You*)
Cocktails for Two (*Everyone Says I Love You*, *Celebrity* and *Small Time Crooks*) (* for *Celebrity* and *Small Time Crooks*)
Crazy Rhythm (*Crimes and Misdemeanors* and *Bullets Over Broadway*)
La Cumparsita (*Radio Days* and *Alice*)*
Darn That Dream (*Alice* and *Melinda and Melinda*)
Easy to Love (*Stardust Memories* and *Anything Else*)
Fascination (*Celebrity* and *Small Time Crooks*)
I Can't Believe That You're in Love with Me (*Everyone Says I Love You* and *Anything Else*)
I Love My Baby, My Baby Loves Me (*Zelig* and *The Purple Rose of Cairo*)
I Remember You (*Hannah and Her Sisters* and *Alice*)
I'll Be Seeing You ("Oedipus Wrecks" and *Crimes and Misdemeanors*)*
I'll See You in My Dreams (*Stardust Memories* and *Sweet and Lowdown*)
I've Found a New Baby ("Oedipus Wrecks" and *Mighty Aphrodite*)*
If I Had You (*Hannah and Her Sisters* and *Everyone Says I Love You*)
In a Persian Market ("Oedipus Wrecks" and *The Curse of the Jade Scorpion*)*
It Could Happen to You (*Hannah and Her Sisters* and *Anything Else*)
Just One of Those Things (*Stardust Memories* and *Radio Days*)
Just You, Just Me (*Hannah and Her Sisters* and *Everyone Says I Love You*)
Let's Misbehave (*Everything You Always Wanted to Know About Sex* and *Bullets Over Broadway*)*
Limehouse Blues (*Alice* and *Sweet and Lowdown*)
Make Believe (*Another Woman* and *Bullets Over Broadway*)
Makin' Whoopee (*Husbands and Wives* and *Everyone Says I Love You*)

Moonglow (*September*, *Alice* and *Melinda and Melinda*)
Night and Day (*Radio Days* and *September*)
No Moon at All (*Hollywood Ending* and *Melinda and Melinda*)
On a Slow Boat to China (*September* and *Celebrity*)
Out of Nowhere (*September*, *Manhattan Murder Mystery*, *Deconstructing Harry* and *Sweet and Lowdown*) (* for *Manhattan Murder Mystery* and *Deconstructing Harry*)
Polkadots and Moonbeams (*Hannah and Her Sisters* and *Crimes and Misdemeanors*)
Poor Butterfly (*Bullets Over Broadway* and *Hollywood Ending*)
Rosalie (*Crimes and Misdemeanors* and *Deconstructing Harry*)
Sing, Sing, Sing (with a Swing) ("Oedipus Wrecks," *Manhattan Murder Mystery* and *Deconstructing Harry*)*
Smiles (*Sleeper* and *Another Woman*)
Sweet Georgia Brown (*Stardust Memories*, *Crimes and Misdemeanors* and *Sweet and Lowdown*)
Take Five (*Manhattan Murder Mystery* and *Mighty Aphrodite*)*
Take the "A" Train (*Radio Days* and *Melinda and Melinda*)*
That Old Feeling (*Radio Days*, *Husbands and Wives* and *Celebrity*) (* for *Husbands and Wives* and *Celebrity*)
The Way You Look Tonight (*Hannah and Her Sisters*, *Alice*, *Deconstructing Harry* and *Anything Else*) (* for *Alice* and *Deconstructing Harry*)
When Day Is Done (*September*, *Shadows and Fog* and *Sweet and Lowdown*)
When the Red, Red Robin Comes Bob, Bob Bobbin' Along (*Bullets Over Broadway* and *Deconstructing Harry*)
Who? (*September* and *Bullets Over Broadway*)
Will You Still Be Mine? (*Alice*, *Celebrity* and *Melinda and Melinda*)*
Wolverine Blues (*Sleeper* and *Interiors*)
You'd Be So Nice to Come Home To (*Radio Days* and *Another Woman*)

# Appendix 5: List of Songs and Jazz

A Frangesa (*Broadway Danny Rose*)
Abide with Me (*Sweet and Lowdown*)
After You've Gone (*Sweet and Lowdown*)
Agita (*Broadway Danny Rose*)
Ain't We Got Fun? (*Zelig*)
Akh, vy seni, moi seni (*Love and Death*)
Alabama Song (*Shadows and Fog*)
Alabamy Bound (*The Purple Rose of Cairo*)
Alice Blue Gown (*Alice*)
All Hail to You, Glenwood High (*Celebrity*)
All I Do Is Dream of You (*Crimes and Misdemeanors*)
All My Life (*Everyone Says I Love You*)
All of Me (*Sweet and Lowdown*)
All of You (*Broadway Danny Rose*)
All or Nothing at All (*Radio Days*)
All the Things You Are ("Oedipus Wrecks" and *Deconstructing Harry*)
Aloha Oe (*Sweet and Lowdown*)
America the Beautiful (*Zelig*)
American Patrol (*Radio Days*)
American Pie (*Celebrity*)
Anchors Aweigh (*Zelig*)
Aquarela do Brasil (see "Brazil")
As Time Goes By (*Play It Again, Sam*)
At the Jazz Band Ball (*Bullets Over Broadway*)
Auld Lang Syne (*Radio Days*)
Avalon (*Hannah and Her Sisters* and *Sweet and Lowdown*)
Babalu (*Radio Days*)
Back to the Apple (*Hannah and Her Sisters*)
The Band Played On (*Broadway Danny Rose*)
Beautiful Love (*Crimes and Misdemeanors*)
Because (*Crimes and Misdemeanors*)
Begin the Beguine (*Radio Days* and *Broadway Danny Rose*)
The Best Things in Life Are Free (*Manhattan Murder Mystery* and *Melinda and Melinda*)
Bewitched, Bothered and Bewildered (*Hannah and Her Sisters*)
Big Eternity (*Melinda and Melinda*)
The Big Noise from Winnetka (*Manhattan Murder Mystery*)
The Bilbao Song (*Another Woman*)
Blues for Allan Felix (*Play It Again, Sam*)
Body and Soul (*Stardust Memories* and *Radio Days*)
Brazil (*Stardust Memories*)
Breezin' Along with the Breeze (*Alice*)
But Not for Me (*Manhattan*)
By the Sleepy Lagoon (*Annie Hall*)
Ca c'est Paris (*Zelig*)
Canal Street Blues (*Sleeper*)
Caravan (*Alice* and *Sweet and Lowdown*)
The Carioca (*Radio Days*)
Catskill Cha Cha (*Broadway Danny Rose*)
'Cause I Believe in Loving (*Bananas*)
Chameleon Days (*Zelig*)
Chanel No. 5 (*Celebrity*)
The Changing Man Concerto (*Zelig*)
Charleston (*Zelig*)
Cheek to Cheek (*The Purple Rose of Cairo*)
Chella llà (*Broadway Danny Rose*)
Chicago (That Toddlin' Town) (*Zelig*)
Chinatown, My Chinatown (*Radio Days* and *Everyone Says I Love You*)
Chiquita Banana (*Everyone Says I Love You*)
Ciribiribin (*Broadway Danny Rose*)
Clarinet Marmalade (*Sweet and Lowdown*)
Cocktails for Two (*Everyone Says I Love You*, *Celebrity* and *Small Time Crooks*)
Come Back to Sorrento (see "Torna a Surriento!")
Come On (*Melinda and Melinda*)
Comin' at Ya (*Melinda and Melinda*)
Could It Be? (*Small Time Crooks*)
The Courier (*Alice*)
Crazy Rhythm (*Crimes and Misdemeanors* and *Bullets Over Broadway*)
Cuban Mambo (*Crimes and Misdemeanors*)
Cuddle Up a Little Closer (*Everyone Says I Love You*)
La Cumparsita (*Radio Days* and *Alice*)
Dancing in the Dark (*Radio Days*)
Dancing on the Ceiling (*Crimes and Misdemeanors*)

Darn That Dream (*Alice* and *Melinda and Melinda*)
Descarga (*Hollywood Ending*)
Diane (see "Tropical Mood — Rhumba")
Did I Remember (To Tell You I Adore You)? (*Celebrity*)
Do, Do, Do (*Manhattan*)
Doin' the Chameleon (*Zelig*)
The Donkey Serenade (*Radio Days*)
Don't Get Around Much Anymore (*Melinda and Melinda*)
Dream a Little Dream of Me (*Deconstructing Harry*)
Easy Lovin' (*Play It Again, Sam*)
Easy to Love (*Stardust Memories* and *Anything Else*)
Embraceable You (*Manhattan*)
Enjoy Yourself (It's Later Than You Think) (*Everyone Says I Love You*)
España Cañi (*Zelig*)
Everyone Says I Love You (*Everyone Says I Love You*)
Die Fahne Hoch (*Zelig*)
FAO Schwarz Clock Tower Song (see "Welcome to Our World of Toys")
Fascination (*Celebrity* and *Small Time Crooks*)
A Fine Romance (*Another Woman*)
Five Foot Two, Eyes of Blue (*Zelig*)
Flatbush Flanagan (*The Curse of the Jade Scorpion*)
The Flight of the Bumble Bee (*Radio Days*)
Flight of the Foo Birds (*Alice*)
For All We Know (*Celebrity*)
Freedonia Is Going to War (*Hannah and Her Sisters*)
Frenesi (*Radio Days*)
Funiculi Funicula (*Broadway Danny Rose*)
Gat I (*Anything Else*)
The Girl from Ipanema (*Deconstructing Harry*)
Glory Hallelujah (*Everything You Always Wanted to Know About Sex*)
God Rest You Merry, Gentlemen (*Annie Hall*)
Going Hollywood (*Hollywood Ending*)
Gone with the Wind (*Anything Else*)
Goodbye (*Radio Days*)
Great Day (*Crimes and Misdemeanors*)
Grindhouse (A Go-Go) (*Hollywood Ending*)
Guys and Dolls Overture (*Manhattan Murder Mystery*)

Happy Birthday to You (*Crimes and Misdemeanors*)
A Hard Way to Go (*Annie Hall*)
Have You Met Miss Jones? (*Manhattan Murder Mystery*)
He Loves and She Loves (*Manhattan*)
Hebrew School Rag (*Stardust Memories*)
Home Cookin' (*Crimes and Misdemeanors*)
Honeysuckle Rose (*Anything Else*)
Hooray for Captain Spaulding (*Everyone Says I Love You*)
Hooray for Hollywood (*Hollywood Ending*)
Hopak (*Crimes and Misdemeanors*)
Horos Tou Sakena (*Mighty Aphrodite*)
Horst Wessel Lied (see "Die Fahne Hoch")
Hot Lips (*Sweet and Lowdown*)
How High the Moon (*The Curse of the Jade Scorpion*)
The Hukilau Song (*Small Time Crooks*)
I Believe My Heart (*Match Point*)
I Can't Believe That You're in Love with Me (*Everyone Says I Love You* and *Anything Else*)
I Can't Get Started (*Anything Else*)
I Could Write a Book (*Deconstructing Harry*)
I Don't Want to Walk Without You (*Radio Days*)
I Double Dare You (*Radio Days*)
I Dream Too Much (*Alice*)
I Got Rhythm (*Celebrity*)
I Hadn't Anyone Till You (*Mighty Aphrodite*)
I Happen to Like New York (*Manhattan Murder Mystery*)
I Know That You Know (*Crimes and Misdemeanors*)
I Let a Song Go Out of My Heart (*Melinda and Melinda*)
I Love My Baby, My Baby Loves Me (*Zelig* and *The Purple Rose of Cairo*)
I Remember You (*Hannah and Her Sisters* and *Alice*)
I Want a Girl ( Just Like the Girl That Married Dear Old Dad) ("Oedipus Wrecks")
Ice Cream (I Scream, You Scream, We All Scream For) (*Sleeper*)
If Dreams Come True (*Stardust Memories*)
If I Didn't Care (*Radio Days*)
If I Had You (*Hannah and Her Sisters* and *Everyone Says I Love You*)

If You Are but a Dream (*Radio Days*)
I'll Be Seeing You ("Oedipus Wrecks" and *Crimes and Misdemeanors*)
I'll Get By (*Zelig*)
I'll See You Again (*Crimes and Misdemeanors*)
I'll See You in My Dreams (*Stardust Memories* and *Sweet and Lowdown*)
I'm a Dreamer, Aren't We All? (*Everyone Says I Love You*)
I'm Confessin' (That I Love You) (*September*)
I'm Forever Blowing Bubbles (*Sweet and Lowdown*)
I'm Gettin' Sentimental Over You (*Radio Days*)
I'm in Love Again (*Hannah and Her Sisters*)
I'm in the Mood for Love (*Manhattan Murder Mystery*)
I'm Old Fashioned (*Hannah and Her Sisters*)
I'm Sitting on Top of the World (*Zelig*)
I'm Thru with Love (*Everyone Says I Love You*)
The Impossible Dream (*Celebrity*)
In a Mellotone (*Melinda and Melinda*)
In a Persian Market ("Oedipus Wrecks" and *The Curse of the Jade Scorpion*)
The "In" Crowd (*Mighty Aphrodite*)
In the Mood (*Radio Days*)
Indiana (Back Home Again In) (*Sweet and Lowdown*)
L'Internationale (*Zelig*)
Isn't It Romantic? (*Hannah and Her Sisters*)
It Could Happen to You (*Hannah and Her Sisters* and *Anything Else*)
It Don't Mean a Thing (If It Ain't Got That Swing) (*Sweet and Lowdown*)
It Had to Be You (*Annie Hall*)
It's Been So Long (*Hollywood Ending*)
It's the Same Sad Story All Over Again (*Play It Again, Sam*)
I've Found a New Baby ("Oedipus Wrecks" and *Mighty Aphrodite*)
I've Got a Crush on You (*Manhattan*)
I've Got a Feeling I'm Falling (*Zelig*)
I've Got You (*Crimes and Misdemeanors*)
I've Heard That Song Before (*Hannah and Her Sisters*)
Ja, ja, die Frau'n sind meine schwache Seite (*Shadows and Fog*)

Jack's the Lad (see "The Sailor's Hornpipe")
Joe Avery (*Sleeper*)
June in January ("Oedipus Wrecks")
Just a Gigolo (*Sweet and Lowdown*)
Just in Time (*Small Time Crooks*)
Just One More Chance (*September*)
Just One of Those Things (*Stardust Memories* and *Radio Days*)
Just Say I Love Her (*Everyone Says I Love You*)
Just You, Just Me (*Hannah and Her Sisters* and *Everyone Says I Love You*)
Keep Italian in Your Heart (see "My Bambina")
Keepin' Out of Mischief Now (*Interiors*)
Kumbayah (*Celebrity*)
Land of the Gay Caballero (*Manhattan*)
Lazy River (*Bullets Over Broadway*)
Leonard the Lizard (*Zelig*)
Lester Lanin Cha Cha (*Small Time Crooks*)
Let's All Sing Like the Birdies Sing (*Radio Days*)
Let's Call the Whole Thing Off (*Manhattan*)
Let's Misbehave (*Everything You Always Wanted to Know About Sex* and *Bullets Over Broadway*)
Liebestraum No. 3 (*Sweet and Lowdown*)
Li'l Darlin (*Mighty Aphrodite*)
Limehouse Blues (*Alice* and *Sweet and Lowdown*)
Looking at You (*Everyone Says I Love You*)
Louise (*Everyone Says I Love You*)
Love Is Here to Stay (*Manhattan*)
Love Is Sweeping the Country (*Manhattan*)
Love Me (*Melinda and Melinda*)
Lovely to Look At (*Another Woman*)
Lullaby of Birdland (*Celebrity*)
Lullaby of Broadway (*Radio Days*)
Lulu's Back in Town (*Sweet and Lowdown*)
Luna mezzo mare (*Broadway Danny Rose*)
Ma! (He's Making Eyes at Me) (*Bullets Over Broadway*)
Mack the Knife (*Alice* and *Shadows and Fog*)
Mairzy Doats (*Radio Days*)
Make Believe (*Another Woman* and *Bullets Over Broadway*)
Makin' Whoopee (*Husbands and Wives* and *Everyone Says I Love You*)

Manhattan (*Mighty Aphrodite*)
Les Marseillaise (*Play It Again, Sam*)
La Mattchiche (*Zelig*)
La Maxixe (see "La Mattchiche")
Memories of You (*Melinda and Melinda*)
Miami Beach Rumba (*Deconstructing Harry*)
Mimi (*Everyone Says I Love You*)
Mine (*Manhattan*)
Misty (*Manhattan Murder Mystery*)
Moonglow (*September, Alice* and *Melinda and Melinda*)
Moonlight Becomes You (*Alice*)
Moonlight Serenade (*Stardust Memories*)
M-O-T-H-E-R (A Word That Means the World to Me) ("Oedipus Wrecks")
Mountain Greenery (*Small Time Crooks*)
Murder He Says (*Crimes and Misdemeanors*)
Music Makers (*Small Time Crooks*)
My Baby Just Cares for Me (*Everyone Says I Love You*)
My Bambina (*Broadway Danny Rose*)
My Ideal (*September*)
Mystery Pacific (*Sweet and Lowdown*)
Nagasaki (*Bullets Over Broadway*)
National Emblem March (*Broadway Danny Rose*)
Neo Minore (*Mighty Aphrodite*)
Nevertheless (I'm in Love with You) (*Sweet and Lowdown*)
Night and Day (*Radio Days* and *September*)
No Lover, No Friend (That's the End) (*Everyone Says I Love You*)
No Moon at All (*Hollywood Ending* and *Melinda and Melinda*)
O Christmas Tree / O Tannenbaum (*Annie Hall* and *Alice*)
O Sole Mio (*Broadway Danny Rose*)
Oh, Lady, Be Good! (*Manhattan*)
Old Devil Moon (*Small Time Crooks*)
Old Fashioned Love (*Sweet and Lowdown*)
On a Slow Boat to China (*September* and *Celebrity*)
On the Sunny Side of the Street (*Another Woman*)
One Day at a Time (*The Purple Rose of Cairo*)
One O'Clock Jump (*Stardust Memories*)
One, Two, Three Kick (*Radio Days*)
Opus One (*Radio Days*)
Out of Nowhere (*September, Manhattan Murder Mystery, Deconstructing Harry* and *Sweet and Lowdown*)

Palesteena (*Stardust Memories*)
Paper Doll (*Radio Days*)
Paree! (see "Ca c'est Paris")
Parlez-moi d'amour (see "Speak to Me of Love")
The Peanut Vendor (*Sweet and Lowdown*)
Penthouse Serenade (When We're Alone) (*Mighty Aphrodite*)
Perdido (*Another Woman*)
Pistol Packin' Mama (*Radio Days*)
Pleasure Mad (see "Viper Mad")
Polkadots and Moonbeams (*Hannah and Her Sisters* and *Crimes and Misdemeanors*)
Poor Butterfly (*Bullets Over Broadway* and *Hollywood Ending*)
A Pretty Girl Is Like a Melody (*Sleeper*)
Queens Club Trio (*Broadway Danny Rose*)
Quiero la noche (*Bananas*)
Recurrence (*Everyone Says I Love You*)
The Red River Valley (*Everything You Always Wanted to Know About Sex*)
Re-Lax Jingle (*Radio Days*)
Remember Pearl Harbor (*Radio Days*)
Rosalie (*Crimes and Misdemeanors* and *Deconstructing Harry*)
Roses of Picardy (*Another Woman*)
Runnin' Wild (*Zelig*)
'S Wonderful (*Manhattan*)
A Sailboat in the Moonlight (*Zelig*)
San (*Sleeper*)
Satan Takes a Holiday (*Everyone Says I Love You*)
The Sailor's Hornpipe (*Radio Days*)
Schlof, mein Kind (*Radio Days*)
Seems Like Old Times (*Annie Hall*)
September Song (*Radio Days*)
Serenade in Blue (*Hollywood Ending*)
She's Funny That Way (*Deconstructing Harry*)
S-H-I-N-E (*Sweet and Lowdown*)
Since My Best Gal Turned Me Down (*Sweet and Lowdown*)
Sing, Sing, Sing (with a Swing) ("Oedipus Wrecks," *Manhattan Murder Mystery* and *Deconstructing Harry*)
Singin' the Blues (Till My Daddy Comes Home) (*Bullets Over Broadway*)
Slip into the Crowd (*Hannah and Her Sisters*)
Smiles (*Sleeper* and *Another Woman*)

Softly, as in a Morning Sunrise (*Hollywood Ending*)
Somebody Stole My Gal (*Melinda and Melinda*)
Someone to Watch Over Me (*Manhattan*)
The Song Is You (*Husbands and Wives*)
Soon (*Celebrity*)
Sophisticated Lady (*The Curse of the Jade Scorpion*)
La Sorella (see "La Mattchiche")
South American Way (*Radio Days*)
Southern Comfort (*Alice*)
Speak to Me of Love (*Sweet and Lowdown*)
Star Eyes (*Crimes and Misdemeanors*)
Stardust (*Stardust Memories*)
Steady, Steady (*Small Time Crooks*)
Stompin' at the Savoy (*Small Time Crooks*)
Strike Up the Band (*Manhattan*)
Sugar (That Sugar Baby of Mine) (*Stardust Memories*)
Sunday (the Day Before My Birthday) (*Anything Else*)
Sunny Side Up (*Zelig*)
Sunrise Serenade (*The Curse of the Jade Scorpion*)
Sweet and Lovely (*Hollywood Ending*)
Sweet and Low-Down (*Manhattan*)
Sweet Georgia Brown (*Stardust Memories*, *Crimes and Misdemeanors* and *Sweet and Lowdown*)
Sweet Sue, Just You (*Sweet and Lowdown*)
Tain't Nobody's Biz-Ness If I Do (*Sleeper*)
Take Five (*Manhattan Murder Mystery* and *Mighty Aphrodite*)
Take the "A" Train (*Radio Days* and *Melinda and Melinda*)
Taking a Chance on Love (*Crimes and Misdemeanors*)
Tangerine (*Celebrity*)
Tarantella (*Broadway Danny Rose*)
Tequila (*Small Time Crooks*)
That Certain Feeling (*Bullets Over Broadway*)
That Jungle Jamboree (*Bullets Over Broadway*)
That Old Feeling (*Radio Days*, *Husbands and Wives* and *Celebrity*)
There'll Be Another Spring (*Anything Else*)
There'll Be Some Changes Made (*Sweet and Lowdown*)
There Will Never Be Another You (*Anything Else*)

They're Either Too Young or Too Old (*Radio Days*)
Thinking About Bix (*Zelig*)
This Could Be the Start of Something Big (*Small Time Crooks*)
This Year's Kisses (*Crimes and Misdemeanors*)
Thou Swell (*Bullets Over Broadway*)
3:00 AM Blues (*Sweet and Lowdown*)
Three Little Words (*Stardust Memories*)
Tickle Toe (*Stardust Memories*)
Tico-Tico (*Radio Days*)
Till We Meet Again (*Sleeper*)
Too Close for Comfort (*Hollywood Ending*)
Toot, Toot, Tootsie! (Goodbye) (*Bullets Over Broadway*)
Torna a Surriento! (*Broadway Danny Rose*)
Top Hat, White Tie and Tails (*Husbands and Wives*)
Tra Veglia e Sonno (*Broadway Danny Rose*)
Tropical Mood — Rhumba (*Stardust Memories*)
The Trot (*Hannah and Her Sisters*)
Truckin' (*Celebrity*)
Tuxedo Junction (*The Curse of the Jade Scorpion*)
Twelfth Street Rag (*Sweet and Lowdown*)
Twisted (*Deconstructing Harry*)
Two Sleepy People (*The Curse of the Jade Scorpion*)
Tzena, Tzena, Tzena (*Deconstructing Harry*)
Unfaithful Woman (*Sweet and Lowdown*)
Venetian Scenes (*Everyone Says I Love You*)
Viper Mad (*Sweet and Lowdown*)
Waiting (*Deconstructing Harry*)
Walking My Baby Back Home (*Mighty Aphrodite*)
The Way You Look Tonight (*Hannah and Her Sisters*, *Alice*, *Deconstructing Harry* and *Anything Else*)
Welcome to Our World of Toys (*Mighty Aphrodite*)
We Wish You a Merry Christmas (*Annie Hall* and *Alice*)
West Coast Blues (*Husbands and Wives*)
What a Little Moonlight Can Do (*Everyone Says I Love You*)
What Is This Thing Called Love? (*Husbands and Wives*)
What'll I Do? (*September*)
Wenn de Weiße Flieder Blüht (see "When the White Lilacs Bloom Again")

When Day Is Done (*September*, *Shadows and Fog* and *Sweet and Lowdown*)
When the Red, Red Robin Comes Bob, Bob Bobbin' Along (*Bullets Over Broadway* and *Deconstructing Harry*)
When the White Lilacs Bloom Again (*Shadows and Fog*)
When You're Smiling (*Mighty Aphrodite*)
When Your Lover Has Gone (*Mighty Aphrodite*)
Where or When (*Hannah and Her Sisters*)
Whispering (*Mighty Aphrodite*)
The White Cliffs of Dover (*Radio Days*)
Who? (*September* and *Bullets Over Broadway*)
Will You Still Be Mine? (*Alice*, *Celebrity* and *Melinda and Melinda*)
With Plenty of Money and You (*Small Time Crooks*)
Wolverine Blues (*Sleeper* and *Interiors*)
World Music (*Alice*)
Wrap Your Troubles in Dreams (*Sweet and Lowdown*)
Yes, Sir, That's My Baby (*Sleeper*)
You and I (*Radio Days*)
You Are Too Beautiful (*Hannah and Her Sisters*)
You Brought a New Kind of Love to Me (*Everyone Says I Love You*)
You Do Something to Me (*Mighty Aphrodite*)
You Have Such Reptile Eyes (*Zelig*)
You Made Me Love You (*Hannah and Her Sisters*)
You May Be Six People, but I Love You (*Zelig*)
You Oughta Be in Pictures (*Celebrity*)
You Took Advantage of Me (*Bullets Over Broadway*)
You Were Meant for Me (*Sweet and Lowdown*)
You'd Be So Nice to Come Home To (*Radio Days* and *Another Woman*)
You'll Never Know (*Radio Days*)
You're Getting to Be a Habit with Me (*Radio Days*)
You're Nobody Till Somebody Loves You (*Broadway Danny Rose*)
You've Got to See Mamma Ev'ry Night (*Bullets Over Broadway*)
Zelda's Theme (*Small Time Crooks*)

# APPENDIX 6: CLASSICAL MUSIC BY COMPOSER

As already mentioned, Allen's love of jazz and its inclusion in his films has, to some extent, overshadowed his liking and use of classical music. However, as you will see from the following list, Allen has incorporated classical music into his films on a regular basis throughout his career. The most predominate composer is Bach (especially during the late 1980s), who appears in six films. Unlike with jazz and popular music, Allen does not tend to use the same piece twice, the only repetition to date being Mussorgsky's *Night on Bald Mountain*.

## Bach, Johann Sebastian

Cello Sonata No. 2 in D Major, BWV 1028 (*Another Woman*)
Cello Sonata No. 3 in G Minor, BWV 1029 (*Another Woman*)
Cello Suite No. 2 in D Minor for Solo Cello, BWV 1008 (*Small Time Crooks*)
Cello Suite No. 6 in D Major, BWV 1012 (*Another Woman*)
Concerto for Two Violins in D Minor, BWV 1043 (*Hannah and Her Sisters*)
English Suite No. 2 in A Minor, BWV 807 (*Crimes and Misdemeanors*)
Harpsichord Concerto No. 5 in F Minor, BWV 1056 (*Hannah and Her Sisters*)
Partita No. 3 in A Minor, BWV 827 (*Melinda and Melinda*)

Prelude No. 2 in C Minor, BWV 847 (*Melinda and Melinda*)
Violin Concerto No. 1 in A Minor, BWV 1041 (*Alice*)

## Bartók, Béla
String Quartet No. 4 (*Melinda and Melinda*)

## Beethoven, Ludwig van
Piano Sonata No. 17 in D Minor, "Tempest," Op. 31 No. 2 (*Sleeper*)
Symphony No. 5 in C Minor, Op. 67 (*Celebrity*)
Symphony No. 7 in A Major, Op. 92 (*Melinda and Melinda*)
Violin Sonata No. 5 in F Major, "Spring," Op. 24 (*Love and Death*)

## Bizet, Georges
*The Pearl Fishers* ("Mi par d'udir ancora") (*Match Point*)

## Boccherini, Luigi
String Quintet in E Major, Op. 13, No. 5 (*Love and Death*)

## Donizetti, Gaetano
*L'Elisir d'amore* ("Una furtiva lagrima") (*Match Point*)

## Gershwin, George
*Rhapsody in Blue* (*Manhattan*)

## Gomes, Antonio Carlos
*Salvator Rosa* ("Mia piccirella") (*Match Point*)

## Handel, George Frideric
*Messiah* ("And the glory of the Lord shall be revealed") (*Sleeper*)

## Hassler, Hans Leo
*Missa Secunda* ("Gloria") (*Hannah and Her Sisters*)

## Herbert, Victor
*Naughty Marietta* ("Tramp! Tramp! Tramp!") (*Bananas*)

## Leoncavallo, Ruggero
*Pagliacci* ("Vesti la giubba") (*Zelig*)

## Liszt, Franz
Liebestraum No. 3 (*Sweet and Lowdown*) (in a jazz version)

## Mahler, Gustav
Symphony No. 4 (*Another Woman*)
Symphony No. 9 (*Husbands and Wives*)

## Malotte, Albert Hay
"The Lord's Prayer" (*A Midsummer Night's Sex Comedy*)

## Marshall, Scott
"The Modern Dance" (*Small Time Crooks*)

## Mendelssohn, Felix
*A Midsummer Night's Dream*, Op. 61 (*A Midsummer Night's Sex Comedy*)
Piano Concerto No. 2 in D Minor, Op. 40 (*A Midsummer Night's Sex Comedy*)
Piano Trio No. 1 in D Minor, Op. 49 (*Love and Death*)
Symphony No. 3 in A Minor, Op. 56 "Scottish" (*A Midsummer Night's Sex Comedy*)
Violin Concerto in E Minor, Op. 64 (*A Midsummer Night's Sex Comedy*)

## Mozart, Wolfgang Amadeus
*The Magic Flute*, K. 620 (Overture) (*Love and Death*)
Symphony No. 40 in G Minor, K. 550 (*Manhattan*)
Symphony No. 41 in C Major, "Jupiter," K. 551 (*Annie Hall*)

## Mussorgsky, Modest
*Night on Bald Mountain* (*Stardust Memories* and *Deconstructing Harry*)

## Prokofiev, Sergei
*Alexander Nevsky*, Op. 78 (*Love and Death*)
*Lieutenant Kijé Suite*, Op. 60 (*Love and Death*)
*The Love of Three Oranges Suite*, Op. 33a (*Love and Death*)
*Scythian Suite*, Op. 20 (from *Ala et Lolly*) (*Love and Death*)

## Puccini, Giacomo
*Gianni Schicchi* ("O mio babbino caro") (*Bananas*)

## Classical Music by Composer / 187

*Madam Butterfly* (Introduction to Act I) (*Hannah and Her Sisters*)
*Manon Lescaut* ("Sola, perduta abbandonata") (*Hannah and Her Sisters*)

### Rachmaninov, Sergei
Prelude in B Minor, Op. 32, No. 10 (*Small Time Crooks*)

### Rimsky-Korsakov, Nikolai
"The Flight of the Bumble Bee" (*Radio Days*) (in a jazz version)

### Rossini, Gioacchino
*William Tell* ("Arresta ... Quali sguardi") (*Match Point*)

### Satie, Erik
*Gymnopédie No. 1* (*Another Woman*)

### Schubert, Franz
*Die schöne Müllerin*, D 795 (No. 2, "Wohin?") (*A Midsummer Night's Sex Comedy*)
String Quartet No. 15 in G Major, D 887 (*Crimes and Misdemeanors*)

### Schumann, Robert
*Dichterliebe*, Op. 48 (No. 7, "Ich grolle nicht") (*A Midsummer Night's Sex Comedy*)

### Strauss, Johann (II)
*Voices of Spring*, Op. 410 (*Small Time Crooks*)

### Stravinsky, Igor
Concerto in D for String Orchestra (*Melinda and Melinda*)

### Tchaikovsky, Peter Ilyich
1812 Overture, Op. 49 (*Bananas*)

### Varèse, Edgard
*Ecuatorial* (*Another Woman*)

### Verdi, Giuseppe
*Macbeth* ("O figli, o figli miei! ... Ah, la paterna mano") (*Match Point*)
*Il Trovatore* ("Mal reggendo all'aspro assalto") (*Match Point*)
*La Traviata* ("Un dì felice, eterea" and Valse from Act I) (*Match Point*)
*Otello* ("Desdemona rea!") (*Match Point*)
*Rigoletto* ("Gualtier Maldè! ... Caro nome") (*Match Point*)

### Wagner, Richard
*The Flying Dutchman* ("Wie oft in Meeres tiefsten Schlund") (*Manhattan Murder Mystery*)
*Lohengrin* ("Bridal Chorus") (*Celebrity*) (in a piano version)

### Weill, Kurt
"Alabama Song" (*Shadows and Fog*) (in a dance band version)
"The Bilbao Song" (*Another Woman*) (in a piano version)
*Kleine Dreigroschenmusik* (Little Threepenny Music) (*Shadows and Fog*)
"Mack the Knife" (*Alice*) (in a jazz version)
*Die sieben Todsünden* (The Seven Deadly Sins) (*Shadows and Fog*)
"September Song" (*Radio Days*) (in a jazz version)

# NOTES

## Preface

1. Sancton, p. 30.

## Introduction

1. Sancton, p. 30.
2. Björkman, p. 37.
3. Quoted in Guthrie, pp. 126–7.
4. Björkman, p. 197.
5. Woody Allen, transcript of interview with Tom Sancton, October 30, 2002.
6. Kaplan, p. 118.
7. Woody Allen, interview with David Geffner, *DGA Magazine* 27 (May 2003).
8. Björkman, p. 34.
9. Kaplan, p. 118.
10. Ibid.
11. Björkman, p. 34.
12. Kaplan, p. 122.
13. Sancton, p. 29.
14. Ibid. Note that here Allen overlooks the fact that he had used Bechet's "Tropical Mood — Rhumba" in *Stardust Memories* (1980). His remarks to Fred Kaplan about using Sidney Bechet's music twice is correct, however, as by that time (2001) he had used another Bechet recording "Viper Mad" in 1999 for *Sweet and Lowdown*.
15. Ibid.
16. Björkman, p. 66.
17. Sancton, p. 30.
18. Lax, *Woody Allen: A Biography*, p. 399.
19. Kaplan, p. 122.
20. For an interesting analysis of this subject, see Carol Goodson's essay *Song As Subtext: The Virtual Reality of Lyrics in the Films of Woody Allen* in *Woody Allen: A Casebook*, edited by Kimball King.
21. Benayoun, p. 174.
22. The numerous recordings of Erroll Garner in Allen's films perhaps provide the best example of this, where Garner's idiosyncratic introductions are invariably omitted.
23. Woody Allen, interview with Melvyn Bragg, *The South Bank Show*, January 16, 1994.
24. Björkman, p. 200.
25. Thomas Fahy, *Dissonant Harmonies,* in *Woody Allen: A Casebook*, edited by Kimball King, p. 81.
26. Lax, *Woody Allen: A Biography*, p. 263.

## Alice

1. Lax, *Woody Allen: A Biography*, p. 321.
2. Hirsch, p. 242.
3. Björkman, p. 232.
4. Paul Weston was known as the "Master of Mood Music" and made a significant contribution to this style of music during the 1950s with albums such as *Music for Dreaming*, *Music for Romancing* and *Dream Time Music*.
5. Although it is implied, "Darn That Dream" does not actually appear on this album (see appendix 1).
6. Allen may be making a subtle reference here, as this recording of "La Cumparsita" featured in Columbia's 1951 biopic of the famous dancer/actor. Valentino contributed heavily to the dance's fame in 1921 when he danced the tango in *The Four Horseman of the Apocalypse*.
7. Brode, p. 279; Schwartz, p. 102.
8. Only Danny Alguire, Ward Kimball and Frank Thomas are credited in the film.

## Annie Hall

1. Björkman, p. 76.
2. Allen, interview with Bragg, *The South Bank Show*, January 16, 1994.
3. Yacowar, p. 173.
4. Björkman, p. 92.
5. Quoted in Rosenblum and Karen, pp. 288–9.

6. This piece of music is not included in the end credits.

## *Another Woman*

1. Bach's three "cello sonatas" (BWV 1027-29) were originally written for viola da gamba and harpsichord.
2. *Gymnopédie No. 3* is given in the end credits, but what we actually hear is No. 1. This confusion is due to the fact that Debussy — who only orchestrated Nos. 1 and 3 — inadvertently reversed the order upon publication. As a result, a number of recordings (including the one used by Allen; see appendix 1) list these two pieces the wrong way round.
3. Björkman, p. 200.
4. Brode, p. 267.
5. Pauline Kael, *The New Yorker*, quoted in Brode, p. 267.
6. Baxter, p. 361.
7. This scene is similar to one in *Manhattan* where, again, two couples are listening to classical music at a concert and two of the people are having an affair with each other.

## *Anything Else*

1. Schuller, *The Swing Era: The Development of Jazz, 1930–1945*, p. 532.
2. Oscar Peterson does not actually play on this track.

## *Bananas*

1. Rosenblum and Karen, p. 259.
2. Björkman, p. 45.
3. Rosenblum and Karen, p. 251.
4. *Viewpoint,* the Washington Post's live discussion forum, October 10, 2000.
5. Yacowar, pp. 134–5.

## *Broadway Danny Rose*

1. The two also collaborated on *Leader of the Band* (1988) and *The Lemon Sisters* (1990).

## *Bullets Over Broadway*

1. This is the first time Allen has used a Gershwin song in one of his films since *Manhattan* fifteen years earlier.
2. It is interesting to note that Allen uses Bix Beiderbecke (whose chronic alcoholism hastened his premature death) to accompany the two scenes that emphasize Helen Sinclair's drink problem — in the speakeasy when she orders two martinis (both for her!) and on a train drinking paint remover.

3. All of the studio musicians were invited to be in the band seen on screen except the banjoist, Cynthia Sayer, for authenticity reasons — there would have been no women playing in bands at this time. She offered to wear a wig and a moustache, but was told that she could only appear if she cut her hair like a man. She refused! Marty Grosz is seen miming her part in the film.
4. The Harlem Footwarmers was one of Duke Ellington's many pseudonyms. In the end credits to the film only Duke Ellington is given.

## *Celebrity*

1. Schwartz, p. 56.
2. Schwartz, p. 57.
3. Hirsch, p. 260.
4. Hirsch, p. 257.
5. Schwartz, p. 57.
6. Bailey, p. 263.
7. It is interesting to note that the nautical imagery in this song, which accompanies the most positive event in Robin's life, parallels that of "On a Slow Boat to China," which attends the most negative episode in Lee's life: his abortive affair with Nola and the resulting break-up with Bonnie and loss of his novel.

## *Crimes and Misdemeanors*

1. Brode, p. 272.
2. Björkman, pp. 217–219.
3. Björkman, p. 213.
4. Lax, *Woody Allen: A Biography*, pp. 367-8.
5. Ibid. It is interesting to note that "I Dream Too Much" is listed in this quotation. This song actually appears in *Alice* — which follows *Crimes and Misdemeanors* — so either Allen or Lax are mistaken here, unless Allen had already chosen this song for his next film, which is unlikely.
6. The end credits give only the personnel of the "Jazz Band" but not the instruments they play. Major Holley Jr. is listed incorrectly as "Major Halley Jr."
7. This song appears in the end credits, but the clip we see from *This Gun for Hire* is not of Veronica Lake singing. I have included the song here for the sake of completeness.
8. This film music is not included in the end credits.
9. As with the "Jazz Band" above, only the names of the performers in the "Wedding Band" are given in the end credits, but not the instruments they play.
10. This piece of music is not included in the end credits.

## The Curse of the Jade Scorpion

1. Official Dreamworks Web site, www.dreamworks.com/jadescorpion.
2. Ibid.
3. Ibid.
4. Susan Wloszczyna, "Woody Allen, in the Mood," *USA Today*, August 1, 2001.
5. Ibid.
6. One wonders if Allen considered using de Paris's recording of "Madagascar" in this film, owing to the title being one of the trigger words used by the hypnotist.

## Deconstructing Harry

1. Woody Allen, interview with John Lahr, *The New Yorker*, December 9, 1997.
2. Kaplan, p. 122.
3. Lee, p. 206.
4. *New York Times*, December 12, 1997.
5. Girgus, p. 151.
6. Schwartz, p. 84.
7. Schwartz, p. 85.
8. "Christopher Columbus" was written by tenor horn player Leon "Chu" Berry with lyrics by Andy Razaf for Fletcher Henderson's orchestra in 1936. Despite its inclusion in the end credits to *Deconstructing Harry*, I have omitted it from this section list (and other places in the book where "Sing, Sing, Sing" appears), as technically it is not heard as a separate piece.
9. This is the exact same track previously used in *Manhattan Murder Mystery*. However, in the film's end credits only Django Reinhardt is acknowledged.
10. This is the sixth film in succession in which a Cole Porter song has appeared on the soundtrack.

## Everyone Says I Love You

1. Kaplan, p. 121.
2. With *Evita* being released in the same year, some thought that this could be the moment that the film musical saw a revival. At the time, the musical was the only film genre not to sustain a comeback. Of the few modern examples, *The Little Shop of Horrors* (1986) had moderate success, but *Newsies* (1992) was a complete turkey. More recently, films such as *Moulin Rouge* (2001) and *Chicago* (2002) have done much to restore the musical as a viable film genre.
3. Paul Power, "The Film Music of Woody Allen," *Film West*, May 28, 1997, pp. 40–41.
4. Taken from the production notes posted on Edward Norton's Web site, www.edward-norton.org.
5. Bruce Kirkland, "Everyone Sings I Love You," review, *Toronto Sun*, February 1, 1997.
6. Kaplan, p. 121.
7. Hirsch, pp. 274–5.
8. Lax, *Woody Allen: A Biography*, p. 401.
9. Taken from the production notes posted on Edward Norton's Web site, www.edward-norton.org.
10. Quoted on the Edward Norton information page, www.edward-norton.org/everyone.html.
11. Bruce Kirkland, "Everyone Sings I Love You," review, *Toronto Sun*, February 1, 1997.
12. Woody Allen, interview with Brandon Judell for *indieWire*, December 7, 1999.
13. Richard Schickel, "They Sorta Got Rhythm," review, *Time*, December 9, 1996, p. 81.
14. Lax, *Woody Allen: A Biography*, p. 399.
15. Taken from the production notes posted on Edward Norton's Web site, www.edward-norton.org.
16. Potter's script was later taken up by Hollywood and released as a film in 1981 starring Steve Martin, directed by Herbert Ross, who had directed *Play It Again, Sam*.
17. On the original sheet music published by Famous Music Corporation in 1932, this song is spelt using an apostrophe: "Ev'ryone Says I Love You." However, throughout the book I have chosen to use the title as it appears in the film.
18. The performers are given in the film as listed, however, in the film the other instruments have been mixed out as much as possible in order to emphasize the piano.
19. Allen uses this symphony in *Another Woman*, a film that shares a similar plot device with "Everyone Sings I Love You," where a psychoanalyst's sessions are overheard.
20. Dick Hyman, correspondence with author, November 14, 2003.
21. Ibid.
22. This song first hit the airwaves in 1944. It was written to help teach Americans how to ripen and use bananas, which were at the time an exotic tropical fruit. At its peak, the jingle was played 376 times a day on radio stations across the United States. It was one of the most successful commercial jingles of all time.
23. An English version of this song was also recorded for the film but not used.

## Everything You Always Wanted to Know About Sex

1. The use of "As Time Goes By" in *Play It Again, Sam* can be discounted, as this would

most likely have been Billy Goldenberg or Herbert Ross's choice.

## Hannah and Her Sisters

1. Girgus, pp. 117–118.
2. Allen, *Hannah and Her Sisters*, p. 144.
3. Carol Goodson, *Song as Subtext: The Virtual Reality of Lyrics in the Films of Woody Allen*, in *Woody Allen: A Casebook*, edited by Kimball King, p. 4.
4. Robert Lindner, correspondence with author, October 26, 2005.
5. Although the Rome Opera Chorus is credited, we do not actually hear them, as only the instrumental introduction to this opera is used in the film.
6. The film credits state that this song was written by Michael Bramon and performed by "Michael Bramon and The 39 Steps." However, apart from these credits — and subsequent references based upon them — I can find no link between Michael Bramon and the band. The song was actually written by the band's vocalist, Chris Barry, and guitarist, Pierre Major, as given on the EP release of this song in 1986 on Gate Records. Nor is Bramon a member of the band, even though he is credited as being the drummer (this is in fact Andre Gagne). The band's involvement in *Hannah and Her Sisters* came about after they answered a cattle call for a punk band to appear in the film. They sent a tape and photo, auditioned for Allen and performed this song at CBGB live to camera. Note also that the band's name does not include a definite article.
7. This piece of music is not included in the end credits.
8. This piece of music is not included in the end credits.

## Hollywood Ending

1. ©1942 (Renewed) WB Music Corp. All rights reserved. Used by permission.
2. Woody Allen, interview with Tom Sancton, October 30, 2002.
3. Woody Allen, interview with Robbie Rozelle in 2003, www.robbierozelle.com.
4. The end credits also give Dick Powell, Frances Langford, Johnny "Scat" Davis and Gene Krupa, but I have omitted these, as the extract we hear contains no singing.

## Husbands and Wives

1. Björkman, p. 66.

## Interiors

1. Björkman, p. 101.
2. Allen, *Four Films of Woody Allen*, p. 170.

## Love and Death

1. Rosenblum and Karen, pp. 269–270.
2. Björkman, pp. 70–1.
3. The piece finishes before the end credits, which appear without music. This anticipates Allen's musical approach in his next two films.
4. For most of the appearances of this piece, the music has been altered to meet the tempo requirements and length of each respective scene. Certain cues have been slightly speeded up (which affects the pitch), several bars have been repeated, and on two occasions, the opening and closing sections have been spliced together. These modifications have made it impossible to identify with certainty which actual recording Allen and Rosenblum used. The speeding up of the music also applies to the "The Battle on Ice" extract heard later.

## Manhattan

1. Allen, *Four Films of Woody Allen*, p. 181.
2. Kaplan, p. 118.
3. Björkman, p. 35.
4. Ibid.
5. Kaplan, p. 118.
6. Baxter, p. 272.
7. Tom Pierson, correspondence with author, March 24, 2005.
8. Ibid.
9. Kaplan, p. 118.
10. Tom Pierson, correspondence with author, December 30, 2004.
11. Lax, *Woody Allen: A Biography*, pp. 298–9.
12. Yacowar, pp. 202–3.
13. Brode, p. 186.
14. Allen, *Four Films of Woody Allen*, p. 194.
15. Hirsch, p. 56.
16. In order to accommodate this sequence, Gershwin's *Rhapsody* has been carefully edited to include both the opening and closing sections, seamlessly joined together.
17. Gershwin, p. 261.
18. This piece of music is not included in the end credits.

## Manhattan Murder Mystery

1. Björkman, p. 255.
2. Allen, interview with Bragg, *The South Bank Show*, January 16, 1994.

3. The end credits understandably list this as being performed by "Bob Crosby and His Orchestra and Bob Cats," the band to which both Bob Haggart and Ray Bauduc belonged. However, this song is purely a duet for bass and drums, with added whistling.
4. This film music is not included in the end credits.

## Match Point

1. Woody Allen, interview with Douglas McGrath (Allen's co-writer on *Bullets Over Broadway*), December 5, 2005 at the Directors Guild of America in New York, available at www.aintitcool.com.
2. Production notes taken from the official *Match Point* Web site, www.matchpoint.dreamworks.com.
3. The whole recording is 5:26 and would have been too long for this purpose if it had been heard complete.
4. The soprano, Janis Kelly, is also seen on stage, but is not heard singing.
5. Possibly owing to financial reasons, the arias "Un dì felice, eterea" and "Caro nome"— seemingly seen performed at the Royal Opera House—were accompanied by piano rather than orchestra. It was originally proposed that Tim Lole would later arrange and conduct the music once the film was made, but in the end, the versions with only piano accompaniment were retained. Note that, as a result, Tim Lole's name appears erroneously in the end credits as arranger and conductor. Interestingly, neither extract was actually filmed at Covent Garden, but on a mock-up opera set at Ealing Studios. At the time of shooting, access to the stage was not possible due to conflicting schedules between the Royal Opera House and the film company.
6. This recording also features the alto Louise Horner, but the music is faded out before her appearance.
7. This piece of music is not included in the end credits. Tim Lole played the "Waltz" straight out of a vocal score, "with maybe the odd extra note!" (Tim Lole, correspondence with the author, May 16, 2006).
8. This extract is so short that we only actually hear Martin Crewes sing the first word of the song ("Whenever...").

## Melinda and Melinda

1. Julian Roman, "Woody Allen gives you two for one in Melinda and Melinda," interview, *Movieweb*, March 17, 2005.
2. Björkman, p. 71.

3. Strangely, the third movement appears (unlisted) on the soundtrack album, but is not actually used in the film.
4. Dick Hyman used a similar type of lunar reference in his score for *Moonstruck*, which also includes the standard "Moonglow" as well as an original composition named "Mr. Moon."
5. This tune is spelt incorrectly as "In a Mellow Tone" in the end credits.
6. The end credits list this piece incorrectly as the "Sapphic Ode" by Brahms.

## A Midsummer Night's Sex Comedy

1. Björkman, p. 131.
2. Ibid.
3. Björkman, p. 132.
4. Ibid.
5. Ibid.
6. Brode, pp. 201–2.
7. Björkman, pp. 132.
8. The Philadelphia Orchestra is given incorrectly in the end credits for this recording. Furthermore, the name of the soloist, Rudolf Serkin, has been omitted, as the piano is not actually heard in the extract used.

## Mighty Aphrodite

1. The Benny Goodman Orchestra is given incorrectly in the end credits.

## "Oedipus Wrecks" (from *New York Stories*)

1. Brode, p. 269.
2. Björkman, p. 203.
3. Dennis Potter also used this song in his 1974 BBC play *Schmoedipus*, which takes its title from an old Jewish joke: "One Jewish lady was talking to the neighbor, and she said, 'The psychoanalyst who is treating my son has said that my son suffers from an Oedipus complex.' And the neighbor lady said, 'Oedipus schmoedipus! Doesn't matter as long as he is a good boy and loves his mother!'"
4. Wernblad, p. 134.
5. Fuld, p. 290, quoting from "Intermarriage: Abnormal or Normal" by Dr. Nathaniel Lehrman in *The Psychological Implications of Intermarriage* (New York, 1966, p. 45).
6. Lax, *Woody Allen: A Biography*, p. 349.
7. Allen, *The Floating Light Bulb*, pp. 75, 104.
8. Allen may well have been influenced subconsciously by Fellini here, as this piece

(though not the Wilbur de Paris recording) is used in a similar fashion to accompany a magic show in *Le notte di Cabiria* (1957).
9. Spignesi, p. 407.
10. Lax, *Woody Allen: A Biography*, p. 261.

## Play It Again, Sam

1. Anobile, p. 7.
2. Bendazzi, p. 72.
3. Brode, p. 102.
4. Yacowar, p. 56.
5. Anobile, p. 7.
6. Anobile, p. 67.

## The Purple Rose of Cairo

1. Björkman, p. 148.
2. Björkman, p. 149.
3. McCann, p. 210.
4. McCann, pp. 212–13.
5. Although Allen eventually decided in favor of period orchestral arrangements, he had originally requested some other combinations, including a three-piano version of "Try It On for Size." This, along with some other music that was recorded for the film but not used, appears on the soundtrack album (see appendix 1).
6. In the film, there are no strings. Allen preferred the starkness of solo piano. However, as the producer of the album, Hyman laid claim to the accompanied version that appears on the soundtrack recording.
7. Dick Hyman is an expert in this field. He has researched and recorded the music of Scott Joplin, Eubie Blake and Jelly Roll Morton, and arranged the music for the film *Scott Joplin: King of Ragtime* (1977).

## Radio Days

1. Björkman, p. 158.
2. Björkman, p. 164.
3. Ibid.
4. Björkman, p. 169. Sharing a similar sentiment, "I'll Be Seeing You" is another well-known song during World War II. Allen actually shot some footage that was to include this song being sung by a radio singer, while Mia Farrow's character, Sally, is seen kissing goodbye to a marine at Grand Central Station, but this sequence was eventually cut. The song was used later by Allen in both "Oedipus Wrecks" and *Crimes and Misdemeanors*.
5. Björkman, p. 160.
6. Ibid.
7. Carol Goodson, *Song as Subtext*, in *Woody Allen: A Casebook*, edited by Kimball King, p. 3.

8. Dick Hyman, correspondence with author, July 11, 2002.
9. Schwartz offers several comparisons (pp. 210–11).
10. Björkman, p. 164.
11. Schwartz, p. 211.
12. This piece of music is not included in the end credits.
13. Note the similarity here to the sequence near the beginning of *Annie Hall*, where Alvy Singer relates some of his childhood memories to the strains of Tommy Dorsey. On the second hearing, we even see a rollercoaster, which also recalls the earlier film.
14. Artie Shaw's 1940 recording sold over three million copies.
15. This piece was also a number one hit for Glenn Miller in 1941. Interestingly, it began life as the theme tune to a real-life radio show for Maxwell House Coffee Time.
16. This song was the biggest selling record of 1943, and is currently cited as one of the biggest selling records in American recorded history.
17. This is the only pre-existent recording used in the film that is not historically accurate, as it was recorded in 1959. The play is unnamed, but Jewish music would be appropriate to accompany *The Cherry Orchard*, which mentions a Jewish band in Act II.
18. This piece of music is not included in the end credits. Hyman and his orchestra recorded this in an impromptu performance following various other titles they had completed.

## September

1. Björkman, p. 179.
2. The recording in question is volume 8 of *The Tatum Group Masterpieces* on Original Jazz Classics/Pablo. This session turns out to be an Allen favorite (see appendix 1).

## Shadows and Fog

1. Björkman, p. 237.
2. Quoted in *Woody Allen: A Biography*, p. 380.
3. Björkman, p. 243.
4. This melody is repeatedly whistled by the killer (played by Peter Lorre) just before he commits a murder, a habit that eventually leads to his capture.
5. The Kafkaesque nature of the story has prompted some commentators (Owen Gleiberman in *Entertainment Weekly*, for example) to suggest Prague.
6. Björkman, p. 243.

7. This tune was originally written under the title "Panama" and was also known as "Madonna." In 1926 it was taken to America and given its more familiar title and English lyric by Buddy DeSylva, and later became Ambrose's signature tune.

8. The extract we hear in the film is taken from the 1956 recording with Lotte Lenya; the name of the orchestra is not given. Presumably, Lotte Lenya's name was omitted from the credits as we only hear the opening bars of the "Prologue," before the singer enters.

9. This extract is listed as coming from *The Threepenny Opera* in the end credits; however, the piece we hear is actually taken from the instrumental suite to Weill's opera, as with "The Cannon Song."

## Sleeper

1. Brode, p. 133.
2. Björkman, p. 67.
3. Quoted in Bendazzi, p. 95.
4. Benayoun, p. 174.
5. Bendazzi, p. 95.
6. Fox, p. 74.
7. Björkman, p. 68.
8. Tom Sancton, "Play It Again, Woody," *Time*, October 23, 1989.
9. Woody Allen, interview with Robert Greenfield, *Rolling Stone*, September 30, 1971.
10. Sancton, p. 130.
11. Lax, *On Being Funny*, p. 136.
12. Ibid., p. 139.
13. Kaplan, p. 119.
14. Björkman, p. 67.
15. This 12-bar blues riff is named after the New Orleans trombonist who played with, among others, Jimmy "Kid" Clayton's band during the 1950s. Alternative titles include "Joe Avery's Blues" and "Joe Avery's Piece."

## Small Time Crooks

1. Stephen Holden, "Just Take the Money and Run? Nah, She Wants Class and Culcha," review, *New York Times*, May 19, 2000.
2. Quoted in Lax, *Woody Allen: A Biography*, p. 408.
3. David in *Small Time Crooks* is not unlike his namesake in *Hannah and Her Sisters*, where the Sam Waterston character introduces Holly and April to the delights of architecture and opera.

## Stardust Memories

1. Nancy Pogel (pp. 133–150) gives the most detailed analysis on the connections between the two films.

2. Fellini, like Allen, often included classical music in his films and, perhaps more interestingly, also incorporated examples of American popular standards. In *La dolce vita*, for instance, we hear "Stormy Weather" and a Dixieland version of "Yes, Sir, That's My Baby," while *Otto e mezzo* contains "Blue Moon."

3. Brode, p. 193. Julian Fox later restated the same view (p. 119).
4. Björkman, p. 123.
5. Sinyard, p. 60.
6. Allen, *Four Films of Woody Allen*, pp. 371–2.
7. Bendazzi, p. 157.
8. Allen, *Four Films of Woody Allen*, p. 356.
9. In the end credits, this piece is given incorrectly as "Tropical Mood Meringue" and is listed as being written by Sidney Bechet. In fact, this is just one of several pieces of traditional Haitian music recorded in New York in 1939. The name of the band is sometimes given as the Willie "The Lion" Smith — Sidney Bechet Orchestra.
10. This film music is not included in the end credits.

## Sweet and Lowdown

1. Taken from the *Sweet and Lowdown* official Web site: www.sonypictures.com/classics/sweetandlowdown/
2. Ibid.
3. Woody Allen, "Mild Man Views," interview with Pamela Harland and Jenny Peters, *If* 10.3 (December 23, 1999).
4. Lax, *Woody Allen: A Biography*, p. 404.
5. Gershwin, p. 183.
6. Woody Allen, interview with Brandon Judell, *indieWire*, December 7, 1999.
7. Jude Hibler, "Howard Alden — An Engaging Explorer," *20th Century Guitar*, December 1999, p. 98.
8. Taken from the *Sweet and Lowdown* official Web site.
9. Hibler, p. 98.
10. Taken from the *Sweet and Lowdown* official Web site.
11. Woody Allen, interview with Brandon Judell, *indieWire*, December 7, 1999.
12. Ira Gitler, "Sweet and Lowdown: A Jazz History Perspective," *Sweet and Lowdown* official Web site.
13. The end credits give only Django Reinhardt, who was in the Warlop orchestra for this session.
14. The word "viper" is African-American slang for "drug dealer." There was an abun-

dance of "reefer songs" during this period, of which this is a good example.

## Take the Money and Run

1. *Current Biography*, quoted in Brode, p. 73.
2. Björkman, p. 16.
3. Hamlisch and Gardner, p. 92.
4. Rosenblum and Karen, p. 250.
5. Hamlisch and Gardner, p. 93.
6. Lax, *Woody Allen: A Biography*, p. 262.
7. Rosenblum and Karen, p. 249.
8. Kaplan, p. 119.
9. Rosenblum and Karen, p. 249.
10. Allen, interview with Bragg, *The South Bank Show*, January 16, 1994.
11. Interestingly, in the aforementioned interview for *The South Bank Show*, this scene is shown with (presumably) the original Hamlisch music underneath it. The music we hear is actually "Hearts and Flowers" performed on solo piano in the style of a silent movie accompaniment. This piece is one of those melodies that everybody recognizes, but usually cannot name. It was composed in 1893 by Tobias Tobani and was frequently used during the silent era to express sadness. It is implied that this is actually the music that Hamlisch originally intended for this scene. It could be, however, that this was simply added by the television company in order to emphasize Allen's point. Indeed, it seems more likely that Hamlisch would have used original music here, possibly his own melancholy waltz theme.
12. Quoted in Lax, *Woody Allen: A Biography*, p. 261.
13. Rosenblum and Karen, pp. 250-1.

14. Quoted in Lax, *Woody Allen: A Biography*, p. 261.

## Zelig

1. Björkman, p. 142.
2. Allen, *Three Films of Woody Allen*, p. 55.
3. Hyman, p. 46.
4. During this sequence, Allen filmed Dick Hyman conducting a dance band with a large plastic chameleon impaled on his baton, but this was eventually cut from the picture.
5. Mae Questel did the voice for Betty Boop (another Helen Kane parody) and also played Allen's mother in "Oedipus Wrecks."
6. This charming piece was originally composed as a more rhythmic orchestral arrangement and was meant to be used under the opening credits. Ultimately, these credits were presented in silence, and the composition itself is used minimally in the film, in slower versions. It has subsequently had an independent life as a piano solo, which Hyman still occasionally performs, and as a movement in his "Novelties for Piano and Saxophone Quartet." In the latter version it is included in Hyman's 1987 score for the television drama "Pat Hobby Teamed with Genius," one of the six *Tales from the Hollywood Hills*. A solo piano rendition can be found on the *Dick Hyman in Recital* album (Reference Recordings 015084).
7. The original title by Hyman for this cue was "Lindy Gets a Medal from Hoover" but the shot of Lindbergh receiving his medal from the President was moved during the editing process to the opening "jazz age" sequence.
8. Hyman, p. 46.
9. Allen, *Three Films of Woody Allen*, p. 129.

# SELECT BIBLIOGRAPHY

Allen, Woody. *The Floating Light Bulb*. New York: Random House, 1982.
_____. *Four Films of Woody Allen*. New York: Random House, 1982. (Contains *Annie Hall, Interiors, Manhattan* and *Stardust Memories*.)
_____. *Getting Even*. New York: Random House, 1971.
_____. *Hannah and Her Sisters*. New York: Vintage, 1987.
_____. *Side Effects*. New York: Random House, 1980.
_____. *Three Films of Woody Allen*. New York: Random House, 1987. (Contains *Zelig, Broadway Danny Rose* and *The Purple Rose of Cairo*.)
_____. *Without Feathers*. New York: Random House, 1975.
Anobile, Richard J., ed. *Woody Allen's "Play It Again, Sam."* New York: Grossett and Dunlap, 1977.
Bailey, Peter J. *The Reluctant Film Art of Woody Allen*. Lexington: The University Press of Kentucky, 2001.
Baxter, John. *Woody Allen: A Biography*. London: Harper Collins, 1998.
Benayoun, Robert. *The Films of Woody Allen*. New York: Harmony, 1986.
Bendazzi, Giannalberto. *The Films of Woody Allen*. Horsham: Ravette, 1987.
Björkman, Stig, ed. *Woody Allen on Woody Allen*. London: Faber and Faber, 1995.
Brode, Douglas. *The Films of Woody Allen*. New Jersey: Citadel Press, 1991.
Byrnes, Christina. *Woody Allen's Trilogy of Terror: A Study of "Interiors," "September" and "Another Woman."* Nottingham: Paupers' Press, 1997.
Cowie, Peter. *Annie Hall*. London: BFI Film Classics, 1996.
De Navacelle, Thierry. *Woody Allen on Location*. London: Sidgewick and Jackson, 1987.
Fox, Julian. *Woody: Movies from Manhattan*. London: Batsford, 1996.
Fuld, James. *The Book of World-Famous Music*. New York: Dover Publications, 1995
Gershwin, Ira. *Lyrics on Several Occasions*. Omnibus Press: London, 1977.
Girgus, Sam B. *The Films of Woody Allen*. Cambridge: Cambridge University Press, 2002.
Guthrie, Lee. *Woody Allen: A Biography*. New York: Drake, 1978.
Hamlisch, Marvin, with Gerald Gardner. *The Way I Was*. New York: Scribners/Macmillan, 1992.
Hirsch, Foster. *Love, Sex, Death, and the Meaning of Life: The Films of Woody Allen*. Cambridge: Da Capo Press, 2001.
Hyman, Dick. *Dick Hyman: Piano Pro*. New York: Ekay Music, 1992.
Jasen, David J. *Tin Pan Alley*. London: Omnibus Press, 1990.
Kaplan, Fred. Interview. *The Perfect Vision* 34 (January–February 2001), pp. 117–122.
Kapsis, Robert E., and Kathie Coblentz (eds.). *Woody Allen Interviews*. Jackson: University Press of Mississippi, 2006.

King, Kimball, ed. *Woody Allen: A Casebook*. New York: Routledge, 2001.
Kinkle, Roger D. *The Complete Encyclopedia of Popular Music and Jazz 1900–1950*. 4 volumes. Westport: Arlington House, 1974.
Lax, Eric. *On Being Funny: Woody Allen and Comedy*. New York: Charterhouse Press, 1975.
_____. *Woody Allen: A Biography*. Cambridge: Da Capo Press, 2000.
Lee, Sander H. *Eighteen Woody Allen Films Analyzed*. Jefferson, N.C.: McFarland, 2002.
McCann, Graham. *Woody Allen: New Yorker*. Cambridge: Polity Press, 1990.
McKnight, Gerald. *Woody Allen: Joking Aside*. London: W.H. Allen, 1982.
Meade, Marion. *The Unruly Life of Woody Allen*. London: Weidenfeld and Nicolson, 2000.
Nichols, Mary P. *Reconstructing Woody*. Lanham: Rowman and Littlefield, 1998.
Pogel, Nancy. *Woody Allen*. Boston: Twayne, 1987.
Rosenblum, Ralph, and Robert Karen. *When the Shooting Stops ... The Cutting Begins*. New York: Viking Press, 1979.
Sancton, Tom. Interview. *Jazz Times*, September 1996, pp. 27–29, 130–131.
Schickel, Richard. *Woody Allen: A Life in Film*. Chicago: Ivan R. Dee, 2003.
Schuller, Gunther. *Early Jazz: Its Roots and Musical Development*. New York: Oxford University Press, 1968.
_____. *The Swing Era: The Development of Jazz, 1930–1945*. New York: Oxford University Press, 1989.
Schwartz, Richard A. *Woody: From Antz to Zelig*. Westport: Greenwood Press, 2000.
Sinyard, Neil. *The Films of Woody Allen*. Leicester: Magna Books, 1987.
Spignesi, Stephen J. *The Woody Allen Companion*. London: Plexus, 1994.
Wernblad, Annette. *Brooklyn Is Not Expanding: Woody Allen's Comic Universe*. Rutherford, N.J.: Fairleigh Dickinson University Press, 1992.
Yacowar, Maurice. *Loser Take All: The Comic Art of Woody Allen*. New York: Continuum, 1991.

# INDEX

Numbers in ***bold italic*** indicate a major entry or section covering the subject.

"A Frangesa" *33*
Aaron, Caroline 45, 52
Aaronson, Irving 62; and His Commanders 36, 62
Abascal, Natividad 31
"Abide with Me" *143*
Abraham, F. Murray 100
Abreu, Zequinha 116
Academy of the Overrated 81
*Across the Pacific* 107
Adair, Thomas M. 18, 41, 93
Adamson, Harold 40, 71
Addinsell, Richard 151
Adler, Jerry 86
*The African Queen* 105
"After You've Gone" *142*
"Agita" *32*
Aiello, Danny 110, 117
"Ain't We Got Fun?" *153*
Akers, Karen 111
"Akh, vy seni, moi seni" *77*
"Alabama Song" *see* Weill, Kurt
"Alabamy Bound" *112*
Alda, Alan 44, 59, 60, 86
Alden, Howard 48, 139–140, 141, 142, 143, 144, 145
Alderhold, Olin 136
Alexander, Edna 138
Alguire, Danny 189
Alhert, Fred E. 100, 156
*Alias Smith and Jones* 105
Alice *13–18*, 22, 27, 37, 51, 52, 70, 92, 115, 134
"Alice Blue Gown" *17*
*Alice in Wonderland* 14
"All Hail to You, Glenwood High" *41*
"All I Do Is Dream of You" *45*
"All My Life" 56, *59*, 60
"All of Me" *143*, 144
"All of You" *33*

"All or Nothing at All" *116*
"All the Things You Are" 8, 51, *52*, 103, *104*
Allen, Steve 131, 132
Allen, Woody: as actor 9, 11, 19, 29, 30, 31, 42, 44, 48, 50, 58, 63, 64, 66, 70, 73, 76, 85, 97, 99, 102, 105, 106, 124, 128, 130, 133, 146, 149; and black and white titles 12, 58, 125; childhood 5, 113–114; and classical music 12, 91, 134; favorite classical composers 12; favorite films 54, 85, 115; favorite songwriters 28, 35; and jazz 5, 7, 12, 91, 133, 138–139; importance of music in his films 6; influence of Ingmar Bergman 19, 73, 74; likes and dislikes 8, 85; liking for pre–War era 34, 47; magic and Eastern-flavored music 103, 134; musical tastes 5, 12, 34–35, 54, 56, 71, 85, 91, 120–121, 133; as performer 5, 91; preference for instrumental music 9, 10, 48, 56; preference for pre–1950 music 8, 12, 28, 56, 70, 99; and traditionalist views on music 8, 71; use of American standards 7–8, 13, 50, 54, 64, 85, 92; use of big band music 7, 19, 20, 113, 130, 134; use of classical music 10–12, 21–23, 42, 64–65, 73, 75, 87–88, 91–92, 96–97, 130–131, 134; use of cocktail music 8, 13, 37; use of composers to score films 6, 62, 105, 125; use of jazz 7, 8, 13, 22, 28, 42, 64, 85, 91, 99, 103, 126, 133, 134, 138; use of music as frame for films 10, 27, 39, 47, 73, 77, 82, 89, 102, 130; use of own record collection to score films 6–7, 102, 148; use of scoring 13, 22, 26–27, 39, 43, 47, 64–65, 70, 79, 85, 88–89; use of song as *leitmotif* 51, 64–66, 102–103, 130, 135; use of song as subtext 9, 14, 22, 27, 28, 35, 39–40, 43, 45, 46, 51–52, 56, 62, 64–66, 70, 80–81, 88–90, 92, 99, 114, 119–120, 131, 134–135, 141; use of source music 9, 11, 12, 18–9, 22, 38, 39, 42–43, 70–71, 73, 74, 85, 96–97, 105, 119–

199

## 200 / Index

120; use of upbeat music to score comedic scenes 9, 11, 85–86, 99, 104, 127, 141
"Aloha Oe" *143*
Alstyne, Egbert van 45
Altman, Arthur 116
"Always" 43
*Amarcord* 115, 151
Ambrose, Bert 13, 14, 99, 195; and His Orchestra 16, 101, 121, 144
"America the Beautiful" *155*
*An American in Paris* (Gershwin) 79, 152
*An American in Paris* (Minnelli) 54, 59
"American Patrol" *118*
"American Pie" *41*
"Anchors Aweigh" *154*
"And the Glory of the Lord Shall Be Revealed" (Handel) *128*
Anderson, Maxwell 114, 115
Andre, Fabian 54
The Andrews Sisters 117
*The Andromeda Strain* 126
Angulo, Rafael 46
*Animal Crackers* 57
*Annie Hall* *18–21*, 73, 74, 81, 119
*Another Woman* 8, 9, 11, 12, 13, 17, 18, *21–26*, 37, 39, 42, 44, 73, 87, 92, 130
Ansermet, Ernest 53
Antell, Peter 46
Anthony, Eugene 112
Anthony, Lysette 74
Anthony, Ray 20
*Anything Else* *26–29*, 51
Anzell, Hy 53
"Aquarela do Brasil" *see* "Brazil"
Argerich, Martha 25, 26
Arlen, Harold 57
Armenian, Raffi 124
Armstrong, Louis 6, 7, 81, 133, 135–136; and His Orchestra 138
Arnheim, Gus 71
Arnone, Don 32
Arodin, Sidney 36
"Arresta ... Quali sguardi" (Rossini) *90*
"As Time Goes By" 44, *106*
Astaire, Fred 54–55, 56, 57, 108–109, 110
"At the Jazz Band Ball" *37*
*At the Movies* 35
Atherton, David 124
"Auld Lang Syne" *119*
Auriacombe, Louis 24
"Avalon" 67, *69*, *142*
Aykroyd, Dan 49
Azaria, Hank 41

"Babalu" *118*
Bacall, Lauren 47
Bach, Johann Sebastian 3, 11, 12, 13, 17, 22, 25, 26, 42, 45, 64, 65–66, 67, 68, 91, 92, 93, 94, 95, 120, 130, 132; Cello Sonata No. 2 in D Major 12, 22, *25*; Cello Sonata No. 3 in G Minor *26*; Cello Suite No. 2 in D Minor *132*; Cello Suite No. 6 in D Major *26*; Concerto for Two Violins in D Minor 65, *67*; English Suite No. 2 in A Minor *44*; Goldberg Variations 136; Harpsichord Concerto No. 5 in F Minor 12, 65, *68*; Partita No. 3 in A Minor *93*; Prelude No. 2 in C Minor *94*; Violin Concerto No. 1 in A Minor *17*
Bacharach, Burt 28
"Back to the Apple" *67*
Badev, Georgi 67
Bagley, Edwin Eugene 34
Bailey, Buster 16, 72
Bailey, Peter J. 39
Baker, Chet 25
Baker, David Aaron 95
Baker, Joséphine 152
Balaban, Bob 53
Baldwin, Alec 14
Balthazar restaurant, New York 72
Banana, Milton 52
*Bananas* 11, *30–31*, 146
"The Band Played On" *32*
Barbetta's, New York 16
Barbirolli, Sir John 68, 73
Barney Google's, New York 5
Baron, Sandy 31
Barrault, Marie-Christine 135
Barroso, Ary 136
Barry, Chris 68
Barrymore, Drew 55, 58
Bartók, Béla 91, 92, 94, 107; String Quartet No. 5 107; String Quartet No. 4 91, *94*
Basie, Count 5, 7, 13, 64, 67, 133, 137; and His Orchestra 18, 67, 100, 136
Bassman, George 118
Bates, Katherine Lee 155
*The Battle of Austerlitz* 76
Bauduc, Ray 85, 86
Baxter, John 23
Beal, John 32, 33
"Beautiful Love" *45*
"Because" 40, *46*
Bechet, Sidney 5, 7, 102, 103, 133, 134, 136, 141, 143, 189, 195
Beck, John 128
Beethoven, Ludwig van 12, 38, 39, 40, 76, 77, 95, 129, 136; Piano Sonata No. 17 in D Minor, "Tempest" 11, *129*; Symphony No. 5 in C Minor 11, 38–39, *40*; Symphony No. 7 in A Major *95*; Violin Sonata No. 5 in F Major, "Spring" *77*
"Begin the Beguine" *34*, *116*
Behar, Joy 86
Beiderbecke, Bix 7, 35, 36, 37, 144; and His Gang 37, 144
Bell, Vinny 32
Belmont Park race track, New York 93, 94
Bemelman's Bar, New York 71, 72

Benayoun, Robert 10, 126
Bendazzi, Giannalberto 105, 126
Benjamin, Richard 52
Bergman, Ingmar 6, 19, 21, 42, 73, 74, 75, 81, 96, 97, 126, 129
Bergman, Martin 42
Berigan, Bunny 7, 40, 141; and His Orchestra 144
Berlin, Irving 5, 8, 43, 44, 45, 54, 57, 73, 74, 87, 109, 110, 121, 129
Berlin Philharmonic Orchestra 73
Berlin Staatsoper 125
Bernie, Ben 45, 138, 142, 149; The Ben Bernie Orchestra 156
Bernstein, Leonard 26, 44, 97
Bertini, Umberto 34
"The Best Things in Life Are Free" **86**, 92, **93**
Betty Boop 196
Beverley Hills 21
"Bewitched, Bothered and Bewildered" 44, 65, **66**
Bhooka 95
Big Apple Circus 16; The Big Apple Circus Band 17
big band *see* Allen, Woody, use of big band music
"Big Eternity" **95**
"The Big Noise from Winnetka" 9, 85, **86**
*The Big Pond* 61
*The Big Sleep* 47
Biggs, Jason 27
"The Bilbao Song" *see* Weill, Kurt
*Billy Jack* 62
Bizet, Georges 88, 89
Björkman, Stig 12, 23, 91
Black, Johnny S. 117
black and white titles *see* Allen, Woody, black and white titles
*The Black Cat* 95
Blake, Eubie 94, 112, 147, 194
Blake, Sydney A. 118
Blakey, Art 18
Block, Jerry 72
Bloom, Claire 45
"Blue, Blue, Blue" 80
"Blue Moon" 195
"Blues for Allan Felix" 7, 106, **107**
Boccherini, Luigi 76, 78
Bodner, Phil 118, 153, 155
"Body and Soul" **115**, 135, **137**
Bogart, Humphrey 105–106, 108
Bohemian Caverns, Washington 100
Bonham Carter, Helena 99
Bonx, Nat 117
Bordo, Edwin 33
Borel-Clerc, Charles 152
*Born to Dance* 28
Bosco, Philip 22
Boulez, Pierre 26

bouzouki music 99
Bow, Clara 152
Bowman, Euday L. 143
Boyer, Lucien 152
Braff, Ruby 16, 72
Braff, Zach 87
Bragg, Melvyn, 19, 85, 147
Braham, Philip 16, 141
Brahms, Johannes 129; Hungarian Dance No. 5 129; "Sapphic Ode" 193
Brammer, Julius 144
Bramon, Michael 192
Branagh, Kenneth 38
*A Brave New World* 125
"Brazil" 134, **136**
Brecht, Bertolt 18, 24, 25, 124, 125
"Breezin' Along with the Breeze" 14, **16**
Brice, Fanny 149, 152
Brickman, Marshall 20, 127
Bricktop's nightclub 149
Broadbent, Jim 37
Broadway 8, 34, 57, 69, 79, 99, 132
*Broadway Danny Rose* **31–34**
Brockman, James 142
Brode, Douglas 23, 42, 81, 96, 105–106, 125–126, 134
Brolin, Josh 92
"Bronco Busters" 80
Brooker, Stephen 90
Brooklyn, New York 78, 83
Brooks, Harry 36
Brooks, Norman 154
Brown, Lawrence 16, 72
Brown, Lew 41, 58, 74, 86, 93, 118, 143, 154
Brown, Nacio Herb 45, 71, 145
Brown, Ray 29, 41, 74
Brubeck, Dave 7, 8, 24, 37, 40, 67, 86, 100; Quartet 24–25, 40, 67, 86, 100
Brückner-Rüggeberg, Wilhelm 124
Bucher, John 127
Buckingham Palace, London 89
Buffalo Philharmonic Orchestra 79, 82, 84
*Bullets Over Broadway* 9, **34–37**, 38, 47, 56, 57, 62, 99, 129, 138
Burbank, Albert 5, 127
Burke, Johnny 17, 29, 46, 69
Burton, Nat 118
Burton, Val 100, 109
Busse, Henry 141, 145; and His Orchestra 145
"But Not for Me" 80, **84**
Butler, Artie 20, 119
"By the Sleepy Lagoon" 19, **20**
Byrd, Charlie 140
Byrne, Anne 82
Byrne, Bobby 151

"Ça C'est Paris" **152**
*The Cabinet of Dr. Caligari* 123
Caesar, Irving 37, 46, 144
Café Carlyle, New York 5, 66, 68, 71, 72, 86

Cahn, Sammy 66
Caine, Michael 12, 65
Caiola, Al 16, 72
Caldwell O'Dea, Anne 44
Calhoun, Eddie 25, 86, 93, 94, 101
*California Suite* 105
Callahan, J. Will 25, 129
Callender, Red 53, 87, 121, 122
Camacho, John A. 53
Campari, Angelo 68
Campbell, Jimmy 60, 68
Campbell's funeral parlor, New York 60
*Can Can* 54
Canadian Chamber Ensemble 123, 124
"Canal Street Blues" 126, *128*
Canoro, Luigi 33
Cantor, Eddie 35, 55, 152
Capua, Eduardo di 34
Capurro, Giovanni 34
"Caravan" *17*, 141, *144*
Carell, Steve 94
Carey, Dave 118
"The Carioca" *116*
Carle, Frankie 26, 49, 102, 104
Carlyle, Kitty 118
Carmichael, Hoagy 36, 48, 135, 138
Carnegie Deli, New York 31, 32, 34
Carnegie Hall, New York 71, 94
Carney, Harry 47
Carradine, John 63
Carroll, Barbara 71–72
Carter, Benny 7, 45, 52, 67, 86, 139
Carter, Ron 25
Caruso, Enrico 88, 89, 90, 150
*Casablanca* 105–106, *107*
Casey, Kenneth 45, 138, 142
The Castilians 13, 16, 116
Casucci, Leonello 144
Catholicism 69
*Cats* 103
"Catskill Cha Cha" *32*
"'Cause I Believe in Loving" 30
Cavallaro, Carmen 8, 37, *42*, 100, 130, 132
Cavanaugh, James 33
CBGB club 192
"C'e la luna" *see* "Luna mezzo mare"
*Celebrity* 8, 11, 27, *37–42*, 70, 92
"Cella luna" *see* "Luna mezzo mare"
Central Park, New York 17, 24, 28, 29, 50, 52, 58, 66, 72, 80, 82, 83
"Chameleon Days" 148, *152*
The Champs 132
Chandler, Raymond 47
"Chanel No. 5" *40*
"The Changing Man Concerto" 109, *151*, 155
Channing, Stockard 28, 29
Chaplin, Charlie 75, 125, 129, 147
Charles, Ray 116
"Charleston" *149*, 150
The Charleston (dance) 151

The Charleston City All-Stars 149, 151, 153, 154
Chase, Newell 121
"Cheek to Cheek" 108–109, *110*
Chekhov, Anton 74, 117, 129
"Chella llà" *34*
Cherry, Vivian 58
*The Cherry Orchard* 194
Chevalier, Maurice 57, 61
Chiara, Maria 68
*Chicago* 191
"Chicago (That Toddlin' Town)" *150*
Chinatown, New York 14, 15, 49
"Chinatown, My Chinatown" 57, *61*, *115*
"Chiquita Banana" *61*
Choir of the Church of the Transfiguration 69
Chopin, Frédéric 60
"Christopher Columbus" 51, 191
Chrysler Building, New York 17, 81–82
Chumley's bar, New York 145
*Chushingura* 83
Cicognini, Alessandro 138
Cinema Studio, New York 83
"Ciribiribin" *33*
Citarella, Paolo 33
Clare, Sidney 35
"Clarinet Marmalade" *141*
Clark, Andrew 116
Clarke, Kenny 68
classical music *see* Allen, Woody, and classical music; Allen, Woody, use of classical music
Clayton, Buck 7, 16, 72
Clayton, Jimmy "Kid" 195
Clayton, Steve 151, 152
Clinton, Larry 60; and His Orchestra 116
*A Clockwork Orange* 125
Clooney, Rosemary 140
Coates, Eric 20
Coburn, Richard 101
"Cocktails for Two" *41*, *61*, 130, *132*
*The Cocoanuts* 54
Cohen, Alexander 111
Cohen, Eric 82, 83
Cohen, Judith 132
Cohen, Lynn 86
Cohen, Ray 42
College of the Pacific 67
*Colombo* 105
Coltrane, John 8, 15
Columbia Records 15, 47, 51
Columbia Symphony Orchestra 98
Columbia University, New York 68
Comden, Betty 133
"Come Back to Sorrento" *see* "Torna a Surriento"
"Come On" *95*
"Comin' at Ya" *95*
Communism 151
Condon, Eddie 35

Coney Island, New York 20
Congo Square Jazz Festival 127
Connelly, Reg 60, 68
Conner, Pierre Norman 61
Conrad, Con 35, 36, 136
Conrad, Lew 73
Coolidge, Calvin 152
Coon-Sanders Nighthawks Orchestra 120
Coots, J. Fred 42
Coppola, Francis Ford 101
Cordle, Owen 139
Corey, Irwin 49
Cortese, Dominic 32, 33, 59
Coslow, Sam 41, 61, 121, 132
Costa, P. Mario 33
Cotton Club, New York 36
"Could It Be" *131*
"The Courier" *17*
Coward, Noël 46
Cragin, Charles 124
Crane, Dagne 31
Cranshaw, Patrick 60
"Crazy Rhythm" *37, 46*
Creamer, Henry 142
Crewes, Martin 90
*Crimes and Misdemeanors* 11, 13, 17, 21, 27, 37, 38, 39, 40, *42-47*, 51, 54, 87, 91, 119, 130
Crosby, Bing 57, 70, 71, 88, 117, 151
Crosby, Bob 7, 85, 86; and His Orchestra and Bob Cats 193
Crotty, Ron 24, 67
Crudup, Billy 60
Crystal, Billy 53
"Cuban Mambo" *46*
Cuccioli, Robert 41
"Cuddle Up a Little Closer" *60*
Cugat, Xavier 46, 119; and His Orchestra 118; and His Waldorf-Astoria Orchestra 119
cummings, e. e. 65, 67
Cummings, Richard 61
"La Cumparsita" 15, *16, 116*
*The Curse of the Jade Scorpion* 9, *47-49*, 54, 70, 103, 134
Curtis, Ernesto de 34
Curtis, Giovanni Battista de 34
Cusack, John 36, 124

Dabney, Ford 143
Dakota Building, New York 65
Dale, Jimmy 59
Damerell, Stanley J. 115
"Dancing in the Dark" 114, *115*, 145
"Dancing on the Ceiling" *44*
Daniels, Charles N. 52, 71
Daniels, Jeff 109, 110
Danner, Blythe 17, 22
*La danza della libellule* (Lehár) 134
Darion, Joe 41
"Darn That Dream" 15, *18*, 92, *94*
Dash, Julian 48

Daugherty, Doc 122
Davern, Kenny 101
Davis, Colin 93
Davis, Eddy R. 41
Davis, Johnny "Scat" 192
Davis, Judy 17, 38, 73
Davis, Lloyd 25
Davis, Lou 145
Davis, Mel 111, 150
Davis, Miles 8
DeAngeles, Gina 34
Death 76-77
*Death* 123
Debussy, Claude 23-24, 190
Decameron, Emil, and His Orchestra 117
*Deconstructing Harry* 8, 9, 14, 22, 27, 38, *50-54*, 103
Degeyter, Pierre 151
DeLange, Eddie 16, 18, 94, 122
Dempsey, Jack 152
Dennis, Matt 18, 41, 93
Dennis, Sandy 22
Denza, Luigi 33
DePaul, Gene 46
The Depression 108
"Descarga" *72*
*Desert Island Discs* 20
Desmond, Paul 24, 25, 40, 67, 86, 100
DeSylva, Buddy G. 58, 69, 86, 93, 112, 122, 124, 141, 142, 154, 195
*deus ex machina* 101
Dexter, Al 117
*Dichteliebe* (Schumann) 97
"Dicitencello Vuie!" *see* "Just Say I Love Her"
Dickson, Glenn 52
"Did I Remember (To Tell You I Adore You)?" 27, 38, 39, *40*
Dietz, Howard 115
Dillon, William 104
Dixieland 7, 13, 30, 48, 99, 125-127, 134, 144
Dixon, Mort 37
"Do, Do, Do" 81, *83*
The Do-Re-Mi Children's Chorus 21
*Dr. Strangelove* 44
*Doctor Zhivago* 151
Dodds, Johnny 7
Dodge, Joe 67
Doelle, Franz 125
"Doin' the Chameleon" 148, *151*, 152
*La Dolce Vita* 195
Dominguez, Alberto 116
Donaldson, Walter 40, 58, 59, 71, 74, 128
Donizetti, Gaetano 88, 89
"The Donkey Serenade" 113, *117*
"Don't Get Around Much Anymore" *95*
Dorati, Antal 77
Dorsey, Tommy 7, 19, 20, 35, 194; and His Orchestra 20, 75, 116, 117, 118
Dorsey brothers 35
Dostoyevsky, Fyodor 75

## 204 / Index

*Double Indemnity* 47, 85, 86
Douglass, Bill 53, 87, 121, 122
Dovzhenko, Alexander 83
Drake, Erwin 24, 116
Drake, Milton 117
"Dream a Little Dream of Me" 52, **54**
Dreiwitz, Barbara 127
Dreiwitz, Dick 127
Dubin, Al 116, 117, 118, 131, 145
Duchin, Eddy 73
*Duck Soup* 54, 69
Duke, Jay 127
Duke, Vernon 27, 29, 44
Dumont, Denise 116
Duncan, Ben 139
Durham, Eddie 48
Duvivier, George 101

*Earth* 83
"Easy Lovin'" **107**
*Easy Rider* 106
"Easy to Love" 27, **28**, 29, 135, **137**
Eaton, Jimmy 116
*Ecuatorial* (Varèse) 23, **26**, 92
Egan, Raymond B. 129, 153
Egen, Austin 124
"Eh Cumpari" 32
Eisenstein, Sergei 75
Ejiofor, Chiwetel 92
Elaine's restaurant, New York 38, 39, 41, 82, 86
Eldridge, Roy 7, 64, 68; Roy Eldridge Quartet 68
Eley, Lewis 82
Eliscu, Edward 46, 116
*L'Elisir d'amore* (Donizetti) 89
Ellington, Duke 7, 17, 35, 36, 44, 47–48, 73, 91, 92, 94, 95, 141, 144; and His Orchestra 48, 93, 94, 95, 118
Elliot, Denholm 121
"Embraceable You" 80, 81, **83**
Empire State Building, New York 81–82
English Chamber Orchestra 17, 93
"Enjoy Yourself (It's Later Than You Think)" **60**
Ensemble InterContemporain 26
Erdman, Ernie 35
Erwin, Lee 116
"España Cañí" **153**
Evans, Paul 58
Evans, Reed 71, 94
Evans, Tolchard 115
*Everybody's Welcome* 106
*Everyone Says I Love You* 6, 9, 32, 35, 51, **54–61**, 113, 139
"Everyone Says I Love You" 57, **58**
*Everything You Always Wanted to Know About Sex* 6, **62–63**, 125
*Evita* 191
"Exactly Like You" 145
Eyton, Frank 116, 137

"Die Fahne Hoch" 151, **155**
Fain, Sammy 41, 47, 61, 74, 104, 118
Falvo, Rudolfo 59
*The Fantastic Planet* 126
"FAO Schwarz Clock Tower Song" *see* "Welcome to Our World of Toys"
FAO Schwarz toy shop, New York 82, 101
Farrow, Mia 14, 24, 31, 44, 65, 73, 97, 104, 108, 112, 116, 117, 118, 120, 124, 150, 155
Farrow, Stephanie 111
"Fascination" **41**, **132**
Fellini, Federico 15, 115, 133–134, 195
Ferland, Danielle 100
Ferrell, Will 92
Ferrer, José 96, 98
Ferret, Pierre Baro 136
Fetter, Ted 44
Field, Todd 116
Fields, Dorothy 16, 17, 25, 29, 53, 69, 86
Fields, Irving 53
59th Street (Queensboro) Bridge, New York 82
*film noir* 47, 54, 86, 87
"A Fine Romance" 22, **25**
Fio Rito, Ted 35
Firehouse Five Plus Two 13, 15, 18
Fisher, Carrie 67, 69
Fisher, Fred 150
Fisher, Mark 101
Fitzgerald, Andy 16, 72
Fitzgerald, F. Scott 81, 149, 156
"Five Foot Two, Eyes of Blue" 110, 149, **153**
El Flamingo Band 40
Flanagan, Tommy 29, 73
*Flash Gordon* 155
"Flatbush Flanagan" 48, **49**
"The Flight of the Bumble Bee" (Rimsky-Korsakov) 10, **115**
"Flight of the Foo Birds" **18**
*The Floating Light Bulb* 103, 134
Folies Bergère 152
*Follow the Fleet* 109
"For All We Know" 40, **42**
Forbes, Chris 129
Forrest, Chet 117
Forte, Nick Apollo 31, 32, 33, 34
Forte, P. 33
Foster, Frank 67
Foster, Jodie 125
*The Four Horseman of the Apocalypse* 189
Fox, Julian 126
Franano, Michael 40
Frazier, Josiah "Cie" 127
Freed, Arthur 45, 71, 145
"Freedonia Is Going to War" **69**
Freeman, Bud 139
Freeman, Russ 101
"Frenesí" 113, **116**
Freud, Sigmund 102
Friedman, Bruce Jay 22

Friesen, Kelly 140, 141, 142, 143, 144, 145
Friml, Rudolf 117
*The Front* 105
Froske, John 101
*Frühlingsstimmen see Voices of Spring*
Fuld, James 102
Fulton, Jack 117
"Funiculi Funicula" 32, *33*
*Funny Face* (Donen) 54
*Funny Face* (Gershwin) 79, 83
Furber, Douglas 16, 141
Fusco, Enzo 59

Gadd, Steve 25
Gallo, Barbara 119
Gallo wines 23
Gamse, Albert 53
Garcia, Jerry 41
Garland, Joe 116
Garner, Erroll 7, 8, 13, 17, 18, 22, 25, 37, 41, 51, 52, 53, 86, 87, 91, 92, 93, 94, 100, 101, 102
Garrett, Brad 144
Gaskill, Clarence 29, 61
"Gat I" *28*
Genetti, Carol 132
Georges-Picot, Olga 77
German Expressionism 54, 123
Gershwin, George 5, 6, 8, 35, 37, 38, 41, 42, 44, 54, 56, 57, 78–84, 87, 96, 139, 152
Gershwin, Ira 27, 29, 37, 41, 42, 56, 82–84, 139
Getz, Stan 7, 8, 37, 41, 52, 74
*Gianni Schicchi see* Puccini, Giacomo
Gibbons, Carroll 53
Gibbs, Arthur Harrington 151
Gibbs, Eddie 49, 100, 103, 104
*Gigi* 54, 57
"Gigolette" (Lehár) 134
Gilbert, L. Wolfe 143
Gilberto, Astrud 52
Gilberto, João 52
Gillespie, Dizzy 50, 139
Gillespie, Haven 16, 45
Gimbel, Norman 52
*La Gioconda* (Ponchielli) 26
Giordano, Jonathan 61
Giordano, Vince 150
Girgus, Sam B. 50, 64
*Girl Crazy* 79, 83, 84
"The Girl from Ipanema" *52*
*Giulietta degli spiriti* 15
Gleason, Jackie 8, 13–14, 15, 26, 37, 39, 70; and His Orchestra 16, 17, 41, 70, 72
Gleason, Joanna 44
Gleiberman, Owen 194
"Gloria" (Hassler) *69*
"Glory Hallelujah" 63
"God Rest You Merry, Gentlemen" *21*
Goehner, Fred 144

"Going Hollywood" *71*
*Going Hollywood* 71
*Gold Diggers of 1937* 130
Golden, John L. 36, 72
The Golden Age 12, 54
Golden Gate Bridge, San Francisco 107
Goldenberg, Billy 105–107
*The Goldwyn Follies* 82
Golschmann, Vladimir 137
Gomes, Antonio Carlos 88, 89
"Gone with the Wind" *29*
"Goodbye" *118*
Goodman, Benny 5, 7, 9, 51, 70, 85, 101, 103, 116, 120, 130, 131, 137, 140, 142, 143; and His Orchestra 53, 71, 87, 104, 118, 131; Swing Quintet 101
Goodman, Hazelle 53
Goodson, Carol 65, 114
Goodwin, Joe 101
Gordon, John 58
Gordon, Mack 29, 72, 119
Gorruso, Anthony 46
Gosh, Bobby 101
Gould, Harold 77
Graham, Ronald 133
Grainger, Porter 128
Gramercy Park, New York 84
Grand Award Records 149
Grand Central Station, New York 49
Grant, Hugh 130
Granz, Norman 8
Grappelli, Stéphane 140, 141
Gray, Diva 58
Gray, Wardell 52
"Great Day" 40, *46*
*The Great Dictator* 75, 129
Greek theater 98–99
Green, Benny 133
Green, Bud 112, 154
Green, John 52, 86, 115, 121, 137, 142
Green, Seth 115
Green, Urbie 110
Greer, Jesse 57, 67
Gregory, Mary 128
Grey, Joe 151
Grieg, Edvard 123
Griffith, Melanie 40
"Grindhouse (A Go-Go)" *72*
Grofé, Ferde 81
Grossberg, Jack 146
Grossman, Julius 53
Grosz, Marty 190
*Guys and Dolls* 54, 85
"Guys and Dolls Overture" *87*

Hackett, Bobby 7, 14, 26, 70; and His Orchestra 72
Hackman, Gene 22
Hagerty, Julie 97
Haggart, Bob, 85, 86

The Haitian Orchestra 136
Hall, Edmond 7, 71; and His Swingtet 71
Hall, Jim 8, 22, 25
Hamilton, Adam 95
Hamilton, George 71
Hamilton, Nancy 49
Hamlisch, Marvin 6, 30–31, 62, 146–148, 196
Hammerstein II, Oscar 25, 36, 37, 52, 72, 74, 104, 122
The Hamptons, New York 73, 94
Handel, George Friedrich 128
Hanley, James F. 143
Hanna, Roland 25
Hannah, Daryl 44
*Hannah and Her Sisters* 5, 8, 9, 11, 12, 13, 21, 28, 35, 37, 42, 44, 51, 54, 56, 57, 60, *64–69*, 71, 85, 92, 102, 120, 130
"Happy Birthday to You" *45*
*Happy Go Lucky* 45, 54
Harbach, Otto 37, 44, 60, 122
Harburg, E. Y. 133
"A Hard Way to Go" *21*
Hardelot, Guy d' 46
Hargreaves, Roger 115
Harlem, New York 120
The Harlem Footwarmers 36
Harper, Jessica 134
Harris, Harry 145
Harris, James, III 95
Harris, Roz 152
Harris, Viola 53
Harris, Will J. 145
Harry Winston, New York 58
Hart, Lorenz 5, 8, 35, 36, 37, 44, 53, 54, 57, 61, 64, 66, 67, 68, 69, 86–87, 99, 100, 132
Hassler, Hans Leo 69
"Have You Met Miss Jones?" 8, 51, *86*
*Hawaii Five-O* 62
Hawkins, Coleman 7, 142; and His All-Star Jam Band 45, 51, 52, 86
Hawkins, Erskine 48
Hawn, Goldie 58, 59
Hayes, Devalle 60
Hayman, Olivia 55, 58, 61
"He Loves and She Loves" 80, *82*, 84
Heard, Eugene "Fats" 17, 18, 41, 87, 93
Heard, J. C. 29
Hearst Metrotone 148, 152, 154, 156
"Hearts and Flowers" 196
Heath, Albert 29, 73
Heath, Percy 29, 73
"Hebrew School Rag" *137*
Hefti, Neal 18, 100
Hegarty, Mary 90
Heifetz, Jascha 71
Helleny, Joel 142, 144
Hemingway, Mariel 81
Henderson, Fletcher 191
Henderson, Ray 58, 86, 93, 112, 153, 154
Henderson, Skitch 140

Hentoff, Nat 138
Herbert, Victor 31
*Here Comes the Hot Tamale Man* 35
Herman, Woody 139
Hershey, Barbara 12, 65
Heusen, Jimmy van 17, 18, 29, 46, 69, 94
Heyman, Edward 38, 40, 52, 86, 115, 121, 137, 142
Hibbert, Edward 58
Higgins, Billy 143
High School Reunion Band 41
High School Reunion Class 41
Hill, Mildred J. 45
Himber, Richard, and His Ritz-Carlton Orchestra 118
Hines, Earl 7, 48, 102
Hinton, Milt 16, 72, 82, 83
Hirsch, Foster 38, 55
Hirt, Al 20
*His Girl Friday* 47
Hitler, Adolf 155
*Hits from Berlin, 1927–31* 123
HMV Victor 152
Hodges, Johnny 47
Hoffman, Al 117
Holiday, Billie 7, 8, 26–28, 29, 39, 40, 62; and Her Orchestra 40
Holland, Loris 60
Holley, Major, Jr. 44
Hollywood 70, 143
*Hollywood Ending* 26, *70–72*, 85
*Hollywood Hotel* 71
Holm, Ian 22
Holmes, Jake 30
Holofcener, Larry 72
"Home Cookin'" *45*
"Honeysuckle Rose" 27, 28, *29*
"Hooray for Captain Spaulding" 57, *61*
"Hooray for Hollywood" *71*
Hoover, Herbert 152
"Hopak" *46*
*Hope* (Klimt) 26
Hope, Bob 47, 48, 75
Hopkins, Claude 16, 72
Horenstein, Jascha 76, 78, 132
Horgan, Patrick 149
Horner, Louise 193
"Horos Tou Sakena" *101*
*Horse Feathers* 57
"Horst Wessel Lied" *see* "Die Fahne Hoch"
Hoschna, Karl 60
Hoskins, Bob 56
"Hot Lips" 141, *145*
Hotter, Hans 86
*House of Exorcism* 21
Houses of Parliament, London 89
"How High the Moon" 48, *49*
Howard, Avery "Kid" 127
Hubbell, Raymond 36, 72
Hudes, Linda 16, 17

Hudson, Will 16, 94, 122
Hudson River, New York 39, 41, 86, 87
"The Hukilau Song" *133*
Humphrey, Percy 127
Hunt, Helen 48
Hunter, Robert 41
Hupfeld, Herman 106
Hurt, Mary Beth 74
Hurt, William 16
*Husbands and Wives* 9, 10, 27, 57, *73-74*, 84, 102, 119
Huston, Angelica 43, 86
Hutton, Betty 45-46
Hylton, Jack, and His Orchestra 123, 124
Hyman, Dick 9, 31, 32, 33, 34, 35, 36, 37, 48-49, 57-61, 63, 64, 67, 68, 69, 79, 80, 82, 83, 92, 94, 95, 99, 100, 101, 108-112, 114-115, 116, 117, 118, 133, 134, 137, 138-145, 146, 148-156, 196; Dick Hyman Chorus and Orchestra 101; *Dick Hyman in Recital* 196; Dick Hyman's Studio Orchestra 33, 34; *Piano Pro* 155
"Hymne" (Vangelis) 23

"I Believe My Heart" *90*
"I Can't Believe That You're in Love with Me" 27, *29*, 61
"I Can't Get Started" 27, *29*
"I Could Write a Book" 52, *53*
"I Don't Want to Walk Without You" 113, *117*
"I Double Dare You" *116*
"I Dream Too Much" 14-15, *16*, 44
"I Got Rhythm" *41*
"I Hadn't Anyone Till You" 99, *101*
"I Happen to Like New York" 85, *86*
"I Know That You Know" *44*
"I Let a Song Go Out of My Heart" *95*
"I Love My Baby, My Baby Loves Me" *112*, 149, *154*
"I Only Have Eyes for You" 43, 44
"I Remember You" 8, 14, *17*, *67*
"I Want a Girl (Just Like the Girl That Married Dear Old Dad)" 10, 102, *103*
"Ice Cream (I Scream, You Scream, We All Scream for)" 126, 127, *128*
"Ich grolle nicht" (Schumann) *98*
*The Icicle Thief see Ladre di Saponette*
"If Dreams Come True" 135, *137*
"If I Didn't Care" *117*
"If I Had You" 57, 58, *60*, 64, *68*
"If I Loved You" 44
"If You Are but a Dream" 113, *117*
"If You Were the Only Girl in the World" 102
"I'll Be Seeing You" 43, 44, *47*, *104*, 194
"I'll Get By" *156*
"I'll See You Again" *46*
"I'll See You in My Dreams" 135, *136*, 140, *142*, 145
"I'm a Dreamer, Aren't We All?" *58*
"I'm Confessin' (That I Love You)" 44, *122*

"I'm Forever Blowing Bubbles" *142*, 145
"I'm Gettin' Sentimental Over You" 114, *118*
"I'm in Love Again" 64, 66, *68*, 69
"I'm in the Mood for Love" 51, *86*
"I'm Old Fashioned" 64, *69*
"I'm Sitting on Top of the World" 149, *154*
"I'm Thru with Love" 56-57, *59*, 60
"The Impossible Dream" *41*
"In a Mellotone" *94*
"In a Persian Market" 48, *49*, 103, *104*, 134
"The 'In' Crowd" *100*
"In the Hall of the Mountain King" (Grieg) 123
"In the Mood" *116*
Inagaki, Hiroshi 83
"Indiana (Back Home Again In)" 141, *143*
The Ink Spots 117
"Innamorata" 32
*Innocents of Paris* 61
*Interiors* 19, 21, 73, *74-75*, 79, 119, 120
"L'Internationale" *151*
"Isn't It Romantic?" 44, 64, *69*
"Isn't This a Lovely Day?" 57
"It Could Happen to You" 28, *29*, 69
"It Don't Mean a Thing (If It Ain't Got That Swing)" *141*, 142
"It Had to Be You" *20*
"It's Been So Long" *71*
"It's the Same Sad Story All Over Again" 106, *107*
"I've Found a New Baby" 9, 99, *100*, *104*
"I've Got a Crush on You" 81, *83*
"I've Got a Feeling I'm Falling" *152*, 154
"I've Got You" *45*
"I've Heard That Song Before" 9, *66*

"Ja, ja, die Frau'n sind meine schwache Seite" *124*
*Jackie Gleason Presents Lazy, Lively Love* 14
"Jack's the Lad" *see* "The Sailor's Hornpipe"
Jackson, Jeanine 154
Jacobs, Paul 81
Jacques, Charles 152
Jaffe, Allan 127
Jaffe, Moe 117
James, Harry 7, 10, 20, 27, 29, 48, 49, 65-66, 117, 130, 131, 132; and His Orchestra 49, 66, 115, 132
James, Henry 132
Janssen, Famke 39
Jarvis, Jane 119
Jason, Will 100, 109
jazz *see* Allen, Woody, and jazz; Allen, Woody, use of jazz
The Jazz Age 148, 149
*The Jazz Baby* 139
The Jazz Band 44
Jazz Heaven Orchestra 136, 137
*Jazz Times* 139
"Jeepers Creepers" 43

Jenkins, Gordon 118
Jerome, Timothy 59
Jerome, William 61, 115
Jewison, Norman 32
Jillian, Sally 139
Jobim, Antonio Carlos 52
"Joe Avery" 126, *128*
Johansson, Scarlett 88
John, Tommy 61
Johnson, Bunk 5
Johnson, Howard 104, 128
Johnson, James P. 144, 149
Johnson, William Luther 48
Johnston, Arthur 41, 61, 121, 132
Jolson, Al 35, 69, 142, 149, 154
Jones, Allan 117
Jones, Hank 136
Jones, Isham 20, 136, 142
Jones, Jo 25, 41
Jones, Quincy 147
Joplin, Scott 112, 194
Joy, Robert 118
Judaism 52, 69
Juilliard String Quartet 45
Jun, Rosemarie 152
"June in January" 103, *105*
"Just a Gigolo" *144*
"Just in Time" *133*
"Just One More Chance" 120, *121*
"Just One of Those Things" 92–93, *119*, 135, *137*
"Just Say I Love Her" *59*
"Just You, Just Me" *57*, 58, *67*, 69

Kael, Pauline 23
Kafka, Franz 129, 194
Kahal, Irving 47, 61, 104
Kahn, Gus 20, 35, 54, 58, 59, 74, 116, 128, 136, 142, 153
Kahn, Roger Wolfe 37, 46; and His Orchestra 37
Kalmanoff, Mark 59
Kalmar, Bert 57, 58, 61, 69, 136, 144
Kane, Helen 149, 152, 196
Katscher, Robert 122, 124, 141
*Katzenjammer Kids* 98
Kavner, Julie 103, 115
Kaye, Sammy 117; and His Orchestra 117
Kazandjiev, Vassil 67
*kazatsky* 46, 77
Keaton, Buster 108, 125
Keaton, Diane 9, 19, 20, 74, 77, 80, 81, 85, 107, 113–114, 119, 128
"Keep Italian in Your Heart" *see* "My Bambina"
"Keepin' Out of Mischief Now" *75*
Kellette, John William 142
Kelly, Gene 56
Kelly, Janis 193
Kemp, Hal, and His Orchestra 131

Kenbrovin, Jean 142
Kendis, James 142
Kent, Walter 118
Keosian, Jessie 103
Kern, Jerome 5, 8, 16, 17, 22, 25, 27, 28, 29, 36, 37, 51, 52, 53, 54, 56, 57, 64, 69, 73, 74, 103, 104, 122
Kessel, Barney 29
Ketèlbey, Albert 49, 103, 104
Keystone Cops 141, 146
Kimball, Ward 189
King, Robert 128
King, Wayne 13; and His Orchestra 17
Kirby, Michael 124
Kirkpatrick, Don 49, 100, 104
Kissell, David 32
Klages, Raymond 57, 67
Klemperer, Otto 125
klezmer music 52, 146
Klimt, Gustav 22
Knee, Bernie 151, 152
Koehler, Ted 145
*Kojak* 105
Koonin, Brian 82
Krall, Diana 28, 29
Krauss, Clemens 86
Krizia, New York 16
Kronsburg, Graeme 106, 107
Krupa, Gene 9, 35, 103, 116
Kubrick, Stanley 10, 125
"The Kugelmass Episode" 108
"Kumbayah" *40*
Kurland, Jeffrey 34
Kurnitz, Julie 116

*Ladre di Saponette* 108
*Ladri di Biciclette* 138
*Lady, Be Good!* 84
*The Lady from Shanghai* 85, 87
Lake, Turk Van 101
Lake, Veronica 48
Lemare, Jules 71
Lancaster, Burt 146
"Land of the Gay Caballero" *84*
Landau, Martin 43
Lane, Burton 133
Lane, Marie 136
Lang, Eddie 7, 141, 142
Lang, Fritz 123
Lang, Stephen 131
Lange, Harry 145
Langford, Frances 192
Lanin, Lester 130, 131, 132, 133
LaPaglia, Anthony 144
"Lara's Theme" 44
Laredo, Ruth 132
LaRocca, D. J. 37
Larrocha, Alicia de 45
Lasser, Louise 30, 63
*Last Action Hero* 108

*The Last Gangster* 46
*The Last of Sheila* 105
LaTouche, John 44
Lavery, Patrick 61
Lawrence, Jack 49, 116, 117
Lawson, Yank 16, 72
Lax, Eric 12, 43, 56, 102, 103, 139, 147
Layton, Turner 142
"Lazy River" 35, **36**
*Leader of the Band* 190
Lecuona, Margarita 118
Lee, Peggy 29, 140
Lee, Sander H. 50
Leerhsen, Erica 29
Lehár, Franz 134
Leibowitz, Rene 40
Leigh, Mitch 41
Leighton, Bernie 9, 24, 25, 44, 46, 67, 68, 69, 74, 104, 121, 122, 149, 151, 153
*leitmotif see* Allen, Woody, use of song as *leitmotif*
*The Lemon Sisters* 190
Lenk, Harry 24
Lenoir, Jean 141
Lenya, Lotte 195
"Leonard the Lizard" 57, 148, 149, **152**
Leoncavallo, Ruggiero 150
Leone, Téa 70
Leonhardt, Gustav 68
Leonhardt Consort 68
Lerer, Shifra 53
Lesh, Phil 41
"Lester Lanin Cha Cha" **133**
*Let 'em Eat Cake* 82
"Let's All Sing Like the Birdies Sing" **115**
"Let's Call the Whole Thing Off" 80, **82**
"Let's Face the Music and Dance" 109
"Let's Misbehave" 35, **36**, **62**
Levey, Stan 41, 74
Levinsky, Ken 117
Levinsky, Walt 44
Lévy, Jacques 25
Levy, Jesse 132
Levy, Lou 41, 74
Lewis, George 5, 7, 126–127
Lewis, Juliette 74
Lewis, Morgan 49
Lewis, Samuel M. 36, 42, 153, 154
Lewis, Ted 5, 7; Ted Lewis's Orchestra 141
Lewis, Terry 95
Liberace 8, 18, 37, 41, 47, 104
"Liebestraum No. 3" (Liszt) 140, **144**
Liebling, Howard 30
*The Life of Emil Zola* 151
Light, Enoch 149
"Li'l Darlin" **100**
Lili'Uokalani, Queen 143
Lima, Leopold di 152
"Limehouse Blues" 13–14, 15, **16**, 17, 134, **141**
Lindner, Robert 65, 66

Lindsey, Canuel 61
Link, Harry 152
Lippen, Renée 118
Liszt, Franz 144
Little, Little Jack 38, 40
The Little Church Around the Corner (New York) 69
*The Little Shop of Horrors* 191
*Lives of the Rich and Famous* 131
Livingston, Fud 59
Livingston, Jerry 117
Lloyd, Eric 53
Lloyd, Harold 125
Lloyd Webber, Andrew 90
Loeb, John Jacob 20, 153
Loesser, Frank 41, 45, 48, 87, 117, 118, 121
Lole, Tim 89, 90, 193
Lombardo, Carmen 20, 153
Lombardo, Guy 149; and His Orchestra 118; and His Royal Canadians 109, 153
Lomita, Sol 151
London Sinfonietta 124
London Symphony Orchestra 77
Long Island, New York 20
"The Look of Love" 28
"Looking At You" 57, **60**
Loquasto, Santo 34, 47
"The Lord's Prayer" (Malotte) 97, **98**
Lorre, Peter 194
Lotrič, Janez 90
Louis-Dreyfus, Julia 52
"Louise" 57, **61**
*Love and Death* 3, 6, 10, 11, 18, 39, **75–78**, 88, 91, 92, 96, 134
"Love Is Here to Stay" 80, **82**, 84
"Love Is Sweeping the Country" **82**
"Love Me" **94**
*Love Me Tonight* 61
"Lovely to Look At" **25**
Lovitz, Jon 131
Lowe, Mundell 6, 62–63
Ludwig, Ray 144
Luke, Keye 14
"Lullaby of Birdland" **41**
"Lullaby of Broadway" **118**
"Lulu's Back in Town" **145**
"Luna mezzo mare" **33**
Lyonne, Natasha 57, 58
Lyte, Henry F. 143

M 123
Ma, Yo-Yo 26
"Ma! (He's Making Eyes at Me)" **35**
*Macbeth see* Verdi, Giuseppe
Maccone, Ronald 33
MacDonald, Ballard 143
Mack, Cecil 143, 144, 149
"Mack the Knife" *see* Weill, Kurt
MacPherson, Elle 18
MacRae, Heather 63

Macy's Thanksgiving Day Parade  34
"Madagascar"  191
*Madama Butterfly see* Puccini, Giacomo
Madonna  124
"Madonna"  195
Magidson, Herb  29, 60
Maguire, Toby  52
*Mahagonny Songspeil see* Weill, Kurt
Mahler, Gustav  12, 22, 73, 81, 92, 93; Symphony No. 2  92, 93; Symphony No. 4  *26*, 59; Symphony No. 9  *73*
"Mairzy Doats"  *117*
Maisky, Mischa  25, 26
Major, Pierre  68
"Make Believe"  22, *25, 36*, 44
"Makin' Whoopee"  57, *59*, 74
Malkovich, John  124
Malneck, Matt  59
Malotte, Albert Hay  97, 98
*The Maltese Falcon*  105, 106
"Manhattan"  99, *100*
*Manhattan*  6, 8, 9, 34, 38, 44, 56, 64, 71, 74, *78–84*, 85, 96, 130, 133, 134, 135, 136
Manhattan Hospital, New York  150
*Manhattan Murder Mystery*  8, 9, 51, 54, *84–87*, 92, 103, 129
Mann, David  71, 94
Manne, Shelly  101
Manning, Dick  41, 132
Mantegna, Joe  14, 38
Marchetti, Filippo D.  41, 132
Margolin, Janet  146, 147
Markell, Jodie  72
Markinson, Brian  131, 142
Marks, Gerald  143
Marlow, Janet  40
Mars, Kenneth  124
"Les Marseillaise"  106, *107*
Marshall, E. G.  74
Marshall, Scott  130, 132
Martell, Arlene  58, 59
Martin, Dean  59
Martin, Kelly  25, 86, 93, 94, 101
Martin, Steve  191
Marx, Groucho  57, 58, 61, 126
The Marx Brothers  54, 57, 61, 69
Maslin, Janet  50
Masso, George  44
*Match Point*  3, 10, 11, *87–90*
"La Mattchiche"  *152*
Maurel-Sithole, Linda  59
"La Maxixe" *see* "La Mattchiche"
May, Elaine  130
Mayol, Felix  152
Mays, Willie  126
McCann, Graham  109
McCarthy, Joseph  17, 66
McGrath, Douglas  139
McHugh, Jimmy  25, 29, 45, 61, 86, 117
McKenzie, Leonard  61

McLean, Don  41
McPhail, Lindsey  129
Meacham, Frank W.  118
*Meet Me in St. Louis*  141
Mehta, Zubin  82, 83, 84
*Melinda and Melinda*  9, 11, *91–95*
"Memories of You"  *94*
Mendelssohn, Felix  6, 10, 76, 78, 95–98; *A Midsummer Night's Dream (Incidental Music)*  96, *97–98*; *A Midsummer Night's Dream Overture*  96, *98*; Piano Concerto No. 2 in D Minor  11, *97*; Piano Trio No. 1 in D Minor  *78*; Symphony No. 3 in A Minor, "Scottish"  96, *97*; Violin Concerto in E Minor  *97*
Mercer, Johnny  17, 40, 67, 69, 71
The Merry Macs  117
*Messiah* (Handel)  128
*Messiah of Evil*  21
Messing, Debra  71
Metro Cinema, New York  69
*Metropolis*  125
Metropolitan Opera House, New York  64, 68
Meyer, Joseph  37, 46
Meyers, Gary Allen  46
MGM Studios  54
"Mi par d'udir ancora" (Bizet)  88, *89*
"Mia piccirella" (Gomes)  *89*
"Miami Beach Rumba"  *53*
The Michael Moon Band  40
Michael's Pub, New York  5, 127
Michelot, Pierre  68
Michels, Walter  129
*A Midsummer Night's Dream* (Shakespeare)  96, 150
*A Midsummer Night's Sex Comedy*  6, 10, 11, 88, *95–98*
*Mighty Aphrodite*  8, 9, 37, 57, *98–101*
Milanova, Stoika  67, 97
Miles, Capt. Alfred H.  154
Miles, Charles  44
Miles, Helen  57, 58, 59; The Helen Miles Singers  58–61
Miley, Bubber  73
Miller, Dick  127, 128
Miller, Glenn  7, 138, 143, 194; and His Orchestra  49, 116, 118, 138
Miller, James "Sing"  127
Miller, Jonny Lee  93
Miller, Mitch  140
Millman, Gabriel  61
Mills, Irving  16, 17, 94, 95, 122, 137, 141–142, 144
The Mills Brothers  117
"Mimi"  *61*
"Mine"  38, 80, *82*
Mingus, Charles  62
Miranda, Carmen  113, 117
Miron, Issachar  53
*Missa Secunda* (Hassler)  69

"Mr. Moon" 193
Mistinguett 152
"Misty" *87*
Mitchell, Radha 92
Mitchell, Sidney D. 59, 138
Moby 29
*The Modern Dance* (Marshall) *132*
Mol, Gretchen 143
Moll, Billy 128, 145
Monaco, James V. 66
Monday, Dick 143
Monk, Thelonious 7, 8, 13, 15, 18
Monk, William H. 143
*Monkey Business* 61
*Monk's Dream* 15
*Monsieur Beaucaire* 75
Monte, Lou 32
Montgomery, Garth 61
Montgomery, Wes 8, 28, 29, 73
"Moonglow" *16*, 92, *94*, *122*
"Moonlight Becomes You" 14, *17*
"Moonlight Serenade" *138*
*Moonstruck* 32, 193
Moore, Demi 52
Morales, Jacobo 31
Morehouse, Chauncey 37, 144
Morello, Joe 40, 86, 100
Moret, Neil 52
Morgan, Russ 33
Morozov, Igor 90
Morris, John Gordon 69
Morse, Susan E. (Sandy) 43–44, 155
Morse, Theodore 104
Mortimer, Emily 89
Morton, Ferdinand "Jelly Roll" 5, 73, 75, 112, 128, 148, 194
Morton, Samantha 141
Mostel, Josh 116
"M-O-T-H-E-R (A Word That Means the World to Me)" 102, *104*
Mother Theresa 18
Mottola, Tony 153
*Moulin Rouge* 191
Mount Sinai Hospital, New York 67
"Mountain Greenery" *132*
Mozart, Wolfgang Amadeus 6, 12, 19, 20, 76, 77, 81, 83, 136; *The Magic Flute Overture* 11, *77*; Symphony No. 40 in G Minor 81, *83*; Symphony No. 41 in C Major, "Jupiter" *20*, 81
Mulligan, Gerry 7, 8, 37, 41, 74
Mundy, Jimmy 51
Munich rally 151, 155
Munich State Opera 86
"Murder He Says" *45*
Murnau, F. W. 123
Murphy, Michael 81
Murray, Don 37, 144
Museum of Modern Art, New York 80–81, 82
*Music from Berlin in the 1920s* 123

"Music Makers" *131*
Musiker, Lee 46
Mussolini, Benito 153
Mussorgsky, Modest 50, 53, 137
"My Baby Just Cares for Me" *58*
"My Bambina" 32, *34*
*My Fair Lady* 54, 141
*My Favorite Blonde* 47
"My Ideal" 8, 51, 120, *121*
"My Melancholy Baby" 145
*My Sister Eileen* 44
"Mystery Pacific" 140, *141*

"Nagasaki" *37*
Napoleon Bonaparte 76–78; campaign in Russia 76, 78
Narro, Pascual Marquina 153
"National Emblem March" *34*
*Naughty Marietta* (Herbert) 31
Nazis 85, 148, 155
Neeson, Liam 73
Neiburg, Al J. 122
Nelligan, Kate 125
Nelson, Ozzie, and His Orchestra 45
Nemo, Henry 95
"Neo Minore" 99, *100*
Nevens, Paul 150
"Nevertheless (I'm in Love with You)" *144*
New Broadway Cast 87
New Leviathan Oriental Fox Trot Orchestra 35, 36
The New Orleans Funeral and Ragtime Orchestra 5, 126, 127–128, 129
New York Philharmonic Orchestra 26, 58, 79–80, 81, 82, 83, 84, 97
New York Rangers 85
*New York Stories* 48, 101
New York Studio Players 58–61
*New York Times* 5, 50
New York Yankees 150
*The New Yorker* 18, 23
Newman, Joy 117
*Newsies* 191
Nichols, Jenny 44
Nichols, Red 7, 35; and His Five Pennies 36, 143
Nickels, Rebecca 117
"Night and Day" 8, 51, *119*, 120, *122*
*Night on Bald Mountain* (Mussorgsky) 50, *53*, *137*
*1984* 125
"No Lover, No Friend (That's the End)" 59, *60*
"No Moon at All" *71*, 92, *94*
"No Strings" 57
Noble, Ray 101
Nolan, Lloyd 65, 66–67
"Non dimenticar" 32
Noone, Jimmie 7
Norris, Melanie 86

## 212 / Index

Norton, Edward 55, 57, 59
Norvo, Red 27, 29
Norworth, Jack 150
*Le notte di Cabiria* 194
"Novelties for Piano and Saxophone Quartet" (Hyman) 196
Nurock, Kirk 136

"O Christmas Tree / O Tannenbaum" **18**, **21**
"O Sole Mio" **34**
Oberlin College 25
Oedipus complex 102
"Oedipus Wrecks" 9, 10, 37, 43, 44, 48, 51, 73, 85, **101–105**, 134
*Of Thee I Sing* 79, 82
O'Farrill, Chico 72
*Oh Kay!* 79, 83
"Oh, Lady, Be Good!" **84**
Oke, Alan 89
*Oklahoma!* 54
"Old Devil Moon" **133**
"Old Fashioned Love" **144**
Oliveira, Aloysio 116
Oliver, Joseph "King" 128
Oliver, Sy 116
Olsen, George, and His Music 37
"On a Slow Boat to China" 39, **41**, 120, **121**, 190
"On the Sunny Side of the Street" **25**
*On the Town* 44
"One Day at a Time" 109, 110, **111**
"One O'Clock Jump" **137**
"One, Two, Three Kick" **119**
"Opus One" **116**
Orchestra of the Regio Theater, Turin 68
Orchestre de la Société des Concerts du Conservatoire 24
L'Orchestre de Suisse Romande 53
Original Dixieland Jazz Band 7, 136
Original Jazz Classics 51
Ormandy, Eugene 97, 98
O'Sullivan, Maureen 65, 66–67
*Otto e mezzo* 15, 133–134, 195
"Out of Nowhere" 9, 51, **52**, **86**, 120, **121**, **142**
Overstreet, W. Benton 143
Owens, Jack 133
Oxtot's, Dick, Traditional Jazz Quartet 127

Padilla, José 152
Page, Billy 100
*Pagliacci* (Leoncavallo) 150
Palace Theater, London 90
"Palesteena" 134, **136**
Palma, Carlo di 34, 54
Palmer, Jack 100, 104
Palmer, John F. 32
Palminteri, Chazz 35
"Panama" 195
"Paper Doll" 113, **117**
"Paree!" *see* "Ça C'est Paris"

Paris, Sidney de 49, 100, 104
Paris, Wilbur de 7, 9, 48, 49, 100, 103, 104
Paris Philharmonic Orchestra 76, 78
Parish, Mitchell 48, 53, 136, 138
Parker, Charlie 50, 62
Parker, Gloria 32, 34
Parker, Mary-Louise 37
"Parlez-Moi d'Amour" *see* "Speak to Me of Love"
"Pat Hobby Teamed with Genius" 196
Pathé newsreels 148
Paul, Les 140
Paul, Walter 36
Pavarotti, Luciano 55
"The Peanut Vendor" **143**
*The Pearl Fishers* (Bizet) 88, 89
Peer, Beverly 68, 86
*Peer Gynt* (Grieg) 123
Peet, Amanda 93
Penn, Sean 138, 139–140, 141
*Pennies from Heaven* 56
Penque, Romeo 111
"Penthouse Serenade" **100**, 109
"Pepino, the Italian Mouse" 32
Peplowski, Ken 140, 142, 143, 144, 145
"Perdido" 8, **24**
Perlman, Itzak 58
Perlman, Navah 58
*Persona* 75
Pestalozza, Alberto 33
Peters, Bernadette 18
Peterson, Oscar 7, 27, 28, 29, 106, 107; Oscar Peterson Trio 27, 29, 107
Pettet, Kristen 61
Pettiford, Oscar 18
Philadelphia Orchestra 97, 98
*The Philadelphia Story* 117
Phonogram Inc. 75
Piano Sonata No. 2 in B flat Minor (Chopin) 60
*Picking Up the Pieces* 105
Pickman A. J. 139, 143
Pierson, Tom 79–80, 82–84
Pine, Larry 39, 93
Pinkard, Maceo 45, 138, 142
"Pistol Packin' Mama" 113, **117**
Pizzarelli, Bucky 140, 141, 142, 143, 144, 145
*Play It Again, Sam* (film) 7, **105–107**, 108
*Play It Again, Sam* (play) 105–106, 108
*Pleasantville* 108
Pleasence, Donald 124
"Pleasure Mad" *see* "Viper Mad"
Plimpton, Martha 25
Pogel, Nancy 195
"Polkadots and Moonbeams" **46**, **69**
Pollack, Sydney 74
Poor, Bray 101
"Poor Butterfly" **36**, 70, **72**
Pope, Ralph 52
Porter, Cole 5, 8, 25, 27, 28, 33, 34, 35, 36,

44, 53, 54, 57, 60, 62, 64, 68, 71, 73, 79, 85, 86, 87, 92, 101, 113, 116, 119, 122, 134, 135, 137, 148, 149
Portman, Natalie 59
Portnow, Richard 118
"Potato Head Blues" 81
Potter, Dennis 56, 193
Pottier, Eugène 151
Powel, Mel 139
Powell, Dick 192
Power, Paul 54
Prado, Perez 132
Pratt, Richie 136
Prelude in B Minor No. 10, Op. 32 (Rachmaninov) *132*
The Preservation Hall Jazz Band 126, 127, 128, 129
Press, Jacques 45
"A Pretty Girl Is Like a Melody" *129*
Previn, André 62, 132
Prima, Louis 53, 87, 104
Prince, Daisy 59
Prokofiev, Sergei 6, 10, 39, 75–78, 92, 120; The Adoration of Veless and Ala *77*; *Alexander Nevsky* 75, 76, 77; The Battle on Ice *77*; The Birth of Kijé *78*; The Enemy God and the Dance of the Spirits of Darkness *77*; *Lieutenant Kijé* 75–78; *The Love of Three Oranges* 75, 76, 78; March from *The Love of Three Oranges* Suite 75, *78*; Romance from *Lieutenant Kijé 78*; *Scythian Suite* 75–77, 92; Song about Alexander Nevsky 10, 39, *77*; Troika from *Lieutenant Kijé* 10, *76*, 78; The Wedding of Kijé *78*
Prune, Ivan de 72
Puccini, Giacomo 31, 32, 64, 67, 68, 92; *La Bohème* 32; "Introduction to Act I" from *Madama Butterfly 67*; *Manon Lescaut* 64; "O mio babbino caro" from *Gianni Schicchi 31*; "Sola, perduta abbandonata" *68*
Puente, Tito 72, 116
*The Purple Rose of Cairo* 47, 54, 56, *108–112*, 148

"Queens Club Trio" *33*
Questel, Mae 102, 152, 196
Quicksell, Howdy 144
"Quiero la noche" 30, 31

Rachmaninov, Sergei 109, 132, 151
Radio City Music Hall, New York 117
*Radio Days* 6, 9, 10, 13, 15, 19, 35, 47, 56, 57, 92, 93, *113–119*, 138
Ragas, Henry W. 141
The Ragtime Rascals 126
Rain, Douglas 125
Rainbow Room, New York 49
Rainbow Room All-Stars 48, 49
Rainger, Ralph 105
Ralph Lauren 18

Ramabhadra, Sanjeev 60
Ramey, Gene 25, 41
Rampling, Charlotte 135
The Ramsey Lewis Trio 100
Randazzo, Steven 100
Rank, Bill 37, 144
Rapaport, Michael 99
*Rashomon* 130
Raye, Don 46, 131
Razaf, Andy 29, 36, 75, 94, 116, 131
RCA Victor 142, 145
"Recurrence" *58*
"The Red River Valley" 63
Redmond, John 95
Redmond, Marge 87
*Reds* 151
Reid, Don 117
Reiner, Rob 37
Reinhardt, Django 3, 6, 7, 45, 52, 86, 133, 135, 136, 138, 139, 140, 141, 143, 144, 191, 195; Quintette du Hot Club de France 80, 137, 140, 141, 144
Reisman, Leo, and His Orchestra 73, 110
"Re-Lax Jingle" 114, *118*
"Remember Pearl Harbor" *117*
Rene, Henri, and His Orchestra 35
Reynolds, Ellis 122
Reynolds, Herb 32
Reynolds, Shauna 72
*Rhapsody in Blue* 80, *81*
Rhys Meyers, Jonathan 88
The Rhythm Boys 151
Ricci, Christina 27
Richardson, Jerome 142, 144
Rifkin, Ron 86
*Rigoletto see* Verdi, Giuseppe
Riley, Dean 48
Rilke, Rainer Maria 22, 25, 26
Rimsky-Korsakov, Nikolai 115
Rio, Chuck 132
RKO Pictures 108, 109
*The Road to Rio* 47
Roane, Kenneth 136
Robbins, Everett 128
Roberts, Judith 136
Roberts, Julia 55, 59
Roberts, Lee S. 25, 129
Roberts, Tony 20, 67, 97, 107, 137
Robin, Leo 61, 105, 121
Robinson, Edward G. 46
Robinson, J. Russell 36, 136
Robinson, Jim 127
Robinson, Sylvia 29
Rodgers, Richard 5, 8, 35, 36, 37, 44, 53, 54, 57, 61, 64, 66, 67, 68, 69, 86, 99, 100, 132
Rodin, Auguste 68
Rodin, Gil 86
Rodriguez, Gerardo Matos 16, 116
Roemheld, Heinz 87, 95
Rogers, Ginger 55, 57, 108, 109

Rogers, Walter 90
*Rolling Stone* magazine 127
Rollini, Adrian 37, 144
Romano, Christy 61
Romberg, Sigmund 72
Rome Opera Chorus and Orchestra 67–68
Romoff, Adam 118
"Rosalie" *44*, 51, *53*
Rose, Billy 35, 36, 152, 153
Rose, David 103; and His Orchestra 104, 105
Rose, Don 79, 82, 84
Rose, Mickey 146
Rose, Vincent 69, 101, 142
Rose, William 46
Rosenblum, Ralph 6, 20, 30, 75–76, 146, 147, 148
"Roses of Picardy" *26*
Ross, Annie 50, 52
Ross, Herbert 105, 106, 191
Rossini, Gioacchino 88, 90
Rostaing, Hubert 140
Rota, Nino 16, 115, 134; "La ballerina del circo Snap" from *Giulietta degli spiriti* 16; "L'illusionista" from *Otto e mezzo* 134; "Vascello di Susi" from *Giulietta degli spiriti* 16
Roth, Tim 55, 58, 60, 61
Rothman, John 134, 154
Rotter, Fritz 125
Rouget de Lisle, Claude 107
Rowlands, Gena 12, 22
Royal Opera House 89, 90, 193
Royal Philharmonic Orchestra 40
Rózsa, Miklós 86
Ruby, Harry 57, 58, 61, 69, 136, 144
Ruby Foo's Chinese restaurant, New York 132
Ruiz, Hilton 45; Quartet 45
"Runnin' Wild" 149, *151*
Runyon, Damon 34
Rush, Deborah 154
Russell, Bob 95
Russell, S. K. 116, 118, 136
Russian Tea Room, New York 82
Russo, Dan 35
Ruther, Wyatt 17, 18, 41, 87, 93
Ryder, Winona 39

"'S Wonderful" 81, *83*
Saatchi Gallery, London 89
Sable, Phil, and His Orchestra 152
"A Sailboat in the Moonlight" 9, *153*, 155
"The Sailor's Hornpipe" *115*
Saks, Gene 53
Salt, Jennifer 107
*Salvator Rosa* (Gomes) 89
Salvo, Anne de 137
Sampson, Edgar 131, 137
"San" 126, *129*
San Simeone 154
Sancton, Tom 6, 126
Sandke, Randy 36, 101

*Satan in High Heels* 62
"Satan Takes a Holiday" *60*
Satie, Erik 12, 23, 24; *Gymnopédie No. 1* 12, 23, *24*, 190; *Gymnopédie No. 3* 23, 190
Savoy Hotel Orpheans 53
Saxe, Phil 36, 62
Sayer, Cynthia 29, 112, 190
Sayles, Emanuel 127
*Scenes from a Mall* 105
Schafer, Milton 133
Scheller, Damion 82
Schertzinger, Victor 17, 40, 67
Schickel, Richard 56
Schiff, András 93
"Schlof, mein Kind" *117*
*Schmoedipus* 193
Schoenfeld, Gerald 33
Schonberger, John 101
Schubert, Franz 11, 27, 42, 43, 45, 88, 97, 98; *Die schöne Müllerin* 97, 98; String Quartet No. 15 in G Major 11–12, 43, *45*, 88; "Wohin?" *98*
Schumann, Robert 97, 98
Schwabach, Kurt 124
Schwandt, Wilbur 54
Schwartz, Arthur 115, 118
Schwartz, Jean 61, 115
Schwartz, Richard A. 38, 39, 50, 115
Scorsese, Martin 101
Scott, Rob 68
*Scott Joplin: King of Ragtime* 194
Scuola di San Rocco 59
Sedric, Gene 5
"Seems Like Old Times" 19–20, *20*
September 8, 9, 21, 22, 39, 42, 43, 44, 51, 73, *119–122*, 123
"September Song" *see* Weill, Kurt
"Serenade in Blue" 70, *72*
Serkin, Rudolf 193
*The Seventh Seal* 75
Severinson, Doc 140
Sevigny, Chloé 92
*Shadows and Fog* 6, 10, 54, 88, *123–125*
Shakespeare, William 96
*Shall We Dance?* 82
Shand, Terry 116
Shanghai Quartet 94
Shankar, Ravi 28
Shapiro, Ted 60, 68
Shaw, Artie 7, 13, 40, 194; and His Orchestra 16, 116
Shaw, Arvell 136
Shaw, Irwin 41
Shaw, Vinessa 92
Shawn, Wallace 49, 93, 119, 124
Shay, Larry 101
Shearing, George 41, 102
Shena 95
Shendell, Earl 136
Sheridan, Richard 86

*Sherlock Jr.* 108
"She's Funny That Way" *52*
Shields, Larry 37, 141
"S-H-I-N-E" *143*
Shirim Klezmer Orchestra 52
Short, Bobby 5, 66, 68, 71, 85, 86
*Shoulder Arms* 75
Shue, Elizabeth 51
Sibelius, Jean 12
Sica, Vittorio de 138
Siever, Bruce 141
Sigman, Carl 60
Signorelli, Frank 37, 144
silent film era 9, 123, 125, 126
Simeon, Omer 49, 100, 104
Simmons, John 17, 29, 52, 53, 86, 100
Simon, Neil 105
Simon, Paul 19
Simons, Moise 143
Simons, Seymour B. 16, 143
Sinatra, Frank 8, 117, 140
"Since My Best Gal Turned Me Down" *144*
"Sing, Sing, Sing (with a Swing)" 9, 51, *53*, 85, *87*, 103, *104*
*Singin' in the Rain* 45, 54
"Singin' the Blues (Till My Daddy Comes Home")" *36*
Singleton, Zutty 49, 100, 104
Sinyard, Neil 135
Sissle's, Noble, Swingsters 143
*Sleeper* 3, 7, 9, 11, 18, 75, 80, 99, *125–129*, 134
*Sleepless in Seattle* 106
"Slip into the Crowd" *68*
Sloane, Everett 87
Slovak Radio Symphony Orchestra 90
*Small Time Crooks* 10, 11, *129–133*
"Smiles" *25*, *129*
*Smiles of a Summer Night* 96, 97
Smith, Ada 149
Smith, Brooke 94
Smith, Derek 35, 37, 44, 59, 68, 69, 118
Smith, Willie "The Lion" 136
Smith Hill, Patty 45
Sofia Soloists Chamber Orchestra 67
"Softly, as in a Morning Sunrise" 71, *72*
"Somebody Stole My Gal" 92, *94*
"Someone to Watch Over Me" 80, 81, *82*
Sommer, Ted 32, 33, 101, 118, 140, 142, 143, 144, 145
song as a subtext *see* Allen, Woody, use of song as subtext
"The Song Is You" *74*
"Soon" 40, *42*
"Sophisticated Lady" 47, *48*
"La Sorella" *see* "La Mattchiche"
Sorvino, Mira 99
Sotos, Tony 46
Soudieux, Emmanuel 136
Soul Avengerz 95
"Soul Bossa Nova" 147

Sour, Robert 116, 137
source music *see* Allen, Woody, use of source music
Sousa, John Philip 146
"South American Way" 113, *117*
*The South Bank Show* 85, 147
"Southern Comfort" 15, *18*
*Soylent Green* 126
"Speak to Me of Love" 44, *141*
Spencer, O'Neil 143
Spielberg, Steven 43
Spignesi, Stephen J. 103
Spikes, Benjamin 75, 128
Spikes, John 75, 128
Springfield, Dusty 28
Stapleton, Maureen 74
"Star Eyes" *46*
"Stardust" 135–136, *138*
*Stardust Memories* 14, 15, 22, 27, 50, 52, 64, 93, 115, *133–138*, 140, 148
"Steady Steady" *133*
Stebbins Hall Band 53, 54
Steenburgen, Mary 97
Stefanov, Vassil 97
Steiner, Max 106, 107
Stept, Sam H. 59
Stern, Daniel 68
Stiers, David Ogden 49
Stillman, Al 119
Stock, Larry 33
Stoller, Alvin 52
"Stompin' at the Savoy" *131*
"Stormy Weather" 195
*The Story of Louis Pasteur* 151
Stothart, Herbert 117
Stout, Mary 143
Strauss, Johann, II 131, 132
Stravinsky, Igor 75–76, 91, 92, 93; Concerto in D 91, *93*; *The Rite of Spring* 76
Strayhorn, Billy 93, 118
Streep, Meryl 84
Strich, Elaine 120, 131
"Strike Up the Band" 82, *84*
*Strike Up the Band* 79, 83, 84
String Quintet in E Major, Op. 13, No. 5 (Boccherini) *78*
Stripling, Bryon 142, 144
Styne, Jule 66, 117, 133
Suesse, Dana 38, 40
"Sugar (That Sugar Baby of Mine)" *138*
"Sunday (the Day Before My Birthday)" 29
Sunjata, Daniel 92
"Sunny Side Up" *154*
*Sunrise* 123
"Sunrise Serenade" *49*
Sunshine, Marion 143
*The Sunshine Boys* 105
Swan, Einar A. 101
"Sweet and Lovely" *71*
"Sweet and Low-Down" 80, *83*

*Sweet and Lowdown* 6, 47, 48, 56, 113, *138–145*
"Sweet Georgia Brown" *45*, 51, *138*, *142*
"Sweet Sue, Just You" 143, *145*
Sweetland Productions 130
*The Swimmer* 146
*Swingtime* 28
Sydow, Max von 68

Taccani, Sandro 34
"Tain't Nobody's Biz-Ness If I Do" 126, *128*
"Take Five" 8, *86*, *100*
"Take Me Out to the Ball Game" 150
"Take the 'A' Train" 92, *93*, *118*
*Take the Money and Run* 3, 6, 7, 9, 30, 31, 129, 138, *146–148*
"Taking a Chance on Love" *44*
*The Tale of Tsar Saltan* (Rimsky-Korsakov) 115
*Tales from the Hollywood Hills* 196
"Tangerine" 8, *40*
Tappan Zee Bridge, New York 84
"Tarantella" *33*
Tate Modern, London 89
Tatum, Art 7, 8, 51, 52–53, 87, 120, 121, 122
Tavern on the Green, New York 44
T-Bone 95
Tchaikovsky, Peter Ilyich 31, 76; *1812 Overture* 11, *31*; *The Sleeping Beauty* 76
Teagarden, Jack 142, 143
Tedesco, Tony 46
"Tequila" 131, *132*
Teschemacher, Edward 46
*Thanks for the Memory* 48
"That Certain Feeling" 35, *37*
"That Jungle Jamboree" *36*
"That Old Feeling" *41*, *74*, *118*
"That's Amore" 32
"There Will Never Be Another You" 27, *29*
"There'll Be Another Spring" 28, *29*
"There'll Be Some Changes Made" *143*
Theron, Charlize 39, 47
*They Got Rhythm* 35
"They Say It's Wonderful" 44
"They're Either Too Young or Too Old" 113, *118*
Thiessen, Tiffani 72
*The Thinker* (Rodin) 68
"Thinking About Bix" *153*
39 Steps 68, 71
"This Could Be the Start of Something Big" 131, *132*
*This Gun for Hire* 45
"This Year's Kisses" *45*
Thomas, Frank 189
Thomas, Michael Tilson 79–80, 82, 84
"Thou Swell" 35, *37*
"3:00 AM Blues" *144*
The Three Deuces Chorus 35, 36, 37
The Three Deuces club, Chicago 35

The Three Deuces club, New York 35
The Three Deuces Musicians 35, 36, 37
"Three Little Words" *136*
Thurman, Uma 140
"Tickle Toe" *136*
"Tico-Tico" *116*
Tierney, Harry 17
"Till We Meet Again" 126, 127, *129*
Tilly, Jennifer 36
Tilzer, Albert von 104
Tilzer, Harry von 150
*A Time for Killing* 62
*Time* magazine 56
Times Square, New York 17, 154
Tin Pan Alley 8, 34, 38, 57, 126
Tintoretto 59
Tiochet, Carlo 33
*Tip-Toes* 83
Tizol, Juan 17, 24, 144
Tobani, Tobias 196
Tobias, Harry 71
Tolkan, James 77
Tolstoy, Leo 75
Tomlin, Lily 125
"Too Close for Comfort" 70, *72*
"Toot, Toot, Tootsie! (Goodbye)" 35
*Top Hat* 54, 57, 108, 110
"Top Hat, White Tie and Tails" *74*
Torme, Mel 140
"Torna a Surriento" 32, *34*
"Tra Veglia e Sonno" *33*
"Tramp! Tramp! Tramp!" (Herbert) *31*
"Tropical Mood – Rhumba" *136*
"The Trot" *67*
*Il Trovatore* see Verdi, Giuseppe
"Truckin'" *41*
Trumbauer, Frankie, and His Orchestra 36
Tsitsanis, Vassilis 99, 100
Tucci, Stanley 52
Tucker, Michael 118
Turca, Tony 33
Turco, Guiseppe "Pepino" 33
Turk, Roy 100, 156
Turpin, Tom 112
"Tuxedo Junction" *48*
TVR Symphony Orchestra 97
"Twelfth Street Rag" *143*
"Twisted" 50, *52*
"Two Sleepy People" *48*
*2001: A Space Odyssey* 125
Tyzack, Margaret 89
"Tzena, Tzena, Tzena" 52, *53*

Ullman, Tracey 37, 130
"Una furtiva lagrima" (Donizetti) 88, *89*
"Unfaithful Woman" *145*
Upper East Side, New York 14, 98

Vaché, Warren 44
Val, Jack 59

Valdes, Miguelito  118
Vale, Jerry  59
Valentino, Rudolf  189
*Valentino: The Lives and Loves of Valentino*  15
Valentino's restaurant, New York  15
Vandenburgh, Craig  34
Vangelis  23
Varèse, Edgard  12, 23, 26, 92
Vassilopoulos, Dimitri  153
"Venetian Scenes"  *59*
Venuti, Joe  7, 142
Vernoff, Kaili  142
Verdi, Giuseppe  88, 89, 90, 92; "Desdemona rea!" from *Otello*  89, *90*; "Gualtier Malde! ... Caro nome" from *Rigoletto 90*; "Mal reggendo all'aspro assalto" from *Il Trovatore 89*; "O figli, o figli miei! ... Ah, la paterna mano" from *Macbeth 90*; *Otello*  89; *La Traviata*  89, 90; "Un dì felice, eterea"  *89*, 90; "Valse from Act I" from *La Traviata 90*
"Vesti la giubba" (Leoncavallo)  *150*
Victor Orchestra  89
Victor Records  88
Vienna State Opera Orchestra  132, 137
Village Vanguard, New York  28, 29
Vincent, Nat  142
Vincent's restaurant, New Jersey  87
Vinicius da Cruz de Melo Moraes, Marcus  52
"Viper Mad"  141, *143*
Vitaphone Orchestra  35
Viterelli, Joe  35
Vochecowizc, Liz  119
*Voices of Spring* (Strauss II)  *132*
Vox / Turnabout Production  75

Wagner, Richard  42, 85, 86; "Bridal Chorus" from *Lohengrin 42*; *The Flying Dutchman*  85, 86; "Wie oft in Meeres tiefsten Schlund"  *86*
"Waiting"  *52*
*Wake Up and Dream*  57
Waldorf-Astoria Hotel, New York  32, 34, 46, 154
Walker, Robert  60
"Walking My Baby Back Home"  *100*
Wall Street Crash  153
Waller, Thomas "Fats"  5, 29, 36, 48, 56, 75, 102, 152
*War of the Worlds*  116
Ward, Charles B.  32
Ward, Edward  46
Ward, Sam  59
Ward, Samuel A.  155
Warden, Jack  36, 121
Warlop, Michel, and His Orchestra  142
Warner Brothers  151
Warney, Leo  136
Warren, Harry  28, 29, 37, 57, 72, 112, 116, 118, 119, 130, 131, 145, 154

Warrilow, David  116
*Warsaw Concerto* (Addinsell)  151
Warwick Hotel, New York  28
Washington, Ned  94, 118
Waterston, Sam  46, 64, 120, 195
Watkins, Earl  48
"The Way You Look Tonight"  *17*, 27, 28, *29*, 51, *53*, *69*
"We Wish You a Merry Christmas"  *18*, *21*
Weatherly, Fred E.  26
Webb, Chick  7, 131, 133; Chick Webb's Savoy Orchestra  137
Webber, Mark  72
Weber, Marek, and His Orchestra  10, 125
Webster, Ben  7, 8, 51, 53, 87, 120, 121, 122
The Wedding Band  46
Weill, Kurt  6, 10, 12, 18, 24, 25, 114, 115, 123–125; "Alabama Song" from *Mahagonny Songspeil 125*; "The Bilbao Song"  24, *25*; "The Cannon Song"  123, *124*; *Happy End*  24; *Kleine Dreigroschenmusik* (*Little Threepenny Music*)  10, 124, 125; "Moritat von Mackie Messer" ("Mack the Knife")  *18*, *125*; "September Song"  10, 114, *115*; *Die sieben Todsünden* (*The Seven Deadly Sins*)  10–11, *124*; *The Threepenny Opera*  10, 195
Weir, Bob  41
Weisberg, Tim  19, 21
Weiss, George David  41, 72
"Welcome to Our World of Toys"  *101*
"We'll Meet Again"  44
Weller, Peter  100
Welles, Orsen  87, 116
Wells, H. G.  116
Wells, Tony  151, 152
"Wenn de Weiße Flieder Blüht" *see* "When the White Lilacs Bloom Again"
Wernblad, Annette  102
Wessel, Horst  155
"West Coast Blues"  *73*
*West Side Story*  54
Westbury Hotel, New York  153
Weston, Paul  13, 15; and His Orchestra  16
*Westworld*  126
"What a Little Moonlight Can Do"  *61*
"What Is This Thing Called Love?"  10, 27, *73*
"What'll I Do"  *121*
*What's Up Doc?*  106
Wheeler, Hubie  29
"When Day Is Done"  *122*, 123, *124*, *141*
"When the Red, Red Robin Comes Bob, Bob Bobbin' Along"  *36*, 51, *53*
"When the White Lilacs Bloom Again"  *125*
"When Your Lover Has Gone"  99, *101*
"When You're Smiling"  99, *101*
"Where or When"  *67*
"Whispering"  *101*
White, Barry  95
"The White Cliffs of Dover"  113, *118*
*White Zombie*  72

Whiteman, Paul 148, 151
Whiting, Richard 16, 52, 61, 71, 121, 129, 153
Whitney Museum, New York 83
"Who?" *37*, *122*
Wiene, Robert 123
Wiest, Dianne 36, 64, 69, 110, 114, 120
Wiggins, Gerald 68
*Wild Man Blues* 5
*Wild Strawberries* 21
*Wild, Wild West* 62
Wilder, Billy 86
Wilder, Gene 63
Wilder, Joe 59, 136, 142, 144
Wildner, Johannes 90
"Will You Still Be Mine?" *18*, 38, 39, *41*, 92, 93
*William Tell* (Rossini) 90
Williams, Clarence 143
Williams, George 16
Williams, Spencer 100, 104
Williams, Tommy 52
Williams, Treat 71
Willis, Gordon 96, 109
Willson, Meredith 117
Wilson, Chuck 142, 144
Wilson, Dooley 107
Wilson, Mary Louise 151
Wilson, Shadow 17, 53, 86, 100
Wilson, Teddy 7, 22, 25, 26–27, 29, 37, 41, 116; and His Orchestra 28, 29
Wilton, Penelope 90
Wirges, William 61
Wiseman, Jack 46
"With Plenty of Money and You" 10, 130, *131*
"Wolverine Blues" *75*, 126, *128*
*The Woman in White* 90
Wood, Haydn 26
Wood, Leo 94, 151
Woodley, Nat 49, 100, 104
Woods, Carol 143
Woods, Harry 36, 53, 61
"World Music" *17*
World War II 113–114, 194
The World's Greatest Jazz Band 75
"Wrap Your Troubles in Dreams" *145*
Wright, Bob 117
Wright, Eugene 40, 86, 100
Wright, James 95
Wrubel, Allie 29

Xarhako, Stavros 101

Yacowar, Maurice 19, 30, 80–81
"Yankee Doodle" 129
*yenta* 102
"Yes, Sir, That's My Baby" *128*, 195
Yomo Toro Trio 30
"You and I" 114, *117*
"You Are Too Beautiful" 44, 60, *68*
"You Brought a New Kind of Love to Me" *61*
"You Do Something to Me" 99, *101*
"You Have Such Reptile Eyes" 148, *152*
"You Made Me Love You" *66*
"You May Be Six People, but I Love You" 148, *152*, 153
"You Oughta Be in Pictures" 38, *40*
"You Took Advantage of Me" 35, *36*
"You Were Meant for Me" *145*
"You'd Be So Nice to Come Home To" *25*, 113, *119*
Youlden, Chris 21
"You'll Never Know" *119*
Youmans, Vincent 44, 46, 116
Young, Joe 36, 153, 154
Young, Lester 7, 26–27, 28, 29, 62, 133, 136
Young, Rider Johnson 31
Young, Victor 45, 94, 145
"You're Getting to Be a Habit with Me" *116*
"You're Nobody Till Somebody Loves You" *33*
"You're the Top" 149
"You've Got to See Mamma Ev'ry Night (or You Can't See Mamma at All)" *36*
Yu Lu 72
Yuenger, Jay 72

Zabar's, New York 83
Zambetas, George 99, 101
Zardis, Chester 127
"Zelda's Theme" *132*
*Zelig* 9, 35, 47, 56, 57, 95, 109, 138, 146, *148–156*
Zenor, Susanne 107
*Ziegfeld Follies of 1934* 38
Zimmermann, Charles A. 154
Zippel, David 90
Zombie, Rob 72
Zukerman, Pinchas 17

www.ingramcontent.com/pod-product-compliance
Ingram Content Group UK Ltd.
Pitfield, Milton Keynes, MK11 3LW, UK
UKHW041953140426
5217IPUK00015B/785